The CRUCIFIXION *of the* KING *of* GLORY

The Amazing History and Sublime Mystery of the Passion

EUGENIA SCARVELIS CONSTANTINOU, PH.D.

ANCIENT FAITH PUBLISHING   CHESTERTON, INDIANA

The Crucifixion of the King of Glory: The Amazing History and Sublime Mystery of the
Passion
Copyright ©2021 Eugenia Scarvelis Constantinou

Published by:
    Ancient Faith Publishing
    A Division of Ancient Faith Ministries
    P.O. Box 748
    Chesterton, IN 46304

Unless otherwise specified, biblical quotations are taken from the Revised Standard Version.

ISBN: 978-1-955890-15-1

Library of Congress Control Number: 2021953562

Printed in the United States of America

To the Father, who so loved the world that He gave us His only begotten Son, to the King of Glory, whose voluntary passion opened paradise for us, and to the All-Holy Spirit, through whom we participate in this gift of new life.

And to my beloved sister, Stella.

Abbreviations

ANF	Ante-Nicene Fathers series
Ant.	Flavius Josephus, *Antiquities of the Jews*
b.	Babylonian Talmud
FOTC	Fathers of the Church series
JW	Flavius Josephus, *The Jewish War*
NPNF-1	Nicene and Post-Nicene Fathers of the Church, First series
NPNF-2	Nicene and Post-Nicene Fathers of the Church, Second series
W. Aug.	Works of Augustine series
y.	Jerusalem Talmud

Tractates of the Mishnah

Berakhoth	*Ber.*
Hagigah	*Hag.*
Megillah	*Meg.*
Menahot	*Men.*
Middoth	*Mid.*
Rosh Hashanah	*Rosh. Hash.*
Shabbath	*Shab.*
Sanhedrin	*Sanh.*
Semahot	*Sem.*
Shekalim	*Shek.*
Sukkah	*Suk.*

Contents

If they had known, they would never have crucified the Lord of glory.
(1 Corinthians 2:8)

Introduction

T ODAY MOST CHRISTIANS IN THE West live relatively safe lives, far removed from the harsh and gruesome realities of daily existence in the Roman Empire. We cannot fully appreciate the power and meaning of the Lord's Passion without a greater appreciation of his time and culture. What message did he bring? Who accepted him and why? Who rejected him and why? He was the pure and spotless Lamb of God, not only blameless of any crime but innocent of any sin at all. Why would anyone seek to destroy Love and Mercy Incarnate? He performed countless miracles and taught with incomparable eloquence and wisdom. He was patient, forgiving, gentle, and loving. Why didn't all Jews accept him as the Messiah? Why were the Jewish leaders determined to kill him?

Let us enter into Christ's world that we might learn how and why the events of Holy Week unfolded as they did, what he endured for our salvation, and the depth of his love, expressed ultimately in his voluntary crucifixion for our sakes.

Why Write This Book?

MANY BOOKS HAVE BEEN WRITTEN over the centuries about the crucifixion of Christ. Why write another one? It is a fair question. Pastors have written inspirational books on the crucifixion focused on theology or the spiritual lesson. Medical doctors have explained the suffering of Christ or the cause of his death, but they lack deep knowledge of advanced biblical studies, Roman culture, or New Testament–era Judaism. Specialists in Roman history have offered their valuable expertise about the crucifixion of Christ, but they lack crucial background in first-century Judaism, Jewish law, and a deep understanding of the Gospels, which are the primary source of information for our subject. Theologians and biblical scholars have analyzed the scriptural text, but their writings are generally technical and unconnected to the mind of the early Church. Many of them dismiss important details in the Gospels as unhistorical.

This book offers a unique perspective on the final week of Christ's life. This perspective is based on my academic background and my Orthodox Christian approach, which is steeped in the mind of the early Church. I hold six degrees, one in law and five in theology, including New Testament, the history of biblical interpretation, early Christianity, and patristics.

I have always been fascinated by trials. Not surprisingly, trials in the Bible occupied much of my research attention as a graduate student of theology and even as a law student. The title of my master of theology thesis at Harvard was "First-Century Roman Criminal Trial Procedures in the Provinces."[1] The research required a deep dive into an entirely different legal system from our own, including the history, presumptions, and framework of Roman law. This thrust me into a surprising world, even more dissimilar to ours than I had imagined, with entirely different assumptions about people, society, and the law.[2] My doctoral research also immersed me in the world of the Roman Empire during its first six centuries. Expertise in biblical studies, the world of the New Testament, and the early Church is essential to any competent analysis of events surrounding the crucifixion of Christ.

The Accessibility of Relevant Information

THIS BOOK EXTENDS FAR BEYOND a simple presentation of the Bible and Church tradition. My comments are grounded in research on ancient society, attitudes, customs, practices, medicine, botany, numismatics, law, and the history of first-century Jewish, Roman, and Christian cultures, as well as

---

1   Harvard Divinity School, 1998.
2   US law is based on English common law, not Roman law.

Orthodox Tradition and the writings of the Fathers of the Church, which are important witnesses to the early understanding of the Gospels.

In reading this book, you will benefit from the expertise and insights of medical doctors, Roman scholars, biblical scholars, archeologists, botanists, philologists, Jewish academics, and others, without having to wade through stacks of articles and books laden with scholarly jargon and quotations in Greek, Hebrew, and Latin. I also hope the book will give you a glimpse into the behind-the-scenes work of scholars and the detailed information necessary for real knowledge of the Bible. I hope it will fascinate you, inspire you, and answer many questions—even some you didn't know you had.

Is the Bible Historically Reliable?

I AM STILL AN ATTORNEY, and even though I no longer work in that field, my legal education and training have never left me. I have always been logical, analytical, and even a skeptic by nature. As a lawyer, I need evidence. I want to know what really happened.

Attorneys also know that eyewitness accounts can be flawed, but they are not meaningless or without value—especially when multiple eyewitnesses testify to the same thing. While conducting investigations and doing legal research, I could not ignore evidence and assume that something different must have happened simply because I had a bias in favor of my client. Unfortunately, many scholars take precisely this position in biblical studies: they ignore the facts in evidence and make statements based on their personal assumptions or religious beliefs.

What does this have to do with the Bible? Simply, the Gospels are historical accounts and deserve to be taken seriously as historical documents. But the details they contain are often overlooked or dismissed as lacking credibility. Every writer has a perspective, a bias, and a purpose for writing. The fact that the Gospel writers had a theological perspective and purpose—to tell people about Jesus Christ—does not eliminate them as credible sources of historical information. Classical historians agree with this approach, and in their analyses they take into consideration the perspective and motivation of ancient authors, rather than automatically dismissing a document as untrustworthy or laden with unhistorical details.

The Importance of First-Generation Witnesses

MOST HISTORIANS BELIEVE THAT ONLY about ten percent of the books that existed in antiquity have survived until today. Furthermore, most ancient books that give us information about important historical figures, such as Alexander the Great, were composed hundreds of years after the famous person lived. Compare that reality to the Gospels. We don't know exactly when the Gospels were written, but probably no earlier than the mid-first century. Most scholars would date them between AD 70 and 90.

While Bible scholars consider those dates to be "late," historians consider the Gospels to be early and extremely credible documents because they were written within the lifetime of people who witnessed the events. Historians call such writings "first-generation" sources. Average life expectancy was much lower in the first century than today due to infant mortality and women dying during childbirth. But the lifespans of ancient people who survived to adulthood almost rivaled those of today. Numerous early writings and grave markers confirm that many people lived to the age of sixty, seventy, eighty— even ninety or more. This means that many eyewitnesses of Jesus Christ were still alive when the Gospels were written.[3]

Why is it important that the Gospels are products of the first century? Skeptics often claim that details in these accounts are legendary additions, theologically motivated but historically untrue. Wouldn't early believers quickly embellish the story of Jesus with legendary or mythological elements? Actually, no. The usual pattern is quite the opposite. Historians prefer earlier accounts because first-generation witnesses are very reliable and less likely to include embellishments than the writers of later accounts. Fictitious details and stories rarely develop during the first generation, because memories

---

3   The last apostle died during the reign of Trajan (AD 98–117), but eyewitnesses to Christ and even people healed by him lived into the time of Hadrian, who succeeded Trajan. Eusebius of Caesarea, *History of the Church* 4.3.2, NPNF-2 1:175.

are fresh and the existence of living eyewitnesses inhibits fabrications and exaggerations.[4]

Classical historians are puzzled by the unwarranted skepticism of many Bible scholars toward the Gospels, since they are first-generation historical sources about Jesus. Historians are much more objective and unbiased toward the use of New Testament books as historical sources and apply the same standards and analyses as they would for any other written source.

Another important factor in the reliability of the Gospels is their plurality. Historians feel lucky if even *one* first-generation written source exists to tell us about a historical person from antiquity. But in the case of Jesus Christ, we have *four* first-generation witnesses—books written during the lifetimes of people who experienced Jesus' ministry firsthand. This is a tremendous amount of credible evidence, and it is supported by multiple sources of corroboration.

Historians accept the Gospels as generally credible for four reasons: First, they are first-generation books, written while eyewitnesses were still alive. Secondly, multiple witnesses exist: four Gospels, not just one. Third, what the Gospels say is supported by other parts of the New Testament, all by authors who wrote independently of one another. Finally, the Gospels are corroborated by other evidence, including ancient writings—Jewish, Greek, and Roman—and archeological discoveries.

Studies of the reliability and credibility of ancient documents occasionally employ the term *verisimilitude*. This long word asks us to consider whether details in the ancient documents (in this case, the Gospels) match what we know from other ancient sources of information. Does the document ring true? Are the statements generally verifiable? Are this document's statements similar to what we read in other documents of the period? As applied to the Gospels, we might ask the following questions: Do the Gospels accurately reflect first-century Palestine? Do the people, lifestyle, customs, practices, attitudes, geographical locations, religious beliefs, and historical figures

---

4   Apocrypha, the false apostolic writings (c. AD 150–250), differ dramatically in style and content. Never considered Scripture, they were not first-generation writings. The stories are sensationalized in contrast to the simple, straightforward style of the Gospels.

mentioned in the Gospels match what we know from other historical sources about those times, places, and persons?

Yes, they do. The Gospels mention countless historical people whose identities have been confirmed, countless places that actually existed, and many events that have been corroborated by other historical sources outside the New Testament. The Gospels present an accurate picture of first-century Palestine. In short, by any objective standard, the Gospels display an extremely high correlation to facts we know to be true about first-century Judaism and the Roman Empire. This means that the Gospels are historically reliable.

Many historical persons and events, such as King David, were at one time dismissed as mythological, until archeological discoveries confirmed their existence. Archeology continues regularly and consistently to prove, not disprove, the accuracy of the accounts of people, places, and events in the Bible. You will learn about some of these in this book.

Biblical Studies and the Postmodern Mind

THOSE WHO REJECT THE EVANGELISTS as biased are biased themselves. Every human being, modern and ancient, has biases. That is inescapable. The only question is whether the Gospels have limited or questionable historical value simply because of the theological motivation and purpose of their authors. If we were to eliminate from historical consideration every source that displays a bias, almost all ancient writings of any kind would be disqualified.

In our era of rampant skepticism, people unrealistically expect everything important to be documented. But people of the past did not rely on writing as we do today. Books were rare and expensive. The first Christians received only oral teachings, not written documents. Even some Bible scholars claim that the Gospels expanded on the events to make it appear that prophecies had been fulfilled.

But the accounts of the crucifixion itself are relatively short, and if the Church had searched for prophecies simply to claim that Christ fulfilled them, the Passion story would contain many more details. Those who knew and loved Jesus vividly remembered what happened to him. His followers endlessly discussed his life and teachings. Rather than contributing to falsehood or distortion, this discussion ensured the preservation of accurate details, because vast numbers of early Christians had met and directly interacted with Jesus Christ. The first Christians experienced something powerful and life altering in Jesus Christ and would not have lied about it.

Living eyewitnesses ensure greater accuracy for another reason: the evangelists cared about their personal reputations, just as we would. Not only would it have been dishonest deliberately to invent stories or details about Jesus, but falsehoods would have been refuted by eyewitnesses, destroying the credibility of the author.

Eyewitnesses were especially important in the early Church since people learned about Jesus from the apostles firsthand. The first Christians preserved everything the apostles taught; we call that knowledge Apostolic Tradition. The church leaders after the apostles did not decide for themselves what to believe or how to behave as Christians. Early Christians learned everything from the apostles, who had learned directly from the Lord himself. There were hundreds of apostles, not just the Twelve.[5] The apostles were constantly traveling, and the first Christians had many opportunities to discuss events in the life of Christ with eyewitnesses. The Gospels were written later, as a supplement to the primarily oral preaching of the gospel message. The first Christians did not learn about Jesus by reading the Gospels. Understanding this requires a paradigm shift in our thinking.

Truth and the Early Christian

ARGUMENTS ARE OFTEN MADE THAT extraordinary events, such as the darkness on the day Christ died, are symbols designed to appeal to ancient readers or recall Old Testament prophecies. We are told that it is illogical to believe such details are factual. The skepticism in our culture subjects everything in the Bible to a test of rationalism and leaves no room for the miraculous. But God is not limited by the laws of nature, and he operates outside the realm of human reason. That is the very message of the cross.

---

5   Initially, the term *apostle* applied to any eyewitness of Christ's Resurrection.

Numerous excellent and respected biblical scholars have unfortunately concluded on the basis of science and rationalism that certain events in the life of Christ did not or could not have happened, or that certain statements attributed to Christ are things he would not have said. Many of these scholars are well-intentioned, intelligent, and sincere Christian believers who no doubt would be greatly offended at being accused of presenting falsehoods in their books. Yet they accuse the evangelists of falsifications, attempting to soften their criticism by attributing such details to the theological reflection of the Church.

The early Christians cared a great deal about truth, especially truths about Jesus Christ. In the prologue of his Gospel, St. Luke assured the recipient of his writing, Theophilus, that he had personally investigated everything he recorded there (Luke 1:1–4). Luke affirmed that it is all true and that he had spoken to the eyewitnesses.

Biblical Scholarship and Orthodox Christianity

BIBLICAL SCHOLARS MAY BE SUSPICIOUS of Apostolic Tradition or lack confidence in it. Perhaps this is because other churches have not preserved Apostolic Tradition, and therefore most scholars have not experienced its power and reliability. Academic circles in contemporary theology and biblical studies tend to accept only that which we can rationally deduce and reasonably prove with our limited human minds. Orthodox Christianity, on the other hand, does not demand that the New Testament conform to the limitations of human reason.

Bible scholars may not lack faith, but they place emphasis on rationalism and the application of human reasoning in theology. This methodology, developed in Western Europe during the Middle Ages, is so entrenched in our culture that these scholars assume there is no other reliable way to think, no other approach to theology or biblical studies. But that manner of thought is completely foreign to the mind of the evangelists and others in the early Church. The New Testament was not written by or for the heirs of medieval theology or the Enlightenment.

What was the mind of the early Church? Christianity was Eastern and apostolic, not Western and rationalistic. It was planted and established among people whose thought processes and assumptions were completely different from those of the average Christian in the world today. The Orthodox Church alone has preserved the mindset of the ancient Church. Orthodox biblical scholars respect Apostolic Tradition, early Church traditions, faith, and spiritual insights, and they consider these factors essential to a correct interpretation of the Bible. That was the mind of the early Church.

Many academics consider Orthodox Christians to be incapable of objective biblical scholarship. Bible scholars who accept the biblical witness as true are frequently regarded as pathetic relics of a bygone era; they are dismissed as narrowminded, stubborn, and hampered by an archaic devotion to the past. In this view the Orthodox are lumped together with fundamentalist Protestants who take every word of the Bible literally. But Orthodoxy is influenced not by Protestant fundamentalism but by Apostolic Tradition. We reject both extremes: academic rationalism on the left and rigid fundamentalism on the right. Orthodox biblical scholars follow an unbroken Tradition that puts us in line with the teachings and mentality of the apostles. If we are to understand the writings of the early Church, especially the New Testament, we must first understand the mind of the early Church.[6]

The Patristic Contribution

THE ORTHODOX CHURCH DOES NOT oppose serious biblical scholarship. The Fathers of the Church were not fundamentalists. They actually applied most of the techniques used in modern scholarship. They examined the biblical text critically, meaning they analyzed the Bible. Their opinions were informed by history, geography, literary analysis, philology, and manuscript evidence. What they lacked that we have today is information gleaned from archeological discoveries and our greater knowledge of first-century Judaism.

---

6   I discuss the differences between Western Christian and Eastern Christian thought in my book *Thinking Orthodox*.

But they had something valuable that we lack and can never recover: they lived in the Roman world and spoke Greek or Latin as their native tongue. They understood the nuances of the language and were immersed in the complex culture of the Roman Empire. They lived in an era closer to the events of the New Testament and were in a much better position than we are to interpret and explain what truly happened. For that reason alone, patristic interpretations are valuable.

Yet another factor makes their contribution of vital importance: the Fathers of the Church applied not only their minds and education to understanding the biblical text but also their lives of holiness and prayer. They had spiritual insight, *theoria,* which is not acquired through books or instruction. This combination of academic knowledge, spirituality, direct knowledge of Greek as a living language, familiarity with Roman culture, and fidelity to ancient Apostolic Tradition is the reason we respect the patristic interpreters.

On one level, the Bible can be understood by anyone. But delving deeply and interpreting it correctly requires serious study, tools, techniques, and knowledge as opposed to mere opinion. Saint John Chrysostom often spoke of the need for real study and expertise to understand the Scriptures. He compared these skills to mining for gold, which requires hard work, the right tools, and specialized knowledge in order to acquire the treasure. Much of what is valuable in the Bible is not found on the surface, Chrysostom said, just as gold is not easily acquired by simply scratching the surface of the ground.[7] He also reminds us that academic study is only part of what is necessary for understanding the Scriptures. It also requires silence, faith, a life of prayer, and especially virtue. The Bible is spiritual and can be correctly understood only by those who are spiritual.

For this reason, bare rationalism and a purely academic approach can never begin to plumb its depths. Even intelligent and sincere scholars who reject a faith perspective and are not engaged in spiritual struggle can never correctly understand or explain the Bible, because their understanding will always remain superficial and limited to the letter of the text, the *historia,* which even in the life of the early Church was considered the lowest level of meaning.

---

7   Chrysostom, *Homilies on Genesis* 21.1–2.

Critical analysis and modern biblical scholarship are important and useful, but the Bible is not a dead object to be dissected, a set of documents whose truth is confined to the surface or to what can be comprehended by the rational mind. The Bible is the inspired word of God, and the Gospels are living testimony about Jesus Christ. They are very much alive, because the life and words of Jesus Christ still live within the Church and speak to each generation.

Along with an Orthodox understanding of the Gospels, this book will employ the fruits of modern scholarship in looking at the early Church and first-century Jewish life, culture, practices, and beliefs. I will exercise some literary license by delving into the psyches of people who participated in these events, so that we might better understand their possible thoughts and motivations. Such scenes do not rest on pure imagination but are based on historical information.

Film and Television Portrayals of the Crucifixion

AT THE OPPOSITE END OF the spectrum from academic analysis, we have popular representations of the events of the Gospels, including the crucifixion. These can be equally problematic in different ways.

Many people expressed significant concerns prior to the release of the 2004 Mel Gibson film *The Passion of the Christ,* anticipated to be the most realistic depiction of crucifixion in cinema to date. First, Jews worldwide were understandably worried that the movie might enflame anti-Semitism. Secondly, questions arose even before its theatrical release concerning the film's accuracy and Gibson's sources of information. Gibson repeatedly stated in media interviews that his sources were "Matthew, Mark, Luke, and John." Unfortunately, that was not true. Gibson, a devout Catholic, supplemented the Gospels with ideas drawn from Catholic traditions, such as the Stations of the Cross and the visions of certain Catholic mystics who described incidents that never happened to Christ. These imaginative events were included in the movie.

Although the cinematography was beautiful, biblical scholars were quite disappointed by *The Passion of the Christ.* Unfortunately, the film was historically and biblically inaccurate in more ways than I could count, a subject

much discussed among scholars at the time. Movies about the Bible are notoriously inaccurate, including the 2013 miniseries *The Bible,* whose producers,
Roma Downey and Mark Burnett, identify themselves as devout Christians
and promised to be faithful to the Bible. The series committed innumerable
historical and biblical errors throughout all the episodes, including obvious
changes to Bible stories that turned out to be comical distortions.

Audiences are usually unaware of these errors and assume that what they
are watching is accurate. Filmmaking requires certain adaptations, and a
degree of poetic license is acceptable, but many inaccuracies serve no purpose
at all. Rather than vividly portraying the Bible narratives for modern audiences, these films often misinform.

Let Us Journey to Jerusalem

GREAT AND HOLY WEEK IN the Orthodox Church looms large in the
annual liturgical cycle, presenting us with an extensive and intensive array
of services, sometimes two or three per day. The week begins the day before
Palm Sunday, on what the Orthodox Church calls the Saturday of Lazarus,
and continues through Pascha and the appearance of the Lord to his disciples
on the evening of Resurrection Day.

Each Holy Week service is unique, thought provoking, emotive, introspec-
tive, deeply historical, profoundly theological, and completely rooted in the
Scriptures. Every detail found in the Gospels is echoed and interpreted in the
eloquent hymns and prayers, which meditate on and then express the meaning of the historical events. Orthodox Christianity has preserved practices,
prayers, divine services, and traditions stretching back to the early Church.
The Orthodox services of Great Week express how the early Church understood the events of Christ's Passion through countless subtle details.

The Lord fulfilled not only prophecies but generations of Jewish hopes,
wishes, ideas, and expectations. The impact and value of Holy Tradition
is never so obvious in Orthodoxy as it is during Great Week, as we hear the
ancient voices of our ancestors in the faith whispering in our ears. Orthodox
services articulate not only our personal, human response to the inexpressible
love and condescension of God, but the profound and insightful theological

reflection of the ancient Church, which deeply experienced and then profoundly expressed the incomprehensible mystery of the Passion to the greatest extent possible in human language.

I wish to thank Dr. George Abouyanni, Dr. Dn. Paul Kalina, and Dr. Maria Lentzou for their helpful suggestions and for reviewing the accuracy of my medical statements. Most of all, endless thanks to my long-suffering husband, Fr. Costas, for his patience as I worked on this book.

Holy Week services are a blessing offered to us year after year, a powerful mechanism through which we are invited to engage and ponder the most monumental and consequential events in history and the way they reveal the unfathomable love, humility, and forbearance of Christ. When we faithfully attend the full sequence of services (being not merely physically present but actively attentive), we dive deeper into the mystery of the cross. We are rewarded with brief flashes of insight, but those moments of sudden illumination ironically also confound our incredulous human minds, leaving us only to ponder the enigma of this impenetrable paradox.

We want to know Jesus. We want to see him, hear him, experience him. Let us journey to Jerusalem. Let us walk the dusty roads of Judea together behind Christ and the apostles. Let us peer into the dark tomb of Lazarus, ascend the staircase inside the Temple Mount, and arrive at the summit to gape at the enormity and opulence of the Temple. We will hear the bleating Passover lambs and the Levites chanting the psalms. We will eavesdrop on the Sanhedrin's deliberations, stand by the charcoal fire with Peter, and witness Pilate's deep apprehensions.

It is my wish that this book will transport you on a journey of discovery, alternating between the dramatic, the informative, the spiritual, and the inspirational. But above all, it is my sincere hope that it will open the world of Christ to you and give you a behind-the-scenes glimpse into the last week in the life of Jesus Christ, leading to a deeper appreciation of his Passion that you will never forget.

We worship your Passion, O Christ!

Eugenia Scarvelis Constantinou
Feast of the Exaltation of the Cross, 2021

On the Jewish People
and the Death of Jesus Christ

T HE DEATH OF JESUS CHRIST is a highly sensitive topic for the Jewish people. Let me be explicit and direct: The Jews as a people, either living at the time of Christ or now, *do not* bear responsibility for the death of Jesus.

Many Jews over the centuries have suffered persecution by so-called Christians who labeled them "Christ killers." This has historically been more common in Western Europe than in traditionally Orthodox countries, but the Christian East has not been immune to this attitude, which all Christians should reject. The Church ultimately held Pontius Pilate responsible for the death of Christ, as indeed he was. We say in the Nicene Creed that Jesus was "crucified under Pontius Pilate." No mention is made of any Jewish participation. Anti-Semitism, hatred toward Jews as a group, persecution of Jews, or indeed the hatred or persecution of *any* group of people is a sin that can never be excused, justified, or condoned.

While I recognize and respect Jewish sensitivity on this issue, the opposite is equally dishonest and inaccurate. We cannot pretend that *no* Jews were involved in the condemnation and death of Jesus. Merely explaining the historical involvement of a small number of Jews in the death of Jesus does not constitute either hatred or anti-Semitism. References in this book to various Jewish leaders and their involvement in the death of Christ are not intended and should not be interpreted as an indictment of *all* Jews, either then or now.

Jesus was not the first Christian. He was Jewish and participated fully in Jewish life. It goes without saying that all the first followers of Christ were devout Jews as well, including his mother, all the apostles, and tens of

14

thousands of Jews who followed him and believed him to be the One whom the prophets had foretold. Thousands were baptized and joined the infant Church in Jerusalem after Pentecost. They did not join Christianity, since it did not exist as a separate religion for decades.[1] The Church was a Jewish movement rooted in Jerusalem and called the Way (Acts 9:2). In other parts of the Roman Empire, thousands more Jews also accepted the preaching of the apostles because the gospel message was spread initially in the synagogues.

During the second century, around AD 150, a Christian presbyter named Marcion argued that the Church should reject everything Jewish, including the Jewish Scriptures. But it was Marcion and his ideas that the Church rejected. To this day we firmly embrace our rich Jewish heritage and cannot imagine our services without the writings of the prophets, the psalms, and Hebrew words such as *amen* and *alleluia*. We use countless psalms in our worship services, and we treasure the Old Testament books as Scripture. We preserve the Jewish roots of our faith in countless practices that Orthodox Christianity still observes in unbroken continuation from the early Church. Our liturgical connections to the Jewish rituals and services are strikingly obvious to any Orthodox Christian who has been to a synagogue service or to any Jew who visits an Orthodox church.

It was not easy to be a Jewish believer in Jesus during the first century, just as it is not easy today. We owe much to our Jewish ancestors in the faith who established the first churches in countless cities and towns in the Roman Empire. The Church of Greece has as its founder a Jewish Christian: St. Paul. The Church has never forgotten this, and Orthodox priests, bishops, and lay people saved many thousands of Jews from Hitler's concentration camps during World War II—by hiding them, by refusing to identify them to the Germans, by producing false baptismal certificates for them, and by other measures.

Saint Paul wondered why more Jews did not accept Jesus as the Christ. He concluded that this was part of God's plan for the salvation of the "Greeks," the word the New Testament uses to refer to all non-Jews. Disbelief on the

---

1   Eventually, around AD 85, the Jews who rejected Jesus excommunicated the Jewish-Christian believers, creating a clear separation between Judaism and Christianity.

part of most of the Jews resulted in Gentiles joining the Church, which was foretold by the prophets. But Paul warned the Gentile Christians not to think of themselves as superior to Jewish Christians. He also warned the Jewish Christians not to despise the "Greek" Christians, who were like a wild olive tree that had been "grafted on" to the cultivated olive tree of Israel, meaning the Church (Rom. 9—11).

The challenges faced by first-century Jewish believers in Jesus still exist for Jewish Christians among us now. The apostles were labeled as blasphemers; today, Jews who convert to the Christian faith are not only considered blasphemers but are reviled as traitors to their own people. They often risk alienating their entire family when they confess faith in Christ. It was no different when the Church first began. For a Jew to accept Jesus as the Messiah demands a great deal of courage, sacrifice, and faith, far more than most of us will ever realize.

Jesus the Messiah came for the Jewish people first of all, and historically his ministry was directed exclusively toward Jews. He loved them, and they loved him. The tragic legacy of anti-Semitism, vile rhetoric, and harassment of Jews by some Christians is responsible for the sad reality that the name of our Savior, who loved his people and died for them, is now associated with hatred and persecution. Many Jews refuse even to pronounce the name of Jesus, nor do they want to hear it spoken. The Talmud refers to Jesus as "Yeshu," an intentional corruption of his Jewish name (Yeshua),[2] and describes Jesus in hell in the worst and most shameful conditions. This is the legacy of Christian anti-Semitism: that even the name of our Lord is rejected—not so much because of what he himself said or did, but because the Jewish people were persecuted in his name.

Some Jews were responsible for rejecting and crucifying Jesus, and they will be judged by God for their involvement. That is neither our business nor our concern. Likewise, Christians who have participated in shaming, condemning, or harassing Jews for the death of Jesus Christ will certainly be judged for their actions. We do not stand as judges of anyone, in the past or today. God alone knows the heart, and he alone is Judge. Christ came into this

---

2   *Yeshu* is an acronym for the words "May his name and memory be obliterated."

world as "the true light that enlightens" every human being (John 1:9). Bringing the light of Christ to all means bringing the love of Christ to all. Both are absolutely incompatible with hatred and anti-Semitism, bigotry, or prejudice of any kind.

But fear of anti-Semitism has compelled most Jews to attempt to distance themselves from the death of Jesus. They have approached the problem by marshaling a variety of defenses. Some point to the fact that Jesus forgave those who executed him, and Christians should follow suit. Others say that if Christians believe the crucifixion of Jesus brought salvation, they should thank the Jews. Some say that Jesus broke the Law, was a blasphemer and a deceiver, and got what he deserved. Many Jews simply deny any Jewish involvement, placing responsibility for the death of Jesus on the Romans alone, which is neither factually true nor intellectually honest. It is patently unfair and inaccurate to hold all Jews responsible for the death of Jesus, but we must also be honest and acknowledge that a small group of Jewish leaders was responsible for orchestrating his death.

Jeremy Cohen provides a balanced assessment of various arguments Jews have employed to defend themselves against anti-Semitic rhetoric concerning the crucifixion. He also notes that one argument never arises: no Jew claims that the events of Jesus' arrest, trial, and crucifixion never occurred. "Jews of late antiquity, the Middle Ages and modern times, have rarely discredited the essential plotline of the Gospels' passion narrative, even as they have rejected the Christian understanding and interpretation of that narrative,"[3] Cohen writes. He observes that the Passion narrative has evoked "ambivalent responses" on the part of Jews throughout the ages and even remarks that some Jews today occasionally reclaim Jesus and parts of his message.

The facts concerning the death of Jesus are incontrovertible. The purpose of this book is not to fix blame but simply to examine the events and circumstances in their historical context and ponder the spiritual lessons of the crucifixion. Specific factors motivated the Jewish leaders of Christ's time to take the actions they did. The story of Christ's Passion is preserved in the Gospels

---

3   Jeremy Cohen, "On Pesach and Pascha," 348–49.

not in order to condemn the Jews—those living then, now, or during any historical period. "Whatever was written in the former days was written for our instruction" (Rom. 15:4), and "all scripture is profitable," wrote St. Paul (2 Tim. 3:16). These stories are written for us, that we may use them to learn, to understand, to be inspired, and to improve ourselves spiritually.

The faith and sacrifice of Jewish believers, including but not limited to the apostles, established churches that became the means of salvation, first for Jewish believers and then for Gentiles as well. Everyone in the world at that time, other than the Jews, worshipped idols. This includes the ancestors of all of us who are not of Jewish descent.

Greeks around the world are proud of their Greek heritage, and rightly so. But in spite of their intelligence, education, and sophistication, the ancient Greeks worshipped idols, and their gods were corrupt, flawed, and extremely immoral—certainly not examples of holiness and virtue! The ancient Greeks gave us many wonderful things—science, mathematics, literature, history, art, theatre, and philosophy. But they did not give us the gospel or the truth about the One True God. Above all, they did not give us the Christ. As the Lord himself said, "Salvation is from the Jews" (John 4:22). *Amin!* Glory to God.

PART I

The Stage Is Set

CHAPTER 1

A Crucified Messiah

I THIRST."

Not a drop of liquid had crossed his lips since the meal he had shared with his disciples the evening before. His blood was now thick and sluggish, and his heart struggled to send the oxygen his body needed. His breathing was rapid and shallow. Severely dehydrated, he felt unbearable thirst as his dry, swollen tongue stuck to the roof of his mouth. Even the most basic humane gesture—a simple drink of water—was denied to him.

Stretched out against rough-hewn beams, his bruised and battered body was bloodied from wounds too numerous to count. His female disciples, powerless to help him, nonetheless faithfully held vigil near the foot of the cross. Standing with them was the "beloved disciple," John. He was stunned. Disbelieving. John could not comprehend the numbing sequence of events. Less than twenty-four hours earlier, he had helped prepare a meal to be joyfully celebrated with the Master and the other disciples. As they ate, the Master said one of them would betray him. Betrayed by one of his own? Impossible! But it happened.

In just a few hours, the lives of the disciples were completely upended. A series of traumatic events struck them in rapid succession, each more shocking than the previous one, enveloping them in a whirlwind of confusion and fear. Just as he had foretold, Jesus was betrayed, arrested, and condemned to the cross. And now John stood incredulous, grieving at his Master's suffering, the sole member of the Twelve to witness the final moments of his horrific and agonizing ordeal. The remaining disciples were hiding from the Jewish authorities, bereft, confused, and bewildered as they pondered this staggering reversal.

Jesus had healed the crippled and the maimed, restored sight to the blind and hearing to the deaf. He fed thousands from a few fish and loaves of bread. He cured lepers, cast out demons, and raised the dead. He knew everything and could do anything. He was at once powerful and gentle. Weren't all these things proof? They had witnessed it all. They knew he was the Christ, the Messiah. Even the crowd welcoming him into Jerusalem had acclaimed Jesus as the Messiah and King of Israel! And yet, now he was being crucified, dying, and with him were dying all their hopes.

For centuries, the Jewish people had found comfort in the shared hope of God's Messiah. Sabbath services at village synagogues reminded them that God was faithful to his promises. Readings of the prophets, especially Isaiah, shaped their expectations about the Messiah. Exactly when he would arrive, no one knew, but that the Messiah would come, they had no doubt. He would be holy and would reign in righteousness (Is. 9:7; 11:4); he would be descended from David, sprung from the root of Jesse (Is. 11:1, 10); and he would come as the servant of the LORD (Is. 42:1; 49:6; 52:13; 53:11). He would inaugurate a New Covenant (Jer. 31:31/38:31 LXX). The Spirit of the LORD would be upon him, the Spirit of wisdom, understanding, counsel, might, knowledge, godliness, and the fear of the LORD (Is. 11:2; 61:1). He would give sight to the blind; the deaf would hear, and the lame would walk again by his power (Is. 29:18; 35:5–6).

Centuries passed, and a variety of messianic expectations developed among different groups of Jews. Rather than diminishing, these hopes and expectations increased over time, especially after the arrival of Roman rule in 63 BC, when the Roman general Pompey entered Jerusalem and claimed the region for Rome. The Jews had enjoyed a brief period of freedom after liberating themselves from the Seleucid dynasty—Greek rulers headquartered in Antioch who had inherited part of Alexander the Great's once vast kingdom. The Maccabees, Jewish freedom fighters, had successfully led a revolt against the Seleucids, inaugurating a brief period of independent rule for the

Jews under the Hasmonean Kingdom. But after only a century of freedom and autonomy, the Jews found themselves again under foreign occupation by the Romans, the latest power to dominate the Mediterranean world.

The Romans allowed a measure of self-government under King Herod the Great and his successors. Herod was actually a foreigner from Idumea, a nation just south of Judea. The Jews suffered under both pagan Roman rulers and Herodian kings, intensifying their entreaties that God would send "the Coming One," the Messiah.

Their prayers would be answered, but not in a manner anyone could have imagined. They knew the Messiah would be a descendant of David, would restore the kingdom of Israel, and would rule in righteousness. But messianic prophecies created confusion, since some prophecies hinted at a suffering Messiah, even a dead Messiah. These ideas appeared to conflict entirely with the concept of a victorious royal leader like King David, for which most Jews hoped. Many assumed that the Messiah Son of David would expel the Romans and restore Jewish self-rule. But some prophecies described an everlasting kingdom, a kingdom of perfect peace. How can a kingdom last forever? How can a kingdom exist in perfect peace?

The answer to this conundrum was both simple and staggering: these messianic prophecies could be fulfilled only by the LORD himself. He would come—not to be served, but to serve. The Shepherd of Israel would become the Perfect Lamb. The Eternal One would consent to die. The Creator would be abused by his creatures, and the King of the universe would suffer at the hands of his servants. The Kingdom he would bring would be the Kingdom of heaven. Though not understood at the time, even this was prophesied:

> For to us a child is born, to us a son is given; and the government will be upon his shoulder, and his name will be called "Wonderful Counselor, Mighty God, Everlasting Father, Prince of Peace." Of the increase of his government and of his peace there will be no end, upon the throne of David, and over his kingdom, to establish it, and to uphold it with justice and with righteousness from this time forth and for evermore. The zeal of the LORD of hosts will do this. (Is. 9:6–7)

For hundreds of years, God's people hoped, prayed, and waited for the Messiah. Philip expressed the exuberant joy of the disciples when he announced to Nathaniel, "We have found him of whom Moses in the law and also the prophets wrote" (John 1:45). Yes, they had found him at last. Jesus of Nazareth was the One. Everything he said, everything he did left no doubt. No one else had ever fulfilled all those extraordinary prophecies. The disciples were so joyful! So confident!

But now all was lost. John stood devasted, overwhelmed, and utterly helpless as he witnessed the final moments of Jesus' suffering. Had he not spent practically every waking moment with Jesus over the past three years, John might not even have recognized the Master. His face was swollen because of beatings. His body was streaked with caked and dried blood, his back mangled and torn by the lashes of the fearsome Roman flagellum. Blood from a crown of thorns, made in cruel jest and forced onto his head, matted his hair and ran down his face. Oh, that gentle face! John had studied that face so carefully as Jesus had shown love, compassion, and mercy toward countless others. He did not deserve this! How did this even *happen*?

John could not imagine that anything could explain or make sense of the crucifixion of Jesus of Nazareth. Life would never be the same.

He was right.

CHAPTER 2

Jesus, the Rabbi Who Taught with Authority

M OST CHRISTIANS DON'T ENCOUNTER RABBIS on a regular basis. We easily forget that the Lord served the people of Israel as a rabbi, an informal Hebrew title that simply meant "teacher."

Around the age of thirty, Jesus began a rather unconventional ministry of teaching and healing, preaching repentance and the nearness of the Kingdom of God. Everyone was welcome to join his movement, including those with a wayward past who had been rejected by establishment Judaism, and others no ordinary rabbi would have accepted as disciples. What a hodgepodge his disciples were: uneducated laborers, fishermen, tradesmen, former tax collectors, the once demon possessed, even women! Some of the most respected leaders in Israel also believed in Jesus, although secretly.

Modern Christians rarely recognize the exceptional and extraordinary nature of the Lord's teachings and actions. Jesus forgave sins, ate with tax collectors and sinners, touched lepers, and taught that virtue—humility, love, patience, forgiveness, mercy—and inner purity of the heart were more important than the outward observance of ritual purity. To Christians this seems perfectly reasonable, even obvious, but Jews presumed that the observation of religious obligations of ritual purity was paramount. They also assumed that being a descendant of Abraham practically guaranteed one would enter the Kingdom of heaven. When the Lord's Forerunner, John the Baptist, and the Lord himself told the Jewish leaders to repent, they objected, saying, "We have Abraham as our father" (Luke 3:8; John 8:39). Jesus taught that simply being Jewish by blood or scrupulously keeping thousands of regulations did not guarantee one would enter the Kingdom of heaven without inner purity.

Today, Judaism embraces a variety of lifestyles and opinions. Modern Jews disagree about the extent of their observance of the Law—meaning not the Ten Commandments but the thousands of rules that govern daily Jewish life, concerning circumcision, Sabbath regulations, dietary rules, ritual washings, and other laws of ritual purity. Most Jews now live primarily secular lives and rarely observe ritual purity to a significant degree. But in the Lord's time, all Jews obeyed at least the most important requirements of the Law, because otherwise they risked rejection by the community.

First-century Judaism encompassed a variety of groups that disagreed on other matters, such as whether oral rules were obligatory, what was the role of the Messiah to come, and which books should be regarded as Scripture.

The largest group in first-century Judaism was the Pharisees, the precursors of modern Rabbinic Judaism. They emphasized observing the Law of Moses to the greatest extent possible. The Torah (the first five books of the Jewish Scriptures) contains hundreds of rules, and for this reason the entire Torah itself is called the Law.

Over the centuries, countless additional oral rules developed to address various situations not mentioned in the Torah. The Pharisees were flexible and willingly adapted the Law of Moses to changing circumstances. But twelve hundred years had passed since the time of Moses, and the Law of Moses had increased dramatically from hundreds of rules to thousands. These additional rules had become a burden. The rules were called "the tradition of the elders" or the "oral Law" because they had never been written down.[1] The Pharisees promoted these additional oral rules, which they regarded as binding (obligatory) for all Jews, and taught that observing these laws made someone more acceptable in the eyes of God.

---

1   Eventually (c. AD 200), the oral laws were written down and became known as the Mishnah. The Talmud is the Mishnah plus its interpretations by famous rabbis and Jewish scholars. Compiled between AD 300 and 600, the Talmud encompasses many volumes.

Sometimes the thousands of rules are called ceremonial laws, because they do not involve spiritual purity or physical cleanliness but *ritual* purity and cleanliness. People might be physically clean, highly moral, or deeply spiritual, but certain actions—even if committed accidentally—rendered them ritually unclean. Ritual purity was determined by what people ate, with whom they associated, what they touched, whether they kept the Sabbath correctly, whether they washed in the prescribed manner, and so forth. Once incurred, a state of uncleanliness remained until it was removed by the performance of detailed rituals: washings, prayers, sacrifices, and the passage of a specified period of time.

The Pharisees sincerely believed that God had called the Jews to a life of righteousness and holiness and that their lifestyle benefited the entire world. Certain actions were considered particularly praiseworthy, including tithing, almsgiving, fasting, and observing certain hours as times of prayer.[2] The intricacies of tithing, fasting, ritual washings, dietary regulations, and Sabbath laws were not just rules to be observed for their own sake but a response to the idolatry and immorality of the Roman culture. In stark contrast to Rome, Israel would present itself as a holy nation, loyal to the One True God and ritually pure.

Christians typically perceive Pharisees negatively because they frequently criticized Jesus. But first-century Jews admired and respected the Pharisees for their devotion and strict adherence to the Law. Unfortunately, Pharisaic emphasis on ritual purity often resulted in the neglect of inner purity and virtue. It also led to a haughty self-righteousness and cool indifference toward average but decent Jews, who often did not even know what the countless regulations were. Many Pharisees had little sympathy or concern for everyday folks whose occupation, lifestyle, or economic status made it difficult or impossible for them to maintain a high level of ritual purity. Some Pharisees even despised ordinary Jews and spoke of them in a derogatory manner,

---

2   Jeremias, *Jerusalem in the Time of Jesus*, 250. Several different groups of Pharisees existed in the first century, and their opinions differed, but generally speaking they promoted and favored an extreme observance of ritual purity. Jeremias, 265.

calling them "the people of the land," a slur similar in meaning to "the igno-rant, unwashed masses."[3]

Imagine the contrast when Jesus appeared, caring for and embracing ordi-nary people, loving and forgiving all, even the worst sinners—those whom some Pharisees disregarded, considered hopeless and destined for hell, with-out even the slightest possibility of salvation. Jesus was not opposed to ritual purity, but he considered the myriad oral laws burdensome and unnecessary. To him, a person was clean or unclean because of what was in his heart, not because of what he ate or touched (Matt. 15:18).

Rabbis, as the teachers of the Law, aligned with the Pharisees. But Jesus, who was a rabbi himself, directly opposed what other rabbis were trying to accomplish. They encouraged ritual purity while Jesus touched lepers (Matt. 8:3) and dead bodies (Luke 7:14), healed on the Sabbath (John 5:16; Mark 3:1–5; Luke 13:10–13), and shared meals with unclean people such as tax collectors and sinners (Luke 15:1–2; Mark 2:15–16).[4] Jesus became ritually unclean in the eyes of the Pharisees by doing these things, but even worse was his forgiveness of sins, which made him guilty of blasphemy (Mark 2:5–7). As a rabbi, a teacher of the people, Jesus was a bad example. The religious authori-ties were aghast at his teaching and behavior, but the people loved him.

The question of Jesus' authority arose for three reasons. First, Jesus never received a formal or traditional rabbinic education. A young man typically studied for years under a recognized teacher (a rabbi), and after he had dem-onstrated his competence, the teacher would acknowledge that his student was adequately prepared and educated. By his teacher's verification, the student was recognized as qualified to be a rabbi, since no rabbinic ordina-tion existed at that time. Jesus had no teacher, no one to vouch for him, and everyone knew that. He had spent his entire youth in Nazareth working as a

---

3   Some Pharisees believed that one should not even share a meal with one of the "people of the land" (the *am ha'aretz*). The term was synonymous with ignorance, boorishness, and not being scrupulously Law observant. Hammer, *Akiva*, 6. The contempt of some of the Jewish leaders toward ordinary Jews is evident in the New Testament: "This crowd, who do not know the law, are accursed" (John 7:4).

4   People ate with their hands and often from the same platter, which implied fellowship and a common way of life. Because he ate with sinners, Jesus was considered to be will-ingly tainted by their ritual impurity.

carpenter, supporting himself and his mother, not sitting at the feet of a rabbi. For this reason, the scribes and Pharisees often scorned Jesus and described him as uneducated (John 7:15).

The second characteristic prompting the question of Jesus' authority was his boldness and unconventional teaching style. Rabbis and scribes typically cited the interpretations of notable teachers of the past. But Jesus never defended his statements by citing earlier rabbinic authorities. Instead, he claimed authority in his own right. Some people regarded him as a prophet, a spokesman for God. Prophets were not expected to have a rabbinic education, since their role was not to teach but to be a mouthpiece for God.

But Jesus was not a prophet and never presented himself as such. The authority behind prophecy was God himself, and the prophets always prefaced their messages with a specific statement: "Thus says the Lord." Jesus never said "Thus says the Lord" because he never claimed to be a prophet; he *was* the Lord. He never claimed to speak on behalf of God since he *was* God. His Jewish critics would have considered this blasphemy. In fact, when he explicitly acknowledged his divinity at his Jewish trial, he was immediately sentenced to death.

The third and most challenging aspect of Jesus' ministry was his amazing signs, his miracles. The scribes and Pharisees were baffled by the combination of extraordinary power and what they considered to be outrageous behavior. Jesus ignored and violated laws of ritual purity that the Pharisees had developed and sincerely believed were essential. The Pharisees were genuinely convinced that they knew the will of God and that the rules they created were God's will for the Jewish people. They were so convinced of their own righteousness that they were adamant: no one who violated their rules could ever be acceptable in the sight of God. Therefore, only one explanation was possible for Jesus' astonishing power: it must come from the devil.

Several different schools of Pharisees existed in the first century, with differences concerning the extent of religious scrupulosity. But Jesus' teachings exceeded even the broadest parameters of Pharisaical opinions. He questioned ritual purity on the one hand and advocated unlimited forgiveness on the other.[5] But while the Pharisees insisted on meticulous obedience to minor rules, they simultaneously ignored major laws, creating legal loopholes and carving out exemptions to avoid fulfilling serious obligations. For example, according to the Pharisees, if someone made a vow by swearing on the Temple, he could break his vow, but if he made his vow on the *gold* of the Temple, he could not break it. Jesus denounced this slippery legalism and warned the Pharisees against "straining out a gnat and swallowing a camel" (Matt. 23:24).

The distinction between man-made rules and the will of God is a modern notion unknown to first-century Jews. Social and religious cohesion and conformity to the Law were important and expected. Religious authorities were revered and obeyed. Scribes and Pharisees were accustomed to honors and praise, a direct contrast to the criticism that Jesus openly leveled against their pride.

Supremely confident of their own righteousness because of their painstaking observance of the tiniest rules of ritual cleanliness, most Pharisees considered Jesus an evil influence, leading the ignorant and gullible masses astray. Pharisees held positions of local leadership and actively plotted Jesus' destruction in the northern district of Galilee long before his arrest in Jerusalem. But many Pharisees resided in Jerusalem and had contacts among powerful national leaders. They undoubtedly alerted their friends in high places to the danger Jesus posed, even if the Pharisees in Galilee could not do much to stop him.

---

5   "I do not say to you seven times, but seventy times seven," which means forgiveness has no limit (Matt. 18:21–22).

CHAPTER 3

The First Catalyst: The Raising of Lazarus

FOR ORTHODOX CHRISTIANS, THE SATURDAY of Lazarus—the day before Palm Sunday—marks the beginning of Holy Week and has done since the early era of the Church. The diary of a fourth-century Western Christian pilgrim named Egeria described Great Week in Jerusalem, including a procession from Jerusalem to Bethany the day before Palm Sunday. On that Saturday:

> Everyone comes to the Lazarium, which is at Bethany, approximately two miles from the city. On the way from Jerusalem to the Lazarium, at about a half mile from that place, there is a church along the road at the very place where Mary, the sister of Lazarus, came forth to meet the Lord. When the bishop reaches this place, all the monks come forth to meet him, and the people go into the church where a hymn and an antiphon are sung and the proper passage from the Gospel is read, describing how Lazarus' sister met the Lord. When a prayer has been said and a blessing given to all, everyone continues on to the Lazarium, chanting hymns; and by the time they have come to the Lazarium, such a multitude has gathered that not only the place itself but all the surrounding fields are filled with people. . . . [After describing the service, she continues.] Because it is written in Scripture that six days before the Pasch this was done in Bethany, therefore on this day this ceremony takes place.[1]

---

1   Egeria, *Diary of a Pilgrimage* 29, 102–3.

In the same way, Orthodox Christians today also remember the raising of Lazarus. The Church provides the historical context for the events of Great and Holy Week through the Scripture readings at the many services, which teach us exactly what happened to Christ and why. By this, the Church affirms that knowing and understanding what happened to Jesus is important.

Only the Orthodox Church celebrates the Saturday of Lazarus, illuminating not only the spiritual significance but the historical connection between the raising of Lazarus and the Lord's entry into Jerusalem. The *apolytikion* (primary hymn) of both the Saturday of Lazarus and Palm Sunday explains, "When you raised Lazarus from the dead before your Passion, you confirmed the common resurrection of us all, Christ God." The raising of Lazarus prompted large crowds to welcome Jesus into Jerusalem on the following day and to hail him as the Messiah. This popular response alarmed the Jewish leaders and became the first catalyst for the arrest of Christ. It motivated the Jewish leaders to take immediate action to eliminate Jesus (John 11:1–48).

Lazarus and his sisters, Mary and Martha, lived in Bethany, a village only two miles outside Jerusalem in the province of Judea. Life in first-century Palestine was difficult. People struggled simply to survive. Some men worked at a trade, but most managed to squeeze a living out of the land as farmers or herders. In the northern region of Galilee was a huge freshwater lake, the Sea of Galilee, from which many earned a living by fishing. Galilee was also greener, more fertile, and better for farming than arid Judea in the south, where Bethany was located.

Judea did not depend on agriculture for its survival since it boasted an unrivaled religious institution, a powerful economic engine that fueled commerce and attracted countless visitors annually: the Temple at Jerusalem. Joyous and colorful celebrations attracted thousands of pilgrims, relieving the dull routine of daily life, giving structure and cadence to the year, marking planting and harvest cycles in a rhythmic fashion that stretched back for countless generations. Passover and Shavuot (Pentecost) aligned with seed planting and the birth of lambs in the spring, while Sukkot (Booths) and Yom Kippur (the Day of Atonement) marked the fall with the harvest of grapes, grain, and other crops.

More intimate than the grand religious festivals were important personal celebrations such as weddings and births, which brought simple joys to village life and hope for a better future. But joys were interspersed with tragedies and loss, such as the sudden illness and death of Lazarus, the beloved brother of two unmarried sisters, Mary and Martha. Lazarus was highly regarded, not only in Bethany but in Jerusalem as well, possessing such an exemplary character that he had become a personal friend of Jesus, who had often stayed with the family during his many journeys to Jerusalem.

When Lazarus fell ill, Mary and Martha sent word to Jesus, asking that he come quickly to heal their brother. But by the time Jesus received the message, Lazarus had already died, and Jesus knew it. Jesus remained two more days where he was before departing for Bethany. Meanwhile, residents of Bethany and Jerusalem streamed to Mary and Martha's home to comfort them. Friends and relatives joined the sisters in making lamentation over Lazarus's body, helping to wash, anoint, and wrap it with strips of cloth.

In the hot Judean climate, the dead were customarily buried the same day they died. The body of Lazarus was placed on a bier or litter supported by two long, horizontal poles, with the four ends carried on the shoulders of four men. As the crowd made its way to the cemetery, funeral musicians and mourners sang dirges. After the procession arrived at the cavelike family tomb and placed the body of Lazarus lovingly inside, a large stone was rolled in front of the entrance to close it off. And that was that.

During the first seven days following a death, family members observed strict rituals of mourning. They were forbidden by the Law to work, bathe, wear shoes, or participate in social activities of any kind. They wore sackcloth, did not comb their hair, and sometimes sprinkled themselves with ashes and dust. They could not leave the house for any reason except to visit the tomb of the deceased. An additional thirty days of mourning followed this initial week, during which restrictions were gradually eased until full participation in society was resumed.[2]

---

2   *Sem.* 6:1, 10.12. The exception to this was that children were expected to mourn their parents for an entire year. McCane, *Roll Back the Stone,* 38; Bromiley, *International Standard Bible Encyclopedia,* "Burial," 1:557.

Jesus arrived four days after the burial to pay his respects and console the sisters—or so everyone assumed. Martha met him on the road just outside the village, most likely returning from the tomb. At the very sight of the Lord, she burst into tears: "Lord, if you had been here, my brother would not have died!" She was not blaming Jesus, only expressing her sadness that he had not arrived in time. But Martha had not lost her faith. "Even now I know that whatever you ask from God, God will give you."

"Your brother will rise again," Jesus replied. Martha nodded her agreement, assuming that the future common resurrection would be her consolation.

But Jesus was not referring to the general resurrection at the end of time. He looked directly into Martha's teary eyes and said firmly, "I AM the resurrection and the life; he who believes in me, though he die, yet shall he live, and whoever lives and believes in me shall never die. Do you believe this?" Martha's eyes returned his steady gaze as she confirmed her faith: "Yes, Lord; I believe that you are the Christ, the Son of God, he who is coming into the world" (John 11:20–27).

Back at the house, Mary sat in mourning. Martha returned and whispered to her that Jesus had arrived and was waiting for her outside the village. Mary abruptly arose and left, kicking up dust as she ran to meet Jesus on the road. Since family members were permitted to leave the house only to weep at the tomb, the friends and neighbors assumed that Mary was going to mourn at the cemetery and ran after her when she suddenly departed.

Falling at the feet of Jesus in tears, Mary expressed the same disappointment as Martha: Jesus had arrived too late. "If you had been here, my brother would not have died." A crowd began to gather on the road to comfort the heartbroken sisters, and Jesus had no further opportunity to speak to them. Deeply moved by their grief and tears, he asked to be led to the tomb, knowing full well where it was and what he was about to do.

Jesus had raised others from the dead, but no one expected that now. The daughter of Jairus was raised, but she had only been dead for perhaps an hour. Upon arriving at Jairus's house, Jesus told the mourners that the girl was not dead, only sleeping, and they laughed at him. Perhaps she *had* only been "sleeping," they reasoned after he brought her out again alive (Luke 8:41–56). On another occasion, Jesus raised a young man in the middle of his own funeral procession in the Galilean town of Nain. He had died only hours before (Luke 7:11–17).

In the case of Lazarus, the reality of his death was beyond question or dispute. Lazarus had been in the tomb for *four* days. He was dead beyond dead. According to Jewish belief, the soul lingered near the body for three days, unwilling to be separated from it. But after three days the soul, seeing its body in the process of decaying, finally departs, never to return.[3] Lazarus was not only physically dead, but his soul was now in Sheol, the place of the dead. Although Jesus had raised the daughter of Jairus and the son of the widow of Nain, that could not possibly happen now. Lazarus had been dead for too long. His soul could never return to his body.

"Where have you laid him?" Jesus asked.

"Lord, come and see," the sisters responded, composing themselves and calmly walking with him to the cemetery. The large crowd trailing behind them knew Jesus was a miracle worker, but after all this time, he could only pray for the soul of Lazarus now.

Seeing the large round stone barring the entrance to the tomb, Jesus issued an order to the men nearby: "Take away the stone." Mary and Martha looked at each other, alarmed, mortified by the idea. After four days, the repulsive smell of decaying human flesh would have filled the tomb. Perhaps Jesus did not realize how long Lazarus had been dead.

Martha spoke up quickly. "Lord, by this time there will be an odor, for he has been dead four days." But Jesus insisted, and when the stone was removed, the stench drifted through the assembled mourners. The crowd covered their noses, looked down, or turned away in embarrassed sympathy for the sisters. Jesus lifted his eyes to heaven and prayed. He did not ask for, nor did he need, the Father's help to raise Lazarus. He prayed so others would hear, know, and believe that God the Father had sent his only Son into the world (John 11:38–42).

Then, unexpectedly, Jesus spoke directly to the dead man: "Lazarus, come out." Everyone's eyes were riveted to the tomb. A long silence of anticipation

---

3   *Leviticus Rabbah* 18.1, commenting on Lev. 15:1–2, and *Qohelet Rabbah* 12.6, sec. 1. Rabbah and Midrash are early Jewish interpretations of the Scriptures.

was punctuated by gasps and shrieks when Lazarus appeared at the entrance, the burial bands of death encircling him from head to foot and the cloth still over his face. The crowd stood dumbstruck in amazement, exchanging astonished looks of disbelief. Jesus said matter-of-factly, "Unbind him, and let him go."

The sisters ran to embrace Lazarus while the disciples sprang into action, untying him as quickly as they could. Before the disciples could even finish removing the burial cloths, Mary and Martha were embracing Lazarus tightly, looking into his open eyes with wonder. They had buried him cold, stiff, and dead, and now he stood before them warm, breathing, and alive! They had prayed and prayed that Jesus would arrive in time to prevent his death, but they had never imagined anything like this!

Tears of mourning became tears of joy streaming down their faces as they jubilantly led Lazarus home. They had seen it with their own eyes, but . . . could it be *real*? The house of mourning became a festival; the funeral lamentations became joyful tunes. Stripping off their funeral attire, the sisters changed into their best clothing and prepared a feast, a celebration like no other.

As word spread, people came from all around to join in the celebration or just to look at Lazarus. There was no disputing it. Jesus had accomplished amazing deeds before, but nothing like *this*! It was the greatest miracle imaginable.

The Council Meets

WHILE MOST ONLOOKERS RETURNED TO the house of Lazarus to join in the celebration, some rushed back to Jerusalem to report to the Pharisees everything that had transpired. Religious authorities in Jerusalem reacted quite differently from those who had witnessed the remarkable event in Bethany. They received the news with alarm and quickly convened a meeting of the Great Sanhedrin, a council composed of seventy leading men of Judea drawn from power groups within Judaism—chief priests, scribes, Pharisees, Sadducees, and elders. All members were prominent, respected, wealthy, and powerful. Without a Jewish king ruling Judea, the Great Sanhedrin was authorized by Rome to manage all Jewish affairs. It operated as the highest ruling body for the Jews, handled political and religious issues, and managed every serious crisis. "Its competence extended throughout the world," and "its reputation as the highest authority guaranteed it the ear of worldwide Jewry."[4]

Administration of the vast Roman Empire required the cooperation of local aristocrats. The wealthy were given authority and benefited from their cooperation with Rome, securing their own power, receiving special privileges, and enriching themselves. Rome benefited also. Upper-class locals controlled the provinces, requiring less tedious Roman involvement and fewer Roman troops to maintain order. The aristocracy ensured that the masses remained submissive both to Rome and to themselves, which facilitated the unimpeded flow of tax revenue. The Sanhedrin had every incentive to preserve the status quo and maintain their authority.

The high priest himself presided over meetings of the Great Sanhedrin, underscoring the supreme status of the council, which met in a special room in the Temple complex constructed from enormous stones: the Chamber of Hewn Stone. The council never forgot one crucial fact: Rome permitted a significant degree of self-rule as long as the Sanhedrin maintained stability. But Jesus was increasingly becoming a threat to the general order, and therefore a threat to the Temple and to their positions of power and influence. If the Sanhedrin did not maintain order, the Romans would surely intervene and remove it from power.

The Great Sanhedrin was a legislative body but also functioned as the highest court in the land, hearing only the most important cases. This would certainly include the case of a man suspected of being a false prophet who leads the people astray. The raising of Lazarus heightened their concerns. Gathering together, they considered their options. John's Gospel gives us an exclusive peek into the private discussions among the most prominent Jewish leaders (John 11:46–53).[5]

"What are we to do? For this man performs many signs." They could not contain their frustration with the silly, senseless people who already believed Jesus was the Messiah. Others concurred: "If we let him go on thus, every

---

4   Jeremias, *Jerusalem in the Time of Jesus*, 74.
5   Jesus had supporters in the council (John 12:42) who no doubt later informed the disciples about the discussions.

one will believe in him, and the Romans will come and destroy both our holy place and our nation." The situation was precarious and volatile, and immediate action was required. But capturing Jesus would be difficult. He was popular, always surrounded by large crowds.

The high priest, Caiaphas, finally interrupted. "You know nothing at all." There was only one way to prevent total disaster: Jesus had to die. "You do not understand that it is expedient for you that one man should die for the people, and that the whole nation should not perish" (John 11:47–49). As high priest, Caiaphas had unknowingly made a prophecy: that Jesus' death would be a sacrifice, not only on behalf of the Jewish nation but for all the peoples of the world. His sobering statement silenced the debate, and the council resolved to put Jesus to death.

The Sanhedrin consisted of prominent men from different Jewish groups, but they agreed on the most important elements of Judaism: God is One and he is the only God. The Lord had made a covenant with their father Abraham almost two thousand years before. He had set Israel apart from other nations, calling them to be a holy people, a light to all the nations. It was a privilege to be among the chosen people of God. Whether they were Pharisees or Sadducees, chief priests, scribes, or elders, all the council members agreed: the Temple and the nation must be protected against any threat.

They also agreed that what had begun as a small local controversy in Galilee had rapidly developed into a significant problem: the teachings and activities of a carpenter turned rabbi named Jesus of Nazareth.

CHAPTER 4

The Second Catalyst: The Entry into Jerusalem

PASSOVER WAS DRAWING NEAR, AND crowds were filling Jerusalem. Jesus was approaching, accompanied by many followers, and it was common knowledge that the religious leaders wanted to arrest him. Meanwhile, news of the raising of Lazarus had excited the crowds, and they turned out to welcome Jesus and escort him into the city.

On Palm Sunday we remember the triumphal entry of the Lord into Jerusalem. Why is this a joyous day? After all, Jesus was going to his death! He knew it, and we all know it today. But on that very first Palm Sunday, there was no hint of the suffering that awaited him. Palm Sunday is marked by an easing of the Lenten fast, a classic Orthodox sign of celebration: we eat fish. We decorate our churches with palm branches. Several Orthodox hymns of the day joyously repeat the acclamation with which the crowd welcomed Jesus on that first Palm Sunday: "Hosanna! Blessed is the One who comes in the name of the Lord!" (Mark 11:9).

We may be mentally anticipating the challenging week of church services ahead, but nonetheless, Palm Sunday morning has a jubilant, festive character. So why does the Church celebrate this day if Jesus is going toward his death? Because this was the only occasion in his life when Jesus was publicly acknowledged as the Messiah. Claiming to be the Messiah was dangerous. The powerful would be threatened, while others would misunderstand his mission and purpose. Even his own disciples did not understand that he had come to suffer and to die.

But now, as he affirmed the crowd's acclamation, he mounted a donkey to enter the city, signaling what kind of Messiah he was: not a conquering, warrior Messiah-King but the peaceful, humble, Suffering Servant of the Lord. Until this point, Jesus had forbidden talk about his identity as the Messiah, but now he openly accepted the cheers and the messianic titles shouted by the crowd.

The Jewish people had never lost hope that one day the Messiah would come. They were not cheering for spiritual salvation but for a political savior. Special titles had evolved for the Messiah over the centuries that expressed their hopeful anticipation, not only "Son of David" or "King of Israel" but "the Coming One" or "the One Who Comes." Jerusalem had similarly welcomed victorious kings in ages past, waving branches and spreading out their cloaks in the path of the king to create a royal red-carpet welcome. The enthusiastic throng shouted, "Hosanna [save us] to the Son of David! Blessed is he who comes in the name of the Lord!" (Matt. 21:19).

The raising of Lazarus alone did not create this excitement. In the history of Israel, only Jesus had healed thousands of people from every conceivable illness and ailment—leprosy, fever, epilepsy, demonic possession, paralysis, deafness, and blindness. Only he had raised people from the dead, healed from a distance, and cast out demons with mere words. The crowd knew the signs the Messiah would perform, especially those foretold by Isaiah. The Messiah would give sight to the blind; the lame would walk, and the deaf would hear. Some of the prophets had performed a few miracles, but nothing like this!

But the chief priests and most Pharisees remained unconvinced. They knew better than the gullible, low-class riffraff who were fooled by Jesus' tricks. "How can a man who is a sinner do such signs?" "We know that this man is a sinner," they insisted (John 9:16, 24), saying, "This man is not from God, for he does not keep the sabbath" (v. 16). Jesus had violated countless laws of ritual purity, not to mention the sabbath laws. He ate with sinners and tax collectors and even dared to tell people that their sins were forgiven! He was a blasphemer and a false prophet who led the people astray. He could not be from God. The Lord's Messiah would keep the Law, not violate it! Therefore, his power could come from only one source: the devil.

As for the crowd, if they had cherished any doubt that Jesus was the Messiah, the raising of Lazarus was the last and greatest sign that confirmed their hopes. As they welcomed Jesus triumphantly into the city, the disciples reveled in the thrilling moment of jubilation, brimming with confidence and exuberance.

They had witnessed his extraordinary powers every single day. Jesus had even admitted to them that he was the Messiah. But he had also told them that in Jerusalem he would be arrested and crucified. How was that even possible? The disciples knew Jesus had enemies, but how could any ordinary person have power over Jesus? No—it was impossible that he would actually be crucified. Jesus must have been speaking figuratively, like those parables he enjoyed telling.

Fueled by their youthful energy and passionate devotion, the disciples were determined to protect their teacher. They had acquired two swords—just in case. And now, with this amazing welcome, it seemed that all of Judea supported him. Yes, the Kingdom was about to be restored. This was the will of God, and no power on earth could prevent it—not even the Romans.

But the disciples' confidence and jubilation would be short-lived.

CHAPTER 5

The Temple at Jerusalem

A Brief History

THE TEMPLE AT JERUSALEM WAS the only Jewish temple in the entire world and unique in many ways. Numerous temples throughout the Roman Empire were dedicated to the same Greek and Roman gods. But only one temple stood for the One God of the Jews.

On that sacred site, Mount Moriah, Abraham had nearly sacrificed his son Isaac.[1] The sacrificial worship of the LORD had been restricted to this spot ever since King David brought the Ark of the Covenant to Jerusalem (c. 1000 BC). David's son Solomon built the first temple dedicated to the God-Who-Had-No-Name-and-No-Image on the highest point in the city. For Jews, the Temple Mount was the epicenter of the world, the meeting place of heaven and earth.

Solomon's Temple was destroyed by the Babylonians in 586 BC, and the Jews were taken away as slaves. After the Babylonian exile ended, they returned from captivity and rebuilt a second temple, around 520 BC. The

---

1 Although doubted by modern scholars, this is firmly entrenched in Jewish tradition. "The idea that Moriah was always another designation of the Temple Mount in Jerusalem is as rare among critical scholars as it is ubiquitous in Jewish tradition." Levenson, *The Death and Resurrection of the Beloved Son*, 121. Associating Isaac's near sacrifice with that particular mountain was the "germ of the rabbinic notion that the binding of Isaac was the origin of the daily lamb offerings (the *tamidim*) and, less directly but more portentously, of the Passover sacrifice as well." Levenson, 174.

Second Temple was functional but far from the opulent, impressive structure built by Solomon. The unique importance of the Temple for Judaism motivated Herod the Great to enlarge and beautify the Second Temple in 20 BC. This ambitious program would continue for over eighty years and guaranteed Herod's legacy. Some incorrectly call the Second Temple "Herod's Temple" because of Herod's considerable improvements and expansions. But worship there never ceased, and the Second Temple was never replaced, only enhanced. The scale of the project and its construction, accomplished without modern machinery, is simply incredible.[2]

The Temple Complex

THE TEMPLE WAS NOT A single building but a large complex, including a massive courtyard, storerooms, archives, a treasury, meeting rooms, colonnades, and porches. The Temple occupied about one-fourth of the land area of Jerusalem and dominated the culture and economy to an extent unrivaled by any edifice in the world today. In Christ's time, the Temple had already stood for over five hundred years, silently bearing witness to the cycle of the Jewish liturgical year, welcoming pilgrims who attended the spectacular celebrations and the steady stream of pious visitors who traveled there for personal reasons, bearing hopes, prayers, and animals as offerings to the Lord.

For all its holiness and beauty, the Temple was not a serene sanctuary of quiet contemplation but a noisy, busy place, its steady hum of activity punctuated by many sounds: coins dropped into the treasury boxes, Levites chanting, people conversing, and trumpets blaring. Worshippers prayed loudly, the priests offered up supplications, animals bleated, shrieked, and squawked,

---

2   All the stone was quarried and prepared off-site so as not to disrupt the daily temple services. Ten thousand construction workers were involved in the project, and one thousand wagons were used to transport the stones. Ritmeyer, "Imagining the Temple Known to Jesus and to Early Jews," 26. The size of the foundation stones is astonishing. Ritmeyer, an architect and archeologist, confirms that some foundation stones measured over 40 feet (12 meters) long and 6–7 feet (2 meters) wide, the size of a city bus. Ritmeyer, 52–53. Some stones weigh over 35 tons, and the largest weighs a mind-boggling 570 tons. Charlesworth, "Jesus and the Temple," 145–81, 147.

burning wood crackled on the altar, while incense and smoke from the burning sacrificial offerings rose heavenward daily.

In its day-to-day operations and within the psyche of first-century Jews, the Temple was a complicated institution as well as the house of the LORD, where God dwelt among his people. This should not be trivialized or misunderstood. The Jews knew very well that God was not confined to a building. Nonetheless, God was *with* his people there in a special way and in a real sense. The Temple also affirmed the Jews' election and importance as his chosen people, providing a sense of security and assurance that God was faithful to the covenant and would protect them.

Countless synagogues served as ordinary meeting places for the Jews. By the first century, the majority of Jews dwelt outside Palestine, having migrated and settled in hundreds of towns from Rome to Libya, from Greece to the Caspian Sea. Alexandria and Babylon boasted especially large Jewish communities. These diaspora Jews, or Hellenized Jews,[3] gathered at their local synagogues for Scripture reading, prayers, hymns, and sermons. Rabbis and scribes encouraged people to dedicate themselves to maintaining ritual purity and observing the Law of Moses, which distinguished the Jews from the immoral pagan world surrounding them.

The Temple, however, was the domain of the priests, not the rabbis. In the whole world, only one Temple served the entire family of far-flung Jews, uniting them as did nothing else. Across the vast Roman Empire, Jewish men contributed an annual tax for the support and maintenance of the Temple.

The Temple at Jerusalem was the largest temple complex in the entire world, its opulence and magnificence unrivaled by any pagan temple. The wealth of the Temple is beyond description—not simply in its decorative embellishments but in the sheer amount of coinage in the Temple treasury, so enormous it could not even be counted.[4] The Temple's uniqueness as a sacred space was likewise beyond compare. It alone was the House of the Lord. It alone was the place where sacrifice could be offered by Jews and where countless rituals

---

3   Hellenized Jews spoke Greek as their native tongue. The vast majority of first-century Jews lived outside Palestine, and most did not know Hebrew.

4   The Roman historian Tacitus confirms that the wealth present in the Temple at Jerusalem was immense. *Hist.* 5.8.1.

required by the Torah could be performed. No pagan temple could equal the importance of the Temple in Jerusalem for the Jewish people: it was the presence of God on earth.

The Economic Impact of the Temple

THE TEMPLE MADE JERUSALEM BOTH the religious center of Judaism and the economic center of the entire region. The city was extremely prosperous and truly international since Jews came from all corners of the empire to offer prayers to God, to complete Nazirite vows, to pay temple taxes, to be purified after childbirth, and to bring their firstfruits. The Law of Moses required Jewish men to come to the Temple three times a year[5] for the "pilgrim festivals"—Passover, Pentecost, and Tabernacles.[6] The constant stream of pilgrims spawned countless shops and services, business opportunities, and professions dependent on observance of temple rituals and requirements. Many different trades provided services for the functioning of the Temple and the personal needs of the priests, including a doctor, barbers, and trench diggers for water.[7] The Temple improvements employed thousands of workers, from engineers and specialized craftsmen to stonemasons and day laborers.[8]

---

5   Jeremias, *Jerusalem in the Time of Jesus*, 75. There were exceptions to this, and women were not required to attend but often did. Those who were exempt from traveling three times annually to the Temple included deaf-mutes, women, unemancipated slaves, "imbeciles," children, the lame, the blind, the sick, the elderly, *tumtums* (androgynous people, or anyone whose gender was not obvious from their physical appearance or clothing), and hermaphrodites. A "child" was defined as one still small enough to ride on his father's shoulders. Attendance was required by a child if he could ascend to the Temple on his own, holding his father's hand. The rule preserved in the Mishnah was that pilgrims must ascend to the Temple on their own legs. For that reason, the sick, lame, and elderly were exempt from the requirement of the thrice-annual attendance. Exemptions for hermaphrodites and tumtums were likely necessary because certain areas of the Temple were restricted according to gender. *Hag.* 1.1.

6   Passover celebrated the Jews' release from slavery in Egypt. Pentecost (Shavuot) was held fifty days after Passover and celebrated the giving of the Law on Mt. Sinai, and Tabernacles (Sukkot, a.k.a. the Feast of Booths) celebrated the forty years of wandering in the wilderness while living in tents.

7   Jeremias, *Jerusalem in the Time of Jesus*, 26.

8   The beautification and enlargement of the Temple was completed after eighty years.

Jerusalem became a mecca for trade in luxury goods since only the highest-quality goods could be used in the Temple. Linen for the high priest's vestments came from India, and costly jewels studded his ephod (priestly breast-plate). The finest and most expensive wine, wood, oil, grain, and incense flowed to the Temple, not to mention countless bulls, calves, sheep, lambs, goats, and doves. The twice-daily mandated sacrifices required lambs, while additional animals were offered for forgiveness of sin and restoration of ritual purity. Certain festivals or special occasions dictated additional animals. Herod the Great had sacrificed three hundred oxen for one important occasion.[9]

The expenditures required for temple ceremonies and rituals kept the economic engine of Jerusalem operating at full speed. Not only the wealthy but ordinary pilgrims were actually obligated by the Law of Moses to spend money in Jerusalem during the festivals, providing not only an economic benefit to the city but also a welcome break from the harshness of daily life. Luxury items such as meat, fish, nuts, oil, spices, alcoholic beverages, and perfumes were purchased, as well as anything else that would increase the enjoyment of the banquets that accompanied the festivities, including new clothing, sandals, jewelry, and souvenirs.[10]

Visiting the Temple

THE TEMPLE STOOD ON THE highest point in the city, Mount Moriah. Herod the Great significantly expanded the Temple Mount with retaining walls on three sides to create a huge outdoor plaza known as the Court of the

---

Everyone rejoiced, but 18,000 men employed for the renovations were suddenly unemployed, creating a tremendous financial crisis in the city.

9   Josephus, *Ant.* 15.422.

10 Spending required for the feasts was called the "second tithe" (Deut. 14:26). Two important contemporary sources of information about first-century Judaism, Philo of Alexandria and Flavius Josephus, both wrote about these lavish expenditures. Abundance was considered an essential element of celebration. Philo, *Special Laws* I.69, in *Works*; Josephus, *Ant.* 4.205, 240ff, 11.119, 15.50. The Mishnah tractate *Maaser Sheni*, 1–2, also describes the meaning of the "second tithe" and the acceptable purchases. See also Jeremias, *Jerusalem in the Time of Jesus*, 102–4.

Gentiles. The Temple complex could be accessed from a number of directions, and several gates admitted worshippers.

The mountain was supported on the west side by the western wall, which loomed above the Tyropean Valley. This massive retaining wall extended some 1,590 feet, nearly one-third of a mile or half a kilometer. A bridge traversed the Tyropean Valley to the west of the Temple Mount, connecting the Upper City with the Temple Mount. Below this bridge, three gates punctuated the western wall: one at an exterior stairway and two that led to interior stairways.[11] A massive exterior staircase in the southwest corner supported by arches allowed visitors to ascend from the street level of the Tyropean Valley to the top of the Temple Mount. Shops lined the base of the western wall, nestled in the openings under the staircase. This important market street served the needs of the throngs visiting the Temple. Along this street at the base of the mountain, two openings at the bottom of the western wall accessed wide, vaulted corridors with interior staircases inside the mountain itself. These underground staircases funneled worshippers from the market at the street level below up to the Temple plaza above.

Visitors coming from the east could enter through the Golden Gate, also known as the Shushan Gate. A large staircase supported by massive arches ran along the eastern wall and led up to the Golden Gate from the valley below. This gate was located at the top, on the same level as the structures of the Temple Mount.[12] Another massive retaining wall supported the Temple Mount on the south side and extended some 912 feet (278 meters) in length. Most pilgrims entered from the south, and this approach offered

---

11   Today only a small portion, about 190 feet (58 meters), of the western wall is visible. The western wall (mistakenly called by some the "Wailing Wall") is considered the most sacred site in Judaism today. No part of the actual Temple itself remains standing.

12   Some Christians believe that when Jesus entered Jerusalem on Palm Sunday, he ascended the Temple Mount from that staircase and entered through the Golden Gate because of a prophecy. Ezekiel was shown the East Gate in a vision and was told that it would remain shut and only the LORD would enter through it (Ezek. 44:1–3). The early Church and Orthodox Christians today have traditionally interpreted this as a prophecy of the virginal conception of Christ and the ever-virginity of Mary. The Theotokos is the East Gate whom only the LORD passed through. The actual Temple gate was used for certain special occasions, and people did pass through it; therefore Ezekiel's prophecy cannot refer to the physical gate of the Temple.

worshippers two means of access to the Temple Mount above: the Double Gate (an entrance with two openings) and the Triple Gate (an entrance with three openings). Both gates were located at the base of the retaining wall, but the base of the wall was not at street level. To reach those entrances, pilgrims first approached the southern retaining wall by ascending the Monumental Stairway, an extremely wide set of thirty steps that ran for hundreds of feet parallel to the wall. A public building and a *mikveh* interrupted the long course of steps.[13]

Approaching from the south and ascending the broad Monumental Stairway, pilgrims entered via the Double Gate. This led to an interior passageway 240 feet (73 meters) long, consisting of strikingly beautiful domed chambers supported by exquisite marble columns. The domed walkways were elaborately decorated with intricate geometric designs, rosettes, grapes, vines, and flower petals. Some scholars and archeologists believe the Double Gate was the one referred to as "the Beautiful Gate" because of its elaborate decorations (Acts 3:2, 10).

Another opening in the southern wall, the Triple Gate, also contained a passageway leading up to the surface of the mountain, but this one primarily accessed storehouses and other functional spaces located deep within the mountain itself. The storerooms and chambers inside the mountain received daylight and fresh air from open shafts that extended all the way up to the plaza level.[14]

Worshippers who ascended through the elaborate domed passageway inside the mountain emerged into the sunlight at the surface near the Royal Stoa, a long, impressive structure that ran the entire length of the south wall. A steeply pitched, copper-tiled roof covered four rows of columns with forty columns in each row. The rows of columns created three long corridors in which merchants offered sacrificial animals for sale and money changers set up their tables to exchange the coinage carried by the throng of worshippers from different lands.

---

13   A *mikveh* is a Jewish bathhouse used for ritual purification. All worshippers were required to be ritually clean to enter the Temple, and several *mikva'ot* (plural for *mikveh*) were located near the main entrances to the Temple Mount.

14   Ritmeyer, "Imagining the Temple," 43.

The Court of the Gentiles and the Porticoes

THE LARGEST AREA ON THE Temple Mount was the Court of the Gentiles, a massive plaza open to the general public that surrounded the Temple Courts proper, which were restricted spaces. The Court of the Gentiles was beautiful and impressive, paved with variegated stones of differing colors and rimmed on three sides by gleaming white marble colonnades. When Herod the Great had built the retaining walls to expand the Temple Mount, he constructed porticoes that rimmed most of the Court of the Gentiles. The porticoes consisted of a double colonnade (two rows of double columns) that ran nearly the entire expanse of the retaining walls. The columns stood over 40 feet (12 meters) high and were crafted from the finest pure white marble. The double colonnade was about 50 feet (15 meters) wide, and a roof above it stretched the full length of the porticoes, creating a massive covered promenade with elaborately carved cedar paneling that lined the entire ceiling overhead.[15] These impressive covered colonnades served as popular gathering places that offered relief from both sun and rain. Jesus would often be found there teaching the multitudes, who could listen in comfort, protected from the elements by the porticoes.[16]

Towering over the Court of the Gentiles at the northwestern corner of the Temple Mount stood the Antonia Fortress, the Roman garrison from which soldiers constantly watched the crowd below for any signs of disturbance.[17] Stairs led directly down from the Antonia to the Court of the Gentiles, giving soldiers rapid and easy access to the plaza.

---

15 Josephus, *JW* 5.190–2.

16 Ritmeyer, "Imagining the Temple," 45–46.

17 The Antonia was dedicated to and named for Mark Antony by Herod the Great, who had aligned himself with Antony and Cleopatra, expecting them to prevail in their war against Octavian, who later became Augustus Caesar. The fact that Herod was able to keep his throne in spite of Octavian's victory at the Battle of Actium in the seventh year of Herod's reign is testament to his political shrewdness and skill.

Entering the Temple Courts

ANYONE COULD MINGLE IN THE Court of the Gentiles, but only ritually pure Jews could proceed farther and enter the Temple Courts themselves. The Temple Courts were surrounded by a low latticed wall or balustrade called the *soreg*. It stood about 5 feet (1.5 meters) high and was interspersed occasionally with openings that allowed Jewish worshippers to pass through to enter the Temple Courts. The soreg kept "unclean" people who might be in the Court of the Gentiles at a safe distance. For a ritually unclean person even to touch the exterior wall of the Temple building would defile it.

Gentiles, Samaritans, and others deemed ritually unclean were denied access to the Temple Courts. Signs written in Greek and Latin were posted at the openings that punctuated the soreg, warning trespassers not to pass through them.[18] Violation of this restriction was punishable by death. This was the only exception to the exclusive right of the Romans to administer capital punishment.

Inside the Temple Courts

AFTER PASSING THROUGH AN OPENING in the soreg, most ritually pure Jews entered the Temple complex through a huge gold door at the east side that led to the first space, the Court of the Women.[19] Numerous additional gates, covered in silver and gold, led to other specific areas of the Temple complex, the names of which suggest their functions: the Gate of the Singers, the Water Gate, the Kindling Gate, and so forth. The entire Temple complex was astonishingly beautiful. All structures of the Temple courts were constructed of the whitest marble, decorated with alabaster and stibium (antimony),

---

18 Josephus, *JW* 5.194; *Ant.* 15.417. Two of the Greek placards were discovered by archeologists. One was discovered in 1871. Clermont-Ganneau, "Une stèle du Temple du Jerusalem," 214–36, 290–96. The other was discovered in 1936. *Corpus Inscriptionum Judaicarum* I and II, Sussidi allo studio della antichità cristiane 1 and 3, J.-B. Frey, ed., Rome, 1936, 1952. They read as follows: "No foreigner is to go beyond the balustrade and the plaza of the Temple zone. Whoever is caught doing so will have himself to blame for his death which will follow." Finegan, *The Archeology of the New Testament*, 197.

19 These large spaces are designated as "courts" because they were courtyards, open to the sky above.

a shiny, silvery stone. Smaller rooms where priests fulfilled various duties flanked the larger courtyards where worshippers congregated. As people proceeded through the Temple precincts, the spaces became both increasingly restrictive and higher in elevation. Steps led upward progressively to the more restricted areas.

All ritually pure Jews could enter the Court of the Women, a large courtyard about 225 feet (68 meters) square, rimmed by a colonnade that created sheltered porticoes on all sides and balconies above.[20] Magnificent ceremonies took place in the Court of the Women. Levites blew trumpets and sang psalms on special occasions. Four huge lampstands dominated the area, each containing four massive bowls that were lit during the Feast of Tabernacles. The light of these enormous bowls could be seen throughout the entire city.[21] There at that feast Jesus proclaimed, "I am the light of the world" (John 8:12).

This area was also called the Treasury, since the Temple treasury was accessed from the Court of the Women. Thirteen boxes for receiving coin offerings from worshippers were located under the colonnade that formed the courtyard. Most receptacles were designated for specific offerings, including gold for the mercy-seat, donations for wood or for offering of sacrificial birds, new temple dues, and old temple dues. Other boxes simply received general freewill offerings. It was into one of these boxes that the Lord observed the poor widow depositing two pennies, the tiniest bronze coins in circulation, which were "everything she had" (Mark 12:44).

Across from the main entrance of the Court of the Women was a staircase consisting of fifteen semicircular steps, associated with fifteen "psalms of ascent."[22] At the top of the steps stood the Nicanor Gate, two massive, gleaming bronze doors about 60 feet (18 meters) high. The Nicanor Gate was so magnificent that it was considered more valuable than all other doors of

---

20 The measurements are approximations using the modern standards of feet/meters rather than the traditional Jewish unit of measurement, the cubit, which is how Flavius Josephus reported these dimensions.

21 *Suk.* 5.3.

22 These same fifteen psalms are read during the Presanctified Divine Liturgy.

the Temple complex, even though the others were plated in silver and gold.[23] Smaller doors on either side of the huge bronze double doors allowed worshippers in the Court of the Women to observe the sacrifices and ceremonies in the more restricted areas of the Temple Court that lay beyond the gate. From that vantage point, for example, new mothers could witness their sacrifice being offered on the altar after giving birth to their first child.

Jewish men offering sacrifice could continue further, up the semicircular steps, through the Nicanor Gate into the next open courtyard, the Temple Court, where the Temple building itself was located.[24] The Temple Court was rimmed with rooms and gates that had different names and functions, such as the Water Gate and the Wood Chamber. One of these rooms was the Chamber of Hewn Stone, where the Great Sanhedrin met. Above these ancillary perimeter rooms, a second story held additional chambers for other functions. Even more rooms were located below ground, including an underground mikveh for the purification of the priests.

Stepping through the Nicanor Gate, men entered into the first section of the Temple Court, the Court of Israel. The Court of the Women was square, but the Court of Israel was long and narrow. It was only about 18 feet (6 meters) deep, but it stretched the entire width of the Temple Court (232 feet or 70 meters). Here Jewish men presented their animals and witnessed the sacrifice from behind a low wall that separated the Court of Israel from the next restricted space, the Court of the Priests. Only ritually pure Jewish men who were offering sacrifice could stand in the Court of Israel.

Just beyond the Court of Israel was the Court of the Priests, a much larger area where the animals were sacrificed and burned on the altar. This space was restricted to priests only. Even the Levites, who were an indispensable part of the Temple operation and performed many duties, could never set foot in that section. Since only priests were permitted in the sacred area, priests were trained for every job that might be required for its repair and maintenance, including carpentry, stone cutting, and metalworking with gold, silver, and bronze.[25]

---

23 Josephus, *JW* 5.201–6, *Mid.* 2.3.
24 This courtyard was about 322 feet (98 meters) long and 232 feet (70 meters) wide.
25 Josephus, *Ant.* 15:390, Ritmeyer and Ritmeyer, *Jerusalem*, 26.

If we were to stand in the Court of Israel and look forward into the Court of the Priests, to the far right we would see the Place of Slaughtering. Stone pillars stood there holding twenty-four rings, into which the animals' heads were placed. After being sacrificed, the animals were hung from iron hooks and then placed on marble tables, where they were divided into pieces. Hides were often removed, and certain parts of a sacrificed animal might be cut off and set aside to be burned, depending on the type of sacrifice. To the far left, a wide ramp led up to the Altar of Sacrifice, a massive platform about 50 feet (15 meters) square that stood at a height of 25 feet (8 meters). Priests walked around the perimeter along a ledge, supervising the sacrifices burning on the huge altar. Behind the Altar of Sacrifice was the Laver, a large brass container of water into which fresh water was pumped daily.

In the center of the Temple Court, past the area where the animals were sacrificed and burned, was the Sanctuary, the actual Temple building itself. The term "Temple" is often used for the entire complex, but properly speaking, the Temple was the enclosed building, also called the Sanctuary. All the spaces previously described—the Court of the Women, the Court of Israel, and the Court of the Priests—were courtyards open to the sky above. But the Sanctuary, the Temple building itself, was an enclosed building that stood within the Temple Court. It was the most sacred space of all. This building also was characterized by progressively more restricted spaces. The Sanctuary consisted of an outer porch, the Holy Place beyond that, and even further within, the Most Holy Place, also known as the Holy of Holies.

The front of the Sanctuary was square in shape, 172 feet (52 meters) wide and equally high, the height of a seventeen-story building. The façade was entirely covered with plates of gold the thickness of a coin. In front of this enormous façade stood four Corinthian columns of pure white marble of the same height. Near the base, a set of twelve steps led up to a wide porch or platform outside the Holy Place that also stretched the entire width of the Sanctuary building.

The entrance to the Holy Place stood in the middle of the four massive columns on the porch. Four additional white marble columns half the size of the porch columns (but still about 90 feet or 27 meters high) flanked the entrance to the Holy Place. This second set of columns was lavishly decorated with grapes and grapevines made of pure gold, twisting and winding down and around their circumference. The sight was breathtaking. Over the years, worshippers brought offerings of gold to the Temple, and priests trained in goldsmithing added to the gold grapevine, continually lengthening it. At one point, three hundred priests were employed to add gold leaves and grapes to the vine decorating the entrance to the Holy Place.[26]

On the lintel that stretched across the entrance to the Holy Place, a massive cluster of grapes six feet (two meters) high, also crafted out of solid gold, framed the entrance to the Sanctuary. The entire top of the building was rimmed with gold spikes to prevent birds from perching at the top and soiling it. The gold ornamentation on the exterior of the Sanctuary was so copious that when the sun shone on the Temple, the sight was too dazzling for human eyes.[27]

Inside the Holy Place was a huge menorah,[28] the Table of Showbread, and the Altar of Incense, all of which were fashioned of solid gold.[29] A curtain separated the Holy Place from the Holy of Holies, also known as the Most Holy Place—a tall, dark, windowless room with walls completely covered in gold. At one time the Ark of the Covenant was kept there, but it had not been seen since Solomon's Temple was destroyed by the Babylonians in 586 BC. Now only a stone platform a few inches high marked the spot where the Ark had once stood. Only the high priest entered the Holy of Holies, once a year on

---

26   *Mid.* 3.8; Jeremias, *Jerusalem in the Time of Jesus*, 203.

27   For descriptions of the opulence and wealth of the Temple, see Josephus, *JW* 5.222–24, 5. 210–11 and *Ant.* 15.395. Josephus explains that all the Jews throughout the Empire contributed to the Temple and had done so for a long time (*Ant.* 15.110). Many historians commented on the immense wealth of the Temple, e.g. Josephus in *Ant.* 15.111–19, and 2 Maccabees 3:6 states that the wealth contained in the Temple was so great that the funds kept there could not even be counted.

28   This menorah was part of the booty taken by Titus after he defeated the Jews in the Jewish War of AD 66–73. The Arch of Titus, which stands outside the Colosseum in Rome, depicts the victorious Roman general's victory parade, along with this menorah and other booty. Titus later became emperor when his father, Vespasian, died. Titus became the patron of Flavius Josephus, the first-century Jewish historian whose writings are the most important historical sources of information about first-century Judaism.

29   Hundreds of utensils, such as bowls and other liturgical items, were needed for the functioning of the Temple and the performance of its rituals. These were all made of gold or silver and had to be cleaned, stored, catalogued, and maintained.

the most solemn day of the year, the Day of Atonement, to sprinkle sacrificial blood and pray for the sins of the people.[30]

The Holy of Holies was separated from the Holy Place by at least one immensely heavy curtain called the veil. It was as thick as a person's hand, and eighty-two girls wove two curtains every year.[31] The number of curtains and the description of the veil have provoked considerable debate.[32]

According to Exodus 26:33–37, Moses was instructed to hang two curtains, one that separated the Holy Place from the rest of the Temple and a second that separated the Holy Place from the Holy of Holies. The inner curtain was to be woven of blue, purple, and scarlet fine linen and decorated with images of cherubim. But the veil of the Temple during Herod's time is described by witnesses as a single curtain decorated with lions and eagles.

The Mishnah (an oral tradition written down long after the destruction of the Temple) describes two staggered veils, each one connected to the wall on one side but not reaching all the way to the other side, with a relatively small space between them.[33] The high priest would go around the first curtain and then walk along the space between the two to the opening at the other side of the second curtain. But first-century witnesses—including Josephus, the Jewish historian who was a priest and very familiar with the Second Temple— mention only one veil.[34] Josephus described a single veil so heavy that three hundred priests were needed to remove it and lower it into a tank of water for purification.[35]

---

30 The Holy of Holies was a tall space, 20 feet (6 meters) wide and 40 feet (12 meters) high. Since only the high priest could enter that space and only once a year, a method was devised to periodically clean and maintain the sacred space: priests were lowered down in baskets that hung from beams overhead.

31 *Shek.* 8.5.

32 This is discussed in chapter 29.

33 *Yoma* 5.1. The Mishnah was not compiled and written down until c. AD 200; therefore, it is not a contemporaneous witness to the activities or appearance of the Temple during the first century. Scholars continually debate the extent to which the Mishnah presents an accurate description of the Second Temple while it still stood.

34 Ritmeyer wonders whether a second curtain was added after the crucifixion of Christ, because when the veil was torn the Holy of Holies was exposed to view. This is an interesting theory, but it remains only speculation.

35 *Shek.* 8.5; Jeremias, *Jerusalem in the Time of Jesus*, 203.

The Fate of the Temple

> As he came out of the temple, one of his disciples said to him, "Look, Teacher,
> what wonderful stones and what wonderful buildings!" And Jesus said to him,
> "Do you see these great buildings? There will not be left here one stone upon
> another, that will not be thrown down." (Mark 13:1–2)

THE LONG PERIOD OF TEMPLE beautification initiated by Herod the Great
had lasted about eighty years. The Temple was completed only a few years
before the Jews revolted against the Romans, prompting the Jewish War
(AD 66–73). For three frustrating years the Romans besieged the city and
attempted to breach the walls of Jerusalem. When they finally succeeded in
entering the city, the Jews fled to the Temple Mount and barricaded themselves within, believing that God would protect them. They were convinced
that God would not allow his Temple to be destroyed.

But the Romans breached the Temple, and in the course of the fighting
a fire broke out, completely destroying the Temple in AD 70.[36] The Romans
seized the priceless treasures and crucified thousands of Jews, many of whom
had never intended to rebel but had merely been trapped inside the city when
the Roman army arrived and encircled it. The very old and the very young
were put to death on the spot, while others were sold into slavery or sent to the
mines, a fate considered worse than death.

The abundant gold that decorated the Temple inside and out melted in the
fire and ran into the cracks between the stones of the Temple buildings. After
the Romans departed, people came from near and far to the Temple Mount to
scavenge the site. They literally took the Temple complex apart stone by stone,
scraping off the gold and silver that had melted in the fire.[37] The Lord had predicted not only the destruction of the Temple but the fact that "there will not

---

36 For all practical purposes, the war ended when Jerusalem was captured and the Temple
    was destroyed in AD 70. But the war did not completely end until 73, because a small
    group of rebels held out for another three years at the fortress of Masada.
37 The quantity of gold recovered from the ruins of the Temple was so enormous that the
    market for gold in the region was entirely glutted. The cost of gold dropped by half,
    according to Josephus, *JW* 6.317.

be left here one stone upon another." This prophecy came to pass precisely as he said.

The enormous significance of the Temple at Jerusalem cannot be over-stated. It was far more than the exclusive location for ritual animal sacrifice, the one Temple for the One God. Regardless of whether Jews lived in Rome, Greece, Babylon, Egypt, or in the very shadow of the Temple Mount, the Temple was an institution that united them all. Nothing rivaled the Temple in beauty, size, or importance. It was the national and religious pride of the Jews, and its destruction by the Romans in AD 70 dramatically changed Juda-ism forever. But while it stood, the Temple was the House of the Lord, revered among Jews as their safety and security, and as a symbol of unity and stability.

The Temple at Jerusalem had stood for centuries as the real and visible presence of God on earth. But now, at the apex of Jesus' ministry, a new reality had appeared, far greater than what Israel could ever have imagined: a Tem-ple Not Made with Hands, One who would render the physical Temple and animal sacrifice unnecessary. The Jews had always regarded the Temple as the presence of God on earth, but God's presence was now with them liter-ally and physically in the person of Jesus Christ. Ironically, the Jewish leaders would seek to destroy that sacred Temple, the incarnate Son of God. Jesus had prophesied to them concerning that as well: "Destroy this temple, and in three days I will raise it up" (John 2:19).

CHAPTER 6

The Jewish Priesthood and Aristocracy

P AGAN PRIESTS AND JEWISH PRIESTS had one primary function in the ancient world: to sacrifice animals.[1] A Jewish priest (Heb. *cohen*) offered sacrifice to the One God according to procedures dictated by the Law of Moses. He did not become a priest by responding to a "calling" but because of family lineage from the tribe of Levi. The tribe had two branches, priestly (descended from Aaron, the first priest) and Levite. A boy born into the Levite branch would eventually serve in the Temple as a Levite. One born into the priestly branch of the tribe would become a priest. Both roles were entirely hereditary and not variable. Levites never set foot in the Court of the Priests. One could not be "promoted" from Levite to priest nor be "demoted" from a priest to a Levite.

The Temple in Jerusalem was a complicated facility requiring many specialized tasks for its administration. Priests and Levites performed different functions, and both groups were essential to the daily operation of the Temple. Let's begin with the Levites.

---

1   Christians never sacrificed animals, and for that reason, Christians did not initially call their religious leader a "priest" but a "presbyter" ("elder"). He presided over the bloodless sacrifice, the spiritual worship of the Lord.

The Levites

ALMOST TEN THOUSAND MEN SERVED the Temple as Levites on a rotating basis. They were divided into twenty-four groups, each of which served in the Temple for one week twice a year. Levites controlled the huge crowds that flocked to the Temple during festivals and served as doorkeepers, barring entry to the sacred precincts by impure Jews, Samaritans, and Gentiles. Every evening, two hundred Levites were needed just to close the enormous Temple doors.[2] Levites patrolled the grounds as night watchmen[3] while sentries stood guard at specific posts in the outer courts.[4] Levites composed the Temple Guard and performed all police functions inside and outside the Temple.[5] They not only made arrests but applied punishments ordered by the Sanhedrin to chastise offenders. They formed the arresting party that seized Jesus.

Sweeping the grounds and assisting priests with their vestments were among the more ordinary tasks Levites performed, while singers and musicians held the most esteemed positions.[6] Harps, flutes, and cymbals accompanied the magnificent Levite choir, which stood on a large platform positioned between the Court of Israel and the Court of the Priests and sang psalms during the sacrifices offered every morning and afternoon. On special occasions, such as the Feast of Tabernacles, when the gigantic lamps were lit in the Court of the Women, the Levite choir sang from the semicircular steps in front of the Nicanor Gate.[7]

---

2   Josephus, *Against Apion*, 2.119; Jeremias, *Jerusalem in the Time of Jesus*, 203.

3   Philo, *Special Laws* I.156; Jeremias, *Jerusalem in the Time of Jesus*, 209–11.

4   Jeremias, *Jerusalem in the Time of Jesus*, 211. A supervisor patrolled the area and periodically checked the sentries to make sure they had not fallen asleep. If they had, the official was allowed to wake the guard by setting fire to his clothes. *Mid.* 1.1–2; Jeremias, *Jerusalem in the Time of Jesus*, 211.

5   Once Levites were sent to arrest Jesus as he taught in the Temple. When they returned without him, the captain of the guard explained to the frustrated Jewish leaders, "No one ever spoke like this man!" (John 7:46).

6   Musicians were the elite among the Levites. Jeremias, *Jerusalem in the Time of Jesus*, 212. To serve as a singer or musician, one had to establish the purity of his Levitical lineage, which had to be certified by the Sanhedrin. *Sanh.* 7.1.425; Jeremias, *Jerusalem in the Time of Jesus*, 215.

7   Jeremias, *Jerusalem in the Time of Jesus*, 208–9.

The Ordinary Priests and Their Duties

PRIESTS WERE ALSO SORTED INTO twenty-four divisions, corresponding to specific priestly clans, and served in the Temple on a rotational basis just as the Levites did—twice a year for one week at a time. While difficult to estimate, the total number of priests was at least ten thousand. All were on duty during the major pilgrimage festivals, such as Passover, which attracted huge crowds. Higher-ranking priests responsible for coordinating their respective divisions lived in or near Jerusalem, and most ordinary priests resided in the region of Judea. Others lived in Galilee, since priests served the Temple only five times a year (twice during their assigned weeks of rotation and at the three festivals all Jewish men were expected to attend).

During their two weeks of regular service, priests were to receive a portion of the sacrificial offerings, both the meat and animal hides, which were quite valuable, as well as a portion of the firstfruits and a percentage of the annual tithe of fruits and vegetables.[8] These allocations were insufficient to sustain a priest and his family year-round, so priests supported themselves through various trades and professions, setting aside their jobs for their sacerdotal duties when their time arrived. Most ordinary priests, such as Zacharias, the father of John the Baptist (Luke 1:5), were not wealthy, high ranking, or influential. Members of elite priestly families, namely the chief priests and high priest, assumed responsibility for the daily management of the Temple. Only those priests actually made their entire living from the Temple.

Duties of the priests included the daily and Sabbath sacrifices on behalf of all Israelites, some assigned by casting lots (Luke 1:9). Offerings made twice daily to the Lord, morning and late afternoon, consisted of incense, a lamb, a food offering, and a baked meal offering. These were in addition to the daily morning purification of the Altar of Burnt Offering. In the evening two priests carried wood to the altar. On the Sabbath, three lambs were offered to the Lord twice daily, and the two bowls of incense and twelve loaves of showbread on the Table of Showbread were replaced.[9]

---

8   Jeremias, *Jerusalem in the Time of Jesus,* 104–8.
9   *Men.* 11.7.

Individual worshippers also brought private sacrifices to the priests for various purposes and occasions. One priest would sacrifice the animal while another collected its blood and sprinkled the blood on the altar. Other priests would burn the animal on the altar whole, or possibly skin it and cut it into pieces, depending on the type of sacrifice.

Priests examined anyone who claimed to be cured of leprosy in a special room next to the Court of the Women. Other priests examined the wood for burning the sacrifices to make sure it was free of insects, which would render it impure and unfit for use in the Temple.[10] One priest blew a silver trumpet late Friday afternoon from a high point of the Temple Mount, notifying everyone that sunset was approaching and soon activities forbidden on the Sabbath must cease.[11]

The Chief Priests

THE CHIEF PRIESTS OCCUPIED THE prestigious and important Temple positions. They regulated and coordinated the activities of thousands of ordinary priests who performed the majority of the tasks in the Temple. In the Greco-Roman world, pagan priests also held positions of authority, power, influence, and honor because of their status in the local cult. It was no different for the Jews in first-century Judaism: priests were revered and respected, and the elite Jewish priests exercised tremendous power and possessed great wealth. The high priest and chief priests were drawn from a small group of influential Jewish families whom the Romans held responsible for maintaining order. The chief priests typically supported harsh treatment of political terrorists and religious fanatics, cooperating with Rome to remove troublesome rabble-rousers or anyone who threatened their positions of wealth and

---

10   Ritmeyer, "Imagining the Temple," 55; Jeremias, *Jerusalem in the Time of Jesus,* 201–3.

11   A trumpet was blown again at sunset on Saturday, indicating that Sabbath had concluded. The location was near the roof by the priests' quarters. Josephus described this particular activity (*JW* 4.582), and a stone placard was discovered on the Temple Mount in 1968 with an inscription in Hebrew that reads "to the place of trumpeting." The original is now in the Israel Museum, but a facsimile is on the Temple Mount today. Ritmeyer and Ritmeyer, *Jerusalem,* 59–60.

influence. The chief priests and high priest were most instrumental in the arrest and execution of Jesus also.

The Levites served as guards and doorkeepers, but the chief priests held the keys to the various doors of the Temple's inner courts (seven in all), and the courts could not be opened until all seven chief priests were assembled. Chief priests held the positions of Temple overseer and Temple treasurer—those who managed the Temple finances and supervised the extraordinary flow of coinage into the Temple coffers from tithes, gifts, and offerings, as well as gold brought by ordinary believers for the embellishment of the Temple.

The chief priests arranged for the purchase of everything needed to maintain the Temple precincts and to perform all sacrifices and offerings, including wood, wine, and flour. They also controlled the sale of sacrificial animals and birds to worshippers. Chief priests maintained the gold and silver containers and other implements needed for worship.[12] They were responsible for supervising the casting of lots; the maintenance, manufacture, and cleaning of the curtains; the vast quantities of wood required for burning the sacrifices; and the showbread, salt,[13] water, and incense. There was also a Temple jailer and a Temple physician.[14]

The Elders and the Jewish Nobility

THE CHIEF PRIESTS FORMED THE heart of the Jewish aristocracy and held political power as a strong permanent voting bloc in the Sanhedrin.[15] The Jewish ruling aristocracy and the Temple establishment were virtually one and the same.[16] However, Jewish aristocracy was not limited to the elite priesthood but included another influential group: the elders.

---

12 Ninety-three vessels were needed simply for the ordinary daily sacrifices. Jeremias, *Jerusalem in the Time of Jesus*, 165–66.
13 Large quantities of salt were needed to process the animal hides that accumulated as a result of the sacrifices.
14 Jeremias, *Jerusalem in the Time of Jesus*, 168–73. Bakers of the showbread and those who manufactured incense were two specific families who had the hereditary right to provide these essentials and became very wealthy as a result of their monopoly. Jeremias, 25.
15 Jeremias, *Jerusalem in the Time of Jesus*, 179.
16 Evans, *Jesus and His Contemporaries*, 322.

This group is much more difficult to define, explain, or categorize. The elders were probably landowners, certainly among the wealthy class, and most likely a relatively small but highly influential group.[17] The Gospels refer to "the elders" but never explain who they were nor their role in Jerusalem society. Old Testament passages refer to elders (*zĕqēnîm*) serving as town leaders, judges, and representatives of various tribes or regions.[18]

The elders became a very powerful group in Jerusalem and served as advisors to kings and priests on important matters facing the nation. This was an aristocracy based on heredity and wealth rather than priestly connections.[19] Elders in the first century seem to follow this same pattern: lay aristocrats, members of the Sanhedrin from the most influential lay families. Joseph of Arimathea was one of them. He was wealthy and a ruler, since he was a member of the council, but he was not a priest, Pharisee, or scribe.

Deteriorating Relationships

EVEN BEFORE THE TIME OF Christ, a tremendous rift had developed between the chief priests and the ordinary priests over whom the chief priests had authority. The chief priests abused their positions to enrich themselves and cement their power. First-century Jewish sources and other early Jewish texts such as the Talmud describe the corruption of the chief priests, who sent club-wielding men to steal the agricultural tithes and valuable animal hides that ordinary priests had earned for their service in the Temple. Many Jewish writings report nepotism and the mistreatment of ordinary priests by the priestly aristocracy, including physical beating.

---

17 Rabbinic writings also refer to laymen as members of the Great Sanhedrin. Jeremias believes that "the heads of the leading Jerusalem families formed a small, close circle that could gather in one room." *Jerusalem in the Time of Jesus,* 225.

18 Brown, *Death of the Messiah,* 2:1428. Elders as town leaders: Judg. 8:14; for the administration of justice: Ruth 4:2, 9, 11; and "elders of Israel" as tribal or regional representatives: 2 Sam. 3:17; 5:3.

19 Certain ancient families were already recognized leaders during the Babylonian exile and continued to hold positions of respect and authority after the enslaved Jews were freed by the Persian king Cyrus the Great in 538 BC. Jeremias, *Jerusalem in the Time of Jesus,* 222–23.

Some ordinary priests deprived of their earnings became so impoverished they literally starved.[20]

Jesus directly challenged the greed and abuse of power by Temple authorities and their misuse of the Temple for personal profit. The stand he took against the greed and corruption of the chief priests—on the Temple Mount itself, the very epicenter of their power—would lead directly to his death.

---

20 Josephus, *Ant.* 20.181, 206ff; Jeremias, *Jerusalem in the Time of Jesus,* 180–81.

CHAPTER 7

The Third Catalyst: The Cleansing of the Temple

JESUS' MOST PROVOCATIVE ACTION WAS driving the merchants and money changers out of the Temple precincts, which unquestionably contributed to his arrest and crucifixion. The cleansing of the Temple is frequently misunderstood by ordinary Christians who are rather uncomfortable with the scene, as though Jesus had lost his temper and trashed the Temple in a fit of anger. No consensus exists among modern interpreters about Jesus' motivation, and they also disagree as to the timing of the event. The synoptic Gospels describe it happening in the last week of Jesus' life, but John's Gospel places the event early in Jesus' ministry—his first action in Jerusalem.[1]

Merchants offered sacrificial animals for sale on the Temple Mount, not simply as a convenience for worshippers, who often traveled long distances to offer sacrifice, but because the priests had to certify animals as fit for sacrifice.[2] The sale of animals and currency exchange occurred at the Royal Stoa.

---

1 Chrysostom suggested that it may have happened twice, but this seems unlikely. This is not a problem or conflict that requires us to force the evangelists to agree. We must respect the right of each evangelist to tell the story in his own way. Since John's Gospel provides us with additional historical information and he is very specific about many details, it is likely that John's chronology is correct. John's Gospel describes many trips by Jesus to Jerusalem, whereas the synoptics (Matthew, Mark, and Luke) focus on Christ's Galilean ministry and describe only one trip to Jerusalem. Exactly when the cleansing of the Temple occurred is not important. All the evangelists agreed that it was significant, and all emphasized that this event led to the arrest and crucifixion of Christ.

2 Animals offered to the LORD had to be perfect, without blemish.

At least one scholar has theorized that Jesus objected to the fact that the chief priests permitted this marketplace to extend outside the Royal Stoa and into the Court of the Gentiles, thereby exceeding the boundaries where such activity was permissible. Some hold the sale of sacrificial animals on the Temple Mount was a new practice introduced by Caiaphas.[3]

It is quite unlikely that Jesus was reacting to some technical violation of certain spaces or rules, since these regulations had been established by men and not by God. The traditional interpretation, and the one best supported by history, Jewish writings, and the Gospels themselves, is that Jesus was protesting the commercialization of the Temple and its corruption by the chief priests. Everything that took place on the Temple Mount was sanctioned by the high priest and chief priests, who received a percentage of the proceeds accumulated by the merchants and money changers and also decided who could do business there.

Currency Exchange

THE TEMPLE CREATED A THRIVING business opportunity in currency exchange. Jews traveled to Jerusalem from all over the Roman world, carrying a wide assortment of coins minted in diverse locations by many different officials and rulers. Money changers sat near the city gates or the gates of the Temple, offering their services in exchange for a fee ranging from four to eight percent. During major feasts they may have set up tables in the Court of the Gentiles to accommodate the crowds of pilgrims streaming into the Temple.

---

3   "Caiaphas may have been the first High Priest to authorize the sale of sacrificial animals in the temple precincts, and may have had a quarrel with the Sanhedrin over it, which may have resulted in the Sanhedrin's expulsion from the Chamber of Hewn Stone." Evans, "Jesus' Action ," 267. Victor Eppstein theorizes that Caiaphas expelled the Sanhedrin from the Chamber of Hewn Stone. The Talmud alludes to this "involuntary expulsion" (*b. Sanh.* 41a refers to it as a period of "exile"). The Sanhedrin moved to a location where sacrificial items were sold. Eppstein theorizes that in AD 30 Caiaphas permitted merchants in the temple area to diminish the religious authority of the Sanhedrin. "Historicity of the Cleansing of the Temple," 55. See also Evans, "Jesus' Action," 265n108. We know that Caiaphas had an argument with the Sanhedrin, and this is an interesting theory, but it is completely unproven.

Coins varied tremendously in weight, size, and purity of the metal, resulting in differing valuations for them.[4] Currency minted by minor rulers or local officials consisted of bronze coins of lower denominations. These circulated widely since bronze coins were in daily use as pocket change for most people.[5] Silver coins had a higher value and would have been too large for ordinary purchases. Currency exchange was essential not only to purchase animals but to pay the annual Temple tax (two denarii, or half a shekel) levied on all adult Jewish men.[6] This tax was to be paid before Passover in the silver coinage of Tyre, deposited in receptacles located in the Court of the Women.[7]

The standard daily salary for a common laborer as well as the daily wage of a Roman soldier was a silver denarius, about the same in value as a drachma. The exclusive silver coinage of the Temple was the silver shekel of Tyre, a large commercial city on the coast near Galilee. The silver shekel was equivalent to four denarii or four drachmas.[8] Tyrian coins were preferred for their consistent weight and higher purity. Roman silver coins were eighty percent silver, whereas coins of Tyre were ninety-four percent silver.[9] Tyrian coins were mandatory because a consistent standard and valuation were essential. Since silver shekels were the exclusive currency for all Temple transactions, the "thirty pieces of silver" paid to Judas would have been silver shekels of Tyre. These coins were so crucial for fulfilling Temple obligations that when their production ceased in Tyre during the first century AD, Jerusalem began to mint identical coins.[10]

---

4   Herodian kings minted coins, and even some Roman procurators and prefects struck their own coins, including Pontius Pilate. These were usually small-denomination coins in bronze. Freedman, *Anchor Bible Dictionary*, s.v. "coinage," 1:1086.

5   Jesus mentions that two sparrows could be purchased for a "penny," the smallest denomination of bronze coin.

6   Matt. 17:24–27. Peter is asked by the temple tax collector whether Jesus pays the temple tax. Peter replies that he does, but apparently, neither of them had paid it yet. Jesus instructs Peter to cast a hook into the sea and open the mouth of the first fish he catches. Inside he finds a shekel coin to pay the tax (half a shekel each owed by Peter and Jesus), so as "not to give offense."

7   *Shek.* 1:3.

8   The shekel of Tyre contained about a quarter ounce of silver (8.26 grams). Three thousand shekels equaled one talent of silver. A talent weighed about 75 to 80 pounds.

9   Jeremias, *Jerusalem in the Time of Jesus*, 36.

10   Friedberg, *Coins of the Bible*, 40.

Jesus' Motivation

And Jesus entered the temple of God and drove out all who sold and bought in the temple, and he overturned the tables of the money-changers and the seats of those who sold pigeons. He said to them, "It is written, 'My house shall be called a house of prayer'; but you make it a den of robbers." (Matt. 21:12–13)

IF SERVICES PROVIDED BY ANIMAL vendors and money changers were necessary, why did Jesus object to them? For many reasons. Rabbinic sources mention that money changers were using dishonest scales and cheating the worshippers.[11] But even when done honestly, the buying, selling, and money exchange on Temple grounds was impious and cheapened the Temple, reducing it to a place of commerce. This activity could have been conducted in the city below rather than on the Temple Mount itself.

Confusion and bedlam ensued as Jesus overturned the tables of the money changers and drove merchants, animals, and birds away. The startled creatures fled while coins tumbled and rolled in every direction and people scrambled after them. Jesus defended his surprising actions by quoting the Scriptures: "'My house shall be a house of prayer'; but you have made it a den of robbers" (Luke 19:46; Is. 56:7; Jer. 7:11). The word for "robbers" here is *lēstēs*, which is striking. A robber is not an ordinary thief but one who *forcibly* takes the property of another. The chief priests were seizing the tithes of the ordinary priests by force for their own enrichment, and Jesus may have implied this also. Many Jewish writings of this era also describe the high priests as "robbers."[12]

The cleansing of the Temple was not an angry outburst, a loss of self-control, or righteous indignation. It was a dramatic statement and a deeply symbolic act. Jesus was not opposing Temple worship or denouncing Temple rituals themselves as empty formalities. On the contrary, he affirmed the sanctity of the Temple, his Father's house, which should be respected and treated with honor and reverence, rather than exploited as an opportunity for financial gain.

---

11 Charlesworth, *Jesus and the Temple*, 155.
12 Evans, "Jesus' Action," 268.

Christ Himself as Temple

JESUS HAD COME TO THE Temple at least a few times per year for his entire life. Why cleanse the Temple now? His public ministry had begun. His crucifixion was approaching, and worship would change completely because of it. Soon people would worship God "in spirit and truth" (John 4:24), not by offering the blood of irrational animals as Jews had done for millennia. When the Romans destroyed the Temple in AD 70, Jesus' prophecy was fulfilled and the Jewish sacrificial system terminated, never to be revived.

The astonished crowd witnessing the cleansing of the Temple could not know of the impending end of animal sacrifice, that Christ would soon sacrifice himself as the spotless Lamb of God who would take away the sins of the world. Christ and the Church he established brought a new Law, a new focus, a new way of worship: spiritual worship. Christians never sacrificed animals; they understood the death of Christ as the perfect sacrifice that fulfilled and infinitely surpassed any and all other sacrifices, because of which the blood of animals became obsolete and unnecessary.

But at that moment, the Temple was the economic, political, and religious center of the nation, on which most people in the city depended for their livelihood, directly or indirectly. It is hardly surprising that any threat to it or any prophecy of its destruction would be viewed with grave concern, even warranting the death penalty, according to rabbinic tradition.[13] Since the Temple represented the real presence of God among his people, to even *say* it would be destroyed was tantamount to saying that God would abandon Israel.

Pious ordinary priests may have approved of Jesus' actions denouncing the corruption of the chief priests, but the chief priests became the primary faction orchestrating his death. In their view, his actions were no righteous protest but a provocation, a disturbance that created instability and challenged their

---

13   *Sanh.* 13:5; *b. Rosh. Hash.* 17a; *y. Ber.* 9:13; Evans, "Jesus' Action," 239. The Prophet Jeremiah was deemed deserving of death for predicting the destruction of Solomon's Temple (Jer. 26:11/LXX 33:11). About thirty years after the time of Christ, another Jesus, Jesus ben Ananias, was "severely chastised" and "flayed to the bone" for predicting the destruction of the Temple. Evans, "Jesus' Action," 239, citing Josephus, *JW* 6.5.300–309.

authority. The first charge leveled against Jesus at his Jewish trial was based on the incident of the cleansing of the Temple, which affirms the extreme serious- ness of his actions.[14]

Temple Corruption

FOR THE JEWISH LEADERS, CONCERN for the survival of the Temple over- shadowed everything else. Their motivation was not piety and a desire that prayers to the Lord remain uninterrupted; rather, they wanted to protect their personal income, power, and prestige. Substantial evidence supports the con- clusion that the Temple leadership was extremely corrupt.[15] The first-century Jewish historian Flavius Josephus, himself an aristocratic Jewish priest, wrote with candor and significant detail about the corruption of the Jewish chief priests and the high priest during this era. Merchants and money changers could not operate on the Temple precincts without the permission of the chief priests, who undoubtedly gave concession space to favored businessmen and received a percentage of the income as a kickback. The sacrificial system had become thoroughly corrupt, and everyone knew it.

Jesus did not condemn the Temple itself nor the worship there, but his words rattled the Jewish establishment. Jesus had a considerable following, and he could not be ignored. His disregard for laws of purity, his claims of authority, and so forth might have caused the chief priests to be angered or offended by him. But it was his threat to the power they wielded in the Temple that led to his arrest.

Temple Authorities Confront Jesus

THE JEWISH AUTHORITIES DIRECTLY CHALLENGED Jesus to justify his behavior: "What sign have you to show us for doing this?" (John 2:18). They were demanding a miracle (which the Jews called "a sign") as proof that Jesus

---

14   It was a false charge. Witnesses claimed that Jesus said he would destroy the Temple and rebuild it in three days (Matt. 26:61; Mark 14:58).

15   Evans, *Jesus and His Contemporaries*, 319–44. Evans presents evidence from Jewish sources of the period detailing significant corruption of the temple establishment.

had the authority to perform such an outrageous deed as driving out the merchants and money changers, disrupting the Temple routine, and usurping the authority of the chief priests.

But Jesus responded cryptically: "Destroy this temple, and in three days I will raise it up" (John 2:19). Jesus was not speaking of the Temple building but of his own body. He had no plans to destroy the physical Temple. It was *they*, the chief priests, who wished to destroy *him*. He knew very well that his actions that day would eventually result in his death, since the chief priests had the greatest financial interest in preserving the Temple, the source of their power and authority. It was the chief priests who conspired with the high priest and the elders to put Jesus to death after the raising of Lazarus, gave money to Judas, sent Temple guards to arrest Jesus, put him on trial before the Sanhedrin, demanded the death penalty from Pilate, and encouraged the mob to shout for the release of Barabbas. It was even the chief priests who asked Pilate for a guard to be placed at the tomb. All of that was yet to come, but Jesus knew the chief priests would soon orchestrate his death.

Only the Gospel of John preserves this brief but important exchange between the most powerful leaders of Israel and a penniless, charismatic rabbi from Galilee. The exact statement is noteworthy because Jesus' words would be completely misrepresented at his trial. But for now, the powerful, pompous Jewish leaders, dressed in their expensive garments, exuding religious authority and political power, flanked by their minions and the Temple guards, arrayed themselves around Jesus, surrounding him and confronting him. "It has taken forty-six years to build this temple, and you will raise it up in three days?" (John 19:20).

The "forty-six years" referred to the ongoing program initiated by Herod the Great in 20 BC to enlarge and renovate the Temple, which was still not completed in Jesus' day. John the Evangelist explains what Jesus meant:

> But he spoke of the temple of his body. When therefore he was raised from the dead, his disciples remembered that he had said this; and they believed the scripture and the word which Jesus had spoken. (John 2:21–22)

The "three days" to which Jesus referred was his time in the tomb awaiting his Resurrection. The temple he would raise up was his body, which the Jewish leaders were determined to destroy. But why does Jesus give that response? Why does he refer to his *body* as a "temple"?

The Temple in Jerusalem was regarded as the presence of God on earth. But now the Temple building no longer played that role, for God himself had become flesh and was physically present on earth, breathing, talking, teaching, healing, walking, living with his creation. The glory and presence of God, which the Jews associated with the Temple building, were present in the *person* of Jesus Christ. Saint John wrote, "the Word became flesh and . . . we have beheld his glory" (John 1:14). The apostles experienced the Son of God in the flesh, and so did everyone who encountered him, whether they realized it or not.

The renovation and expansion of the Second Temple, initiated by Herod the Great before the birth of Christ, took over eighty years. Ironically, the Temple was completed only a few years before the Romans destroyed it in AD 70—remarkably, on precisely the same date that Solomon's Temple was destroyed centuries earlier. The Jews themselves concluded that the ruin of both temples on the same date was no mere coincidence. It must have been the will of God, they realized, but Jews have never agreed why God allowed the Second Temple to be destroyed and never rebuilt. Christians, however, remembered the Lord's prophecy that the Temple would be destroyed (Matt. 24:2; John 4:21) and understood why it happened.

Worship of the Lord would no longer be centered at the Temple, nor would it require the blood of animals, for the Lamb of God poured out his blood, creating the New Covenant that Jeremiah had foretold (31:31). God would be worshipped spiritually, and the Law would be spiritual, written on the people's hearts (Jer. 31:33). The Temple of Jesus' body, which the chief priests had sought to destroy, would become the Body through which the faithful would commune with God in spiritual worship, in every epoch and every conceivable culture, language, and location. The entire world had been sanctified by the presence of God on earth and had become, in its own way, the temple of God, since the Son of God himself was in it. Every individual believer receiving Christ through Holy Communion would become a living, breathing, walking, talking temple of the Living God.

But for now, knowing full well what the chief priests would do to his body, Jesus simply replied, "Destroy this temple, and in three days I will raise it up."

Noone understood the comment.

CHAPTER 8

Escalating Conflict

The Cursing of the Fig Tree

T HE GOSPEL READING FOR BRIDEGROOM Matins of Holy Monday, Matthew 21:18–43, explains the increased conflict between Jesus and the Jewish leaders. The reading begins with Jesus cursing a fruitless fig tree on his way to morning prayers in the Temple.

> In the morning, as he was returning to the city, he was hungry. And seeing a fig tree by the wayside he went to it, and found nothing on it but leaves only. And he said to it, "May no fruit ever come from you again!" And the fig tree withered at once. (Matt. 21:18–19)

Why would Jesus curse a tree? It makes us a little uncomfortable. It seems strange, pointless, out of character for Jesus, not to mention unfair to the tree. The hymns and prayers explain this symbolic act, which powerfully dramatized Jesus' message of judgment that still applies to us today.

Several times the reading mentions that God expects his people to produce fruit. We interpret this as spiritual fruit, meaning that we should not simply attend services, say prayers, or do good deeds, but our faith and love for God should bring about real change in our hearts. Cursing the fig tree means rejection, and Christ vividly dramatized the consequence of being fruitless. The warning was not simply a message for the leaders of Israel long ago but for us as well, lest we too are condemned as fruitless fig trees, merely exhibiting religiosity when in fact we are complacent and indifferent toward God.

The prophets had frequently condemned the people of Israel for their lack of response to God, their unfruitfulness. The Old Testament often symbolically described Israel as a tree or a vineyard.[1] Jesus employed that ancient metaphor, which was very familiar to the Jews. The Jewish leaders were performing the rituals and sacrifices required by the Law of Moses, but merely as external actions not accompanied by an inner disposition of repentance and humility. They were spiritually fruitless. Jesus did not condemn the Temple, rituals, prayers, or sacrifices; he condemned their observance, which was without true piety, devotion, or love for God and without mercy toward others.

"By What Authority Are You Doing These Things?"

> When he entered the temple, the chief priests and the elders of the people came up to him as he was teaching, and said, "By what authority are you doing these things, and who gave you this authority?" (Matt. 21:23)

AFTER CURSING THE FIG TREE, Jesus arrived at the Temple, where he had driven out the money changers and the merchants the day before. People quickly gathered around him. As he began to teach them, the chief priests and elders approached. This was their turf. They were in charge of the Temple and its precincts. They were wealthy, influential, and powerful. Jesus was a nobody. The chief priests and elders made no attempt to hide their exasperation as they confronted him in the presence of the crowd: "By what authority are you doing these things, and who gave you this authority?"

They pressed him for a reply, but Jesus never answered their question. Instead, he countered it with a question of his own: "The baptism of John, where was it from? From heaven or from men?" Responding to a question with another question was not considered evasive. It was a common rabbinic technique designed to make a point or to lead to an obvious conclusion. Jesus

---

1   This is why the entrance to the Temple Sanctuary was decorated with the gold grapevine and grape clusters.

asked them about John the Baptist: Who gave John the authority to baptize, preach repentance, and forgive sins? The chief priests and elders refused to answer the question. They had confronted Jesus in front of the multitude gathered in the Temple, but now they were in an uncomfortable position. They did not believe that John the Forerunner was a prophet, but they were afraid to admit that publicly in the presence of the crowd.

Their silence and refusal to acknowledge the divine origin of John's ministry demonstrated their indifference to God, their pride, their hardheartedness, and their unresponsiveness to John's message, which had come from God, not from John. He had baptized thousands of ordinary Jews who came to the Jordan, repented, confessed their sins, and returned to God. Even tax collectors and sinners had responded to John's call to repent, and they actually changed their lives. John's baptism was from heaven. His ministry could only be the work of God, not of men. The religious leaders had not changed the lives of thousands of ordinary Jews, but John had. They had not motivated thousands to repent, but John had. Yet they refused to acknowledge God working through John, and, convinced of their own righteousness, they refused to repent and be baptized themselves.

The Jews had a notion that if someone was blessed—wealthy, respected, having many children—this meant that God approved of him: he was righteous in the eyes of God. The elite of Jewish society had no reason to repent. Their wealth and status were proof that God approved of them. They assumed, conversely, that the lowly, poor, childless, sick, and disabled were being punished for their sins.

Since the Jewish authorities did not answer Jesus' question about the source of John's authority, he refused to answer their question about the source of his authority. Instead, Jesus posed another question to them in the form of a parable that even more powerfully revealed their attitude.

The Parable of the Two Sons (Matt. 21:28–32)

IN THE PARABLE OF THE Two Sons, Jesus described a father who asked each of his two sons to go work in the vineyard. The first one initially refused to go. But he changed his mind, did as his father asked, and worked in the vineyard. The second son initially seemed to accept his father's request. He said he would go, but then did not go to the vineyard. Jesus asked the Jewish leaders, "Which of the two did the will of his father?" They correctly answered that it was the first son. Jesus replied, "The tax collectors and the harlots go into the kingdom of God before you."

It was a shocking and insulting statement: repentant sinners were more acceptable in the sight of God than the self-righteous religious authorities. The sinners had initially refused to do God's will, but they repented, changed their minds, and obeyed God, like the first son in the parable. However, the chief priests and elders were like the second son, pretending to be obedient but not doing God's will.

The Parable of the Wicked Tenants (Matt. 21:33–41)

JESUS HAD COMPARED THE CHIEF priests and elders to a disobedient son, but he had not finished accentuating their moral and spiritual failure. He offered yet another, even more insulting parable based on a passage familiar to all, sometimes called the "Song of the Vineyard" (Isaiah 5:1–7). Isaiah and other prophets had frequently criticized the Temple and the corrupt priesthood.[2] Other Jewish teachers and sages had used this passage to condemn Jewish leaders' corruption. Aramaic writings from the period of Christ's activity interpreted this passage as a serious criticism of the Temple and the ruling priestly class.[3]

Jesus applied Isaiah's condemnation of unrepentant and fruitless Israel to the religious leaders of his own time. He expanded Isaiah's lesson by adding himself to the story and creating a parable. God had sent many prophets to Israel, but the people had neither repented nor responded. In the Parable of the Wicked Tenants, Jesus not only identified the chief priests as disobedient

---

2   A few examples are Ezek. 34:1–10; Zeph. 3:1–13; Micah 3; and Zech. 11. See also Evans, "Jesus' Action," 250–52.

3   Evans, *Jesus and His Contemporaries,* 328–29. Aramaic was the common form of Hebrew in Jesus' era. Ancient Aramaic commentaries, called "Targums," explained passages from the Jewish Scriptures, sometimes adding details or otherwise modifying details in the stories. Targums are valuable sources of information because they give insight into the issues, concerns, and attitudes among Jews during this time.

leaders who refused to honor God, but he revealed his awareness of their plans to exterminate him.

The parable describes a man who owned a vineyard and did everything necessary to make it useful and productive. The owner represents God the Father, who established Israel and expected the Jews to produce spiritual fruits. He then rented the vineyard out to tenant farmers (representing the Jewish leaders) and went far away on a journey. When harvest time arrived, the owner of the vineyard sent servants to collect his rent, a portion of the fruits. The servants represent the numerous prophets whom God had sent to Israel over the centuries. But rather than giving the fruits rightfully due to the owner, the tenants beat the servants, abused them, and even killed them—precisely what happened to the Jewish prophets. Then the owner sent his son to the vineyard, but the evil tenants in the parable killed the son, just as the Jewish leaders had resolved to kill Jesus, the Son of God.

After telling the parable, Jesus asked the chief priests and elders, "What will [the owner of the vineyard] do to those tenants?" They replied that the owner would destroy the wicked tenants and rent the vineyard out to others who would produce the fruits. They were correct in their interpretation, and the parable was even more accurate than they realized. Israel had historically rejected and killed its prophets, and now its leaders would reject and kill the Messiah, the Son whom the Father, the Planter of the Vineyard, had sent.

The Prophecy of the Cornerstone (Matt. 21:42–43; Luke 20:18)

AFTER PRESENTING TWO DEVASTATING PARABLES—THE Two Sons and the Wicked Tenants—Jesus pointedly drew his conclusion, asking the Jewish leaders:

> "Have you never read the Scriptures:
>> 'The very stone which the builders rejected has become the head of the corner; this was the Lord's doing, and it is marvelous in our eyes'?
> Therefore I tell you, the kingdom of God will be taken away from you and given to a nation producing the fruits of it." . . .

"Every one who falls on that stone will be broken to pieces; but when it falls on any one it will crush him."

The leaders had failed to bear fruit or even to recognize the work of God being done among them by John the Forerunner and Jesus. They rejected Christ and planned to put him to death—he who is the Cornerstone, the foundation and most important stone in the building. But they would be defeated, broken to pieces, and crushed by the Stone they rejected. The reading concludes with the Lord hinting at his own Resurrection and openly declaring that the Kingdom of God will be taken away from the leaders and given to others who will produce fruits.

Undoubtedly the chief priests and elders were highly insulted by the statements of this uneducated village rabbi. They were even more determined than ever to eliminate him. But they must catch him saying or doing something that would provide a solid justification for his arrest. They began to formulate plots to trap him with his words.

CHAPTER 9

Traps Are Set

J ESUS HAD BEEN ON A collision course with other rabbis and various
Jewish authorities since the beginning of his ministry in Galilee. Attempts
to kill him and resolutions to put him to death were not new. Tension between
Jesus and the Jewish leaders escalated during the period immediately preced-
ing his crucifixion. The scribes and the Pharisees posed challenging questions
to Jesus and set a serious trap for him. These two groups shared similar beliefs,
especially their concern for maintaining ritual purity by observing countless
daily regulations in the Law of Moses.[1]

The Jewish leaders had decided long ago that Jesus should die as a false
prophet because he was guilty of leading the people astray, teaching them
to ignore the laws of ritual purity, and flagrantly violating the traditions of
the elders (the Pharisees' oral laws). He was a menace, a threat to order and

---

1   In the Gospels, different combinations of groups appear at different times to challenge
     Jesus. In Galilee, it is usually the scribes and Pharisees, and in Judea it is often the chief
     priests and elders. In Matthew 22:15–16, the Pharisees send some of their disciples
     to question Jesus along with some "Herodians," a group occasionally mentioned in
     the Gospels. The Herodians were most likely associates, advisors, and sycophants of
     Herodian kings. The name Herod became a title for the kings who descended from
     Herod the Great. At this time, Herod Antipas, son of Herod the Great, was king in
     Galilee and Perea, a long, narrow district along the eastern shore of the Jordan River.
     Herodian involvement in the plot against Jesus suggests that Herod was also concerned
     about Jesus' possible influence over the crowds.

stability, and he caused a disturbance in the Temple. The rabble that believed in Jesus might easily be led into a revolt against Rome.

But on what charge could they get Jesus arrested? It would be best if they could catch him violating Roman law. Unsuccessful Jewish revolutionaries had opposed Roman authority, advocating liberation and an independent Jewish state. The Romans had quickly dispatched many of these without hesitation. But Jesus was different: he was not a revolutionary and had no political objectives. He never talked about politics and discouraged rumors about himself as the Messiah. He actually fled when a crowd tried to proclaim him king (John 6:15).

It would not be easy to paint Jesus as a revolutionary. The Pharisees would have to be clever. They decided to set a trap from which escape seemed impossible. But first, Jesus must be softened by flattery. He must not be put on his guard. He must not perceive the trap.

Paying Tribute to Caesar (Matt. 22:16–21)

THE GOSPEL READINGS FOR MATINS of Holy Tuesday describe the scene as the disciples of the Pharisees surrounded Jesus, dripping with insincerity and flattery as they craftily laid their trap. The Pharisees themselves did not approach him but sent their disciples, thinking that perhaps Jesus might be less on his guard. "Teacher," the disciples said, "we know that you are true, and teach the way of God truthfully, and care for no man; for you do not regard the position of men."

Notice the feigned respect, addressing him as "Teacher." Notice the flattery: "We know you are true" and "teach the way of God truthfully." "[You] care for no man" and "do not regard the position of men" meant that Jesus did not take into consideration anyone's status or position when expounding his teachings. That was true, but the statement was an attempt to manipulate him, to encourage him to give a reply without considering how anyone (including the Romans) might react. The Pharisees hoped he would give an offhand response that would be a serious misstep, leading to his downfall.

Believing he was sufficiently softened by their flattery, they now presented their question: "Tell us, then, what you think. Is it lawful to pay taxes to Caesar, or not?"

The form of the question, "Is it lawful . . . ," is typical of a rabbinic question intended to initiate a discussion. "Is it lawful" indicates that this was a theological question concerning the Law of Moses, not Roman law. The tax was certainly required by Roman law, and the Jews had no choice but to pay it. Given that, did paying the tax violate a religious precept? Was it tantamount to recognizing Roman occupation of their land as valid and tacitly endorsing Tiberius Caesar as their rightful ruler?

For pious Jews, God alone was King. Nearly two thousand years before the Romans ever appeared, God had given the land to Abraham and his descendants. The Romans were interlopers, occupiers—not lawful rulers.

The most offensive Roman tax was the tribute, a "head tax," which the Jews considered "tantamount to slavery."[2] Roman taxes of various types were imposed on the locals to force submission. On more than one occasion, Roman armies burned entire towns, including Lydda and Emmaus, to the ground over tax disputes, crucifying or enslaving all the inhabitants. Sepphoris, an important city and the capital of Galilee, was burned down and all its inhabitants killed or sold into slavery because the town failed to raise the taxes levied on it.[3] The Romans considered failure to pay taxes a form of rebellion. The Jewish people had fared no better under Herod the Great, who placed a "nearly impossible" burden on the people, who were "virtually exhausted economically."[4]

---

2   Horsley, *Bandits, Prophets and Messiahs*, 35. The word here is *kēnson*, a Greek version of the Latin word for "census," also the word for the coin used to pay the tax. Use of this word indicates that the tax being discussed is the hated Roman tribute, levied annually on individuals, households, and property. Luke uses the Greek word for tribute tax: *phoros* (Luke 20:22).

3   Josephus, *Ant.* 17.288–89; Horsley, *Bandits, Prophets and Messiahs*, 31. Sepphoris was only about four miles from Nazareth.

4   Horsley, *Bandits, Prophets and Messiahs*, 32. For decades Roman governors turned a deaf ear to the pleas of ordinary Jews who begged for relief from heavy tax burdens. This insensitivity contributed to the rise of Jewish movements of liberation and eventually to outright war against Rome. Horsley, 41–43.

"Is it lawful to pay taxes to Caesar, or not?" Jesus' opponents were convinced this was a perfect trap, since the question has only two possible answers: yes or no. If he were to answer "yes," Jesus would be acknowledging Roman occupation as lawful and Caesar as the true king, not God. Jesus would be a traitor to his own people and would lose credibility as a rabbi and religious leader. On the other hand, saying "no" would constitute treason because he would be advocating the violation of Roman law. The disciples of the Pharisees eagerly gathered around to witness Jesus' reply. They would not hesitate to testify to his treason.

But the Lord was not fooled by their flattery. He rebuked them harshly, revealing his awareness of their malicious plot and insincerity. "But Jesus, aware of their malice, said, 'Why put me to the test, you hypocrites?'"

They despised him. They did not regard him as a teacher and were not genuinely interested in his rabbinic opinion on the tribute tax or anything else. "Hypocrites!" he exclaimed, reproaching them openly so that all who were present would recognize their evil intentions. He first exposed their malice and then revealed his divine wisdom by his brilliant response.

"'Show me the money for the tax.' And they brought him a coin. And Jesus said to them, 'Whose likeness and inscription is this?' They said, 'Caesar's.'"

The coin the Pharisees' disciples produced was probably the denarius of the current emperor, Tiberius Caesar, who over his thirty-three-year reign minted one basic style of coin almost exclusively. Therefore, we can be rather confident about what the coin looked like. As Jesus pointed out, the coin bore the emperor's image and name. The inscription on the front would have read, "Tiberius Caesar son of the divine Augustus," and on the reverse "Pontifex Maximus" (High Priest).[5]

Jesus responded, "Render therefore to Caesar the things that are Caesar's, and to God the things that are God's." He did not say "give" to Caesar, but

---

5   Friedberg, *Coins of the Bible*, 82. Tiberius minted only three different coins. One was very common, and the other two were rarely seen in circulation. The reverse of Tiberius's coin depicted his mother, Livia, holding an olive branch and a scepter, representing Pax, the goddess of peace. Coins served as Roman propaganda. Most emperors struck coins with various designs or titles to commemorate particular events or occasions. Bromiley, *International Standard Bible Encyclopedia*, 3:409.

"*render* to Caesar"—in other words, "give *back*."[6] Since Caesar's name was written on the coin, it could be said that it belonged to him and could be given back. There was nothing unlawful or even immoral about paying taxes to Caesar.

But Jesus did not end his lesson there. A far greater concern should be our obligations to God, so he added, "and to God the things that are God's." His reply left them speechless. They could not conceal their amazement. "When they heard it, they marveled; and they left him and went away."

The Pharisees would be back to test Jesus again, but in the meantime, the Sadducees would attempt to humiliate and discredit him with their own question. The Pharisees seem conservative because of their emphasis on observing even tiny details in the Law of Moses. But in fact, the Pharisees were progressives who continually changed and adapted Judaism to changing circumstances. The conservatives were the Sadducees.

Teaching on the Resurrection (Matt. 22:23–33)

THE NEXT CHALLENGE CAME FROM the Sadducees, a conservative group associated with the upper classes and the Temple (Acts 4:1; 5:17). Most of the chief priests were Sadducees. The Sadducees formed a significant part of the governing class. Politically and religiously conservative because they held political power, the Sadducees had a vested interest in maintaining the status quo. The Temple served as the locus of their power, and they were determined to preserve it and the nation from Roman destruction.

The Sadducees had their own interpretation of the Law and their own scribes but were not obsessed with the minutiae of the Law of Moses. They rejected the thousands of oral rules developed by the Pharisees, just as they rejected other theological developments, including additional Scriptures and belief in the afterlife. The Sadducees accepted only the Torah, the first five books of the Bible, as Scripture. The Torah says nothing about resurrection,

---

6   *Didomi* is the Greek verb for the word "give." But the word here is *apodidomi*, "give back" or "render."

the Sadducees argued; therefore, there is no resurrection. Their opinion was not shared by most Jews.

By the first century, most Jews believed that at the end times there would be a general resurrection of the dead. Everyone would be judged and then rewarded or punished, destined either for paradise or for hell. The Sadducees were unconvinced, insisting that no reference to resurrection could be found in the Torah. Now they saw in Jesus an opportunity to discredit belief in the resurrection by challenging this rabbi everyone was talking about.

The Pharisees had failed to trap Jesus. Now the Sadducees conspired together, asking themselves, "How could Jesus possibly defend such a notion as a resurrection of the dead?" So they approached Jesus and posed a hypothetical question, confident that no rabbi or Pharisee could possibly support belief in the resurrection with the ridiculous scenario they presented:

> "Teacher, Moses said, 'If a man dies, having no children, his brother must marry the widow, and raise up children for his brother.' Now there were seven brothers among us; the first married, and died, and having no children left his wife to his brother. So too the second and third, down to the seventh. After them all, the woman died. In the resurrection, therefore, to which of the seven will she be wife? For they all had her."

The Sadducees described an extreme hypothetical example of a levirate marriage. If a married man died before children were produced from the marriage, the Torah required his brother to marry the widow, fulfilling the dead brother's obligation to provide children so that "his name may not be blotted out of Israel" (Deut. 25:5–10). This was a practical measure intended to ensure that a childless widow would have some means of support and not be left alone and destitute.[7]

---

7   We may find a levirate marriage very peculiar since our culture focuses on marriage for love, out of affection, rather than for practical purposes or survival. But marriage and children were a woman's primary protection and security. Women did not have education or careers and could not be self-supporting. The Law of Moses created this provision to protect a young widow who found herself in this unfortunate circumstance.

"Whose wife will she be?" the Sadducees asked. Remember: the question was about the resurrection. Even though the scenario was extremely unlikely—all seven brothers marrying her and all seven dying in succession without producing even a single child—Jesus did not object to the question. He knew it was designed to ridicule the resurrection as absurd, but the situation was at least theoretically possible. To the Sadducees, however, the question proved that the resurrection is impossible.

Although monogamy had become the norm by the first century, a Jewish man could still have more than one wife. (Herod the Great had ten wives!) But Judaism never permitted polyandry—a woman having more than one husband at a time. Therefore, it was obvious to the Sadducees that Moses would have agreed with them—the existence of an afterlife would mean that in the next life, the seven brothers would be married to the same woman at the same time. This was untenable for two reasons. Not only could a woman have only one husband at a time, but it was forbidden to marry one's brother-in-law or sister-in-law while the brother or sister was still alive (Lev. 18:16–18). Since this hypothetical situation was forbidden, the Sadducees concluded there could be no resurrection.

They were confident that Jesus would have no good response. Christ did not rebuke the Sadducees harshly, as he had the disciples of the Pharisees, even though the Sadducees also sought to discredit him. The previous question about the Roman tax was designed to entrap Jesus so he could be arrested. But the Sadducees' question was only designed to make him look foolish for teaching the resurrection of the dead. The Sadducees assumed that the next life would simply be a continuation of this life. The question was based on their ignorance, not motivated by malice; therefore, he did not reprimand them by calling them hypocrites. He simply said "You are wrong" and explained why.

> But Jesus answered them, "You are wrong, because you know neither the scriptures nor the power of God. For in the resurrection they neither marry nor are given in marriage, but are like angels in heaven." (Matt. 22:29–30)

Christ began by correcting the second reason for their error: they do not accept the power of God. All things are possible with God, including the resurrection of the dead. He corrected their carnal notion about the after-life. People will not marry as they do now. There will be no procreation and therefore no marriage. The next life will be spiritual, not a sensual existence in which we enjoy food, drink, and other physical pleasures.

But what about the first basis for their error, that they do not know the Scriptures? Why would Jesus say that, when they began by citing Moses, the great Lawgiver of Israel, the author of the Torah itself? No one had greater authority in the history of Judaism than Moses. By his response, Jesus proved that Moses did affirm the resurrection of the dead and did so in the Torah:

> "And as for the resurrection of the dead, have you not read what was said to you by God, 'I am the God of Abraham, and the God of Isaac, and the God of Jacob'? He is not God of the dead, but of the living."

The explanation was brilliant, an incontrovertible defense of the resurrection from Moses himself, the author of the Torah. The Lord identified himself to Moses in the burning bush, saying, "I am . . . the God of Abraham, and the God of Isaac, and the God of Jacob" (Ex. 3:14–15). The story is told in the Book of Exodus, the second book of the Torah, which is why Jesus' response is so significant here. The LORD identified himself as the God of Abraham, Isaac, and Jacob, each of whom had died hundreds of years before Moses encountered the LORD on Mt. Sinai. But the Lord did not say, "I *was* the God of Abraham, Isaac and Jacob" but "I *am* the God of Abraham, Isaac and Jacob," indicating by this that the patriarchs are still alive.

Jesus provided scriptural proof of the Resurrection that the Sadducees could not refute because it came from the Torah. But he made another point on an even deeper level: the scriptural proof was not given for Moses, but for *them,* for the Sadducees. Before he quoted that scripture to the Sadducees, Christ did not say, "Have you not read what was said *to Moses* by God," but "Have you not read what was said *to you* by God?" It was written in the Torah for their instruction. The episode concludes with the evangelist describing the amazement of all: "And when the crowd heard it, they were astonished at his teaching."

The Greatest Commandment (Matt. 22:34–40)

THE PHARISEES HEARD THAT JESUS had silenced the Sadducees, and now one of the scribes decided to put him to the test. The term "scribe" in antiquity often referred to a copyist, someone who could write and was educated. But among first-century Jews, a scribe was an expert in the Law of Moses, especially in the oral law—the thousands of rules developed by the Pharisees that had not been written down yet. The scribes were trained experts in these laws, their technicalities and interpretations. Because of that, scribes are sometimes called "lawyers" in the Gospels.

A scribe not only committed to memory thousands of oral laws but also memorized the interpretations and applications of those laws by famous rabbis of the past. Scribes were expected to memorize and pass down the entire tradition of the Torah, including the oral developments, which the Pharisees considered equal to the written Torah. Over the centuries, a legal precedent developed, similar to what we see in our own secular legal systems today.

Scribes were highly respected, and because of their depth of knowledge and extraordinary education they had enormous authority and status. Rabbis, kings, chief priests, and others in power consulted them, especially for the most difficult or complex questions of the Law. Scribes served as judges in criminal trials or civil disputes and had the authority to "bind" or "loose" any Jew by their interpretation of the Law—that is, to require compliance or create an exception to a rule.

Scribes came from a wide variety of backgrounds and could rise to great prominence from even the humblest beginnings.[8] Becoming a scribe was perhaps the only opportunity for significant social advancement for any Jewish

---

8   One of the most famous first-century scribes, Hillel, was from a very poor family. He had walked from Babylon to Jerusalem to study the Law and supported himself as a common day laborer. When he could not afford instruction, sometimes he stood outside a window to listen to the lessons, even in freezing weather. Jeremias, *Jerusalem in the Time of Jesus*, 116.

man not born into an aristocratic or chief priestly family. Ambitious young men came to Jerusalem from all over the Roman world hoping to become scribes. Not all scribes became wealthy. Some were poor, since it was considered inappropriate to profit from the study of the Law or for a scribe to be preoccupied with worldly concerns. For this reason, most scribes depended on gifts and patronage from the wealthy. Some unscrupulous scribes took advantage of the generosity of the Jews they served, even the lower classes.[9]

Scribes wore a special mantle that reached down to the feet and was embellished by a long fringe.[10] When a scribe passed by on the street, people stood out of respect and greeted him with titles such as Rabbi, Father, and Master. At banquets, scribes were given the highest places of honor, and at the synagogue, a scribe sat in the very front, facing the congregation with the Torah behind him in its special cabinet.[11] Their education and status and the honors heaped upon them led many scribes to become proud and interested only in glory. Jesus denounced their pride, their ostentatious displays, and their expectation of honors and exceptional treatment (Matt. 23:5–7). He criticized them for doing good deeds simply in order to be seen and admired by others, feigning piety while remaining inwardly corrupt.

Scribes focused intently on the legal technicalities of the Law and kept the minutiae of the Law with exactitude. But like the Pharisees, scribes could be ritually clean or pure but completely lacking in virtue. They considered themselves righteous because they were obedient to the Law, but many regarded Jesus with contempt since he sometimes violated the Law, lacked their extensive education, and had no rabbinic teacher at all. They considered him an ignorant country preacher who disregarded their interpretations and transgressed the legal precedents established and observed by famous rabbis, Pharisees, and scribes over the centuries.

---

9   Jeremias, *Jerusalem in the Time of Jesus,* 113–14. Jesus condemns the scribes for "devouring the houses of widows" (Mark 12:40), taking money from people who could least afford it. See also Jeremias, 233–36, on the scribes.

10   A mantle was the large cloak that everyone wore, usually draped over one shoulder. It was wrapped around the body in cold weather and used as a blanket at night. Jesus criticized the scribes for ostentatious displays of their status, which they achieved by making the fringe on their mantles extra long.

11   Jeremias, *Jerusalem in the Time of Jesus,* 244.

Jesus emphasized virtue and inner cleanliness. These were more important than observing rules of ritual purity. "Unless your righteousness exceeds that of the scribes and Pharisees, you will never enter the kingdom of heaven," he told his disciples (Matt. 5:20). The disciples must have been shocked by that statement. The scribes and Pharisees were so righteous in their observance of the Law! How could ordinary Jews like Jesus' disciples exceed the scribes and Pharisees in righteousness? This was possible because the righteousness of the Jewish leaders was purely external. It was ritual cleanliness, purity in appearance and outward actions only. Inner purity, the purity of the heart and soul, is far greater than ritual purity. Jesus did not oppose ritual cleanliness, only the keeping of purity rules while neglecting inner virtue and holiness. That was never the purpose of the Law of Moses.

The Pharisees and Sadducees had questioned Jesus unsuccessfully, neither trapping him nor embarrassing him. Now a scribe, a lawyer, also came forward to test Jesus. He disingenuously addressed Jesus as "Teacher," also hoping by flattery to engage him in a discussion, to potentially embarrass him by revealing his ignorance of the law. The lawyer asked Jesus a question:

> "Teacher, which is the great commandment in the law?" And he said to him, "'You shall love the Lord your God with all your heart, and with all your soul, and with all your mind.' This is the great and first commandment. And a second is like it, You shall love your neighbor as yourself. On these two commandments depend all the law and the prophets." (Matt. 22:32–40)

Jesus answered correctly that the greatest commandment is to love God completely and without limit. But he added that the love of neighbor is second, since we cannot love God if we do not love our neighbor, who is made in the image and likeness of God. Everything else is based on these core principles. The scribe who questioned him did not argue with this.

The Son of David (Matt 22:41–46)

PERHAPS THE LORD HAD TOLERATED enough of traps, challenges, and tests, because after the scribe's test, Jesus asked his opponents a question that no one could answer. He expressed a truth about the Messiah that they had never considered: "Now while the Pharisees were gathered together, Jesus asked them a question, saying, 'What do you think of the Christ? Whose son is he?'" (Matt 22:41–42).

The answer was obvious: everyone knew that the Messiah would be descended from David, the ideal king. "They said to him, 'The son of David.'"

In spite of his adultery with Bathsheba, of which he had repented, David was considered the model king, since his devotion to God was absolute. He never worshipped other gods and forbade the worship of any other gods in the then-united kingdom of Israel. All subsequent kings in the Bible were judged in comparison to David. Jesus would now prove that the Messiah would be far greater than David, an idea no one had considered, because the Messiah's importance, his identity, even his title ("Son of David") derived from his relationship to David. The Lord challenged the notion that the Messiah is great because he is David's descendant.

> He said to them, "How is it then that David, inspired by the Spirit, calls him Lord, saying,
>> 'The LORD says to my Lord,
>> Sit at my right hand,
>> till I put thy enemies under thy feet'?"

Jesus quoted from a psalm written by David himself through the inspiration of the Holy Spirit. The Jews regarded this psalm, which foretold the victory of a king over his enemies, as a messianic prophecy.[12] Jesus pointed out that David called the Messiah "my lord." The first use of "Lord" ("the Lord said") refers to God, and the second ("to my lord") is a reference to the

---

12   This psalm (Ps. 109 in the Septuagint numbering or 110 in the Western tradition) was very important in the early Church. At that time, the psalms did not have numbers, so the psalm's title was the first verse: "The LORD says to my lord." Other verses of this same psalm also express important messianic and theological concepts, such as verse 4: "The LORD has sworn and will not change his mind, 'You are a priest forever according to the order of Melchizedek.'"

Messiah. No one disagreed with this, which led Jesus to ask the Pharisees a very simple question: "If David then calls him Lord,' how is he his son?"

Why would the great King David call the Messiah—his descendant—"my lord," a title that places David in a position of subservience? If the Messiah is great because he is David's son, how could the Son of David possibly be greater than David himself? And yet the Messiah must be far greater than David, since David himself calls the Messiah "my lord"!

Jesus demonstrated by his interpretation of the psalm that the Messiah was more than a mere human being descended from David. This prophetic psalm—inspired by the Holy Spirit and acknowledged as inspired prophecy by the Pharisees themselves—showed that the Messiah would be the *Lord*. It also meant that the Kingdom Christ would bring was no mere restoration of David's kingdom. Jesus confounded the Pharisees and all others who sought to challenge him by that simple observation. The Scripture relates, "And no one was able to answer him a word, nor from that day did any one dare to ask him any more questions."

Jesus silenced his opponents, but although they were grudgingly impressed by his brilliant responses, they remained determined to destroy him. Their traps had failed. They would seek another way to eliminate him. But help would come soon, and from a very unlikely source: one of his own disciples.

PART II

The King on Trial

CHAPTER 10

The Betrayal

The Scandal of the Betrayal

T HE BETRAYAL OF CHRIST BY Judas, one of the Twelve, was scandalous. Both Jews and pagans pointed to the disloyalty of Judas as proof that Jesus was not who he claimed to be. Early enemies of the Christian faith suggested that Judas must have realized Jesus was a fraud, which motivated him to betray his master. And thus, the betrayal of Jesus by one of his closest disciples was a source of some embarrassment for the first Christians, not to mention a terrible shock to the other disciples.

The Fathers of the Church noted that because the Gospels include such unfavorable facts, we can have confidence that they are true and reliable. The Gospels are nothing like ancient mythologies that have no historical basis. And unlike ancient royal biographies penned by court-appointed historians, the Gospels do not portray everyone in the most positive light. The evangelists told the truth and hid nothing, not even embarrassing episodes such as Judas's betrayal or Peter's denial.

Christians cannot comprehend anyone betraying the Lord for money. Countless modern movies and books have proposed various rational explanations for Judas's actions. But the only motive given in the Gospels is greed. And Judas approached the Jewish leaders—they did not recruit or entice him. "Then one of the twelve, who was called Judas Iscariot, went to the chief priests and said, 'What will you give me if I deliver him to you?'" (Matt. 26:14–15).

THE CRUCIFIXION OF THE KING OF GLORY

What Does "Iscariot" Mean?

THE BETRAYER IS ALWAYS REFERRED to in the Gospels as Judas Iscariot to differentiate him from the other Judas, a faithful disciple who unfortunately had the same given name. The other Judas is identified as "the son of James" (Luke 6:16). People had no surnames then, so Iscariot was not the last name of Judas. Often people were identified by the name of their father, like James the son of Zebedee, or with a place, such as Mary of Magdala, or by some other defining characteristic, such as Simon the Leper or Alexander the Coppersmith. The moniker Iscariot identified which Judas among the Twelve betrayed Christ, but unfortunately it reveals nothing definitive about the person of Judas Iscariot, his motives, or his background.

Nonetheless, speculations abound concerning the infamous Judas. In Greek, the name is written as *Iskarioth*. But exactly how that name sounded or was written in Aramaic, the common form of Hebrew, is impossible to determine. The Aramaic original of Iscariot could have been *sequarya*, meaning "false one," which certainly would have been an appropriate adjective. If this is the case, perhaps Judas was given the appellation by the other disciples after he betrayed Christ, since, as it turned out, he was indeed a false disciple.

The Hebrew word *qeriyyot*, meaning "a man from Kerioth," also sounds like Iskarioth. If that word is the origin of Iscariot, it would indicate that Judas came from a village in Judea called Kerioth. Iscariot also sounds similar to the Aramaic words for "the dyer" and "the red." Could Judas have been a professional cloth dyer before becoming a disciple? Or did Iskarioth refer to a ruddy complexion, reddish hair color, or some other characteristic?

By far the most popular explanation for Iscariot has been that it identifies Judas as a zealot, a member of a violent revolutionary group, because Iscariot sounds similar to *sikarii*, meaning "dagger man." This theory suggests that Judas became a follower of Christ, but after realizing Jesus would never lead a revolt against Rome, he betrayed him.[1] But this explanation is even more

---

1   Various Jewish revolutionary groups and leaders emerged during the first century and even fought against each other sometimes. Two failed revolutionaries are mentioned in Acts 5:36–37—Judas the Galilean and Theudas, who revolted in AD 6 and 45 respectively. (See Josephus, *Ant.* 18.1 and 20.97–98.) The Zealots organized after the time of Christ when the war against Rome began. The Sicarii, a different violent resistance

speculative than the others. It appeals to our imagination and our desire for intrigue and a rational motivation for the betrayal. It is simply more interesting than "a man from Kerioth."

Among the disciples of Jesus was Simon the Zealot, an epithet given to distinguish him from the other disciple called Simon, who came to be known as Simon Peter.[2] Absolutely no evidence supports the idea that Judas Iscariot was a zealot. If he had been, he probably would have been identified as Judas the Zealot to distinguish him from Judas, son of James. It is much more likely that Judas was given the name Iscariot as either the "false one" or "the man from Kerioth," both of which in Aramaic sound more similar to Iscariot than does *sikarii*.

What Motivated Judas?

JUDAS WAS NOT MOTIVATED BY politics, only by money. Any other suggestion is only groundless speculation. The evangelists explained Judas's motivation, and we should not seek another to satisfy our notion of what makes sense. This only distracts us from the profound lesson of the betrayal, which the hymns of Holy Wednesday Matins eloquently express.

One hymn employs an alliterative wordplay that English cannot capture: "from the closest intimacy with Christ (*Christos*), Judas was drawn away by gold (*chrysos*)." Judas loved money more than Christ, a naked and uncomfortable truth that should prompt us to ponder our own attachment to money and possessions.

---

group, also developed later. This urban gang assassinated Jewish aristocrats who cooperated with Rome, quickly and quietly murdering their targets in broad daylight with a small, hidden dagger (a *sicae*), then escaping into a large crowd. See *JW* 2.254–56; Horsley, *Bandits, Prophets and Messiahs*, 190–243.

2   If the Zealots did not exist as an established organization at the time of Christ, why is one of Jesus' apostles called Simon the Zealot? Either he belonged to a revolutionary group that existed during the time of Christ and was later identified with that specific group, or "zealot" simply described his passionate character of extreme zeal or dedication to a cause. St. Paul identifies himself as *zelotes* in Galatians 1:14, writing that he was a "greater zealot" than his contemporaries, referring to religious zealotry or enthusiasm for Judaism, not political revolutionary activity.

"'What will you give me if I deliver him to you?' And they paid him thirty pieces of silver. And from that moment he sought an opportunity to betray him" (Matt. 26:15–16). The Book of Exodus specifies the precise compensation for certain injuries or losses, including the loss of a slave in an animal attack: "If the ox gores a slave, male or female, the owner shall give to their master thirty shekels of silver" (Ex. 21:32).

Ironically, the numerical equivalent of Judas's name in Hebrew is the number thirty.[3] "Judas" is literally "thirty," and he received the value of his name: thirty pieces of silver. Christ was sold for the price of a slave, an appropriate sum for the One who came "not to be served but to serve" (Matt. 20:28). But the one who actually became a slave was Judas, who sold himself to the Adversary.

Judas did not betray the Lord for any principled motive or out of loyalty to some noble cause. Greed is the most crass and common human motive of all, and John, one of the Twelve, confirms that this alone motivated Judas. John's Gospel informs us that Judas was a thief, an embezzler. He was responsible for safeguarding the money of the disciples, and he stole from the common treasury. It was Judas who objected to the extravagant sum Mary, the sister of Lazarus, spent on her lavish display of love for Christ when she anointed his feet. Judas objected, saying the money should have been spent on the poor:

"Why was this ointment not sold for three hundred denarii and given to the poor?" This he said, not that he cared for the poor but because he was a thief, and as he had the money box he used to take what was put into it. (John 12:5–6)

---

3   Brown, *Death of the Messiah*, 2:1395. All names had a numerical equivalent. Neither Greeks nor Jews had symbols to represent numbers as we do today; they used letters of the alphabet to represent numbers. The Hebrew alphabet contains no vowels. The name Judas would have been *Yhwdh*. The numerical value of those letters in Hebrew adds up to the number 30. "Y" (*yod*) and "W" (*vav*) appear toward the beginning of the Hebrew alphabet, not at the end, where they are found in the English alphabet; hence the low numerical value.

The Lord's Patience with Judas

WHAT AMAZING RESTRAINT THE LORD demonstrated on hearing that disingenuous comment, knowing that he would soon be betrayed by Judas and crucified! Judas objected to Mary's expression of love for Christ, not out of concern for the poor but because he wanted the money for himself. The Lord knew that Judas embezzled from the common purse of the disciples, and yet he deliberately allowed Judas to serve as the group's treasurer. Why? Saint John Chrysostom tells us that the Lord allowed this in order to temper the disciple's insatiable appetite for money.[4]

Christ knew that Judas would betray him and even washed his feet at the Last Supper on Thursday night. Judas had already betrayed him on Wednesday and was carrying the thirty pieces of silver at the very moment his feet were being washed by the Lord! Judas even received Holy Communion, the precious and holy Body and Blood of Christ, on Thursday night, then left the Last Supper to betray the Lord. Marveling in amazement at all these things, we glorify Christ during Holy Week with the words "Glory to your forbearance, O Lord!" Truly, the Lord gave us the paramount example of patience, meekness, humility, and restraint in all his actions before and during his Passion.

We might also ask another, more difficult question concerning Judas: Why did Christ even choose Judas to be one of the Twelve? It was to show that God never abandons us. It is we who depart from him.[5] The Lord sent prophets to preach to unrepentant Israel, already knowing they would not heed the prophets or repent for their idolatry. This showed the Lord's love for his people. He did everything he could to save them, even though he knew they would not repent. Just as the Lord remained faithful to the Israelites and never stopped loving them or trying to save them, Jesus did not deprive Judas of any opportunity to seek salvation.

Judas was accepted among the Twelve so that he would have every opportunity to repent. Christ deprived Judas of nothing at all; therefore, Judas had no excuse for his actions. He was part of that intimate brotherhood. He heard

---

4   Chrysostom, Homily 65, *Homilies on the Gospel of John.*
5   Chrysostom, Homily 68, *Homilies on the Gospel of John.*

every sermon, witnessed the healings, and beheld Jesus walking on water, stilling the storm, and multiplying the loaves. He heard the Lord confirm that he was indeed the Messiah, the Son of God, and foretell his arrest and crucifixion. Judas had the same knowledge and experiences as all the others: the marvels, the love, the mercy, the foreknowledge, the power, the wisdom, the grace, and the humility of Christ. Yet in spite of those extraordinary experiences, Judas betrayed Christ, rendering his treachery inexcusable.

Saint Cyril of Alexandria remarked on the importance of Judas being consistently identified as "one of the Twelve":

> This is also a matter of great importance to demonstrate more fully the guilt of the traitor's crime. For he who had been equally honored with the rest and adorned with apostolic dignities; he, the elect and beloved, deigned admittance to the holy table, and the highest honors, became the pathway and the means for the murderers of Christ. What lamentations can suffice for him, or what floods of tears must not each shed from his eyes when he considers from what happiness that wretched being fell into such utter misery![6]

Didn't Judas Have to Betray Jesus?

SOME ASSERT THAT IF JUDAS had not betrayed Christ, the crucifixion would never have happened, implying that his betrayal was a good thing or at least necessary. This is theologically incorrect and even perverse, because if that were true, Judas would have been necessary for, or at least contributed to, our salvation! His betrayal was neither good nor necessary.

Others say Judas had no free will: he had to betray Christ since it was prophesied. Saint John Chrysostom explained the relationship between prophecy and fulfillment. The prophet or his prophecy is never the cause of the event. The event did not occur because the prophet foretold it. The prophecy was made because the prophet saw what would happen in the future.[7] Judas was not forced to betray Christ because a prophecy had been made. Judas was

---

6   Cyril of Alexandria, Homily 148, *Commentary on Luke*, 587–88.
7   Chrysostom, Homily 68, *Homilies on the Gospel of John*.

not a victim of the prophecy or a pawn in the plan of salvation. He was never deprived of his free will.

It was never necessary that anyone betray Christ in order for him to be crucified, which is why Judas's betrayal is particularly tragic. Attempts were made on Christ's life as early as his first sermon at the synagogue in Nazareth. In Jerusalem, at least twice after he spoke in the Temple, some of the Jews attempted to stone him. The Gospels record many occasions when the Pharisees, scribes, and others plotted to destroy Jesus.[8] As we have seen, the Jewish leaders had formally resolved to put Jesus to death at the meeting of the Sanhedrin after the raising of Lazarus (John 11:47–53). All these attempts took place before Judas had approached the chief priests.

The only difficulty the chief priests faced was how to accomplish his arrest and eliminate him in the most efficient and least disruptive manner. The Jewish authorities were concerned about creating a disturbance among the people by arresting Jesus publicly (Matt. 26:3–5). Judas provided inside information concerning Jesus' whereabouts. He led the guards to Jesus late at night, far from the adoring crowds. Betrayal by Judas was not necessary; he simply made the arrest of Jesus much easier.

Christ's Gesture of Love

JUDAS BELONGED TO THE INNER circle of disciples. He knew Jesus' movements and where the group slept during Passover week. Suddenly and inexplicably, he left the group earlier that evening when they gathered in the upper room for what would be their last supper.

Jesus had announced that one of the disciples would betray him. The other eleven disciples were confused and puzzled by this. Why would any of them betray the Master? Their confidence in Christ's foreknowledge was so absolute that some of them actually asked Jesus individually, "Is it I?" Everyone wondered who it could possibly be. Judas was cold and indifferent in spite of

---

8   Attempts in Nazareth: Luke 4:29. Attempts to stone him in the Temple: John 8:59; 10:31. Various plots in the synoptic Gospels: Matt. 12:14; Mark 3:6; 11:18; Luke 6:7, 11; 19:47. Numerous attempts were made to arrest Jesus, but he always escaped (John 7:32, 44; 10:39).

Christ's remarkable revelation: "One of you will betray me." John, the beloved disciple, leaned close to Jesus and asked, "Lord, who is it?"

> Jesus answered, "It is he to whom I shall give this morsel when I have dipped it." So when he had dipped the morsel, he gave it to Judas, the son of Simon Iscariot. Then after the morsel, Satan entered into him. Jesus said to him, "What you are going to do, do quickly." (John 13:26–27)

Christ loved Judas too and demonstrated that to the end. His last gesture to Judas was to offer him a morsel of food, an act of care and friendship. The Lord did not do this because he hoped to avoid the cross. Christ knew what Judas would do, and he would not interfere with his disciple's free will. But he gave Judas one final opportunity to change his mind. However, when Judas accepted the food from the hand of the Lord, "Satan entered into him," John relates—a truly chilling comment.

The bit of food Judas received from the Lord was probably a piece of bread dipped in a sauce. That "Satan entered" Judas should not be misunderstood. John included this detail to reveal the depth of Judas's perversion. Christ made a simple gesture of kindness and friendship: sharing a bit of food. But Judas received Satan. The Lord did not cause Satan to enter Judas by handing him the food. Rather it was Judas's perverse spiritual state that allowed Satan to enter.

Christ was looking at Judas when he handed him the morsel. The power of human free will was on full display at that moment. God does not interfere with our ability to choose him or to reject him. We are absolutely and completely responsible for our choices and for our eternal destiny, because it is we who chose in this life whether to be with God or to be apart from him. Christ neither inhibited Judas's decisions nor denied him any opportunity to repent. This is the case for each of us, which is why Judas is an important figure to contemplate, lest we betray the Master in our own way.

Satan entered Judas not because of the morsel, but because of Judas's disposition. Judas was receptive to Satan's influence, not Christ's, because of the evil that dwelt in his heart. No doubt the Lord saw that Satan had entered him, and then, knowing the prophecy would be fulfilled, simply said, "What you are going to do, do quickly."

The Farewell Discourse

THE OTHER DISCIPLES THOUGHT NOTHING of that comment nor of Judas's abrupt departure that night. If they had known, they would certainly have prevented Judas from leaving. But God does not interfere with the exercise of our free will, and the Lord would not prevent Judas's action.

After his departure, the Lord turned his attention to the faithful Eleven and tried to prepare them for disturbing events to come—not only his arrest and crucifixion but all the challenges they would face in the future. The exchange between the Lord and his disciples that night was tender, deep, and affectionate. He calls them "little children" and "friends." He gives them one commandment: to love one another. This remarkable final conversation, known popularly as the Farewell Discourse, is heard during the first of twelve Gospel readings in the Passion Gospels service on Holy Thursday night in the Orthodox Church.[9]

Jesus tells the faithful disciples that he is about to leave them, saying that where he is going, they cannot follow. The disciples are distressed and confused; they cannot bear the thought of being separated from him. They all insist they will follow him anywhere. Peter swears that he is willing to die for Christ, and all the others say the same. But the Lord shockingly predicts that rather than dying for him that night, Simon Peter will show himself to be anything but a rock. He will deny not only that he is a disciple but that he even knows Jesus.

The Lord knows the disciples are about to endure a traumatic experience, and he assures them they will see him again. They will weep and mourn, but their mourning will become joy, which no one will ever be able to take from

---

9   The farewell discourse is from John 13:31—16:33. This first Holy Thursday reading concludes with a prayer (John 17), popularly known as the High Priestly Prayer, in which Christ prays to the Father for his disciples and consecrates himself for his upcoming sacrifice.

them. In this life there will be tribulations, but they should not be afraid, because he has conquered the world.

But Judas was not present to hear those beautiful words. Satan had entered him. Judas had gone out into the night, into the darkness, to lead an arresting party to an obscure oil press on the Mount of Olives: Gethsemane.

CHAPTER 11

Agony in the Garden

J UDAS RUSHED TO THE CHIEF priests to carry out his plan while the Lord was giving final instructions to the Eleven. After comforting the disciples and attempting to prepare them, Jesus led them out of the city, down a deep ravine known as the Kidron Valley, and up to the Mount of Olives, a hill opposite Jerusalem where he and his disciples had been spending their nights. It was Passover week, and the city overflowed with pilgrims. The population of Jerusalem, normally about fifty thousand, had swelled to two hundred thousand or more. Not enough accommodations existed within the city for all the worshippers. Many lodged in nearby towns or outdoors in shelters.

The large crowds prompted the Sanhedrin's decision to put Jesus to death before Passover. An arrest in a public place such as the Temple, while he was surrounded by a crowd that considered him the Messiah, might lead to a riot. Only five days earlier the crowd had shouted, "Hosanna to the Son of David! Blessed is he who comes in the name of the Lord!" when Jesus entered the city (Matt. 21:9). The authorities knew his charisma and crowd appeal. A revolt against Rome could easily develop among the enthusiastic and impassioned crowds. Even if Jesus had no political ambitions, insurrection remained a possibility; Jewish religious and national fervor were at their peak as the Jews remembered their deliverance from slavery in Egypt. Jesus was a danger who must be eliminated before Passover. As the high priest had said, "It is expedient for you that one man should die . . . and that the whole nation should not perish" (John 11:49).

Judas was extremely helpful to the Jewish authorities and certainly well worth the money. He knew exactly where to find Jesus and the disciples. Jesus spent his days preaching in the Temple and nights with his disciples in Gethsemane, a secluded olive grove on the Mount of Olives, which contained a cave that housed a working olive press.[1] In the springtime the press and cave were not in use, so Jesus and his disciples took shelter there during the chilly April nights. The cave had often provided a quiet place of refuge and retreat for them.[2]

For the Jewish authorities, the timing and location were perfect for an arrest. It was a secluded spot, and by the time they reached the Mount of Olives, it was past midnight. Jesus could be arrested quietly in the middle of the night and would not be able to disappear into the throng as he had before. No devout worshippers would witness their religious leaders arresting him. A handful of his supporters were nearby to protect him, but the arresting party far outnumbered the disciples in men and weapons.

The Fear Shown by Christ

AS JUDAS AND THE ARRESTING party wound their way down the Kidron Valley and up the Mount of Olives, through the many groves from which the place took its name, Jesus prayed to his Father with intense emotion. He did not need help from God the Father, for he *is* God the Son. Cyril of Alexandria

---

1   *Gethsemane* means "oil press." The synoptic Gospels do not describe Gethsemane as a "garden." John refers to a *kēpos*, which means "garden" but in the ordinary sense—a small cultivated plot or simply a place with trees or other greenery.

2   John 18:4 states that Jesus "came forward" (presumably from the cave) to meet the soldiers. Through oral tradition, the early Christians preserved knowledge of the precise location of Jesus' arrest. Christians have lived continuously in Jerusalem since the first century, and they knew and visited the cave of Gethsemane. Egeria's fourth-century diary mentions visiting Gethsemane, not as a grove of trees but as a dimly lit place. A sixth-century pilgrim to Jerusalem described it specifically as a "cave." (See Theodosius, *De Situ Terrae Sanctae* 10.) A chapel located there is one of the most ancient sites venerated by pilgrims. Murphy-O'Connor, "Where was Gethsemane?" 35–36.

remarks that even at this moment, Christ gave us an example not to rely on ourselves, but always to turn to God in every circumstance.

> And let no man of understanding say that he offered these supplications as being in need of strength or help from another—for He Himself is the Father's almighty strength and power—but it was that we might hereby learn always to put away from us carelessness when temptation harasses and persecution presses upon us, and treachery contrives its snare for us and makes ready the net of death. For it is the very means of our salvation to watch and fall upon our knees and to make constant supplications and to ask for the aid from above . . . for it is an act of utter ignorance to be over confident . . . and should any temptation befall us, our mind will be prepared to resist it bravely.[3]

Saint Cyril observes that Christ showed us not only *that* we ought to pray but *how*.

> Behold, then and see the pattern of your conduct depicted for you in Christ the Savior of all. And let us also observe the manner of his prayer. *Father*, He says, *if You are willing, remove this cup from me*. . . . And if, therefore it happens that we also at any time fall into unexpected troubles, and have to endure any mental conflict, let us beseech God, not so much that it may end according to our will, but rather let us ask that whatever He knows to be fit and expedient for the benefit of our souls may be brought to pass.[4]

Jesus did not doubt the Father or the plan of salvation. His desire to live and the fear and anxiety he felt as he anticipated facing the cross are not sins but human nature. Saint John of Damascus distinguished two kinds of fear, natural and unnatural. The fear shown by Christ was appropriate to his created human nature because all creatures naturally seek to preserve their lives.

---

3   Cyril of Alexandria, Homily 147, *Commentary on Luke*, 584–85.
4   Cyril of Alexandria, Homily 147, *Commentary on Luke*, 585.

There is a natural fear when the soul is unwilling to be separated from the body because of the natural feeling of affinity and kinship implanted in it by the Creator from the beginning. On account of this it is naturally afraid and distressed and shrinks from death. . . . If all things have been brought into existence from non-existence by the Creator, they naturally do not have the desire for non-existence. . . . This kind of fear, fright and distress belongs to the passions which are natural and blameless and are not subject to sin. There is still another kind of fear which arises from loss of reason, from mistrust and from not knowing the hour of one's death. . . . This is unnatural. . . . Unnatural fear is an unreasonable withdrawal. This kind the Lord did not have.[5]

His recoiling from the cross reveals Jesus' true humanity perhaps more than any other moment in his life. Today people doubt the divinity of Christ, not his humanity, but the early Church faced exactly the opposite problem. Many ancients could never accept that God or a god would become a human being, especially not to die on a cross. Docetism, the first serious heresy the Church faced, denied the humanity of Christ. Chrysostom agrees that it was important for the evangelists to depict the human fear and anxiety of Jesus as he awaited his arrest.

For had He not uttered any of these things, it might have been said that if He were a man, He ought to have experienced human feelings. And what are these? In the case of one about to be crucified, fear and agony, and pain in being torn from this present life; for a sense of the charm which surrounds present things is implanted in human nature; on this account wishing to prove the reality of the fleshly clothing, and to give assurance of the incarnation He manifests the actual feelings of man with full demonstration. . . . And He prayed as instructing us to pray, and even to seek deliverance from distress; but, if this be not permitted, then to acquiesce in what seems good to God.[6]

---

5   John of Damascus, *Exact Exposition of the Orthodox Faith*, 3.23, FOTC 37:327–28.
6   John Chrysostom, *Homily on the Passage*, "*Father, if it be possible, let this cup pass from me*," in *Homily against Marcionists and Manicheans*, NPNF-1, 9:205–6.

Matthew and Mark give us a hint of Jesus' mental state when he began to pray. He went a short distance away from the other disciples, taking only Peter, James, and John with him. "He said to them, 'My soul is very sorrowful, even to death; remain here, and watch with me.' And going a little farther he fell on his face and prayed, 'My Father, if it be possible, let this cup pass from me'" (Matt. 26:38–39).

Such was Christ's state of mind as he prayed passionately and fervently to the Father while his closest friends slept soundly nearby, unaware of the extreme crisis he faced at that moment. He appealed to them to keep watch with him, but they failed him. What is translated as "very sorrowful" (*peril-ypos*) literally means "encompassed with grief," a state of mind so profoundly sorrowful as to cause death.[7]

Hematohidrosis: The Bloody Sweat

JESUS WAS UNDER EXTREME STRESS. This state of mind would have produced the nervous system's automatic response to a life-threatening situation: cold, pale skin, profuse sweating, a pounding heart, and tightening muscles. He was not simply facing death but death by slow torture in the most painful manner ever devised. This moment in Christ's life has traditionally been called the agony in the garden.

The level of courage, determination, and obedience to the will of God that was necessary for him to remain in the garden awaiting his arrest, with complete knowledge of what would soon transpire and without any human support or consolation, is truly incomprehensible. We might begin to appreciate the magnitude of his stress by noting an interesting detail preserved only by the evangelist Luke: "And there appeared to him an angel from heaven, strengthening him. And being in agony he prayed more earnestly; and his sweat became like great drops of blood falling down upon the ground" (Luke 22:43–44).[8]

---

7 Mark uses the words *ekthambeō* and *adēmoneō*, "greatly distressed and troubled" (14:33), which could even be translated as "terrified" or "thoroughly alarmed and distressed."

8 Some manuscripts of Luke's Gospel do not contain these verses, and for this reason they

The bloody-sweat detail reveals the tremendous stress Jesus experienced, knowing he would be crucified and forcing himself to remain there waiting. Under this severe strain, he may have literally sweated blood in a rare but documented medical condition known as *hematohidrosis*. This can occur when a person is subjected to "extreme physical or emotional stress" and "capillary blood vessels that feed the sweat glands rupture, causing them to exude blood."[9] This "extreme anxiety triggered by fear" is also described as "acute fear or intense mental contemplation."[10]

Each of us has an autonomic nervous system that controls various functions of the body. Its two components are the sympathetic and parasympathetic responses. The amygdala is the area of the brain sometimes called the fear center. When we are afraid, the nervous system sends an alarm triggering a fight-or-flight response (sympathetic response). The ensuing reaction comprises symptoms of anxiety, rapid heart rate (tachycardia), heart palpitations (awareness of own's own heartbeats), rapid breathing (tachypnea), sweating, trembling, and tension. Blood pressure rises; blood is diverted away from the skin and sent to the muscles, which is why people look pale when suddenly frightened. The brain goes on alert and sends blood to the arms and legs to prepare them for a fight or flight. After the threat subsides, the opposite reaction occurs, restoring previous functions. This is the parasympathetic response. The extra blood leaves the muscles and returns to the skin, the body relaxes, the heart rate is restored to baseline, and breathing returns to normal.

---

are omitted in some translations and versions of the New Testament. Were these verses original to the Gospel, actually written by Luke, then later omitted in some copies? Or were they not originally included in the Gospel but added later by a copyist? The weight of the evidence is in favor of the verses being written by Luke himself. They are written in his style and are found in the earliest manuscript copies. It is more likely that they were omitted by later copyists who were uncomfortable with the idea of Jesus exhibiting such distress and being comforted by an angel.

9   Jerajani, Jaju, Phiske, and Lade, "Hematidrosis." Hematohidrosis is also spelled "hematidrosis" and "hemidrosis," but all mean simply "blood sweat." See National Center for Biotechnology Information, https://www.ncbi.nlm.nih.gov/pmc/articles/PMC2810702/. See also the US Department of Health and Human Services website, "Hematohidrosis," https://rarediseases.info.nih.gov/diseases/13131/hematohidrosis.

10   Zugibe, *Crucifixion of Jesus*, 9.

The primary sweat glands are the exocrine glands.[11] The human body has about two million tiny sweat ducts that emerge at the surface of the skin. Below the surface, these glands look like a mass of tangled coils. Each gland has a single duct that channels the sweat up to the surface of the skin. But wrapped around and intertwined with the tangled coils are tiny blood vessels that provide the nourishment those glands and cells need.

The extreme distress Jesus was experiencing led to the fight-or-flight reaction of his nervous system, causing the blood to rush to his heart and muscles, away from his skin. This lasted for a long time, the Gospels tell us, as he wrestled with what he was facing, asking God to remove the cup. After about three hours in agonizing prayer, he accepted the will of his Father.

He was totally exhausted, but eventually the fight-or-flight reaction of the nervous system, which had drawn blood away from the skin, yielded to acceptance, and the opposite reaction occurred. His muscles relaxed, his blood pressure dropped, and the blood that had accumulated in the muscles went rushing back to his skin, causing severe dilation and rupture of the blood vessels that are intertwined with the sweat glands. Thus great drops of blood emerged from those glands.

As we ponder this scene, let us remember that Christ, just like any human being, suffered not only physically but emotionally as well. His mental suffering, his anxiety over what was to come, his anguish as he struggled to accept the cross were not easier for him because of his divine nature. In his human nature, he was like us in every way except that he never sinned.

Jesus was already physically and emotionally drained, but the night was only just beginning. Already in the distance he heard the muffled sound of a crowd approaching the olive grove.

---

11   These glands produce substances such as sweat, tears, saliva, digestive juices, and milk.

CHAPTER 12

The Akedah

JESUS FERVENTLY PRAYED TO HIS Father as he awaited the arrival of Judas and the arresting party. He knew what crucifixion entailed, and he asked the Father to take the cup of suffering away from him. Something similar to this had occurred once before, about two thousand years earlier, when Abraham faced the greatest test of his faith: the Lord asked him to sacrifice his beloved and only-begotten son, Isaac. In an unparalleled act of faith, Abraham trusted the Lord completely, bound his son for sacrifice, and lifted the hand holding the knife. But an angel stopped his hand before he actually sacrificed Isaac, and Abraham offered a ram whose horns were caught in a nearby thicket in place of his beloved only son.

Christians call the story the Sacrifice of Isaac, but Jews call it the Binding of Isaac, or the *Akedah*.[1] That remarkable event was a type, a foreshadowing of the later event that would occur as its fulfillment: the sacrifice of the Only and Beloved Son of God. The Akedah may be the Bible's earliest hint of how our salvation would occur, but its complete significance would not be entirely understood until the crucifixion of Christ.

The Akedah has been pondered, discussed, and debated by Jews for centuries. The very idea of sacrificing one's child is unimaginable. How could God even ask this of Abraham, and why did he ask it? Abraham's extraordinary faith and complete obedience to God are admirable beyond words, but that

---

1   Also spelled *Aqedah*. The story is told in Genesis 22.

does not minimize the horror of the idea. Sacrificing one's own child is so horrendous, monstrous, and inconceivable that it fills us with revulsion. To this day, Jewish scholars remain divided as to why this event happened and what it means.

Abraham, Isaac, and the Passover

THE BINDING OF ISAAC IS closely associated with Passover in Jewish tradition. Jews celebrate Moses and the Exodus at Passover, but the Akedah is also associated with Passover because Jews believe that Abraham (who died hundreds of years before Moses) preserved the Israelites from the angel of death during the Exodus.[2] Various rabbinic texts explain that the Jews' deliverance at Passover was God's reward for the piety of the Patriarchs.[3] Jewish tradition specifically links Isaac and the Passover lamb in the noncanonical Jewish literature popular during the first centuries BC and AD, such as the Book of Jubilees.[4] The crucifixion of Jesus at Passover is no mere coincidence.

The Father's Willingness to Sacrifice His Son

ABRAHAM AND ISAAC WALKED TOGETHER for three days to Mt. Moriah, carrying everything necessary for the sacrifice. Isaac carried the wood on his back but wondered why they had no lamb. When he questioned his father, Abraham replied, "God will provide the lamb," knowing all along that Isaac was to be the sacrifice. As Abraham lifted his hand holding the knife, he was stopped by the Angel of the Lord, who told him not to harm his son. A ram

---

2   Hayward, "The Sacrifice of Isaac," 297.
3   Abraham, Isaac, and Jacob, Gen. 15, 22, and 28 respectively. Hayward, "Sacrifice of Isaac," 297.
4   Tabory, "The Crucifixion of the Paschal Lamb," 396. Jubilees 17–18 states that God instructed Abraham to sacrifice Isaac on the twelfth day of the month of Nisan. Abraham and Isaac walked for three days to the place of sacrifice, and by Jewish counting (which includes the first day and the last day), Isaac was bound for sacrifice on 14 Nisan, the exact month and day when Passover lambs were sacrificed and Jesus was crucified.

was caught by its horns in a nearby thicket, and Abraham offered the ram instead of Isaac.[5]

Abraham remains the greatest model of faith and obedience in the Jewish Scriptures. Many Second Temple Jews additionally considered Abraham praiseworthy, righteous, and blessed because he obeyed the Law of Moses even though it had not yet been written. But his ultimate act of faith and obedience was his willingness to sacrifice even his beloved son.[6] This gave Abraham "meritorious power," and his name reverberates throughout Judaism in many situations that Christians do not normally associate with Abraham, including the Exodus, the parting of the Red Sea, the receiving of the Law at Mt. Sinai, and the blowing of the ram's horn (the *shofar*) at Rosh Hashana (Jewish New Year).

The Son's Willingness to Be Sacrificed

THE AKEDAH IS IMPORTANT IN Jewish thought and tradition not only because of Abraham's willingness to offer Isaac as a sacrifice, but because of Isaac's willingness to be sacrificed. First-century Jewish commentaries on Genesis describe Isaac as encouraging his father to carry out the sacrifice, the result being that at least for some Jewish authors, "the near sacrifice was thought to be meritorious or atoning."[7] As one of the Dead Sea Scrolls retells the story, Isaac encouraged Abraham to accomplish the sacrifice: "Bind my hands," he said. First-century Jews firmly believed that God tested Isaac too, and because Isaac passed the test, he was righteous and blessed by God.[8] Several Jewish documents of the first centuries BC and AD emphasized Isaac's voluntary cooperation.[9]

---

5   Abraham did not offer a young lamb but a ram, a fully grown male sheep, just as Christ was not a child but a fully grown man when he offered himself up. Both the ram and Jesus were sacrifices provided by God.

6   Das, *Paul and the Stories of Israel*, 95.

7   Das, 95.

8   4Q225. Some Jewish commentators describe Isaac as begging his father to bind him tightly lest he become afraid and the sacrifice be invalidated. *Sanh.* 89b.

9   This includes the Book of Jubilees, 4 Maccabees, and one of the Dead Sea Scrolls, 4Q225.

The Akedah tradition emphasizes Isaac's willingness to be offered and "regards his act as if it had been a real sacrifice, utterly without blemish, as effective as none other to procure God's mercy, forgiveness and help in times of need."[10] Some rabbis describe Isaac as a "perfect burnt offering," and moreover, they assert that some of his blood was actually shed.[11] Even in the first century, some Jewish traditions referred to the *ashes* of Isaac, asserting that Abraham actually sacrificed Isaac and burnt him as an offering to the Lord, but he was then resurrected.[12] Because Isaac was willing to be sacrificed, the sacrifice was regarded as if it had actually taken place, and Isaac's near sacrifice was considered "expiatory," according to first-century rabbinic midrash.[13]

"The merits of Isaac assist his descendants and counterbalance their sins."[14] The ram's horn is blown that the Lord might remember the sacrifice of Isaac and credit it to all Jews as if they too had also allowed themselves to be bound for the Lord.[15] The ram's horn also proclaims "Messianic redemption," and the "expiating power of the Aqedah is known from ancient times."[16] According to some rabbis, "God remembers the Aqedah for the benefit of *all* men, Gentiles as well as Jews,"[17] and at least one Jewish tradition connects the binding of Isaac to the future resurrection: "Through the deserts of Isaac, who offered himself on the altar, the Holy One, praised be his name, will eventually raise the dead."[18]

---

10 Hayward, "Sacrifice of Isaac," 292.

11 *Cant. Rabba* (ad1,4) states explicitly, "Isaac lay bound on the altar as the expiator of Israel's sins." Schoeps, "Sacrifice of Isaac," 389.

12 Hayward, "Sacrifice of Isaac," 292. Rubenstein, "What Was at Stake in the Parting of the Ways Between Judaism and Christianity?" 84; Levenson, *Death and Resurrection*, 199. See Spiegal, *Last Trial,* for a comprehensive study of the Akedah throughout history, including medieval Jewish interpretation.

13 Isaac's action forgave sins. Midrash is Jewish interpretation of the Scriptures. Das, *Paul and the Stories of Israel*, 96.

14 Schoeps, "Sacrifice of Isaac," 388. Schoeps provides extensive citations to these rabbinic traditions.

15 Schoeps, 388. The ram's horn, the shofar, is blown on Rosh Hashana, the Jewish New Year, and prayers on Rosh Hashana, which go back to the first century, reflect a connection to the Akedah. Schoeps, 388–89.

16 Schoeps, 389, citing ancient Jewish sources. This concept was discussed in the famous first-century rabbinic schools of Hillel and Shammai.

17 Schoeps, 390.

18 *Pesikta of R. Kahana*, Piska 32 [200a]; Schoeps, "Sacrifice of Isaac," 390.

Some rabbinic writings connected the "blood of Isaac (!) with the blood of the paschal lamb when the Jews left Egypt."[19] Even crucifixion was connected to the sacrifice of Isaac. The rabbis described Isaac as carrying the wood for his own sacrifice just as "one who carries his cross on his back."[20] Isaac was bound and not sacrificed, but Jesus was actually sacrificed on 14 Nisan. The first Christians easily recognized the parallel between Isaac and Jesus. Isaac was the type, the sketch or shadow, and the sacrifice of Christ was the fulfillment.

Did Christianity Inspire Jewish Views of the Akedah?

THESE VARIOUS NOTIONS ABOUT THE Akedah were not universally held or even necessarily widespread in first-century Judaism. Nonetheless, these concepts existed before the time of Christ and flowed within Jewish currents of thought during his lifetime. Some modern scholars have attempted to refute this, claiming that Jewish interpretations referring to the blood of Isaac or suggesting that the Akedah was expiatory were inspired by Christian claims about Jesus and his sacrifice. But a deeper examination reveals that this is not correct.[21]

A famous first-century Jewish philosopher and contemporary of Christ, Philo of Alexandria, discussed the willingness of Isaac to be sacrificed. Jews discussed these ideas before the rise of the Christian Church, and Jewish writings reflect this.[22] The idea of the salvific nature of the binding of Isaac—that it provided either spiritual assistance or forgiveness of sin—was unrelated to any Christian claims about Jesus and was established well before the

---

19   Tabory, "Crucifixion of the Paschal Lamb," 405.

20   Tabory, "Crucifixion of the Paschal Lamb," 405.

21   The main proponents of this view are Davies and Chilton, "The Aqedah: A Revised Tradition History," 514–546. But as Leroy Huizenga pointed out, Davies and Chilton base their position on a strict and unrealistic definition of Akedah that would apply only to a later and more developed stage of the tradition. Davies and Chilton also ignore the connection of the Akedah with the Passover and other Exodus parallels found in the Book of Jubilees, which dates back to the second century BC. "Obedience unto Death."

22   Das, *Paul and the Stories of Israel*, 112, citing Philo, *On the Life of Abraham* 33.177. See also Hayward, "Sacrifice of Isaac," 301, and Huizenga, "Obedience unto Death," 510–15.

destruction of the Temple in AD 70. Jews would not have adopted Christian concepts, and no evidence supports that theory. Jewish belief is that God favors the Jews, and spiritual benefits flow to them because of Abraham's outstanding act of faith and Isaac's willing participation. [23]

Did the Akedah Inspire Christian Ideas about Jesus?

BUT WHAT ABOUT THE OPPOSITE effect? Did early Christians derive their ideas about who Jesus was and the meaning of his sacrifice from Jewish ideas about Isaac? Certainly not. Jesus was not simply a rabbi who died prematurely and whose followers developed ideas. Christians did not employ the Isaac-Jesus parallel to create ideas about Jesus. They knew him and directly experienced the person of Jesus, hearing his teachings and witnessing his miracles and his bodily Resurrection.

Jewish ideas about the Akedah are significant because many strange or mysterious concepts in first-century Judaism converged and were fulfilled in the person of Jesus Christ. What the apostles taught about Jesus was not new or strange to the Jews of their time. These concepts were already present in Judaism and had prepared the Jewish people for the coming of Christ.

The Voluntary Sin of Adam and the Voluntary Death of Jesus

CHRIST COULD EASILY HAVE AVOIDED arrest, but he came to his passion willingly. Orthodox hymnology repeatedly emphasizes the voluntary Passion of the Lord and almost never calls him a "victim." He was not a victim but willingly ascended the cross. Adam was indifferent to God and lost paradise because he followed his self-will and chose the fruit of the Tree of the

---

23 Hayward, "Sacrifice of Isaac," 301. It is more likely that any similarity between Isaac's and Jesus' sacrifice was suppressed by the Jews rather than created to respond to Christian claims. Jewish traditions about the Akedah became more elaborate after the destruction of the Temple, but Christian claims did not inspire it. Segal, "'He who did not spare his own son . . .': Jesus, Paul and the Akeda," 182. Ideas about the merits of Isaac continued to develop later, but emphasis on the benefits from the willingness of Isaac is clearly present by the first century. See Fitzmyer, "The Sacrifice of Isaac in Qumran Literature."

Knowledge of Good and Evil. But the true fruit of his choice, the bitter knowledge he acquired, was knowledge of sin and death. Christ accepted the cross and experienced the bitterness of death, but the result would be our return to paradise and eternal life. Christ as the New Adam reversed the sin of Adam by his complete obedience to the Father's will.

The Orthodox Church repeatedly emphasizes the voluntary nature of Christ's suffering, a point St. Paul also articulated in one of the most famous passages of the New Testament. Christ "humbled himself and became obedient unto death, even death on a cross" (Phil. 2:8). He could have avoided the cross, and he prayed to the Father, as any human being would, to take the cup away. But by accepting it, he taught us humility, obedience, and courage in the face of death. Saint John Chrysostom remarked, "It was to teach us this lesson by His example that Christ went to His Passion, not by compulsion or by necessity, but willingly."[24]

The Death of Christ as Sacrifice

JESUS' DEATH WAS NEITHER A mistake nor an accident. It was a sacrifice, but Jesus was not a victim. It was a sacrifice, but it was not required. It was a sacrifice, but it was a gift, freely given, the supreme paradox in the plan of salvation. The meaning of the cross is perverted when Christians assert that the Father required the sacrifice of the Son, whose blood was necessary to pay a price demanded by the Father. This theology of the cross makes God a cruel, legalistic tyrant, and it is hardly surprising that people reject such views or even reject God entirely because of this notion. This understanding of the death of Christ infinitely impoverishes the cross, and it was not the view of the early Church.[25]

Paul reminded the Corinthians that "Christ died for our sins" (1 Cor.15:3), but this should not be reduced to a legalistic vicarious atonement for the sins

---

24   St. John Chrysostom, Homily 83, *Homilies on the Gospel of John*, FOTC 41:399.

25   The idea that the death of Christ on the cross served primarily to make payment for sin demanded because of divine justice arose during the Middle Ages out of a legalistic view of sin and salvation that developed in Western Europe. This was foreign to the early Church and is still alien to Orthodox Christianity.

of humankind. Christ accomplished perfect obedience to God the Father. Many Jews speculated that if a man could live without sinning, in perfect obedience to God, he would not die.[26] But St. Paul realized that it is not possible to live a perfect life. Humans can never achieve salvation by our own efforts. At some point we all sin. But Christ's perfect obedience reversed the effects of Adam's sin and our own. The cross is our redemption, not because the Father demanded or required someone to pay the price for our sins, but because sin had its roots in Adam's assertion of his self-will. The voluntary death of Christ reversed what Adam caused. Christ did not *have* to die; he *chose* to die, not to pay a price but to destroy death by death.

Although Jesus had agonized in the garden, he fully accepted the cross, and when the arresting party arrived, he was composed and prepared. Judas had also acted voluntarily in his betrayal. He was not forced into betrayal because of the prophecy. He had not been tricked or entrapped. He had approached the chief priests on his own initiative. Jesus never regretted his choice, but Judas would. Almost immediately.

---

26   Rubenstein, "What Was at Stake," 96.

CHAPTER 13

The Arrest

S OON THE QUIET OF THE olive grove was disrupted by sounds of tense, furtive voices and many footsteps rapidly approaching. A large crowd appeared on the scene, carrying torches that illuminated the night. Jesus stood upright and faced them. He was ready. The disciples awoke in a foggy haze. "What's going on?" they wondered.

> Judas came, one of the twelve, and with him a great crowd with swords and clubs, from the chief priests and the elders of the people. Now the betrayer had given them a sign, saying, "The one I shall kiss is the man; seize him." And he came up to Jesus at once and said, "Hail, Master!" And he kissed him. (Matt. 26:47–49)

The Kiss

THE JEWS CUSTOMARILY KISSED THE hand of a rabbi, an expression of respect, obedience, and recognition of their master's authority.[1] Judas addressed Jesus as "Rabbi," translated here into English as "Master," and kissed him. Was it a kiss on the hand, a disciple's gesture of deference and esteem for his teacher? Or was it a kiss on the cheek, a gesture of friendship and goodwill? Regardless, it was a kiss of treachery and the height of hypocrisy. The ordinary

---

1   Brown, *Death of the Messiah*, 1:255.

Greek word for "kiss" is *phileo*, but the Greek word here for Judas's kiss is *kata-phileo*, which means "to kiss tenderly, to kiss earnestly or repeatedly." It is the same word used to describe the kisses the sinful woman lavished on Christ's feet (Luke 7:38, 45) or the way the loving father kissed the returning prodigal son (Luke 15:20). Jesus endured Judas's corruption and hypocrisy even to this last moment.

Jesus was fully aware of the fate that awaited Judas, and his love and concern for his betrayer at that moment astonishes St. John Chrysostom:

> He bewails those who were upon the point of killing Him, and is troubled and confounded at seeing the traitor, not because He was going to be crucified, but because he was lost. He was troubled then as having foreknowledge of the hanging, and the punishment after the hanging. And though He knew his wickedness, He bore with him to the last hour, and thrust not away the traitor, but even kissed him. Thy Master kisses, and with His lips receives him who was on the very point of shedding His precious Blood.[2]

"But Jesus said to him, 'Judas, would you betray the Son of man with a kiss?'" (Luke 22:48). The Lord looked at Judas with knowing eyes of deep sadness, aware of his betrayer's impending demise. Jesus was still trying to amend Judas by his mild statement, teaching us by his example to pity those who seek to do us harm. Chrysostom assumes that Jesus kissed Judas in response.

> Just consider what Christ did near the Cross itself, wishing to amend by His kiss the traitor by whom He was on the point of being betrayed. And see with how much power to shame him. For He says, "Judas, you betray the Son of Man with a kiss?" Who is there He would not have softened? Who is there that this address would not have made yielding? . . . And therefore do not hate, but bewail and pity him that plots against you. For such a one deserves pity at our hands, and tears. For we are the servants of Him Who kissed even the traitor (I will not leave off dwelling over that continually), and spoke words to him more

---

2   Chrysostom, Homily 21, *Homilies on Romans,* NPNF-1, 11:505.

gentle than the kiss. For He did not even say, O you foul and villainous traitor, is this the sort of recompense you return us for so great a benefit? But in what words? "Judas," using his own name, which is more like a person bemoaning, and recalling him, than one angry at him.[3]

Luke brings out the tenderness and disappointment of the Lord and his sadness at the loss of Judas's soul. "Judas, would you betray the Son of man with a kiss?" (Luke 22:48). But Matthew highlights the hypocrisy of the kiss by the words of Christ. "Jesus said to him, 'Friend, why are you here?' Then they came up and laid hands on Jesus and seized him" (Matt. 26:50).

Jesus knew why Judas was there. The question "Why are you here?" expressed incredulity at the depth of Judas's hypocrisy: the sign to identify the Master would be a *kiss*? A kiss is incompatible with betrayal. It was a mild remark, as Chrysostom noted, but perhaps Jesus was also saying, "Why are you here? Do what you came to do! You came here to betray me. Let's not have any more pretense."

Were the Arresting Soldiers Jews or Romans?

Then Jesus, knowing all that was to befall him, came forward and said to them, "Whom do you seek?" They answered him, "Jesus of Nazareth." Jesus said to them, "I am he." Judas, who betrayed him, was standing with them. When he said to them, "I am he," they drew back and fell to the ground. (John 18:4–6)

JUDAS "PROCURED A BAND OF soldiers," the evangelist John writes (John 18:3). Now Judas stood with soldiers, opposite the disciples, signifying that he was no longer a disciple. Were the soldiers who arrested Jesus Jews or Romans? This question is a matter of some debate. Some scholars believe they were Roman troops, because John writes that Judas procured a *speira*, the Greek military term for a company of six hundred men.[4] But just as a modern

---

3   Chrysostom, Homily 21, *Homilies on Romans*, NPNF-1, 11:504.
4   A speira is a tenth of a legion, or 600 men, since a legion has 6,000 men. Some commentators have actually suggested that 600 men were brought to arrest Jesus. This did not

nonmilitary person might use a word like "battalion" or "troop" as a general expression, John was not using the word with precision. He employed *speira* here to indicate a group of soldiers of indefinite number.

These soldiers must have been from the Temple guard. The objective was to arrest Jesus quietly, which could not happen if six hundred Roman soldiers were marching in the middle of the night. Secondly, six hundred Roman soldiers could not have been mobilized without Pilate's knowledge; but when Jesus appears before Pilate, we learn that he has never heard of Jesus before (John 18:35).

Furthermore, Jesus identifies himself to the arresting party with the divine name "I AM," and immediately all the soldiers fall to the ground. Christ's words are often translated as "I am he," but the Greek words are "I am." Roman soldiers would not have reacted that way, since they would not have recognized or respected the divine name. When the sacred name was pronounced by the high priest in the Temple on Yom Kippur, the Jews would fall to the ground and prostrate themselves. No Roman soldiers participated in Yom Kippur. They would not recognize the divine name if they heard it, and they would never have heard it since it was spoken aloud only in the Temple on Yom Kippur. Therefore, the arresting soldiers must have been Jews.

Christ was not identifying himself as Jesus of Nazareth but as the eternal Son of God, who had revealed himself to Moses in the burning bush with this name, I AM (Ex. 3:14). Cyril of Alexandria asks why the Lord revealed himself with the divine name:

> It was that they might learn that his passion did not happen to him without his own will, nor could they have seized him, had he not consented to be taken. For it was not the effect of their own strength that they took Christ and brought him to the wicked rulers, but he yielded himself up to suffer, as well as knowing that his passion on the cross was for the salvation of the whole world.[5]

---

happen.

5   Cyril of Alexandria, Homily 148, *Commentary on Luke*, 588.

Jesus also reproached the crowd that came to arrest him for cowardice, treating him like a violent criminal and arresting him secretly in the middle of the night:

Then Jesus said to the chief priests and officers of the temple and elders, who had come out against him, "Have you come out as against a robber, with swords and clubs? When I was with you day after day in the temple, you did not lay hands on me. But this is your hour, and the power of darkness." (Luke 22:52–53)

Chrysostom is so overwhelmed by Christ's patience and meekness, he spontaneously glorifies the Lord:

Blessed art Thou, O Lord! What lowliness of mind, what forbearance have you given us examples of! And to Judas He behaved thus. But to those who came with staves and swords to Him, was it not so too? What can be more gentle than the words spoken to them? For when He had power to demolish them all in an instant, He did nothing of the kind, but as reproving, addressed them in the words, "Why, have you come out as against a thief with swords and staves?" And having cast them down backwards as they continued insensible, He of His own accord gave Himself up next, and forbore while He saw them putting manacles upon His holy hands, while He had the power at once to confound all things, and overthrow them.[6]

The Disciples Flee

JESUS HAD PREDICTED THAT THE disciples would abandon him, but they all insisted they would fight for him. Peter was so determined to protect Jesus that he carried a sword, confident that he was ready for any threat. When trouble began, he drew his sword and even cut off the ear of the high priest's servant Malchus, who was with the arresting party (John 18:10).[7] But

---

6   Chrysostom, Homily 21, *Homilies on Romans,* NPNF-1, 11:504.
7   Malchus is identified in John 18:10, and the ear is healed in Luke 22:51.

Jesus immediately put a stop to the violence, healed the servant's ear (Luke 22:51), and reprimanded Peter for using the sword to defend him: "Put your sword back into its place; for all who take the sword will perish by the sword" (Matt. 26:52). "Shall I not drink the cup which the Father has given me?" (John 18:11).

Peter was at a loss. He did not know what to do. All the disciples, now in a quandary, could only watch helplessly as Jesus was bound with a rope. He would not allow them to defend him. But as the soldiers turned toward the disciples, Jesus abruptly stopped them. The disciples had vowed to protect Jesus, but now it was he who would protect them: "'If you seek me, let these men go.' This was to fulfil the word which he had spoken [in prayer to the Father], 'Of those whom thou gavest me I lost not one'" (John 18:8–9).

Seeing themselves unable to help Jesus and recognizing their chance to escape, the disciples fled into the night. Only three years before, they had left everything to follow Jesus; but now they fled from him, leaving him to face an unimaginable ordeal alone. But Peter and John lurked behind the mob and quietly followed Jesus and the arresting party to the home of the high priest, Caiaphas.

When Jesus had foretold his arrest and crucifixion, Peter had insisted that Jesus should not go to Jerusalem. But Jesus replied, "Get behind me, Satan! You are a hindrance to me; for you are not on the side of God, but of men" (Matt. 16:21–23). Now Peter's worst fears were realized: Jesus was in custody. Maybe he could help his Master somehow if he remained in close proximity. So Peter stood warming himself by the fire, hoping to mingle inconspicuously with the others in the courtyard on that chilly spring night.

CHAPTER 14

Regrets and Denials

Judas's Regret

JUDAS SOON REGRETTED HIS DECISION and returned to the Temple with the thirty pieces of silver, admitting Jesus' innocence to the chief priests and elders. "When Judas, his betrayer, saw that he was condemned, he repented and brought back the thirty pieces of silver to the chief priests and the elders, saying, 'I have sinned in betraying innocent blood'" (Matt. 27:3–4).

The response was cold and callous: "What is that to us? See to it yourself" (Matt. 27:4). In other words, "We don't care! That's your problem." The response demonstrates that the guilt or innocence of Jesus was irrelevant to them. At worst he was a blasphemer and deserved to die. At best he was an annoyance, a source of aggravation, a problem to be eliminated.

Did Judas really believe he could change his mind, reverse what he had done, and undo the deal he had struck to hand over Jesus? In fact, he probably did. There was a legal basis for such a cancellation, a grace period during which a seller could change his mind. Jewish tradition, later codified as law in the Mishna, held that a sale could be cancelled by a seller within one year of a transaction, even a large sale such as a house or a field. Buyers who were happy with their purchase would sometimes go into hiding so the seller could not find them and revoke the sale at the last minute. A famous rabbi, Hillel the Elder, created a remedy to counteract this: If a buyer hid in order to avoid a seller seeking to cancel the sale and regain his property, the seller could come to the Temple and leave the purchase money there. This would legally rescind the sale.[1]

"And throwing down the pieces of silver in the temple, he departed" (Matt. 27:5). Judas attempted to nullify the sale, to reverse what he had done. The item that was sold was Jesus. The chief priests were the buyers. They were not in hiding, but they refused to accept a return of the funds and rescind the deal they had made, so Judas threw down the money in the Temple. This was not an act of frustration but Judas's only option for undoing what he had done. It may be significant that the term used here for "Temple" is *naos*, rather than the more general word *ieron*, which could refer to any location in the entire Temple complex, including outer courtyards.[2] The naos was the sanctuary, the dwelling of God. Did Judas stand in the Court of Israel and throw the coins into the Holy Place? Perhaps. He threw the coins into the Temple, not into the treasury.

Judas realized he had no power to change the outcome for Jesus. Perhaps he hoped to avoid any moral or legal responsibility for betraying him by returning the purchase price. But he could not escape his conscience. He "went and hanged himself" (Matt. 27:5).

The money that induced his actions brought Judas no joy. Within two days his conscience scourged him, and he returned the money to the chief priests. Why? Chrysostom remarks that initially Satan prevents us from recognizing the evil we are doing. Then he prevents our repentance, or our repentance is spiritually unprofitable, as in this case. Judas did not enjoy the money, nor this life, nor the life to come; he lost everything because of greed. "For the devil led him out of his repentance too soon, so that he should reap no fruit from there; and carries him off, by a most disgraceful death, and one manifest to all, having persuaded him to destroy himself."[3]

"But the chief priests, taking the pieces of silver, said, 'It is not lawful to put them into the treasury, since they are blood money'" (Matt. 27:6–9). Money

---

1   Jeremias, *Jerusalem in the Time of Jesus*, 139.

2   *Naos* and *ieron* can be and often are used interchangeably. However, *naos* often indicates more precisely the dwelling place of God. Charlesworth, *Jesus and the Temple*, 149.

3   Chrysostom, Homily 85, *Homilies on Matthew*, NPNF-1, 10:488.

acquired through sin or illegal activities, or which was simply stolen property whose owner could not be ascertained, was never comingled with other coins in the treasury. These were tainted funds and could be used only for some public benefit. In this case, the money returned by Judas was used to purchase land for a cemetery.

In fulfillment of prophecy (Zech. 11:13), the chief priests refused to return the funds to the treasury, a tacit recognition that their actions were murderous. The money had secured someone's death. Now they would pick up each coin that had been cast into the sacred space, one by one. When he cleansed the Temple, Jesus had underscored the corruption of the chief priests. Like the Pharisees, "straining out a gnat and swallowing a camel," they carefully segregated the blood money from other Temple coinage while ignoring a monumental commandment: Thou shalt not kill.

> So they took counsel, and bought with them the potter's field, to bury strangers in. Therefore that field has been called the Field of Blood to this day. Then was fulfilled what had been spoken by the prophet Jeremiah, saying, "And they took the thirty pieces of silver, the price of him on whom a price had been set by some of the sons of Israel, and they gave them for the potter's field, as the Lord directed me." (Matt. 27:7–10)[4]

In the course of Christ's Passion, certain people attempted to distance themselves from their deeds—including Judas, who returned the money, and Pilate, who washed his hands. But to this day, we still say that Christ was "crucified under Pontius Pilate." Likewise, long after the betrayal, the name of the plot of land purchased with Judas's silver pieces—the Field of Blood—stood as silent witness to his betrayal and to the fact that this silver was "blood money," payment for condemning an innocent man.

Chrysostom points out that the chief priests revealed their guilt, unaware that they were condemning themselves by their actions. "For if they had cast

---

4   Although he only mentions Jeremiah, the better-known prophet, Matthew actually combines two prophetic images and references here: first, the wages paid to Judas from Zech. 11:12, and images from Jeremiah. His prophetic activities were associated with potters (Jer. 18; 19), and he was instructed to purchase a field (Jer. 32:25).

it into the treasury, the thing would not have been so clearly discovered; but now having bought a piece of ground, they made it all manifest even to subsequent generations." The truth about Christ could never be hidden and would inevitably be manifested, "shining forth on every side," since even his adversaries unwittingly revealed the truth as they themselves fulfilled the prophecies by giving thirty pieces of silver to Judas, by purchasing the potter's field, and in countless other ways. Judas's suicide also silently testifies to the innocence of Christ. How can anyone argue against the complete innocence of Jesus, Chrysostom asks, when even the betrayer refuted the council's guilty verdict against Jesus by passing sentence on himself?[5]

Peter's Denials

MEANWHILE, PETER AND JOHN TRAILED at a safe distance behind the arresting party and followed it all the way to the house of Caiaphas, where the crowd funneled into the gated courtyard alongside the house. Jesus, still bound with ropes and accompanied by guards, was immediately taken to see Annas, while the rest of the mob remained outdoors, a location more appropriate for their status. A teenage servant girl guarding the gate had admitted the throng but closed the gate behind John, leaving Peter outside. This was the private residence of a very important person, the high priest himself. She was the gatekeeper and admitted only people she knew.

The sounds of shuffling feet, twitters of laughter, and casual conversation about the evening's events filled the chilly air as the crowd set down their clubs and torches to relax by the charcoal fire. John, the beloved disciple, realizing that Peter was not admitted to the courtyard, went to the gate. He knew the household servants and intervened with the girl gatekeeper to vouch for Peter: "He's okay. He's with me." John was admitted because he was "known to the high priest," as he would later explain in his Gospel (John 18:16).[6]

---

5   Chrysostom, Homily 85, *Homilies on Matthew*, NPNF-1, 10:489–90.

6   This surprising statement by the evangelist has led people to question whether or not John was in fact the author of the Fourth Gospel. Although John and James, the sons of Zebedee, met Jesus in Galilee and were fishermen by trade, their father must have been a priest, a status that was inherited. Some priests lived in Galilee, since most priests

The servant girl must have known that John was a disciple and may have seen John and Peter with Jesus at the Temple or elsewhere in Jerusalem. When she opened the gate to admit Peter, she thought she recognized him and remarked, "Aren't you one of this man's disciples, too?"

Peter replied, "No, I'm not." (One.)

As Jesus was being interrogated, the servants and members of the high priest's retinue huddled around the glowing chunks of charcoal, chatting and keeping warm. Peter was also warming himself when someone casually asked him, "Aren't you one of his disciples?"

Peter shook his head. "No, I don't even know the man." (Two.)

John must have looked at Peter, remembering the Lord's prediction earlier in the evening. But Peter was too fearful of the imminent danger to remember the prophecy when yet another servant, one related to the man whose ear Peter had cut off, said, "Didn't I see you in the garden with him? You even have a Galilean accent!"

Peter swore an oath and called down curses upon himself if he should be lying. "I do not know him!" (Three.) Immediately a rooster crowed.[7]

Peter must have frozen in shock as he realized the significance of his own words, the memory of Jesus' prediction suddenly flooding his mind. Luke tells us that Jesus, who was inside the house but within sight of Peter, turned and looked directly at him (22:61). Perhaps he slowly shook his head, not to say "I told you so," but to give Peter a glance of loving concern and compassion.

It was too much for Peter to bear. John had silently witnessed each denial but could not even offer a word of comfort as Peter, unable to restrain his tears, fled from the courtyard into the empty streets, where he wept bitterly.

---

did not earn their livelihood through fulfilling their priestly duties but had their own profession, trade, farm, or flocks. Exactly how this particular family was known to the high priest we cannot say; however, that John was a Jewish priest is preserved in early Christian correspondence. When John died, Polycrates, the Bishop of Ephesus, wrote to Victor, the Bishop of Rome, that John was buried as "a priest and wore the sacerdotal plate," a reference to the vestments worn by Jewish priests. Eusebius of Caesarea, *History of the Church*, 3.31.3. John died in Ephesus during the reign of Trajan (98–117).

7   Dialogue in this section has been paraphrased from Matt. 26:69–75; Mark 14:66–72; Luke 22:56–62; and John 18:25–27.

It was a hard lesson for Peter to learn: not to be confident in himself. The Lord could not console him now, but he had already prayed for Peter not to lose faith during this heart-wrenching and agonizing night. At the Last Supper Jesus had said to Peter, "Simon, Simon, behold, Satan demanded to have you, that he might sift you like wheat, but I have prayed for you that your faith may not fail; and when you have turned again, strengthen your brethren" (Luke 22:31–32).

But Peter insisted, "Lord, I am ready to go with you to prison and to death!" Jesus simply replied, "I tell you, Peter, the cock will not crow this day, until you three times deny that you know me" (Luke 22:33–34).

The offense was not simple disloyalty to a friend. Peter denied knowing the Lord. He denied being a disciple of Christ, the worst transgression any Christian can commit. We must never deny the Lord, even at the cost of our lives. He said, "Whoever denies me before men, I also will deny before my Father who is in heaven" (Matt. 10:33).[8]

Saint Cyril comments on the lessons we can learn from Peter's denials.

It is worth our while observing in what way his sin was forgiven and how he put away his fault. For the event might prove no slight benefit to us also. He did not therefore defer his repentance, nor was he careless about it. For as rapid as his descent was into sin, so quick were his tears because of it; nor did he merely weep but wept bitterly. . . . If temptation assails us and we prove weak, let us weep bitterly, let us ask forgiveness of God. For he heals those who are contrite. He raises up the fallen. He stretches out his saving hand to those who have gone astray, for he is the Savior of all.[9]

Christ forgave him, but Peter would never forget the lesson of that night. Cyril of Alexandria reminds us that stories such as these are included in the

---

8   Of course, the Lord forgave Peter and restored him when he asked Peter three times, "Simon, son of John, do you love me more than these?" (John 21:15–17). The Fathers of the Church always understood this to be a restoration of Peter, not a special commissioning of him to be "the first pope" as is often claimed by the Roman Catholic Church. "A triple confession is paid back to the triple denial." St. Augustine, *Tractates on the Gospel of John,* Tractate 123.5, FOTC 92:77.

9   Cyril of Alexandria, Homily 149, *Commentary on Luke,* 592–93.

Scriptures to give us hope, that we might learn from the shortcomings of the saints. Even if we fall, we should not despair but rise again and recover our spiritual health through repentance.[10]

Peter, the most boisterous, enthusiastic, and passionate disciple, was confident in himself, but he was "sifted," tested by Satan, during the worst night of his life. Everything was black and bleak. He was despondent and despairing. When Christ asked his disciples, "Who do you say that I am?" Peter had immediately confessed boldly, "You are the Christ, the Son of the living God," and Jesus had confirmed the truth of that statement (Matt. 16:15–17). How could Jesus now be arrested and facing death?

Christ could not explain or comfort Peter now. Perhaps later Peter would remember that the Lord had prayed for him to recover from his denials. But at that moment, all he remembered was that Jesus was right. He was *always* right. One by one, roosters began heralding the dawn in every corner of the city, and each exclamation was like a knife to Peter's heart. He had denied the Lord. *Koo-koo-Rhoo-koo-Rhooooo! Koo-koo-Rhoo-koo-Rhooooo!* The roosters themselves seemed to accuse him. *YOU-deNIED-the-Loooord! YOU-deNIED-the Loooord!* As the roosters crowed again and again and again, Peter could not escape their condemnation.

As Peter wept bitterly in the streets because he had denied him, Christ stood before the Great Sanhedrin and the high priest, Caiaphas, whose words would echo Peter's great confession of faith.

---

10   Cyril of Alexandria, Homily 149, *Commentary on Luke*, 592.

CHAPTER 15

Interrogation by Annas

So the band of soldiers and their captain and the officers of the Jews seized Jesus and bound him. First they led him to Annas; for he was the father-in-law of Caiaphas, who was the high priest that year. (John 18:12–13)

WHEN JESUS ARRIVED AT THE home of Caiaphas, he was immediately brought to Annas, the father-in-law of Caiaphas, for a private interrogation. Only John's Gospel recounts this scene. John described Annas as "the high priest" because Annas had once held the position.[1] Not only had Annas served as high priest, but five of his sons became high priests, and now his son-in-law, Caiaphas, held that office. The family of Annas dominated the high priesthood during the first century, thereby controlling the Temple and the Sanhedrin. Through those institutions, this one powerful family controlled the nation and its political relationship with Rome.[2]

The High Priesthood in First-Century Judea

FOR THE JEWS, THE HIGH priest (kōhēn gādōl) was authorized by God to offer sacrifices for the sins of the people and had "lifelong sanctity" as an

---

1   Annas was high priest from AD 6 to 15. Josephus, *Ant.* 18.2.1. His name is recorded by Josephus as "Ananus, son of Seth."
2   Jeremias, *Jerusalem in the Time of Jesus*, 197–98.

133

indelible characteristic.[3] Anyone who had served as high priest even for one day kept the title and enjoyed significant authority for his entire life. Regardless of his personal sins or the corruption of the office itself, the high priest was the only human being permitted to enter the unspeakably sacred space, the Holy of Holies, on the Day of Atonement and pronounce the sacred Name of God.[4] This alone gave him an awe-inspiring cultic status surpassing all others.[5]

By the time of Christ, many ancient traditions and important laws regarding the high priest were no longer observed. The high priesthood had ceased being hereditary, and high priests no longer served for life. Instead of being consecrated by anointing with holy oil, as required by the Torah (Ex. 29:7), they were presented with vestments. No one is certain why or how this change occurred.[6] The position of high priest was considered so sanctified that the death of the high priest had the power to atone for sin. If anyone committed a negligent homicide (an accidental killing), he could avoid the legal consequences and escape revenge on the part of the victim's family by fleeing to a "city of refuge" (Num. 35:9–15; Deut. 19:1ff; Ex. 21:23). When a high priest died, anyone who had fled to a city of refuge could return home and face no legal consequences, because the death of the high priest had expiated the guilt of the accidental killing—even if the high priest was not in office at the time of his death.[7]

Because no Jewish king ruled in the province of Judea for most of the first century AD, the high priest had the title *ethnarch*, meaning that he represented the Jewish people in religious matters before God and in all political

---

3   Jeremias, *Jerusalem in the Time of Jesus*, 148.

4   Jeremias, *Jerusalem in the Time of Jesus*, 149. The sacred Name is not actually God's name, for he has no name. Rather, it was the LORD's reply to Moses at the burning bush when Moses asked, "what shall I say?" to those who ask for God's name. The LORD said, "I AM WHO I AM. . . . I AM has sent me to you" (Ex. 3:13–14). Thus, the statement "I am" is considered the sacred Name of God and is represented in Hebrew with four letters: YHWH (*Yahweh*). This word is not pronounced by Jews when they read the Scriptures aloud. Instead, out of reverence for the Name, they substitute the word *Adonai*, which means "my Lord."

5   Jeremias, *Jerusalem in the Time of Jesus*, 160.

6   Jeremias, *Jerusalem in the Time of Jesus*, 158. A ceremony of investiture conferred the office. The vestments consisted of eight different pieces, and each piece was believed to possess power to atone for specific sins. Jeremias, 148.

7   Jeremias, 157.

matters with Rome.[8] Jewish high priests held a significant level of authority to keep the peace and to ensure that taxes would be paid. This was a political arrangement between Rome and the Jewish aristocracy, whose mutual interests in their own self-preservation and self-enrichment would serve the interests of Rome.

Lifestyle of the High Priests

THE HIGH PRIESTS AND CHIEF priests belonged to the wealthy aristocracy. Caiaphas's house was large enough to accommodate an emergency meeting of the Sanhedrin, and his household would have included numerous servants.[9] High-priestly families were extraordinarily wealthy. Brides were given enormous dowries, and wives of high priests and chief priests had special allowances for perfumes, jewelry, and other extravagances. High priests and their widows received generous pensions from the Temple treasury.[10]

High-priestly families had many sources of income from farms, as landowners, and from trading, as shipowners. However, kickbacks, nepotism, and bribery were rampant. Anyone who held a key Temple position was appointed by the high priest and was almost always a relative. The high priest had ceremonial rights to perform rituals and offer certain sacrifices not permitted for other priests. But his responsibilities also involved considerable expenditure, including the purchase of costly vestments and large sacrificial animals such as bulls, which he was required to provide out of his own pocket.[11]

In his daily life, the high priest also faced numerous restrictions not imposed on other priests. He could not enter a house in mourning nor exhibit any signs of mourning, such as disheveling his hair or tearing his clothes, even on the death of a parent. Temple officials went to great lengths to quarantine the high priest and keep him in strict isolation for seven days prior to Yom Kippur, so

---

8   Josephus, *Ant.* 20.251; Horsley, "High Priests," 30. Horsley correctly notes that Palestinian Judaism at this time made no distinction between religious and political aspects of life. Horsley, 33.

9   Jeremias, *Jerusalem in the Time of Jesus*, 96.

10   Evans, *Jesus and His Contemporaries*, 322.

11   Jeremias, *Jerusalem in the Time of Jesus*, 97–98.

that nothing unclean could touch him and render him unable to perform his sacred duties. Observing the rituals for sacrifice with exactitude was so important that high priests carried out their duties terrified of divine retribution should they make any mistakes. Even corrupt high priests were said to have had visions and other extraordinary experiences while in the Holy of Holies.[12]

The Corruption of the High Priesthood

BY THE TIME OF CHRIST, the high priesthood had become thoroughly corrupt, but the office was already being obtained by bribery in the second century BC.[13] After the Hasmonean Kingdom arose,[14] the Hasmonean family seized both the throne and the high priesthood for themselves, consolidating their power. Later Herod the Great and Roman governors regularly appointed and removed the high priest. One Roman governor appointed and deposed three high priests in a single year.[15] Because the high priesthood was powerful, the position became very political. Simony prevailed as aristocratic priestly families literally bid against each other for the position of high priest.[16]

According to the Torah, the high priest was to serve for life, but this had ceased to be the practice long before the first century. From Herod the Great's reign until the destruction of the Temple (37 BC–AD 70, a period of 106 years), twenty-eight different men served as high priest, almost every one of whom belonged to one of four powerful families. None were legitimate descendants of the correct high-priestly family of Zadok.[17] These four families also inter-

---

12 Jeremias, 149–53.

13 2 Macc. 4:7–8 mentions that Jason acquired the high priesthood by bribing the Seleucid king Antiochus IV while the Jews were under Greek rule.

14 The Jews won independence from the Seleucid dynasty when the Hasmonean family led a successful revolt called the Maccabean War, 167–160 BC. "Maccabee" was a nickname. They were conquered by the Romans in 63 BC.

15 Valerius Gratus, governor from AD 15 to 26, the immediate predecessor of Pilate. Gratus became known for frequently changing the high priest. Josephus, *Ant.* 18.2.2.

16 Simony is the sale or purchase of a religious position or sacrament.

17 Horsley, "High Priests," 30; Jeremias, *Jerusalem in the Time of Jesus*, 194. Twenty-five of these high priests actually came from ordinary priestly families, not from high-priestly lineage. Compare this number (28 high priests in 106 years) to the period just before the reign of Herod the Great, when only *eight* men had served as high priest during 115 years

married, preserving and solidifying the power and wealth of the high priesthood and further enriching themselves, their relatives, and their friends.[18]

Ruling authority and political power were achieved by violence, intrigue, and control of the important positions for the administration of the Temple, not to mention the Temple funds, finances, and sacrificial offerings. The high priests and chief priests appropriated more from the Temple and the sacrificial offerings than was legally permitted. The chief priests stole the valuable hides of sacrificial animals that were supposed to be divided among the ordinary priests after they had served their rotation in the Temple. The high priests sent their servants to take by force the heave-offerings (tithes given in money or in produce) belonging to the ordinary priests, beating them with wooden staves. Deprived of their income, some ordinary priests starved to death.[19] The Jewish aristocracy increasingly resorted to "predatory behavior against their own people."[20] "Greed, nepotism, oppression and violence, according to these rabbinic traditions, characterized the leading aristocratic priestly families," and the family of Annas was "particularly criticized by the rabbis."[21]

A popular first-century Jewish writing known as the *Assumption of Moses* or the *Testament of Moses* levels a devastating critique of the priestly aristocracy during the first century, describing them as "treacherous men, self-pleasers, dissemblers in all their own affairs and lovers of banquets at every hour of the day, gluttons, gourmands . . . filled with lawlessness and iniquity." Their hypocrisy was noted sarcastically: "Though their hands and their minds touch unclean

---

of Hasmonean rule. Jeremias, *Jerusalem in the Time of Jesus*, 190. After they prevailed in the Maccabean War, the Hasmoneans, a family of ordinary priests, seized the monarchy and the high priesthood. They were neither legitimate high priests nor legitimate kings. However, the high priesthood was more stable and ethical than with Herodian kings and Roman governors, under whom the high priesthood became increasingly corrupt and politicized to an unimaginable degree.

18 Evans, *Jesus and His Contemporaries*, 323; Jeremias, *Jerusalem in the Time of Jesus*, 158–59.

19 Josephus, *Ant.* 20.181, 20.206–7. These actions by the high priests are corroborated by comments in the Babylonian Talmud *Pesahim* 57a. See also Horsley, "High Priests," 45–46; and Evans, "Jesus' Action," 259. The high priests were not supposed to share in the revenue allocated for ordinary priests. Jeremias, *Jerusalem in the Time of Jesus*, 97–98.

20 Horsley, "High Priests," 44.

21 Evans, *Jesus and His Contemporaries*, 335; Horsley, "High Priests," 24.

things, yet their mouth will speak great things and they will say furthermore: 'Do not touch me, lest you should pollute me in the place where I stand.'"[22]

The religious aristocracy maintained and supported the imperial system that served only Rome's interests and their own.[23] The arrangement benefited those already holding power, but corruption and injustice flourished. Ordinary Jews were well aware of this and bitterly resented the fact that high-priestly families cooperated with Rome to preserve power and wealth in the hands of a few. Decades of corruption created pent-up frustration that eventually exploded. When Jewish revolutionaries finally revolted against Rome, they also rebelled against the Jewish aristocracy, executing and imprisoning wealthy Jews, murdering one of the high priests, and burning Temple archives, which contained the records of debts owed to the Temple.[24]

High priests had maintained their grip on power by bribing Roman officials and retaliating with violence against any Jew who opposed them.[25] Annas and his family wielded this extraordinary power. Now Jesus was brought before Annas, the most formidable figure in first-century Judaism.

The Interrogation of Jesus by Annas

ANNAS AND CAIAPHAS MUST HAVE prearranged this private questioning of Jesus. Perhaps they strategized that if Annas were to engage in an informal conversation with Jesus prior to his appearance before the entire Sanhedrin, Jesus might make a mistake and say something incriminating that could be reported to the full council.

The high priest then questioned Jesus about his disciples and his teaching. Jesus answered him, "I have spoken openly to the world; I have always taught

---

22 *Assumption of Moses* 7, 24–28. This book and others such as the *Book of Jubilees* were popular in Second Temple Judaism but were never included in the Jewish canon of Scripture. However, they are historically useful for understanding ideas within Judaism at that time. The correct term for Jewish religious books that were not accepted into the Jewish canon of Scripture (the Old Testament) is "pseudepigrapha."

23 Horsley, "High Priests," 24.

24 Evans, *Jesus and His Contemporaries*, 324; Josephus, *JW* 2.426–27.

25 Evans, *Jesus and His Contemporaries*, 324, 332–33.

in synagogues and in the temple, where all the Jews come together; I have said nothing secretly." (John 18:19–20)

Jesus' reply is important. First, it shows us that he had no secret teachings, a claim later made by heretics such as gnostics, who wrote apocrypha (false books) claiming that these contained secret teachings of Jesus. Secondly, his remark shows that Jesus had a public ministry. His message was for everyone, and he often called upon people to really listen ("He who has ears to hear, let him hear!"). He invited everyone to believe, to pay attention, and to respond to what he said, not simply to hear his words. But as Jesus continued his response to Annas, he made yet another point. This one would be a legal point of order regarding the procedure: "I have said nothing secretly. Why do you ask me? Ask those who have heard me, what I said to them; they know what I said" (John 18:20–21).

This comment reveals that Jesus refused to respond to Annas's questions because the process was not fair. This private, preliminary questioning by Annas was a sham, and it violated established Jewish legal procedure. Jesus indicated that he would not respond to these questions because Jewish criminal procedure required that prior to any interrogation, witnesses must first be brought forward to testify to what a defendant had said or done. If two witnesses testified to the same facts, then a charge could be leveled against someone. It was unfair to question Jesus when no witnesses had been produced and he had not been charged with a crime. This interrogation by Annas was not a trial, and Jesus should not have been expected to respond to anything. The Lord knew they would convict him, but he would not make it easy. He would not participate in their charade.

"When he had said this, one of the officers standing by struck Jesus with his hand, saying, 'Is that how you answer the high priest?'" (John 18:22). This officer who struck the Lord was an ordinary Temple guard, one among those who had arrested Jesus. The Temple had its own large security organization. Temple guards were needed to control the huge crowds that assembled for feasts and to provide security for the chief priests, the high priest, and other dignitaries. They were also essential to guard the tremendous wealth in the Temple treasury in the form of coinage as well as the solid gold embellishments and sacred utensils used for worship services and ceremonies.

High priests adjudicated cases and meted out punishments for those convicted of crimes. Those who disobeyed the high priest were considered worthy of punishment as though they had insulted God himself.[26] But this anonymous officer who struck Jesus may not have reacted as he did merely because Jesus seemed disrespectful. This officer was employed by the Temple establishment. This particular guard may have been genuinely indignant, or perhaps he wished to demonstrate loyalty or devotion to his superior, the captain of the Temple.

The Temple guards served under the captain of the Temple, the second-highest-ranking priest in the entire Temple institution, subordinate only to the high priest himself. He had the power to make arrests and enact punishments. However, the captain of the Temple was not only a law enforcement position but one that wielded tremendous priestly authority. He was responsible for overseeing the thousands of priests who came to serve in the Temple. He was literally the right-hand man of the high priest, standing to his right at all important Temple rituals and ceremonies. As the second-ranking priest in the Temple, the captain of the Temple usually succeeded the high priest; therefore, whoever held that position would have been a close relative, usually a son.[27]

The Lord's response—"Why do you ask me? Ask those who have heard me"—was an objection to the unfair procedure. Jesus stood before Annas bound as a prisoner, surrounded by guards. He was not brought there for a friendly conversation but for a trial. If they wished to accuse him of a crime, what were the charges? Where were the witnesses? His response to Annas was fair and not at all disrespectful or deserving of a hard slap. It was Jesus who should have been indignant. But we marvel at the Lord's restrained and mild response to the guard who struck him: "'If I have spoken wrongly, bear witness to the wrong; but if I have spoken rightly, why do you strike me?' Annas then sent him bound to Caiaphas the high priest" (John 18:23–24).

---

26 Josephus, *Against Apion*, 2.194.
27 Jeremias, *Jerusalem in the Time of Jesus*, 160–63.

Annas never elicited an incriminating statement from Jesus. Acquiring evidence sufficient to justify a death sentence would take some time. Witnesses would have to be summoned, and Jesus would be put on trial before Caiaphas and the Great Sanhedrin.

CHAPTER 16

The Jewish Trial

I T WAS THE DAY OF Preparation. In less than twenty-four hours, Passover would begin. But the members of the council were summoned to an urgent meeting at the house of Caiaphas in the middle of the night. They usually gathered on the Temple Mount in the Chamber of Hewn Stone. Perhaps the choice of venue was made for their comfort on a cold night. Perhaps it was more convenient, as Caiaphas's house was located in the Upper City, the wealthiest neighborhood in Jerusalem, where most members also would have resided. But it is equally likely the council members were called to the house of Caiaphas because the entire operation must be carried out in secrecy, lest the crowds—who regarded Jesus as at least a prophet, if not the Messiah—discover that he had been arrested by their own religious leaders.

The city was packed with pilgrims who were full of religious zeal and enthusiastic for freedom from the Romans as they celebrated their deliverance from slavery in Egypt long ago. The religious remembrance and fervent hopes of the crowd, coupled with the charismatic presence of Jesus of Nazareth, could not be allowed to spark a revolt, whether intentionally or accidentally. Jesus must be put to death before the beginning of Passover. This was the Sanhedrin's only chance to accomplish that goal.

The Trial of Jesus Violated Jewish Law

"THEN THOSE WHO HAD SEIZED Jesus led him to Caiaphas the high priest, where the scribes and the elders had gathered" (Matt. 26:57). Both the time and the place of this trial violated Jewish law. According to the Mishnah, the Jewish legal code,[1] a Jewish criminal court could convene only during the day and was required to adjourn at sunset.[2] Basic standards of fairness require that civilized societies hold public trials during the day for the impartial administration of justice, rather than secret trials at night. Jewish law specifically forbade trials at night, making the trial of Christ clearly illegal. However, the Gospels also mention a morning meeting of the council involving the same people in a proceeding that seems to echo the condemnation of the previous night.[3] This strongly suggests that, at least in the eyes of the Sanhedrin, the proceedings during the night were not a formal trial but a preliminary procedure. The morning trial was quick and perfunctory, merely an official confirmation of Jesus' condemnation the previous night.

But even if the morning meeting was the official Jewish trial, that trial would also have violated Jewish law for two reasons. First, criminal trials were not permitted on the eve of the Sabbath or the eve of a holiday. This Friday morning trial officially condemning Jesus was doubly illegal since that day was both the eve of the Sabbath and the eve of Passover.[4] Secondly, the condemnation of Christ violated another provision designed to promote justice, or at least to prevent a rush to judgment: a guilty verdict could not be pronounced the same day as the trial. Under Jewish law, judges were required to

---

1   The trial procedures were written down after AD 200. Some rules may not reflect actual practices during the first century, but scholars believe that they generally do.

2   *Sanh.* 4.1.

3   "When morning came, all the chief priests and the elders of the people took counsel against Jesus to put him to death" (Matt. 27:1). See also Mark 15:1, which mentions an extremely brief morning trial. Luke describes only the morning trial during which Jesus was officially condemned (Luke 22:66).

4   Whether the official trial of Jesus was held late Thursday night or after midnight early Friday morning, for the Jews it was already Friday in either case, since the Jewish day began at sunset rather than at midnight.

consider a guilty verdict overnight. They could issue an immediate decision only if the decision was an acquittal.[5]

Therefore, whether the trial we are about to discuss was the official trial or some sort of preliminary procedure, the proceeding violated basic Jewish law. This was irrelevant to the religious authorities, who were determined to eliminate Jesus before the Passover. He was alone, in their custody, and they would do as they pleased. And so the trial began.

The Judicial Role of the Great Sanhedrin

"NOW THE CHIEF PRIESTS AND the whole council sought false testimony against Jesus that they might put him to death" (Matt. 26:59). The Great Sanhedrin, the preeminent ruling body of the Jews, was a council of seventy prominent and influential men responsible for the political and religious life of the nation. The Gospels say that Jesus appeared before "the whole council," which is presumed to be the Great Sanhedrin for two reasons. First, the person presiding over the trial was the high priest, Caiaphas, and secondly, the Great Sanhedrin had exclusive jurisdiction over anyone accused of being a false prophet. It was also the only court under Jewish law that could try a king or a high priest. Undoubtedly, Jesus was being tried as a false prophet, but ironically the person who stood before them was the King of the angels and the Great High Priest of heaven.

The Need for Witnesses

"THE WHOLE COUNCIL WAS SEEKING false testimony against Jesus." Use of the continuous past tense ("they were seeking" instead of "they sought") suggests that the search for witnesses to convict Jesus took some time, perhaps much of the night. Matthew emphasizes the untruthfulness of the witnesses and the council's disregard for truth or justice. The outcome was predetermined. Truthful witnesses would have been welcomed, but even false testimony would be received.

---

5   *Sanh.* 32a.

"But they found none, though many false witnesses came forward. At last two came forward" (Matt. 26:60). At first glance, this verse seems strange. In the search for witnesses, how can there be "none" when "many" came forward? Then Matthew writes that "at last two came forward." The requirement that a conviction be based on the testimony of at least two witnesses was sacrosanct under Jewish law. The testimony could be accepted only if at least two witnesses agreed on all details. This requirement hindered false convictions.

"Many" came forward, Matthew reports, indicating that countless witnesses offered testimony. But their testimony conflicted and could not be accepted. We can only imagine the frustration of the religious authorities, who heard witness after witness, all contradicting one another. The trial was going nowhere. Convicting Jesus was surprisingly more difficult than the Jewish leaders had anticipated.

"At last," Matthew's Gospel states, "two came forward," indicating that the testimony of two witnesses agreed. After a long, tiresome night of hearing useless testimonies, it is entirely possible that these final two witnesses had been coached and had rehearsed their stories.

"At last two came forward and said, 'This fellow said, "I am able to destroy the temple of God, and to build it in three days"'" (Matt. 26:60–61). This statement sounds familiar and may seem correct, but Jesus did not say this, and it is not found in any Gospel. He said something similar that was misunderstood by the Jewish authorities and had an entirely different meaning.

After Jesus cleansed the Temple, driving out the merchants and money changers, the Jewish leaders confronted him and asked, "What sign have you to show us for doing this?" Jesus replied, "Destroy this temple, and in three days I will raise it up again" (John 2:18–19). When they questioned his authority, he implied that it would be proven by his Resurrection. He knew that they would kill him, thus destroying his physical body, which he referred to as "this temple." But they considered his actions to be a warning about the Temple building and interpreted his statement as a threat to destroy it.

But the authorities did not take Jesus' words seriously even in their misunderstanding at the time. They replied, "It has taken forty-six years to build this temple, and will you raise it up in three days?" (John 2:20). No one could rebuild the Temple in three days. But even if it appeared impossible and was not understood literally, now at the trial the false statement was alarming. The witness testimony was inaccurate, but the trial could now commence, and Jesus' alleged statement about the Temple prompted a specific question by the high priest, Caiaphas.

Caiaphas

"AND THE HIGH PRIEST STOOD up"(Matt. 26:62; Mark 14:60). Roman governors appointed the high priest every year, ensuring his cooperation with Rome. Choosing the high priest also created an opportunity for financial gain for the governor, who could look forward to an annual bribe.

The Romans knew that the Temple rituals were essential to the Jews. For that reason, the Romans controlled the high priest by keeping his vestments in their custody in the Antonia Fortress, the Roman garrison that overlooked the Court of the Gentiles. This, perhaps more than anything else, was the worst offense of Roman occupation. Certain ritual sacrifices could be performed only by the high priest. His sacred vestments being handled and kept in the custody of the immoral, swine-eating, idol-worshipping pagans was shameful and repulsive beyond imagination. The Jews were forced to accept this bitter reality.[6]

Caiaphas was high priest when Pilate arrived, and he remained in office through Pilate's tenure and beyond. He held the office of high priest for eighteen years, while Pontius Pilate was governor of Judea for only twelve years. The remarkable length of Caiaphas's tenure reveals his tremendous wealth, political power, and shrewdness. He must have cooperated well with the Romans and must have paid a sizable sum to Pilate and other governors to secure his position. No doubt his family connections also played a role.

---

6   Josephus, *Ant.* 20.1.1. The Jews were forced to request the vestments from the Romans in advance of any feasts so the vestments could be ritually cleansed after being defiled by idolators. This practice began in AD 6 and persisted until the Roman governor Vitellius returned the vestments to Jewish custody in 37. When a subsequent procurator, Cuspius Fadus, attempted to confiscate them again in AD 44, a Jewish delegation traveled to Rome and appealed to Emperor Claudius to end this offensive practice. Claudius issued an order allowing the vestments to remain under Jewish control.

Jewish high priests were not chosen by Roman governors because they had the requisite family lineage, nor because they were pious and devout. They attained this position through wealth, influence, political savvy, ruthlessness, and brutality. Jesus was nothing to Caiaphas except an annoying pest to be exterminated. But Jesus was different from those who had threatened their religious authority before. He was immensely charismatic and had the ability to perform amazing signs. The crowds hailed him as the Messiah, yet he never sought political power nor advocated revolution. Finding grounds to hand him over to face Roman justice would be a challenge.

Questioning Begins, and Jesus Is Silent

"AND THE HIGH PRIEST STOOD up and said, 'Have you no answer to make? What is it that these men testify against you?'" (Matt. 26:62). Caiaphas's initial statement shows that the witnesses' testimony formed the basis for the charge. The assertion that Jesus would destroy and rebuild the Temple in three days was serious but not sufficient to call for his death. Caiaphas sought some pronouncement from Jesus that would unambiguously justify the death penalty. At this point, Jesus could have extricated himself from the situation. He could have corrected the inaccurate statement the witnesses alleged or explained that he was referring to their destruction of his own body, not making a threat against the Temple. But he did not.

"But Jesus was silent" (Matt 26:63). Jesus was not intimidated by the high priest nor by the members of the Great Sanhedrin. He knew they were determined to put him to death, so he made no defense nor attempted to save himself. Later the Church would understand his silence as fulfillment of the prophecy made by Isaiah: he was "like a lamb that is led to the slaughter, and like a sheep that before its shearers is dumb, so he opened not his mouth" (Is. 53:7). He was obedient to the will of God and answerable only to his Father. Far from being a victim, Jesus placed himself above the proceedings and showed that he was in control of his own destiny. He saw no point in defending himself to people who were not interested in hearing the truth. This is brought out most clearly in the trial account in Luke's Gospel, when Jesus replies to the question of whether he is the Christ by responding, "If I tell you, you won't believe me" (Luke 22:67).

The crowd that hailed him when he entered Jerusalem believed Jesus to be the Messiah. But did Jesus believe that himself? He never said so explicitly or publicly, but the high priest was determined to find out.

The Link between the Temple and Messianic Expectations

AFTER THE WITNESSES CLAIMED THAT Jesus had threatened to destroy the Temple, Caiaphas immediately asked him to respond. Caiaphas suspected that Jesus was claiming to be the Messiah. The Sanhedrin believed he was fomenting revolt against Rome because of Jewish messianic expectations at that time. A prophecy in Zechariah foretold that the Messiah would build a new Temple:[7] "Thus says the LORD of Hosts, 'Behold, the man whose name is the Branch; for he shall grow up in his place, and he shall build the temple of the LORD" (Zech. 6:12).

"Branch" was a title for the Messiah not only in Zechariah but in other prophets, such as Isaiah and Jeremiah. The Branch will come from the root of Jesse, David's father. "There shall come forth a shoot from the stump of Jesse, / and a branch shall grow out of his roots" (Is. 11:1). "Behold, the days are coming, says the LORD, when I will raise up for David a righteous Branch, and he shall reign as a king and deal wisely, and shall execute justice and righteousness in the land" (Jer. 23:5).

Jesus had predicted the future destruction of the Temple at Jerusalem by the Romans, but he never threatened to destroy it himself. Ironically, it was the actions and attitudes of the religious leaders, so intent on preserving their own wealth and power, that would ultimately lead to the destruction of the Temple. The immense greed and corruption of the Temple authorities, their callous disregard for the average Jew struggling under poverty, would spark a revolt by the desperate populace, not only against Rome but against their own priestly leaders.

---

7   See also Jer. 33:15 (missing from LXX) and Zech. 3:8.

But that was yet to come. At this moment, the Jewish leaders understood neither Jesus' words nor his intentions, but many factors convinced them he was a threat to their survival: (1) his act of cleansing the Temple, (2) the inaccurate accusation that he had threatened to destroy the Temple, (3) his entry into Jerusalem on a donkey,[8] (4) the crowd welcoming him by shouting the messianic titles "Son of David" and "King of Israel," and (5) the fact that the people overwhelmingly considered Jesus to be the Messiah, or at least a prophet, because of his astonishing powers.

The Jewish authorities did not believe that Jesus was the Messiah, but a promise to destroy and rebuild the Temple was associated in the Jewish mind with the coming of a Messiah-King, a descendant of David who would reign as wise, just, and righteous. Was Jesus claiming that role? Caiaphas demanded an answer.

Caiaphas Compels Jesus to Speak

"AND THE HIGH PRIEST STOOD up and said, 'Have you no answer to make? What is it that these men testify against you?' But Jesus was silent." Jesus' silence frustrated Caiaphas, who was determined that Jesus would answer him whether he was willing to or not. He would force Jesus to respond to the ultimate question about his identity: Was Jesus claiming to be the Messiah, and even greater than the Messiah? To compel him to answer, Caiaphas placed Jesus under oath, using a specific formula: "I adjure you by the living God, tell us if you are the Christ, the Son of God" (Matt. 26:63).

The Greek word translated as "I adjure you" is *exorkizō*, which is even stronger than the ordinary word for swearing an oath, *orkizō*. This particular word, *exorkizō*, was a legal formula that placed someone under an oath and forced a response.[9] When a question was preceded by that formulaic statement, "I adjure you by the living God," a defendant was compelled to respond. He had no right to remain silent and no right to avoid self-incrimination. This technique was considered a guarantee of truthful testimony because the Jews

---

8   An obvious fulfillment of another prophecy, Zech. 9:9.

9   The formula is also found in the Mishnah, as well as in the Old Testament (Gen. 24:3; 1 Kin. 22:16).

believed that a defendant questioned in the name of God would fear divine retribution and would not lie. If the defendant remained silent and did not respond, his silence would be considered an admission of the accusation against him, and he would be condemned on the basis of his silence.

The Christ

"TELL US IF YOU ARE the Christ, the Son of God." Jesus had once asked his disciples, "Who do you say that I am?" Peter replied, "You are the Christ, the Son of the Living God" (Matt. 16:15–16). Peter was praised for having recognized and expressed the true identity of Jesus. Now, at Jesus' trial, ironically, the high priest's question exactly echoes Peter's confession of faith, the deepest mystery and most exalted confession of the Church: Jesus is the Messiah and the Son of God. Jesus will be rejected by the Jewish leaders, finally and completely, for precisely who he truly is, not on the basis of a misunderstanding on their part or a failure to fully reveal the truth about himself.

Let us consider first the title *Messiah* (*Christos* in Greek). Jesus had consistently avoided using the term because a variety of messianic prophecies had created diverse expectations among the Jews for what the Messiah would be: priest, prophet, righteous judge, glorious king, suffering servant. Occasionally people claim that Jesus was simply one of many messianic pretenders who arose during this period and who were arrested by the Romans and suffered the same fate. This turbulent period of history indeed spawned many failed political revolutionaries who stoked public hostility toward Rome and the Jewish aristocracy. But those seeking political power or societal change need not claim to be the Messiah, and most of them did not.

The Jewish historian Josephus lists different types of activists, including "prophets, would-be kings, priests, agitators," but he never calls any of them "Christos" (Messiah), which means they did not claim that title. Revolutionaries are often lumped together by scholars today as messianic pretenders. But while the Second Temple stood, Jesus was the only person whom thousands considered to be the Messiah. The Jews knew the messianic prophecies well. To be recognized as Messiah was extremely difficult, since one must fulfill those prophecies, including healing the blind, deaf, and lame. It is highly significant that no one in this period of history other than Jesus claimed to be the Messiah. In the centuries before Jesus, "there seems to be no identifiable Jew hailed as the kingly Messiah other than Jesus of Nazareth."[10] Jesus was unique in that he never grasped for power or political authority either as a high priest or as a king, and yet he alone was regarded as the Messiah by a significant number of people.

The Son of God

CONCERNED THAT MESSIANIC FERVOR WOULD lead to civil unrest, the Jewish authorities sought to eliminate the threat they believed Jesus posed. But he was not condemned to death for claiming to be the Messiah. That was neither a crime nor blasphemy. But claiming to be the Son of God was. The term "son of God" was used occasionally for human beings, as Jesus himself had previously pointed out to his critics,[11] and was equivalent to calling someone a "child of God." We express the same idea today, that God is the Father of us all in an adoptive sense.

But Jesus was not claiming to be *a* son of God. He claimed to be *the* Son of God in a unique sense, in a truly divine sense, and that is why he was condemned to death. "Messiah" and "Son of God" were not synonymous. "Son of God" was not a messianic title, and the Jews had generally not anticipated that the Messiah would be God himself. Some prophecies, however, did allude to this,[12] and recent discoveries suggest that at least some first-century Jews may have expected a divine Messiah.[13] This does not mean that the Church

---

10 Brown, *Death of the Messiah*, 1:475.

11 John 10:34. The expression is found in the Old Testament, "You are all sons of the Most High" (Ps. 82:6).

12 He will be called "Emmanuel" (Is. 7:14) and "They shall all be taught by God" (Is. 54:13; John 6:45), as well as other prophecies that speak of the perfect righteousness and holiness of the Messiah.

13 A fragment was discovered among the Dead Sea Scrolls that refers to the Messiah as "Son of God." This caused a great stir in the scholarly world and provoked a great deal of debate. Some scholars claimed that it was a sarcastic reference to an enemy of Israel, but that view has been rejected because that does not fit the context. The language in this particular document also strongly echoes statements in Luke's Gospel that refer to the Messiah as Son of God. Fitzmyer, "4Q246."

invented doctrines about Jesus because certain messianic expectations already existed in first-century Judaism, but the reverse: God had planted these seeds among his people through the Scriptures so the Jews would be prepared for the Messiah Jesus when he arrived and would recognize him.[14]

"'Tell us if you are the Christ, the Son of God.' Jesus said to him, 'You have said so'" (Matt. 26:63–64). Jesus decided to respond. Silence would be considered an admission. He would have been condemned for not denying it, so he might as well speak. Now he openly acknowledged his identity and further clarified it.

Initially, Jesus responded by saying, "You have said so." This strikes the modern reader as evasive. Modern commentators have interpreted this statement in three ways—as affirmative, negative, or neutral—an ambiguous response. But it is not ambiguous in the least, and Jesus was being neither evasive nor obscure. "You have said so" is clearly an *affirmative* answer and seems to have been a characteristic expression of Jesus'.

Earlier that evening, Jesus had announced to his disciples that one of them would betray him. One by one, the startled disciples asked, "Is it me, Lord?" When Judas Iscariot asked, "Is it I, Master?" Jesus answered with the same words: "You have said so" (Matt. 26:25). It was obviously an affirmative answer, since Judas was indeed the betrayer.

Later Jesus replied in a very similar manner to Pilate when he asked, "Are you the King of the Jews?" Jesus answered, "You say so" (Matt. 27:11; John 18:37). "You say so" or "You have said so" may have been a characteristic way for Jesus to indicate "yes." But it was far more powerful than a simple "yes," because whether it was Judas, Caiaphas, or Pilate speaking, the truth had come from the speaker's own mouth, whether he wished to acknowledge it or not. These three men are most responsible for the death of Jesus, but none can claim ignorance about who Jesus was or what they were doing because they themselves testified to the truth. They said so. They incriminated themselves.

---

14 The Jewish Scriptures contain many prophecies about a divine Messiah, but they were not understood as such by all Jews. This is why Christ raised the question about who the Messiah truly was when he challenged the Pharisees about the psalm that begins, "The Lord said to my Lord." See chapter 9.

Now Caiaphas demanded that Jesus respond: "I adjure you: Tell us if you are the Messiah, the Son of God." Jesus responded, "You have said so," affirming that Caiaphas himself had explicitly stated his true identity, even though that was clearly not the high priest's intention.

Jesus now openly declared his divine identity to the Sanhedrin. Previously he had only hinted at his divinity by claiming authority to forgive sins and to change the Law of Moses, by calling himself "the Son," and so forth. Saint John Chrysostom wondered why Christ bothered to answer his accusers at all. They already knew who he believed himself to be. Through countless interactions with Jesus, the Jewish leaders constantly challenged him and attempted to trap him. Why respond to them now? Chrysostom concluded that it was "to take away all their excuse, because unto the last day he taught that he was Christ."[15] But Jesus was not finished. He would make one more statement, a clear and undeniable declaration of his divinity: "You have said so. But I tell you, hereafter you will see the Son of man seated at the right hand of Power, and coming on the clouds of heaven" (Matt. 26:64).

The additional statement after "you have said so" is absolute confirmation that Jesus affirmed himself as truly the Son of God. He knew that after this key statement he would be condemned to death, and he was right. Immediately the high priest tore his robes, and the whole assembly pronounced Jesus guilty of blasphemy. Let's analyze his statement and why it was considered a claim of divinity.

The expression "Son of Man" had different meanings. First, it was a known substitution for the pronoun "I," a way to refer to oneself in the third person. Jesus often referred to himself as "the Son of Man," usually when he foretold his future suffering or when claiming divine authority to forgive sins, judge humanity, and so forth.

"Son of Man" is not the opposite of "Son of God." It is not a reference to his humanity. In fact, "Son of Man" also hinted at Jesus' divinity. The title appears in the Book of Daniel, which undoubtedly was the inspiration for Jesus' use of the term during his ministry and here at his trial. The prophet Daniel

---

15   Chrysostom, Homily 84, *Homilies on Matthew*, NPNF-1, 10:485.

described a vision in which he saw the Ancient of Days (God the Father) give all glory and dominion to "one like the son of man":

> I saw in the night visions, and behold, with the clouds of heaven there came one like a son of man and he came to the Ancient of Days and was presented before him. And to him was given dominion and glory and kingdom, that all peoples, nations, and languages should serve him; his dominion is an everlasting dominion, which shall not pass away, and his kingdom one that shall not be destroyed. (Dan. 7:13)

By describing himself as "Son of Man," Jesus identified himself as the person whom Daniel had seen in his vision, the one co-ruling with God, whom Jesus referred to here at his trial as "the Power."[16] All these expressions meant the same thing: Jesus was claiming that he would be seated at the right hand of God. This expression, also found in Psalm 110:1, is a powerful biblical image that indicates co-rule, equal authority, and equal divinity. This is why we use the expression in the Creed, "and he ascended into heaven and is seated at the right hand of the Father." No mere human being co-rules with God. No one reigns with God unless he himself *is* God. Jesus was telling them that he was the "Son of Man" whom Daniel had seen in his vision.

Reference to "the clouds" was not poetic embellishment. The Jews associated clouds with divine revelations, appearances, and theophanies.[17] All these details reinforced Jesus' acknowledgment that he was the Son of God. The Sanhedrin would see "the Son of Man," Jesus of Nazareth, "sitting at the right hand of Power, and coming on the clouds of heaven." Jesus was the one who would receive from God dominion, glory, and an everlasting Kingdom. All people on earth would serve him, and his Kingdom would never end.

---

16   The Jews refer to God indirectly, using various substitutes such as "the Power," "the Almighty," "Heaven," or the "Mighty One."

17   At the Transfiguration, the voice of God came from the cloud (Matt. 17:5). God accompanied the Israelites in the form of a cloud in the wilderness (Ex. 13:21). God "makes the clouds [his] chariot" (Ps. 104:3). At his ascension, Jesus disappeared into the clouds (Acts 1:9), and St. Paul also describes his return with clouds (1 Thess. 4:17).

Some people say that Jesus never claimed to be God. Nothing could be further from the truth. He implied it in countless ways during his ministry, and here at his trial he openly stated it. His claim of divinity is exactly the reason he was condemned to death. The Jewish leaders admitted this to Pilate: "We have a law, and by that law he ought to die, because he has made himself the Son of God" (John 19:7). It was not a crime under Jewish law to claim to be the Messiah. Jesus was not condemned for being the Messiah, but for acknowledging his identity as the Son of God, a title that has never been applied to anyone else.

The Jewish leaders may have been extremely angered or disturbed by his statement, but they were also relieved: they finally had the incriminating statement they had hoped he would provide. Now at last he could be put to death.

Jesus made a surprisingly candid statement. Caiaphas's response was predictable: "Blasphemy!" He tore his garments in the traditional Jewish ritual expression of grief and anguish. The high priest was forbidden to tear his robes, even upon the death of his own parents, and if they tore, his garments were never to be mended. Caiaphas tore his robes, even though that was forbidden, to accentuate the seriousness of Jesus' statement. God had been egregiously offended, and Caiaphas intended to underscore the blasphemy in the most dramatic fashion. Chrysostom recognized the symbolism of the act: "The High Priest rending his clothes was done to add force to the accusation, to aggravate what the Lord had said by the act, for what Jesus had said moved the hearers to fear."[18]

"Then the High Priest tore his robes, and said, 'He has uttered blasphemy. Why do we still need witnesses? You have now heard his blasphemy.'" Blasphemy was the most serious crime and required the death penalty. In earlier times, a person was accused of blasphemy only when he pronounced the sacred four-letter name of God (YHWH). Jesus did not pronounce the name of God here but used a typical reverential substitute, "the Power." Laws developed later to allow someone to be charged with blasphemy for other statements or actions considered offensive to the power or majesty of God, whether directly or indirectly. The Pharisees had often accused Jesus of blasphemy for merely

---

18   Chrysostom, Homily 84, *Homilies on Matthew*, NPNF-1, 10:485.

saying that someone's sins were forgiven, since this seemed to encroach on the exclusive prerogatives of God. A claim of actual divinity would certainly qualify as blasphemy and warrant the death penalty. "Caiaphas asked, 'What is your judgment?' They answered, 'He deserves death'" (Matt. 26:65–66).

Saint John Chrysostom astutely observed that the behavior of the high priest encouraged the desired response from the Sanhedrin. He tore his robes, announced that Jesus had committed blasphemy, and even pronounced the sentence against Christ before asking members of the council for their opinion,[19] although it is hard to imagine that they would have reached a different conclusion.

Once he was found guilty, the physical abuse of Christ began. After the many unsuccessful efforts to trap him, stone him, arrest him—at last, he was formally proclaimed guilty of blasphemy and deserved the worst treatment. The hatred, jealousy, fury, and frustration that had steadily accumulated within the authorities was unleashed against Jesus and found its mark. No one could stop them now—there were no strong young disciples to protect him, no adoring, misguided crowds for the chief priests to fear. He stood before them alone, and the leaders of Israel—elders, chief priests, Pharisees, Sadducees, and scribes—could not moderate their contempt or restrain their rage. "Then they spat in his face, and struck him; and some slapped him, saying, 'Prophesy to us, you Christ! Who is it that struck you?'" (Matt. 26:67–68).

The Evangelist Luke concurs: "Now the men who were holding Jesus mocked him and beat him; they also blindfolded him and asked him, 'Prophesy! Who is it that struck you?' And they spoke many other words against him, reviling him" (Luke 22:63–65).

The Prophet Isaiah foretold this abuse: "I gave my back to the smiters, and my cheeks to those who pulled out the beard; I hid not my face from shame and spitting" (Is. 50:6).

We cannot say exactly what the Jewish authorities or Temple guards did to the Lord by that night, but he certainly received a beating. Not only would they have considered a beating appropriate, but he would have received a very severe lashing at their hands, but they intended to take him to Pilate in the

---

19   Chrysostom, Homily 84, *Homilies on Matthew*, NPNF-1, 10:485.

morning. Saint Cyril of Alexandria eloquently expressed the extraordinary contrast between the demeanor of the Lord and the actions of his creatures:

> The Lord of earth and heaven, the Creator and Artificer of all, the King of Kings and Lord of Lords, he who is of such surpassing greatness in glory and majesty, the foundation of everything and that in which all things exist and abide . . . is scorned like one of us, and patiently endures the buffetings and submits to the ridicule of the wicked, offering himself to us as a perfect pattern of longsuffering, or rather manifesting the incomparable greatness of his godlike gentleness. Or perhaps he endures this to rebuke the infirmity of our minds, to show that the things of men fall as far below the divine excellencies as our nature is inferior to his. For we who are of earth, mere corruption and ashes, attack at once those who would mistreat us . . . but He, who in nature and glory transcends the limits of our understanding and powers of speech, patiently endured those officers when they not merely mocked but even smote him.[20]

The outcome of the trial is not surprising. The Sanhedrin had resolved to kill Jesus even before the trial began. Almost any Jew would consider it his duty to put Jesus to death after hearing his shocking statement claiming divinity. But the irony of the Jewish trial is that Jesus is condemned to death precisely for who he truly is: the Messiah and Son of God.

The council was outraged by his statements yet pleased that they had elicited the confession that irrefutably justified his execution. But they were not quite finished. They had no legal authority to put him to death. Although they could have secretly executed him, the people still regarded Jesus as a prophet. They would be angry if their leaders put him to death. Furthermore, a quiet, secret murder was too good for Jesus. His blasphemous claims and his perverse teachings must be completely discredited. Jesus must be crucified. Everyone must see him on the cross. Everyone must know that he was not the Son of God but in fact was cursed by God. Such was their reasoning.

But accomplishing this would require the cooperation of the Romans.

---

20   Cyril of Alexandria, Homily 150, *Commentary on Luke*, 594.

CHAPTER 17

The Roman Trial

Jesus Appears before Pilate

T HEN THEY LED JESUS FROM the house of Caiaphas to the praetorium"
(John 18:28). The praetorium was located in the Antonia Fortress, the
Roman garrison constructed by Herod the Great, who had built and dedicated it to Mark Antony when he supported Antony's alliance with Cleopatra.
It included the Roman governor's residence and public spaces for conducting
official business. The Antonia stood in a strategic location: on the northwest
corner of the Temple Mount overlooking the Court of the Gentiles. Roman
soldiers kept constant watch over the large open courtyard, scanning the
crowd for any signs of riot or rebellion.

Normally the governor resided at the provincial capital, Caesarea Maritima, the magnificent Roman seaport built by Herod the Great in honor of
Augustus Caesar. Many scholars believe that when in Jerusalem, Pilate may
have resided at Herod the Great's former palace in the posh district of the
Upper City. But this is unlikely, since Pilate was in Jerusalem for Passover for
one purpose: to observe and control the crowd on the Temple Mount. From
Herod's former palace he would not have been able to respond immediately to
any unrest at the Temple by commanding the troops garrisoned at the Antonia. Furthermore, the Antonia provided more security, and Pilate's protection
was always a concern, particularly at Passover.

The Administration of Criminal Justice in the Roman Provinces[1]

THE ROMANS MANAGED THEIR VAST empire by embracing many different forms of government in a variety of jurisdictions: provinces, colonies, independent cities, and kingdoms, all under the umbrella of Rome. Each jurisdiction encompassed people of varying legal statuses: slaves, former slaves, Roman subjects, Roman citizens, citizens of cities, citizens of colonies. Justice was administered according to one's wealth, social status, legal status, and domicile. Independent cities, Roman colonies, and allied kingdoms enjoyed almost unfettered self-administration, including their own completely independent courts and assemblies. The Jews also had their own laws and independent courts where Jews pursued justice and settled disputes. In fact, the Sanhedrin was performing precisely that function and was within its legal rights to put Jesus, a fellow Jew, on trial.[2]

The Powers of the Provincial Governor

THE PROVINCIAL GOVERNOR WAS RESPONSIBLE for the administration of justice in his area. The Latin word *provincia* literally means "the sphere of action of a magistrate." Roman provinces were subjected to the sweeping authority of a single magistrate, the governor, whose responsibilities

---

1   Drawing conclusions about the Roman administration of criminal justice in Judea
     is difficult for a number of reasons. Little information exists about routine criminal
     justice in the provinces versus the City of Rome itself. Secondly, Roman law and legal
     procedures were constantly developing. Sources of information for Roman criminal law
     and procedure might come from speeches of Cicero during the late republican period or
     from jurists writing during the imperial period of the second and third centuries, such
     as Ulpian, Paulus, and Gaius. Even the later legal digests, the Codes of Justinian and
     Theodosius, include laws and interpretations that developed over many centuries. I use
     republican-era sources that reflect attitudes and practices that continued into the impe-
     rial period, and the later digests if the laws and procedures presented are corroborated
     by first-century sources.
2   When the Great Sanhedrin functioned as a court, it was the highest court among the
     Jews. But there were also "lesser" Sanhedrins of twenty-three members and smaller local
     tribunals consisting of three judges in towns and villages. Jewish courts served Jewish
     inhabitants and applied Jewish law. Goodman, *The Ruling Class of Judea*, 70–71; Schürer,
     The History of the Jewish People in the Age of Jesus Christ, 2:184–90, 220–21.

encompassed a wide range of military, administrative, and judicial duties. The Romans established the first province during the Roman Republic, and provincial governors were responsible for maintaining law and order. They administered justice, including the death penalty, for provincial inhabitants.[3]

A governor would arrive in the province as the emperor's representative, bearing the authority of the emperor himself. This authority, called the *imperium*, can be described as the supreme administrative power within a specific area. The governor could exercise the imperium only within his own province during his tenure, usually two years. As soon as his successor reached the province, the former governor's powers were at an end. A governor's powers were extensive but not unlimited. If he abused his position, he could be removed and might even face criminal prosecution. Nonetheless, corruption, extortion, and abuse of power by provincial governors was a continuous problem.

A governor heard both criminal cases and ordinary civil cases. Many actions that are criminal offenses in our society—such as theft—under Roman law would be considered a private matter between two parties.[4] The administration of justice demanded a great deal of a governor's time and attention; governors frequently traveled around the province hearing cases.[5]

The Roman governor's authority included the *ius gladii*, "the right of the sword," the authority to execute anyone in his province. This power of life and

---

3 Lémnon, *Pilate et le Gouvernement de la Judée*, 76.

4 Roman administration of criminal justice in the first century also heavily involved the administration of the *ius civile*, civil law. At this time, Roman criminal law was extremely narrow. Many offenses against persons and property, including most thefts, embezzlement, property damage, and even assault, were not considered crimes but *delicts* (a violation of private law), corresponding more closely to what we would call a "tort," a civil action that does not arise out of a breach of contract. Nippel, *Public Order in Ancient Rome*, 2; Strachan-Davidson, *Problems of the Roman Criminal Law*, 39–41.

5 These were called "assize tours." Since large provinces had many cases, the governor might delegate this responsibility to lower-ranking officials, especially for simple cases. Presiding over every trial was simply too time-consuming for a governor. Burton, "Proconsuls, Assizes and the Administration of Justice under the Empire," 102. Cicero criticized his predecessor, Appius, for continuing to hear cases after Cicero had arrived in the province as governor. This was illegal, but Cicero remarked that at least Appius saved him almost one month's work. *Ep. ad Fam.* III.6.5.

death extended to virtually every person in the province, whether he was a citizen or not, although the governor could not *summarily* execute a citizen. Roman *subjects* could be executed without a trial, but if the accused were a Roman *citizen*, proper judicial procedures would be observed since citizens had special legal rights and privileges.[6] The Romans encouraged local self-administration of justice, respected local laws and customs, and generally allowed community tribunals to handle their own matters. But the governor retained supreme judicial authority in a provincial territory, especially the right to exercise capital punishment.[7] Since the governor had the "right of the sword," the Jews did not have the legal right to administer capital punishment, with one exception.[8]

Roman Concerns during Passover

PASSOVER CELEBRATED THE EXODUS, WHEN Moses liberated the Hebrews and led them out of slavery in Egypt. Now the Jews longed for their liberation again, this time from the Romans. Both Jewish and Roman authorities feared potential disruption among the huge crowds that assembled in Jerusalem for the feast. Nervous Romans knew that the masses, already excited by religious and nationalistic passions evoked by the feast, could easily be stoked into a full-blown rebellion. The Romans always arrived in Jerusalem for Passover week bolstered by additional troops, just in case trouble arose.

---

6 Only about ten percent of the inhabitants of the Roman empire were citizens. Non-citizens (*peregrines*) like Jesus had virtually no protection against a magistrate's absolute power, but a Roman citizen could not be killed, scourged, tortured, condemned, or put into bonds without following legal procedures. Garnsey, *Social Status and Privilege in the Roman Empire*, 263; Jones, *Studies in Roman Government and Law*, 54. Nonetheless, we know of many examples in which the rights guaranteed to citizens were flagrantly ignored by provincial governors.

7 Garnsey, "Criminal Jurisdiction of Governors," 51.

8 One exception remained: Any non-Jew could be put to death immediately by the Jewish authorities if he passed the low wall (*soreg*) that defined the sacred areas of the Temple precinct restricted to ritually pure Jews. See chapter 5.

The Motivation of the Chief Priests

"THEN THEY LED JESUS FROM the house of Caiaphas to the praetorium. It was early. They themselves did not enter the praetorium, so that they might not be defiled, but might eat the Passover" (John 18:28).

Jesus was in Jewish custody all night. He could have been illegally executed by stoning, just as happened to St. Stephen, the protomartyr (Acts 7:58). No one could have prevented the Jewish authorities from murdering Jesus, and it is likely that no one would have challenged them or prosecuted them if they had. The Romans would not have objected if the Sanhedrin had discreetly killed someone who threatened political stability. But the Sanhedrin did not want Jesus eliminated *quietly*. They wanted him crucified *publicly* in order to totally disgrace and discredit him, to leave no doubt that Jesus was a false prophet and cursed by God.

Crucifixion was the only way to prove to the people that Jesus was not the Messiah but a false prophet. The Law of Moses states, "Cursed be every one who hangs on a tree" (Gal. 3:13, referring to Deut. 21:23). Crucifixion was considered a form of hanging. The effectiveness and lasting impact of the Sanhedrin's strategy is indisputable: to this very day, the primary reason Jews reject Jesus as the Messiah is that he died by crucifixion. They still assume that he was cursed by God and therefore cannot be the Messiah.[9]

"It was early" (John 18:28). By early Friday morning, Jesus was brought before the Roman authorities. A typical Roman workday began about six AM and concluded around noon. Romans preferred a short workday and, in the hot Judean climate, starting early and ending before the afternoon heat set in suited them perfectly. The religious leaders knew that the Roman governor, Pontius Pilate, would already be at work. This was advantageous. Jesus could be convicted and sentenced to death by Pilate early and quickly, before most people in the city even realized that he had been arrested during the night while they slept.

---

9   A Qumran text (from the Dead Sea Scrolls), a commentary on Deut. 21:22–23, lists the reasons one might be hanged, which include "doing evil to one's people." The Sanhedrin described Jesus to Pilate as an "evildoer." 4QpNah, col. 64 lines 6–13; Fitzmyer, "Crucifixion in Ancient Palestine," 503–4.

"They themselves did not enter the praetorium, so that they might not be defiled, but might eat the Passover. So Pilate went out to them" (John 18:28–29). Passover and the Sabbath would begin at sunset, in less than twelve hours. The chief priests and elders would not enter the praetorium since entering a Gentile structure would defile them, rendering them unable to enter the Temple later or even participate in the feast. Ritual defilement could be removed, but not enough time remained to remove it before the start of Passover at sunset. The Temple delegation consisted primarily of chief priests, and preserving ritual purity was an absolute necessity.

Saint John Chrysostom noted the irony of their concern for ritual purity when they were participating in such a corrupt process: "They who paid tithes on mint and anise did not consider that they were defiled by becoming murderers but thought that they defiled themselves by merely entering the court of Pilate."[10] Pilate would have to go outside to meet with the Sanhedrin delegation while Jesus remained inside the praetorium. The Sanhedrin authorities could not hear Jesus' conversations with Pilate.

The Governor: Pontius Pilate

PONTIUS PILATE WAS A PREFECT, not a procurator, a title that would be given to Roman administrators of Judea later on.[11] He was an equestrian, a rank of nobility just below the highest level of Roman aristocracy, occupied by the senatorial rank. Pilate held office in Judea for ten years, AD 26–36, a surprisingly long time since a governor's term was normally two years. Pilate had a great deal of experience in dealing with Jews and their leaders. A general attitude of mutual cooperation existed between them. For this reason, and because of Pilate's reputation for brutally repressing dissent, the Sanhedrin expected Pilate to rubber-stamp their request to execute Jesus.

Pilate's five consecutive two-year terms indicate that he was an effective administrator, successful at least in maintaining the peace and collecting

---

10 Chrysostom, Homily 83, *Homilies on the Gospel of John*, FOTC 41:409.

11 A stone was discovered in 1961 at Caesarea Maritima with an inscription that mentions Pontius Pilate as the prefect, leaving no doubt regarding his exact title and status. Finegan, *Archeology of the New Testament*, 138–39.

tax revenue. However, Pilate made some serious blunders; two actions in particular roused Jewish protest. He brought several busts of the emperor Tiberius into Jerusalem, most likely in an effort to curry favor with Tiberius. The images were considered idolatrous, and the populace begged Pilate to remove them. He initially refused, but later he relented.[12] The second episode occurred when Pilate appropriated money from the Temple treasury and used those funds to construct an aqueduct for the city.[13]

Judea was not a prestigious or desirable assignment. Pilate's ten-year term suggests that he benefited financially from his time in Judea to a significant degree, probably enriching himself by receiving bribes for appointments to various positions, including the appointment of the high priest, Caiaphas. Roman men of Pilate's equestrian rank accepted assignments in difficult, far-away places like Judea in order to acquire wealth. Bribery was against Roman law, but it was widely practiced nonetheless. A governor who violated the law or exceeded his power could be recalled to Rome, although the Roman Senate tended to treat governors charged with abuse of power with some

---

12   Josephus, *JW* 2.169-74; *Ant*.18.3.55–59; Evans, *Jesus and His Contemporaries*, 339; Horsley, *Bandits*, 38–39. A huge number of Jews spontaneously traveled from Jerusalem and the surrounding countryside to Caesarea, where the Roman administrative buildings were located. They implored Pilate to remove the images of Tiberius from Jerusalem. The crowd was invited the following day to the stadium and expected Pilate to respond to their demands. But instead, he called forward a large number of Roman troops, who entirely surrounded the assembled Jews. He announced that he would slay them all if they did not accept the images of Caesar in the holy city. Then he ordered his soldiers to draw their swords. Pilate was stunned when all the Jews spontaneously fell to the ground and bowed their necks, taking the position of one about to be beheaded, showing that they would rather die than accept the violation of the holy city with idolatry. Pilate was amazed by this and ordered that the images be removed.

13   Josephus, *Ant*. 18.60–62; *JW* 2.175–77. In this case, Pilate did not change his mind or reverse his action. He ordered his soldiers to dress in civilian clothes and mingle with the crowd. When he gave a signal, the soldiers began to beat the Jewish protesters with clubs, even killing some of them. In both instances, these massive and spontaneous protests were led by peasants and ordinary city dwellers who opposed Pilate's actions on religious grounds. No Temple officials, high priests, or chief priests protested, even though preserving the sanctity of the Temple was their responsibility. They became involved only later, when the protests created economic disruption and threatened the payment of Roman tribute. Apparently, desecration of the Temple was a lesser concern than protecting their positions. Horsley, "High Priests and Politics," 39.

deference and leniency. Nonetheless, in a few known cases, provincial governors were convicted of abuse of power or committed suicide prior to their trials.[14]

Roman Governors and Jewish Rebellion

"SO PILATE WENT OUT TO them and said, 'What accusation do you bring against this man?'" (John 18:29). Pilate's question proves that this is the first time he has seen or heard of Jesus. Some New Testament scholars have claimed that the Gospels are not truthful because they depict Pilate as reluctant to execute Jesus, and this could not possibly be true. They say that Pilate must have already heard about Jesus and considered him a threat. They allege that the evangelists were trying to curry favor with the Roman state and place responsibility for Jesus' death on the Jews by highlighting Pilate's reluctance to execute Jesus. To support this theory, they point to Jewish revolutionaries who had revolted against Rome and had received swift and violent Roman justice.

A few revolutionaries attempted to lead revolts against Rome in the first century: three after the death of Herod the Great in 4 BC (Judas the son of Ezekias; Simon, a former slave; and Athronges the Shepherd),[15] and Judas the Galilean in AD 6.[16] Theudas claimed to be a prophet and enticed a large group to follow him in about AD 45. He was captured in the desert and executed by the governor, Cuspius Fadus.[17] Josephus described additional "imposters and deceivers" as being active when Felix was governor (c. 52–60), including an Egyptian false prophet mentioned in Acts 21:38.[18] Under the next governor, Festus (60–62), another revolutionary attracted a following, and he was also destroyed by Roman troops.[19]

---

14   Horsley, "High Priests and Politics," 28.

15   Josephus, *JW* 2.39-79; Horsley, "Popular Messianic Movements around the Time of Jesus," 484–86.

16   Josephus, *JW* 2.118 and *Ant.* 18.3–6.23.

17   Josephus, *Ant.* 20.97–99.

18   Josephus, *JW* 2.258–63, *Ant.* 20.167–72.

19   Josephus, *Ant.* 20.188.

But Jesus' life, ministry, and message bore no resemblance to those men or their movements. The evangelists were truthful and reported the trial accurately. It is obvious here, in Pilate's initial conversation with the Jewish authorities and in his conversation with Jesus, that Pilate had never heard of Jesus before. Regardless of what some imagine must have happened, absolutely no evidence exists that Pilate already knew about Jesus; therefore, unlike actual revolutionaries, he could not have considered Jesus a threat.

Pilate Had No Previous Knowledge of Jesus

IF WE STUDY THE QUESTION from the perspective of that time and place, rather than making assumptions based on Jesus' fame today, we will realize why Jesus was well known only among Jews. A preaching rabbi would not attract Pilate's notice. Gentiles never came to hear Jesus preach. Jesus was a sensation in Jewish circles only. Both his message and the crowds he attracted were peaceful. Nothing about him would have alarmed the Romans or drawn their attention.[20] The motivation for the Pharisees' question to Jesus about paying tribute to Caesar was to elicit a reason to report him to the Romans.

When Jewish insurrectionists were arrested, their followers were arrested and executed as well, because they too were involved in sedition. But Jesus' disciples were not arrested. His movement was not a threat to Roman order, because Jesus' message was not political. Treason was the pretext for the Sanhedrin bringing Jesus to the Romans for crucifixion but not the reason for his arrest by the Jewish leaders. In fact, no Jewish trial would have been required at all if Jesus had truly been undermining Roman authority. The Sanhedrin did not arrest revolutionaries and put them on trial. The Romans would have handled the entire Jesus matter speedily, without any Sanhedrin involvement, if Jesus had undermined Roman authority in the slightest.

---

20 Brian McGing considered whether the evangelists were engaged in a massive cover-up designed to make the Jews rather than the Romans responsible for Jesus' death. After surveying first-century Jewish revolutionaries, their movements, actions, and fate, and other factors, McGing concluded that the Gospels are accurate and no reason exists to find the portrayal of Pilate untruthful. McGing, "Pontius Pilate and the Sources," 423–24.

Since Jesus was not a revolutionary and had no political ambition, his ministry would not have attracted Pilate's attention. Jesus' love for the poor and his preaching about the Kingdom of God do not make him a "zealot," a failed revolutionary like those others. Nothing became of those other men and their movements. But Christ's movement survived because his deeds, his message, his purpose were not of this world. Those scholars who claim the evangelists falsely cast Pilate in a favorable light are the ones who distort the Gospels and the historical record.

Wouldn't Jesus' miracles bring him to the attention of the Romans? No, because Romans did not witness the miracles; Jews did. Jesus almost always healed where he was preaching: in synagogues, at the Temple, in Jewish houses, and in other locations where Jews gathered and Romans were not present. Occasionally we see Gentiles who know of Jesus' miraculous powers, such as the centurion (Matt. 8:5–13) or the Canaanite woman (Matt. 15:21–28). But those incidents occurred in the northern region of Galilee, where Herod Antipas ruled, not down south in Judea, where Pilate was in charge. Pilate was not responsible for the administration of Galilee.

If Romans had heard of Jesus' miracles, they might not have believed the accounts. Even if they did, the accounts were still not worth reporting to Pilate because they were unimportant from his perspective. Pilate had many pressures and concerns. His staff would not have bothered to keep him informed about the activities of a popular rabbi unless his teachings encouraged rebellion. But the reality was quite the opposite: Jesus taught love of enemies, nonviolence, and paying Roman taxes. Since Jesus posed no threat to Roman order, no one had any reason to inform Pilate about his activities.

Law Enforcement and the Role of Accusers under Roman Law

PROVINCES IN THE FIRST CENTURY usually had no professional police force or government prosecutors. In large cities, the military often served a policing function. But crime victims who wanted justice were expected to gather evidence, identify a suspect, arrest that person, accuse him before the authorities, and prosecute the case themselves.[21] This is exactly what the San-hedrin did in the case of Jesus: they arrested him, tried him, and convicted him. Normally, the Sanhedrin would also order punishment to be admin-istered, but since they decided that Jesus deserved the death penalty, they brought him to Pilate.

"'What accusation do you bring against this man?' They answered him, 'If this man were not an evildoer, we would not have handed him over'" (John 18:29–30). Pilate asked the Jewish authorities to state their case "against this man," yet another indication that he knew nothing about Jesus. They imme-diately reveal that they have no case against Jesus under Roman law. Accus-ers were expected to arrest a suspect, bring him to trial, and prosecute their own case. Here the Jewish authorities did not even state a crime, only a vague claim that Jesus is an "evildoer." Without a professional police force or gov-ernment prosecutors, the Roman criminal justice system depended heavily on private prosecution of criminal cases. One predictable consequence was abuse of process because criminal prosecutions were not initiated by unbi-ased, disinterested state prosecutors but usually by an enemy of the accused.[22] Accusations were sometimes made solely out of spite, hatred, or jealousy. The chief priests sincerely believed Jesus deserved to die, but undoubtedly they were also motivated by their own self-interest to prevent unrest and protect their positions.

The Roman imperial system depended on collaboration between local rul-ing aristocrats and Roman officials. Local power relationships were observed and preserved, to the advantage of the Romans and the local aristocracy but to the disadvantage of the less privileged. The upper class maintained its power through loyalty to the Roman state.[23] Pilate expected Jewish authorities to alert him to any troublemakers, but they failed to articulate a crime here.

The elders and chief priests appear to have been unprepared to prosecute the case against Jesus when they presented him to Pilate. Because they ambig-uously described Jesus as an "evildoer," Pilate immediately realized their com-plaint could not be sustained under Roman law.

---

21   Nippel, *Public Order in Ancient Rome*, 95.
22   See Tacitus, *Annals*, 3.37; 4.31; 4.36; 4.66; 11.5–7; 13.5; 13.23; 15.33.
23   Horsley, "High Priests and Politics," 28–29.

The Application of Jewish Law and Punishment in the Empire

"PILATE SAID TO THEM, 'TAKE him yourselves and judge him by your own law'" (John 18:31). Pilate's initial reaction raises two points. First, as explained above, the Jews had their own courts and generally handled their own issues, complaints, and controversies—including criminal matters— according to their own laws. The Jews had the right to administer justice as they saw fit, not only in Jerusalem or in Judea, but in their communities throughout the Roman Empire. Secondly, the case of Jesus was clearly a religious dispute and did not involve Roman law. With no underlying Roman crime even alleged, Pilate's immediate reaction was dismissive, equivalent to "Don't waste my time! Handle this yourselves!" The Jewish authorities had already judged Jesus, and they could legally have administered severe physical punishments, including beating him with rods or whipping him up to forty times. Those punishments were permitted by Jewish law and even by Roman law, since they fell short of a death sentence.

When he was persecuting the Church, Saul of Tarsus (later known as St. Paul) was deputized by the chief priests to arrest followers of Jesus who had fled from Jerusalem to Damascus to avoid arrest (Acts 9:1–2). Today some doubt this and say this would never have happened. However, all Jews worldwide were under the religious jurisdiction of the high priest and the Temple authorities. Local Jews in Damascus or elsewhere would have cooperated with Jerusalem and assisted in arresting and returning to Jerusalem any Jews whom Temple authorities considered blasphemers, such as the followers of Jesus. The Romans would not have interfered and would have no incentive to become involved in such matters. In fact, the Jews would have complained if the Romans had prevented the exercise of their religious authority. If Jewish leaders decided that someone was a blasphemer and deserved to be punished, the Romans would not have objected to that.[24]

---

24 In Acts 16:20–23, Jews began beating Paul and Silas. Roman officials were actually present and not only did not stop the beating but joined in. Sosthenes, a Jewish member of the Church in Corinth, was beaten by other Jews for believing in Jesus, and the beating took place in front of Gallio, the Roman tribune. Gallio refused to hear complaints brought by Jews against Sosthenes since he considered it a Jewish religious issue. He did not stop the beating of Sosthenes before his very eyes (Acts 18:15–17) since the Jews

Details in the Bible that do not reflect practices or expectations people have today should not be summarily dismissed as untrue. The Roman Empire was a brutal and violent society. We should not doubt the biblical witness by naively projecting our norms, sensitivities, and presumptions back into the first century, because their customs were different from ours. They would have considered our norms, ideas, and legal procedures, such as equal justice under the law, preposterous.

"Pilate said to them, 'Take him yourselves and judge him by your own law.' The Jews said to him, 'It is not lawful for us to put any man to death'" (John 18:31). The Jewish leaders wanted Jesus dead, and Pilate alone held the ius gladii, "the right of the sword." The chief priests now admitted what they really wanted from Pilate: Jesus must die. But convincing Pilate to cooperate with them would require a much stronger case than describing Jesus as an "evil-doer," which was not a crime and therefore not a charge Pilate could entertain. Jesus must be accused of a specific crime under Roman law.

As Jesus waited inside the praetorium, the Jewish leaders stood outside conversing with Pilate. A few days earlier the crowds had hailed Jesus as a king when he entered Jerusalem. Based on this, the chief priests accused Jesus of the worst possible crime under Roman law, one that carried the death penalty: treason. This is clear from Pilate's first statement to Jesus when he began questioning him. "Pilate entered the praetorium again and called Jesus, and said to him, 'Are you the King of the Jews?'" (John 18:33).

Cognitio: *Roman Judicial Examination*

THE ROMAN TRIAL OF JESUS began with a judicial examination or inquiry conducted by the governor. Known as *cognitio,* this procedure was considered an extraordinary form of justice, meaning outside (*extra*) or different from the

---

were judging a fellow Jew by their own laws. Saint Paul mentioned many punishments he received from the Jews, including thirty-nine lashes on five occasions and even being stoned (2 Cor. 11:24–25). The apostles and other Jewish Christians consistently preached about Christ in synagogues, and occasionally they were punished according to Jewish law. Jewish Christians were not immune from Jewish penalties inflicted by Jews in other parts of the empire outside of Palestine.

ordinary legal process. A trial by cognitio did not follow specific procedures and penalties created by Roman statute.[25] Trials held in the provinces were likely to be conducted by cognitio, allowing the governor to dispense justice freely in almost any manner he pleased.

Cognitio was an inquisitorial system, and Pilate completely controlled the proceedings. Governors who received a report of an individual's criminal activity might order that person immediately executed without even a perfunctory trial.[26] If he believed a person to be innocent, the governor could order him immediately released. If he was not sure whether the accused was guilty, he would question the parties, interrogate witnesses, and render a final judgment.

Cognitio was unstructured, quick, and efficient, freeing the governor from many of the requirements and constraints of legal procedures or specific laws. But the flexibility to proceed by cognitio also had a negative aspect: governors could dispense justice in an arbitrary and capricious manner. Acting under cognitio, a provincial governor assumed a far more active role in the trial than did impartial judges who presided over trials conducted according to statutory regulations. Penalties imposed under cognitio could be either relaxed or aggravated, solely at the discretion of the judge. Justice was often not fair and certainly not blind. The poor and lower classes were typically treated far more severely than those with wealth and position. Litigants, accusers, and defendants expected that penalties and even the quality of evidence needed to convict would vary according to social status. Slaves had no rights, and the worst punishments were reserved for them.

---

25   Operating outside the system in which crime was prosecuted by following specific procedures was referred to as proceeding *extra ordinem*. A magistrate's exercise of cognitio functioned outside the system of the *ordo*. Robinson, *Criminal Law of Ancient Rome*, 157.

26   This is the treatment Christians received from pagan Romans for over two hundred years, until Christianity was legalized in 313. The writings of early believers and the accounts of martyrdom repeatedly show early Christians objecting to the fact that they were denied even a trial or hearing before being summarily executed. See especially Justin Martyr's *First Apology to the Roman Emperor* 2–4, dated around 150. The first complaint Justin made to the emperor was that Christians were denied trials. Saint Polycarp made the same point prior to his martyrdom around 155. When Roman officials questioned him about his beliefs before the crowd in the arena, Polycarp replied, "Give me a hearing." But this was denied. *Martyrdom of Polycarp* 10.

Because he was a provincial subject of Rome, Jesus would have been considered a *peregrini*, a "foreigner," even though he was Jewish and living in Jewish lands. Lower-class peregrini were treated almost at the level of slaves, except that Romans believed certain forms of punishment should not be applied to one who was freeborn.[27] Wealthy peregrini usually fared better, since Romans believed that punishment should reflect one's status, *pro qualitate dignitatis*.[28] Roman citizenship offered the highest legal status and gave special privileges, including not being subject to physical punishment without a trial and the right to have one's case heard by Caesar. Roman citizens were not forced into a trial by cognitio.[29]

"Are You the King of the Jews?"

THE JEWISH LEADERS HAD LEVELED the one political charge they could think of: treason. Now Pilate reentered the praetorium and asked Jesus, "Are you the king of the Jews?" It was a ridiculous question and completely without basis. Pilate was being sarcastic. Jesus did not look like a king, had no army, had never claimed to be a king, and fled when an enthusiastic crowd tried to make him a king after he fed a large group of people with a small amount of bread and fish (John 6:15). Jesus was a poor, itinerant preacher who was clearly not claiming kingship.

> Jesus answered, "Do you say this of your own accord, or did others say it to you about me?" Pilate answered, "Am I a Jew? Your own nation and the chief priests have handed you over to me; what have you done?" (John 18:34–35)

---

27 Aubert, "A Double Standard in Roman Criminal Law?", 100.

28 "According to quality of honor." The *Sententiae Pauli*, a legal compilation by the Roman jurist Julius Paulus Prudentissimus ("Paulus"), lists gradations of punishment according to the crime and the status of the offender. Aubert, "Double Standard," 109.

29 Only about ten percent of the population held Roman citizenship, including very few Jews. The earliest historical documentation of a Roman citizen exercising his right to appeal to Caesar is found in the New Testament when Paul makes use of this right (Acts 25:11–12). Laws giving citizens special privileges dated back to the *lex Valeria* in the late 500s BC and the *leges Porciae* in the second century BC. But even laws that protected citizens were sometimes violated or ignored by provincial governors. Aubert, "Double Standard," 100.

Jesus questioned the source of Pilate's information in order to make a point. Pilate knew that Jesus had not heard the accusations of the chief priests as they stood outside the praetorium to avoid becoming defiled. Jesus asked the question to help Pilate realize that the charges were baseless, since Pilate himself had not heard about Jesus except from his accusers. Governors were aware of rebellious movements and seditious leaders in the region. Spies, informers, sycophants, and political opportunists would have immediately reported any treasonous remarks or claims of kingship made by Jesus. This new accusation of treason had been concocted by the Jewish authorities to ensure the death penalty since the weak "evildoer" charge had failed.

By his question, Jesus demonstrated the lack of evidence against him. Pilate's response proves the lack of Roman knowledge about Jesus; hence the Romans were not involved in his arrest.

Accusation of Treason: The Kingship of Jesus

"'ARE YOU THE KING OF the Jews?' Jesus said, 'You have said so'" (Matt. 27:11). Matthew, Mark, and Luke report the same accusation, and all confirm that Jesus admitted to Pilate that he was a king, using his characteristic expression to acknowledge that the questioner had spoken the truth. "You have said so" eliminates any excuse that the questioner was ignorant about Jesus' identity. John's Gospel preserves the longest and most detailed account of the dialogue between Jesus and Pilate, including a discussion of his kingship: "My kingship is not of this world; if my kingship were of this world, my servants would fight, that I might not be handed over to the Jews; but my kingship is not from the world" (John 18:36).

Pilate understood "not of this world" to mean that Jesus' kingship was metaphorical or spiritual. Jesus also said that his followers were not fighting for him. He posed no threat to the state; the evidence for this is irrefutable. Furthermore, Jesus told his followers not to fight for him (Matt. 26:52), he did not oppose the paying of Roman tribute (Matt. 22:20–21), and he fled when the crowd tried to make him a king (John 6:15).

Pilate said to him, "So you are a king?" Jesus answered, "You say that I am a king. For this I was born, and for this I have come into the world, to bear witness to the truth. Everyone who is of the truth hears my voice." Pilate said to him, "What is truth?" After he had said this, he went out to the Jews again, and told them, "I find no crime in him." (John 18:37–38)

Pilate had tried many cases, and Jesus' demeanor also revealed his innocence. He showed no signs of guilt. Jesus was not nervous or afraid. He did not behave like a person fearing execution but was calm and dignified, saying nothing that suggested criminal activity or treason. His accusers had provided no evidence whatsoever—merely an accusation.

Jesus said that his purpose was to bear witness to the Truth. This statement could just as easily have been made by a wandering Greek philosopher. Itinerant philosophers had become a growing presence in the Roman Empire during the first century and were part of an "unstructured and unfocused" movement of truth seekers.[30] Pilate's reply, "What is truth?" suggests that he saw Jesus as one of these itinerant philosophers.

The Right to Confront Witnesses under Roman Law

"BUT WHEN HE WAS ACCUSED by the chief priests and elders, he made no answer. Then Pilate said to him, 'Do you not hear how many things they testify against you?'" (Matt. 27:12–13). Even in proceedings against noncitizens like Jesus, the accused was allowed to speak on his own behalf or to have an advocate speak for him, often a professional orator or rhetor, if the accused could afford it. Romans believed in the basic fairness of allowing an accused person to confront witnesses and defend himself (see Acts 25:16).

Witnesses were usually present since no professional prosecutors existed. Ordinary people usually prosecuted their own case and also bore witness against the one they accused of a crime, which is precisely what we see in the case of Jesus. The opportunity to confront one's accuser was common and expected, but a judge could proceed even without an accuser present, on the

---

30   Montiglio, "Wandering Philosophers in Classical Greece," 86.

basis of an anonymous accusation (though this was discouraged). "But he gave him no answer, not even to a single charge; so that the governor wondered greatly" (Matt. 27:14).

Pilate's Wife

JESUS REMAINED MOSTLY SILENT BEFORE Pilate, just as he had in the Jewish trial. Pilate was accustomed to defendants vigorously defending themselves, pleading for their lives, begging for mercy or leniency. Jesus' silence and calm demeanor must have greatly perplexed him. Pilate was reluctant to act, already convinced that Jesus had committed no crime and that the Jewish leaders were motivated by self-interest or animosity. Then Pilate received a message from his wife, providing yet another reason to distance himself from the case.

> For he knew that it was out of envy that they had delivered him up. Besides, while he was sitting on the judgment seat, his wife sent word to him, "Have nothing to do with that righteous man, for I have suffered much over him today in a dream." (Matt. 27:18–19)

According to early Church tradition, Pilate's wife, Procla or Procla Claudia, later became a Christian. The first written reference to this is found in Origen (early third century), and she is listed among the saints in the Orthodox Church. As she was a Gentile, her sensitivity to the message she received in a dream contrasts with the attitude of the Jewish leaders, who were not open to the voice of God but resolute in their objective.

The Fate of Pilate

THE ULTIMATE FATE OF PILATE is unknown. One tradition holds that he too became a Christian, although this is unlikely. Another states that he was exiled to Gaul. Eusebius relates yet a third tradition that Pilate committed suicide. Eusebius wrote in the fourth century; no earlier Church tradition mentions a suicide, and even Eusebius is doubtful about it.[31]

We do not know when or how Pilate's life ended, but we do know that after spending ten years in Judea as governor, he was recalled to Rome to answer charges of cruelty and oppression for killing a large number of Samaritans. Committing an unlawful act while serving as governor would be considered an abuse of the imperium. But while Pilate was en route from Judea to answer the charges in Rome, the Emperor Tiberius died. Under these circumstances, it is unlikely that any Samaritans would have traveled to Rome to prosecute their case against Pilate, although he could still have been held accountable for abusing Tiberius's imperium. Gaius Caligula, Tiberius's successor, could have prosecuted Pilate, but the case was dismissed. It was a lucky break for Pilate, but he might have avoided a conviction regardless, since the senate and emperors generally supported governors and presumed they were acting appropriately.

After his case was dropped, we never hear of Pilate again in any Jewish or Roman sources. It is possible that, finding himself back in Rome and without a job, he simply retired. It is unlikely that tragedy such as suicide or exile befell him, since early Christians would have mentioned this.

In the second century, a famous pagan named Celsus penned a book against the Christian faith. One of his arguments against the divinity of Christ was that nothing terrible happened to Pilate, who had scourged and crucified Jesus. If Jesus had in fact been a god, Celsus argued, Pilate would certainly have met with divine retribution from the gods. This constituted a rock-solid argument in the Roman view.[32] The most famous early Church author and thinker, Origen (c. 185–254), responded to Celsus to defend the Christian faith in a famous work known as *Contra Celsum* (*Against Celsus*). Origen responded point by point to many of Celsus's arguments against Christ but

---

31 Eusebius, *History of the Church*, 2.7. In another one of his works, *Chronicon*, Eusebius admits that as a historian he had difficulty confirming that Pilate had committed suicide.

32 In Roman literature and lore, anyone who offended the gods always suffered severe consequences.

said nothing about Pontius Pilate,[33] indicating that the early Church had no tradition regarding his fate.[34]

But as Jesus stood before him, Pilate had no idea that his name would forever be remembered and that this little trial would become the most famous trial in world history. He did not even know that he would be recalled to Rome in the future to face charges about his administration of the province. For now, he simply attempted to extricate himself from the pressure being applied by the Jewish leaders to execute Jesus. He would try to pass the problem off to another ruler: Herod.

---

33   Origen, *Contra Celsum* 2.34.
34   Maier, "The Fate of Pontius Pilate," 370.

CHAPTER 18

Jesus Appears before Herod

THREE TIMES PILATE STATED THAT he did not find Jesus guilty of any crime (John 18:38; 19:4, 6). All the evangelists report the same thing. "Pilate said to the chief priests and the multitudes, 'I find no crime in this man.' But they were urgent, saying, 'He stirs up the people, teaching throughout all Judea, from Galilee even to this place'" (Luke 23:4–5).

The Jewish leaders insisted that Pilate convict Jesus, who had been "stirring up" trouble from Galilee down to Jerusalem. In their words, Pilate identified a way he could extricate himself from this unwelcome business they had thrown into his lap. "When Pilate heard this, he asked whether the man was a Galilean. And when he learned that he belonged to Herod's jurisdiction, he sent him over to Herod, who was himself in Jerusalem at that time" (Luke 23:6–7).

Jesus had not broken any Roman laws; Pilate was certain of that. If the Jewish authorities had complaints about Jesus regarding either religious issues or claims of kingship, Jesus should be taken before his own king for trial— Herod Antipas, the king in Galilee. Jesus was not a resident of Judea, and since he had not committed any crime in the province of Judea, Pilate actually had no legal jurisdiction over him. Pilate must have thought, "If the Jewish authorities want Jesus dead because he has violated some Jewish law, let Herod execute him!" The timing was perfect, since Herod was in Jerusalem for Passover. Happy to be relieved of this annoyance, Pilate sent the delegation off to Herod Antipas, who had heard of Jesus and wanted to meet him.

The first Herod, Herod the Great, had been recognized as king of the Jews by the Romans in 37 BC, even though he was not Jewish at all but hailed from Idumea, a tribal kingdom south of Judea.[1] The Romans were unconcerned that Herod the Great was not of Jewish ancestry, since their goal was order and stability. All kings in the empire were puppet kings, or client kings, appointed and ultimately controlled by Rome. Herod the Great was survived by three sons, and the name Herod became a title for all the kings who were his descendants, including the son who ruled Galilee at this time, Herod Antipas.

Herod Antipas became king of Galilee, a region west of the Sea of Galilee, on the death of his father in 4 BC. His territory also included Perea, a long strip of land on the east side of the Jordan River. Herod Antipas married his brother Philip's wife, Herodias, and John the Forerunner denounced the marriage as an incestuous violation of Jewish law because Philip was still alive.[2] John's outspoken condemnation eventually cost the Baptist his head through the machinations of Herodias (Matt. 14:1–12). Jesus rose to prominence after the death of John, and a superstitious Herod Antipas wondered whether he might actually be John the Baptist risen from the dead. John had not been a miracle worker, but Jesus was, and Herod knew of his many wondrous signs. He was eager to see Jesus perform a miracle in front of him, displaying his powers like the magicians who entertained Herod's court.

"When Herod saw Jesus, he was very glad, for he had long desired to see him, because he had heard about him, and he was hoping to see some sign done by him" (Luke 23:8). Unlike Pilate, Herod had heard many things about Jesus. But even Herod had never heard that Jesus claimed to be king. Jesus was often in Galilee, where Herod had many informants and sycophants who

---

1 The Idumeans had been forcibly converted to Judaism when the region was governed by Jewish Hasmonean kings during a period lasting about a hundred years, not long before the Roman conquest in 63 BC.

2 Some scholars, however, say that Herodias was not married to the half brother of Herod Antipas but to another member of the Herodian family, also named Philip, an uncle of Antipas. Male relatives such as uncles and cousins were often referred to as "brother." That fact, along with sharing the same name, has contributed to confusion about the exact family connection. Regardless of the precise blood relationship, the marriage would have been considered incestuous and adulterous, and John denounced it because her husband was still alive.

would have wasted no time in notifying him of any threat to his rule. Herod knew that Jesus preached humility, love of enemies, and nonviolence, and the wife of his chief steward was even a disciple of Jesus.[3] "So he questioned him at some length; but he made no answer. The chief priests and the scribes stood by, vehemently accusing him" (Luke 23:9–10).

Jesus remained characteristically silent as he now stood before Herod Antipas. He had accepted his Father's will, knew what the outcome would be, and saw no point in defending himself. No doubt he prayed silently as the Jewish leaders furiously accused him of blasphemy, treason, and anything else they could think of to achieve their desired result. If Pilate was reluctant to execute Jesus because he had not committed a Roman crime, Herod was under no such restrictions. The chief priests and scribes labored hard to persuade him to execute Jesus. Herod Antipas had put others to death for far less.

So why didn't Herod put Jesus to death? The first and most important reason was that Jesus was never a threat. Jesus had grown up in Galilee and established his ministry there, traveling to every village and town, preaching and healing in public places. Herod Antipas ruled and controlled Galilee ruthlessly. He had his own army with contingents of soldiers, such as the centurion whose servant Jesus healed, keeping the peace in his kingdom. Herod could have given orders to arrest Jesus long before, but he never did because the reports he received were that Jesus was harmless.

Secondly, Herod had beheaded John, whom the people considered a prophet. They were still angry about that. It might not be wise to kill Jesus, whom the populace also held in high regard, particularly since he never expressed any political ambitions and posed no threat. "And Herod with his soldiers treated him with contempt and mocked him; then, arraying him in gorgeous apparel, he sent him back to Pilate" (Luke 23:11).

The frustrated chief priests and scribes tried every argument to persuade Herod to kill Jesus, but he refused to become involved. Herod was interested only in seeing a miracle, something to entertain him. But Jesus refused to perform a miracle, and since his life was at stake, Herod must have reasoned that

---

3   Luke mentions Joanna, one of the Myrrhbearers, as a disciple and the wife of Chuza, Herod's chief steward (Luke 8:3). This means that he was in charge of running the day-to-day operations in Herod's household, the palace.

Jesus was a fraud. The reports of his powers must have been exaggerations or outright lies. Jesus was just a harmless charismatic preacher. So rather than killing him, Herod toyed with Jesus, entertaining himself and his entourage. "Jesus? A *king*? Look at his clothes!" They must have laughed as they dressed him up in luxurious garments and sent Jesus back to the praetorium for Pilate's amusement.

CHAPTER 19

The Scourging and Mocking

P ILATE HAD SENT JESUS, A Galilean, to be tried by the king of Galilee, Herod Antipas, who had jurisdiction over him. "And that is that," Pilate assumed. It was a lucky break that Herod was in Jerusalem for Passover. If Jesus deserved to die for claiming to be a king, Herod would render expedient judgment. Pilate need not be bothered with this issue, which had already consumed too much of his precious time.

Many other pressing matters demanded his attention. Passover was to begin at sunset, and soon the entire Temple Mount would be swarming with people and their lambs. The city was packed with ardent Jewish pilgrims gathered from throughout the Roman world. His troops must be prepared to manage the throng that would soon congregate on the mountain. The Sanhedrin's interruption was unwelcome on the day before Passover, when Pilate's paramount concern and responsibility was to maintain crowd control. Having dispatched Jesus to Herod, Pilate assumed that the case of the obscure rabbi the Sanhedrin had abruptly thrust upon him was over. He had no time for their petty jealousies and religious quarrels.

Imagine Pilate's surprise when once again the chief priests and elders disrupted his morning duties, along with the Temple guard, who escorted Jesus back to the praetorium. Pilate might have chuckled at the sight of Jesus, now attired by Herod in expensive clothes fit for royalty. He got the joke, but he had hoped to be rid of the Jewish authorities and of Jesus. But the chief priests and elders simply would not take no for an answer. Herod would not handle the matter, so once again, Jesus was Pilate's problem.

Herod's action of returning Jesus to him for judgment confirmed for Pilate that Jesus was innocent. Pilate knew he could not avoid involvement, but he also knew that Jesus was not guilty of any crime. He had already expressed that—three times. But the Jewish authorities wanted Jesus dead. Perhaps, Pilate reasoned, if he scourged Jesus, that would satisfy their desire for his blood. Although three of the Gospels merely imply this strategy, the Gospel of Luke is explicit.

> Pilate then called together the chief priests and the rulers and the people, and said to them, "You brought me this man as one who was perverting the people; and after examining him before you, behold, I did not find this man guilty of any of your charges against him; neither did Herod, for he sent him back to us. Behold, nothing deserving of death has been done by him; I will therefore chastise him and release him." (Luke 23:13–16)

Pilate attempted to pacify the Jewish leaders by scourging Jesus. Although it is cruel to inflict such a horrible punishment on an innocent person, Pilate preferred it to crucifixion. This action could spare Jesus' life if it satisfied the religious leaders.

The Scourging and Coercitio

AN IMPORTANT TOOL OF ROMAN criminal justice and law enforcement was the power of *coercitio*, which essentially was a governor's right to punish, force compliance, or compel obedience without first engaging the legal process. Coercitio encompassed a variety of measures, including beating, scourging, imprisonment, fines, and summary execution. Coercitio was an extrajudicial power, different and distinct from the governor's judicial powers, because it was used not only to punish a crime but to force compliance or cooperation. It is the root of our English word "coercion." One important privilege Roman citizens enjoyed was freedom from coercitio. It was a basic tenet of Roman law that citizens were not subject to a magistrate's *coercitio*, but everyone else was.[1]

A scourging could be administered simply to punish an accused or give him a warning, but scourging always accompanied crucifixion as a precursor to the execution itself.[2] Crucifixion was a slow form of death that involved very little blood-letting. Scourging inflicted tremendous pain and led to a more rapid death from the loss of blood and the shock to the body.

A Roman scourging was a much more severe punishment than a whipping.[3] The Jews employed whipping as a punishment, but a whip is merely a long strip of leather that creates a single, smooth wound like a ribbon across the back. Next to crucifixion and being burned alive, scourging was the most feared Roman punishment. Romans administered a scourging with a *flagellum* (or *flagrum*), which was far more brutal than a whip. The flagellum had a stubby handgrip that held several strands of leather braided together. About halfway up this portion, the braid separated into individual strands. Each strand had small metal balls attached to it at intervals along its length. The balls made the flesh more tender by repeatedly bruising the person with each stroke. Attached to the end of each strand of leather was a sharp piece of metal that dug into the body.

The accused criminal was stripped of his clothes and tied facing a pillar, either with his hands above his head or bent over a lower pillar. Two Roman soldiers, alternating on the left and right sides, struck the accused with the flagellum with full force. With each blow the victim received multiple wounds to the back, legs, and buttocks. The metal tips at the ends of the strands would

---

1   This privilege is illustrated in the case of Paul and Silas, who, although Roman citizens, were beaten and imprisoned in Philippi without a trial. When the magistrate learned that they were Roman citizens, he became fearful and immediately apologized. Roman authorities hoped they could simply escort the apostles quietly out of town, but St. Paul insisted on an apology (Acts 16:35–39). To apply coercitio to a Roman citizen without a trial was a serious violation and could be severely punished.

2   With one exception: women sentenced to crucifixion were not scourged. They were also crucified facing the wood of the cross.

3   According to Zugibe, scourging is so incomparably worse than a whipping that the difference between them is like the difference between receiving an electric shock and being struck by a bolt of lightning. Zugibe, *Crucifixion of Jesus*, 19.

dig deep into the flesh, tearing the skin, muscles, and nerves, and ripping small blood vessels.[4]

The individual strands of the flagellum could also whip around the body, striking the front. Repeated strikes could tear open the abdomen, and sometimes the intestines and other internal organs of a scourging victim became visible. As the scourging continued, the injuries grew worse as the small metal balls repeatedly pounded muscles and the sharp metal tips dug into the body, removing more skin and muscle. Eventually the back was reduced to ribbons of bleeding flesh.[5] Scourging caused tremendous blood loss from the visible trauma but also significant injury to the rib cage in the form of fractures, making breathing painful and difficult.[6] The intercostal muscles (the muscles in between the ribs that allow the ribcage to expand when we breathe) would also become bruised and bleed. A single rib fracture can account for a loss of up to half a cup of blood.[7] A person could easily die from a scourging, which was excruciating and exhausting. Josephus describes a flogged man who was "whipped until his bones were laid bare."[8]

The Roman objective was to punish or prepare the accused for crucifixion, not to kill him by the scourging. They were experts in the procedure and usually knew how severely they could scourge without causing death. It is commonly assumed that Jesus received thirty-nine lashes, but this is not correct. The Scriptures do not tell us how many strokes he received from the flagellum. First, he did not receive "the lash" but a scourging, which is much worse than a whipping, as we have established. Second, the custom of limiting strokes to

---

4   Zugibe, *Crucifixion of Jesus*, 20.

5   "After a scourging, large black and blue and reddish purple bruises, lacerations (tears), scratches, welts and swellings appear all over the front and back of the victim's body." Zugibe, *Crucifixion of Jesus*, 21.

6   A blow to the ribs results in shallow breathing because it is painful to take a full breath. Zugibe, *Crucifixion of Jesus*, 21.

7   Zugibe describes the effects of the scourging and its impact on the body. "Periods of severe sweating would occur, intermittently. The victim would be reduced to an exhausted, mangled mass of flesh with a craving for water. The scourging propelled Jesus into an early stage of shock. Over the next few hours there would be a slow accumulation of fluid (pleural effusion) developing around the lungs, adding to his breathing difficulties." Zugibe, *Crucifixion of Jesus*, 22.

8   Josephus, *JW* 6.304, 742.

thirty-nine was a Jewish limitation for whippings administered by the Jews themselves. Under Jewish law, a person could be whipped with up to forty strokes maximum. If that number was exceeded and the victim died from the lashing, the person administering the punishment was liable for murder under Jewish law. To ensure they would not be liable for murder, Jews stopped at thirty-nine lashes, one short of the maximum.[9]

We do not know how many strokes the Lord received from the Roman soldiers since they had no limitations. Details in the Gospels suggest that the scourging Christ received was severe, since he was unable to carry his cross to the site of execution in spite of the fact that he was young, healthy, and strong.

The Mocking and the Crown of Thorns

Then the soldiers of the governor took Jesus into the praetorium, and they gathered the whole battalion before him. And they stripped him and put a scarlet robe upon him, and plaiting a crown of thorns they put it on his head, and put a reed in his right hand. And kneeling before him they mocked him, saying, "Hail, King of the Jews!" And they spat upon him, and took the reed and struck him on the head. And when they had mocked him, they stripped him of the robe, and put his own clothes on him, and led him away to crucify him. (Matt. 27:27–31)

JESUS WAS MOCKED AS A pseudo-king, dressed in a mock royal robe, handed a mock scepter in the form of a reed, in a coronation topped off with a crown of thorns. A large number of soldiers participated in the abuse, not simply the two or three who might have been responsible for carrying out the scourging itself. The mocking provided entertainment and was a welcome break for the soldiers.

---

9   When St. Paul described his sufferings for Christ, his words show that the Jews administered these punishments to him, in particular the whippings: "Five times I have received at the hands of the Jews the forty lashes less one" (2 Cor. 11:24).

Mocking was common, since crucifixion was designed to humiliate and shame the victim.[10] Plays and Roman circuses also commonly depicted mocking, and Roman soldiers played a game of mock kingship, something like a board game, during Saturnalia. Scratches made in the stone pavement at the Antonia Fortress showed that the soldiers garrisoned there played that very game.[11] The mocking reflected the crime for which Jesus was condemned: treason, for claiming to be a king. The soldiers' words and genuflections imitated how Caesar would have been honored. The mockery was also fulfillment of prophecy. Isaiah refers to the mocked "servant of the Lord" tolerating beating and spitting. "I gave my back to scourges, and my cheeks to blows; I hid not my face from the shame of the spittings" (Is. 50:6, LXX).

We can relate to the mocking since everyone has been maligned, unfairly used, treated with contempt or disrespect. But in ancient cultures, especially for the Romans, honor and glory were so highly valued that preserving personal honor and avoiding shame were considered more important than money and even more important than life itself. Better to die with honor than to live with shame. The humiliation that accompanied crucifixion was one of the primary reasons it served as a deterrent—people did not fear the pain alone.

The Mocking as Proof of Gospel Truth

TODAY A SENSE OF SHAME is often absent in our culture, or it is discouraged, even shame for sin. Today, we consider it admirable and virtuous that Christ willingly suffered such humiliation. But when the Gospels were written, these details were highly embarrassing. The culture in which the Church was established was a society that valued honor. But the Church never attempted to hide the mockery that accompanied the crucifixion, and the Scriptures honestly describe even shameful things done to Christ.

---

10   Even slaves sentenced to be crucified were given over to their fellow slaves to be ridiculed and shamed by their peers prior to their execution. Collins, "Exegetical Notes," 157.

11   Brown, *Gospel of John*, 2:888–89.

The honesty of the Gospels concerning the mocking should be noted for another reason. Today people might readily dismiss the accounts of Christ's miracles as myths, exaggerations, or fabrications, arguing that such stories were invented simply to persuade people to believe in and follow Jesus. This seems plausible to modern people who pride themselves on reason, rationalism, and the immutable laws of science. But if the evangelists, or any early Christians, had been dishonest and lied about the miracles of Christ, the Resurrection, the Virgin Birth, and so forth so that people would believe in Jesus, they would never have included details that were humiliating for Christ and that allowed people to call his divinity into question. In ancient stories, gods and heroes did not suffer shame and humiliation—certainly nothing like crucifixion—and not with Christ's attitude of meekness, humility, and forbearance. Even today, Muslims reject the historical record that Jesus was crucified because they see it as humiliation and weakness.

The fact that the Church openly spoke of the mocking and the evangelists wrote these details supports the trustworthiness of everything in the Gospels. Nothing about the crucifixion of Christ was good public relations for the Church, and yet all these details were told and retold.

The Rod

WE RECOGNIZE THE ABUSE AND humiliation of the mocking and the sarcasm, and the disgust of being spat on. But reference to the reed by the evangelists means that Jesus received additional physical beatings at this time. He had already been scourged, and now he was beaten with the rod and by the soldiers' hands. The word often translated as "reed" (*kalamon*) can refer to a slender or supple reed, but it should be translated as "rod," a stiff and strong measuring stick, a form of chastisement in the Roman arsenal of punishments.[12] Jesus would not have been handed a slender, limp reed to serve as his mock scepter. First he was given a rod, and then he was beaten with it. Soldiers

---

12 Saint Paul mentions being beaten with rods three times (2 Cor. 11:25). Acts 16:22 describes Paul and Silas being beaten with rods by a crowd at the instruction of a Roman magistrate in Philippi.

were strong young men who did not restrain either their contempt for him or the physical force of their blows.

The Robe

MATTHEW DESCRIBES THE ROBE PLACED on Jesus as "scarlet," whereas other evangelists use the word "purple." It was certainly intended to serve as a purple robe of mockery, and this must have been what the other evangelists had in mind. The color purple was associated with royalty and wealth because purple dye was extremely expensive. The dye was extracted from deep-water snails, and each snail produced only a few drops of dye. Thousands of snails were needed to produce even a small quantity of dye. The robe was a mock-purple robe, just as the crown of thorns was a mock crown, the reed was a mock royal scepter, and the salutations and genuflections were sarcastic imitations of the greeting and obeisance given to Caesar. Even Jesus' position on Golgotha would become a parody of kingly enthronement as he was lifted up off the ground, with thieves on either side as though installed as advisors, one on his right and one on his left.

The mockery of Christ is laden with deep irony as the King of the universe and Creator of all things, with unimaginable humility and divine forbearance, silently accepts such abuse at the hands of men. Jesus himself was without sin, and yet he experienced in full measure the reality of sin and its expression in fallen humanity. "The Lord became a sport to them," Cyril of Jerusalem noted. But the intention of the soldiers to humiliate him actually served an ironic purpose. Just as Pilate and Caiaphas spoke the truth about who Jesus was, even though they did not believe it, the soldiers' actions expressed the truth of who Christ was—the King of heaven—even though they did not recognize him. In the parody, the truth was revealed. Even though they mocked him, they bent the knee, gave him a crown, and called him "king."[13]

---

13   Cyril of Jerusalem, Lecture 13.17, FOTC 64:16.

The Crown of Thorns

THE CROWN OF THORNS WAS probably not a neatly plaited circlet as is often depicted in the movies. Roman coins show the emperor wearing a crown with large triangular projections radiating from his head like sunbeams. Close-fitting wreaths made of leaves of gold were also worn by Roman emperors. Various theories have been proposed as to precisely which plant was used to create the crown of thorns, but no one can be certain. Most varieties of thorny plants commonly suggested today did not grow in Palestine during the first century. Prickly plants, more like thistles than thorns, have been proposed, but the crown would probably imitate the look of a Roman imperial crown with larger spikes or thorns. The thorns would necessarily be large and strong enough to penetrate the scalp, which is difficult because the skin is tightly bound to the skull.

We understand the mockery aspect of the crown of thorns on an emotional level, but we have little appreciation for the severe pain it inflicted on Christ. The scalp is a particularly sensitive part of the body, with many nerve endings and more blood vessels than any other part of the body. Two major branches of nerves register pain in the head region. The trigeminal (fifth cranial) nerve sends pain signals from the front of the head, and three occipital nerves relay pain from the top and back of the head. These are the two main nerve branches on the scalp, but from these two branches, thousands of fine nerves spread out and cover the entire scalp.[14]

Compression of these nerves causes pain so severe it is described as agonizing.[15] Patients attempt to immobilize themselves to avoid the slightest movement of the head or the slightest touch, either of which can trigger an attack described as "knife-like stabs," "electric shocks," or "jabs with a red-hot poker."[16] It is "particularly painful," "sudden, transient and intense,"[17] and an "excruciating and debilitating pain" that is "shooting, electrical, sharp and

---

14 Zugibe, *Crucifixion of Jesus*, 33.
15 As a chronic condition, this type of pain is associated with a condition known as trigeminal neuralgia.
16 Zugibe, *Crucifixion of Jesus*, 34.
17 Bowsher, "Trigeminal Neuralgia," 409.

stabbing."[18] Many thorns would have penetrated Jesus' scalp, resulting in significant pain, exacerbated by his being struck on the head with the reed while he was wearing the crown of thorns. This pain might have subsided or stopped if he were momentarily standing still, only to flare up again with the slightest touch, movement of the head, or even the blowing of a breeze, any of which would trigger throbbing bolts of pain.

Behold the Man!

AFTER THE SCOURGING AND THE mocking by the soldiers, Jesus was returned to Pilate, who hoped that the sight of a bloody and battered Jesus would placate the Jewish leaders. Again, Pilate pronounced Jesus innocent of any crime.

> Pilate went out again, and said to them, "See, I am bringing him out to you, that you may know that I find no crime in him." So Jesus came out, wearing the crown of thorns and the purple robe. Pilate said to them, "Behold the man!" (John 19:4–5)

"Behold the man!" Pilate exclaimed, as if to say, "Look at him! Isn't this punishment enough for you?" By now Jesus would have been a mass of blood with wounds on virtually every part of his body. Indeed, the bizarre and macabre scene defies adequate description: Jesus dripping blood, a spiky crown on his head and draped in a blood-soaked robe. But the sight of Isaiah's prophesied Suffering Servant did not placate the Jewish leaders but had the opposite effect from the one Pilate had intended. Rather than pacifying the chief priests and elders, the sight of Jesus, beaten, bloody, and now barely able to stand, seemed to fuel their hatred, contempt, and determination to kill him.

---

18   Besi and Zakrzewska, "Trigeminal Neuralgia and its Variants," 405 and 407 respectively. Patients describe the pain as exhausting and so severe that a pain which lasted for "only seconds seemed like an eternity" (406). It could be set off even by light wind or touching a mustache. The pain can be so severe that some patients even committed suicide (407).

"When the chief priests and officers saw him, they cried out, 'Crucify him! Crucify him!' Pilate said to them, 'Take him yourselves and crucify him, for I find no crime in him'" (John 19:6). Pilate was disgusted at the reaction of the Jewish leaders. He knew they did not have the legal right to crucify Jesus, and he was not giving them permission by saying "Take him yourselves and crucify him." If that were the case, the Jewish leaders would have crucified him immediately. But instead, they continued to pressure Pilate. For a second time Pilate proclaimed Jesus not guilty of any crime. By saying "Take him yourselves and crucify him," Pilate expressed his frustration with them, as if to say "He's not guilty! Go away and don't bother me any further!" But the Jewish leaders were relentless.

Then Pilate thought of another way to release Jesus and extricate himself from this problem: by offering clemency. It was Passover, and two prisoners were in Roman custody: Jesus and Barabbas.

CHAPTER 20

Barabbas

J ESUS HAD BEEN BROUGHT BEFORE Pilate early in the morning, accompanied by important and influential Jewish leaders who made it clear they
wanted Jesus dead. The delegation to Pilate consisted of some of the most
prominent men in Jerusalem—elders and chief priests—all members of the
Sanhedrin. It would be embarrassing to them if Pilate rejected their request
and simply released Jesus immediately. Pilate had the power to release Jesus
outright, but that would signal an acquittal. Pilate had already concluded that
Jesus was innocent of any Roman crime, but he had been brought to him by
a very high-level Jewish delegation. Perhaps he could release Jesus by some
other means that would not humiliate the dignitaries. Looking for a way to
avoid embarrassing the representatives of the Sanhedrin, Pilate made them an
offer: "I find no crime in him. But you have a custom that I should release one
man for you at the Passover; will you have me release for you the King of the
Jews?" (John 18:38–39).

Another factor may also have motivated Pilate to release a prisoner. As
noted earlier, Jerusalem during Passover was a political pressure cooker. The
city's ordinary population of fifty thousand swelled to four or five times that
number because of the influx of pilgrims for Passover, which commemorated
the Jews' deliverance from slavery in Egypt and reminded them of their present subjugation. The danger of revolt was especially high at Passover, and the
Romans knew that. They also knew that even bolstered with additional troops

brought in for the occasion, a few hundred soldiers could never squelch an uprising involving two hundred thousand Jews.

The Romans had no custom of releasing prisoners. The Evangelist John is completely accurate as he relates the words of Pilate: "*You* have a custom . . ." The custom of releasing a prisoner at Passover was a Jewish one.[1] The Romans were not required to observe any Jewish customs, but at that moment, releasing a prisoner could serve a dual purpose for Pilate. His act of clemency could release some pent-up steam of religious emotion, lessening the chance that the city would explode in revolt, while also demonstrating the great magnanimity of Rome. Since Jesus was popular, his release could generate goodwill and would also get Pilate out of this predicament. The Jewish leaders must have told Pilate about the enthusiastic crowds that had acclaimed Jesus as a king when he entered Jerusalem. Executing him might inflame anti-Roman sentiment and actually trigger a revolt. But if Pilate released Jesus as an act of clemency, this would be an excellent Roman public-relations move and would also avoid embarrassing the Jewish leaders by an outright acquittal.

Barabbas

"AND THEY HAD THEN A notorious prisoner, called Barabbas" (Matt. 27:16).

Pilate had offered clemency to avoid embarrassing the Sanhedrin. No one needed to know that he had found Jesus innocent of any crime. They could blame Jesus' release on the Romans. But what the chief priests wanted was to blame Jesus' *death* on the Romans. His release on any terms was unacceptable to them.

After cooking up numerous plots against Jesus and making countless attempts simply to arrest him, they had finally done so. He was in their custody. They had convicted him, found him deserving of death, and now he stood before Pilate. They were so close to their goal! They could not allow Jesus to be released. In fact, they would prefer the release of anyone other

---

1   Evidence of the Jewish custom of releasing a prisoner at Passover is found in other Jewish writings of the period. See Chavel, "The Releasing of a Prisoner on the Eve of Passover."

than Jesus. They asked for another prisoner in Roman custody, a man named Barabbas.

"'Will you have me release for you the King of the Jews?' They cried out again, 'Not this man, but Barabbas!' Now Barabbas was a robber" (John 18:39–40).

The evangelist describes Barabbas as a "bandit" or "robber," but he was not an ordinary highway thief. The same Greek word *lēstēs* was also used for revolutionary bandits or guerrilla warriors. Mark confirmed this when he described Barabbas as one of a group imprisoned for having committed murder in an insurrection. Matthew described him as "notorious," indicating that Barabbas was well-known, perhaps the leader of a gang of religious and political fanatics intent on freeing the nation from Roman rule (John 18:40; Mark 15:7; Matt. 27:16).

Neither Roman nor Jewish officials would ordinarily have considered releasing Barabbas. Certainly not Pilate, since Barabbas had probably murdered Roman soldiers. The Jewish authorities worked hand in glove with Rome. Their power, wealth, and influence depended on stability, and they consistently opposed dangerous and destabilizing revolutionaries like Barabbas. But to the Sanhedrin, Jesus was a far greater threat than Barabbas. Pilate had not suggested Barabbas, would not have wanted to release him, and never anticipated that Barabbas would be chosen over Jesus.

"So when they had gathered, Pilate said to them, 'Whom do you want me to release for you, Barabbas or Jesus who is called Christ?'" (Matt. 27:17). Saint John Chrysostom remarks on the bizarre, convoluted order of events and the reversal of roles among the parties. Usually, the people ask for a prisoner to be released, and the judge decides whether to release him. But here, the judge is suggesting the release and asking the people to decide which prisoner to let go.[2] Since Pilate had undoubtedly learned of Jesus' enthusiastic welcome into the city of Jerusalem just days before, perhaps he was confident that Jesus' popularity would lead to his release.

---

2   Chrysostom, Homily 86, *Homilies on Matthew*, NPNF-1, 10:492.

Why the Crowd Asked for Barabbas

"NOW THE CHIEF PRIESTS AND the elders persuaded the people to ask for Barabbas and destroy Jesus" (Matt. 27:20). The Jewish leaders not only prompted the crowd to ask for Barabbas but actually generated the mob, ensuring the desired result.

By now the morning was underway, but it was still early enough in the day that most people were entirely unaware of the previous evening's momentous development: the arrest of Jesus of Nazareth. Arrested and condemned as a blasphemer by the Sanhedrin in the middle of the night, Jesus now awaited the judgment of Pilate. Friday was the day of preparation, the day before the Sabbath and, this year, also the day before Passover. It would have been a very busy day, full of final preparations. People scurried about, cleaning their homes, checking the ingredients for the supper, going to the marketplace, preparing the meal, confirming who would be coming to their homes for the feast and who would be taking the lamb to the Temple.

The chief priests also had important duties, tasks, and responsibilities to fulfill at the Temple. Their effort to ensure the execution of Jesus prior to Passover was taking longer than anticipated. No doubt some members of the Sanhedrin delegation had returned to the Temple while Pilate dragged his feet. Thousands of people would be bringing their lambs for sacrifice that very afternoon. Hundreds of priests must be coordinated, tools and other implements sharpened, organized, and readied. The Levite choir must be rehearsed and instruments tuned. Supplies of wood, water, incense, and bowls must be checked and the Temple guard duly prepared for crowd control.

What Jew would be simply loitering outside the praetorium on a Friday morning, especially on the eve of Passover? If indeed a random, unbiased crowd had been asked to decide between Barabbas and Jesus, the crowd might have asked for Jesus. But at that moment most people were bustling about in the city below preparing for the feast. Who knew that Jesus was in Roman custody and facing the death penalty? Even the disciples may not have known exactly where Jesus was at that moment. They did not know that he was already held before Pilate and that they should assemble to shout for his release. Certainly the crowd that had welcomed Jesus as the Messiah the previous Sunday morning did not know.

Who knew where Jesus was and what was about to take place? Only the high priest, chief priests, and members of the Sanhedrin. Only they knew where Jesus was and that Pilate was going to release one prisoner of the crowd's choosing. They were in a perfect position to control the outcome since the Temple, their domain where they wielded their power, stood just a few hundred yards away from the praetorium. As Pilate delayed, the chief priests generated the crowd, easily summoning friends and supporters from the Temple precincts nearby to rally in the Court of the Gentiles below the Antonia Fortress and shout for Barabbas.

"The governor again said to them, 'Which of the two do you want me to release for you?' And they said, 'Barabbas'" (Matt 27:21). Some Jews would have supported Barabbas regardless of whether the chief priests had prompted the crowd to ask for him. His crime against the Romans was an act of Jewish patriotism. Those who advocated rebellion against Rome would have considered Barabbas a heroic figure, even more so than Jesus, who told people to "turn the other cheek" and "love your enemies." The irony of the demand for Barabbas was not lost on the evangelists. The Hebrew word *bar* means "son" and *abba* is the word for "father," so Barabbas literally means "son of the father." The true Son of the Father was rejected in favor of a counterfeit, one who bore the name Barabbas but was not in fact the Son of the Father.

Pilate was stymied by an outcome he had not anticipated. His plan to release Jesus without humiliating the Jewish authorities had backfired. He had suggested the prisoner release and allowed the crowd to choose, and now he was forced to release Barabbas. But even the release of Barabbas did not require that Jesus be executed. Pilate was forced to release a criminal, but he still had an innocent man in custody.

> Pilate said to them, "Then what shall I do with Jesus, who is called Christ?" They all said, "Let him be crucified." And he said, "Why, what evil has he done?" But they shouted all the more, "Let him be crucified." (Matt. 27:22–23)

The fact that Pilate asks the crowd, "But what shall I do with Jesus?" suggests that he was surprised and unprepared for them to ask for Barabbas. He was even more bewildered when the crowd demanded the crucifixion of Jesus, the worst possible punishment, for no apparent reason. Pilate asks, "Why? What evil has he done?" It is unimaginable that an unbiased crowd would call for the crucifixion of Jesus with no basis or motivation.

Jesus was a well-known and popular figure, and the general public held no animosity toward him. He had healed thousands, and his was an inspirational voice that called for common sense and moderation in keeping the Law rather than strictness and severity. He gave the people hope, reassured them of God's love, and cared about them. He embraced the poor and accepted repentant sinners while openly criticizing the greedy elite, corrupt rulers, and hypocritical religious leadership. Why would a random crowd of typical Jews call for him to be crucified? They would not.

A worn-out and inane theme of too many Christian sermons on Good/ Great Friday has been to highlight the supposed fickleness of the Jewish people. A typical comment is, "On Sunday, the crowd hailed Jesus as the Messiah, but on Friday they shouted, 'Crucify him!'" But that cliché is unfair and completely nonsensical. The crowd that assembled outside the praetorium that morning did not consist of the same people who had welcomed Jesus into the city five days earlier. Instead, the Jewish authorities who controlled the Temple Mount could quickly create and control a crowd when everyone else in the city below was preparing for Passover. This was no arbitrary cross-section of ordinary inhabitants or visitors to Jerusalem. The populace had no motivation to call for Jesus' death, let alone by crucifixion, with such vitriol and animosity.

Pilate was stunned. The crowd had chosen Barabbas, and Pilate compounded the mistake by asking, "Then what shall I do with Jesus who is called Christ?" They all said, "Let him be crucified," shouting the words repeatedly.

Pilate was still not prepared to yield to their demands. He would have to be forced to crucify Jesus, and that would require nothing less than blackmail.

CHAPTER 21

The Sentencing

T HE RELENTLESS CROWD PERSISTED, EVEN demanding the crucifixion. Irritated and frustrated by Pilate's unwillingness to sentence
Jesus to death, the religious authorities finally expressed the *true* reason they
had condemned Jesus to death: he claimed to be God.

> The Jews answered him, "We have a law, and by that law he ought to die,
> because he has made himself the Son of God." When Pilate heard these words,
> he was more afraid; he entered the praetorium again and said to Jesus, "Where
> are you from?" But Jesus gave no answer. (John 19:7–9)

Pilate's misgivings were confirmed, and his previous apprehension now
became fear. Could Jesus be a *god*? Pilate had already scourged Jesus, who had
spoken earlier of a Kingdom "not of this world." Now Pilate was alarmed and
confronted Jesus: "Where—are—you—*from*?"

All four Gospels depict Pilate as reluctant to crucify Jesus, a depiction dismissed and even criticized today by many modern interpreters as unrealistic and unhistorical. Critics presume that Pilate's reluctance cannot possibly
have been authentic; they explain it as a transparent attempt by the evangelists to curry favor with Roman authorities and place blame for the death of
Christ on the Jews alone. But the early Christians had no motive to blame the
death of Jesus on anyone, either on the Jews or on the Romans. And from the

beginning and to this day, the Church has acknowledged Pilate's historical role: Christ "was crucified under Pontius Pilate."

A Roman governor was completely within his rights to release an accused, and in fact this actually happened.[1] Nonetheless, the relationship between the Christians and the Roman state would have been no different, even if the Gospels had portrayed the Jews as the sole responsible party, or the Romans had not been involved with the death of Christ.

Christians were persecuted not because they blamed Romans for the death of Jesus but because they refused to worship the emperor and the Roman gods. Furthermore, Romans would not have been offended by a governor being accused of executing an alleged criminal. In fact, the opposite is true. Romans would have been annoyed by the Gospel portrayal of Pilate's hesitation. Roman culture was harsh, violent, and brutal. They expected Roman governors to treat accused criminals severely. The evangelists had no motivation to soften Pilate's personality or to minimize his involvement in the death of Jesus.

Others say the Gospel depiction of Pilate's efforts to avoid crucifying Jesus is not accurate or truthful because Pilate had a reputation for dealing harshly with people accused of crimes. But Pilate had never before put anyone on trial who claimed to be the Son of God. Jesus' dignified demeanor and unusual responses made Pilate wonder whether the claim just might be true. Greek and Roman culture were replete with stories of gods coming to earth, appearing as ordinary people. For the Romans, these tales were not mythology but reality. Pilate had tried and condemned hundreds of people, but he had never encountered any prisoner like Jesus. Ordinarily, defendants would vehemently deny committing the crime, beg for mercy, or argue passionately that their lives be spared. Others would hire an orator to plead their case or even offer Pilate a bribe. Jesus did none of those things. Suspects accused of insurrection might be fearful, angry, spiteful, hateful, contemptuous, cocky,

---

1   About thirty years later an ordinary farmer, ironically also named Jesus, began to lament unceasingly and predict the imminent destruction of the Temple. At first he was ignored, but the Jewish leaders eventually became so irritated by him they brought him before the Roman governor, Albinus (procurator from 62 to 64), who scourged him and then released him. Josephus, JW 6.300–309.

or defiant. Jesus was calm, peaceful, dignified, self-assured, and composed. And now the Sanhedrin admitted that this unusual prisoner was deserving of death for claiming to be the Son of God. Pilate was genuinely alarmed by the possibility.[2]

Three strong reasons explain why Pilate sought to release Jesus: First, Jesus was clearly not a threat to the general order, since Pilate had never heard of him and no testimony or evidence had been brought forward that he was fomenting rebellion. Second, Jesus had not committed any crime under Roman law. Regardless of the Sanhedrin's private motivation, Pilate could not execute anyone for violating Jewish law. Third, Jesus might be a god. The Sanhedrin rejected that notion, but Pilate preferred not to take any chances.

Now Pilate looked intently at Jesus: "Where are you from?" But Jesus did not reply. His silent nobility and calm decorum must have absolutely unnerved Pilate. He questioned Jesus again, but Jesus remained silent. Pilate must have thought, "This is not normal behavior. This . . . is . . . *bizarre*." He wanted nothing further to do with this case, but Jesus wasn't helping the situation by his lack of cooperation. Pilate momentarily forgot his trepidation. Unaccustomed to the slightest sign of impudence, Pilate became annoyed by Jesus' silence.

"Pilate therefore said to him, 'You will not speak to me? Do you not know that I have power to release you, and power to crucify you?'" (John 19:10–12). "Why isn't this man trying to save himself?" Pilate must have wondered. "Can't he see that I want to *help* him?! Yes, Jesus has been scourged, but he does not have to be crucified!" Pilate reminded Jesus of his power, the absolute power of life and death over everyone in the province: "Do you not know that I have power to release you, and power to crucify you?"

---

2   One example is a famous Greek myth well known from an ancient Greek tragedy penned by Euripides in his play *The Bacchae*, c. 400 BC. Pentheus, the king of Thebes, mistreated the god Dionysus, who had come to earth appearing as a man. Later, Dionysus exacted a terrible revenge against Pentheus. Pilate probably knew the story, or if not, knew of similar stories among the Romans about gods who appeared as ordinary people. Romans would expect that a god who was mistreated would later avenge himself. One argument raised against the divinity of Christ by pagans was that nothing bad happened to Pilate after crucifying Jesus.

Jesus said to him, "'You would have no power over me unless it had been given you from above; therefore he who delivered me to you has the greater sin'" (John 19:10–11). Jesus' response only further alarmed Pilate. What an amazing statement! The one holding the imperium, embodying the power of the emperor himself, in fact has no real power at all. Pilate can exercise power over Jesus only because he has been given power by one higher than the emperor: the Power above. No one had ever dared speak to Pilate like that before.

What did Jesus mean by "he who delivered me to you has the greater sin"? This comment is obscure. It may refer to Judas, the traitor, but most interpreters think this refers to Caiaphas, who had sent Jesus to Pilate to administer the death penalty. If Caiaphas has the "greater sin," this means Pilate is not without sin and will not be entirely absolved of responsibility.

Pilate is startled and shaken by the answer, and more determined than ever to have nothing to do with Jesus, just as his wife had advised earlier. But how?

Pilate Is Coerced

"Upon this Pilate sought to release him, but the Jews cried out, 'If you release this man, you are not Caesar's friend; every one who makes himself a king sets himself against Caesar'" (John 19:12). The Sanhedrin now played its trump card. With these words they terminated any further efforts on Pilate's part to release Jesus.

Pilate had been convinced from the beginning that Jesus had not committed a Roman crime. Although Jesus confessed to being a king, he said his Kingdom is "not of this world." The chief priests admitted that they thought Jesus deserved to die because he had claimed to be the Son of God. Every sign pointed to the fact that Jesus was in fact a god. But now Pilate was being forced to crucify Jesus because the chief priests were threatening to denounce him to Caesar.

"Friend of Caesar" (*amicus Caesaris*) was a title of honor given to leading men of Rome, and Pilate probably held that title.[3] He had governed Judea for

---

3   This idea dated back to earlier Hellenistic eras when an inner circle of supporters who

several years. Clearly he had Tiberius Caesar's trust. But like most emperors, Tiberius was notoriously suspicious and dealt ruthlessly with anyone suspected of disloyalty. Pilate may have attained the coveted title Friend of Caesar, and possibly additional favors, through the efforts of a highly influential Roman named Lucius Aelius Sejanus. The Roman historian Tacitus wrote, "Whoever was close to Sejanus had a claim on the friendship of Caesar."[4]

But Tiberius had recently removed Sejanus and his supporters from power and executed them on a charge of treason. Regardless of the relationship between Sejanus and Pilate, Caiaphas and the chief priests would have known about this development in Roman politics. Now they used it effectively to force Pilate to execute Jesus by threatening to portray Pilate as disloyal to Caesar. It was a curious twist: the man who represented Rome because he was a loyal Friend of Caesar would now be accused of not supporting Caesar by men who represented a nation that passionately hated and despised Caesar. Pilate was fuming as they forced him to do what he had not wished to do. He understood exactly what they were threatening and concluded that he had no choice: it would be either Jesus' life or his own. The effectiveness of this final tactic is proven by the fact that Pilate immediately succumbed to their demand.

> When Pilate heard these words, he brought Jesus out and sat down on the judgment seat at a place called The Pavement, and in Hebrew, Gabbatha. Now it was the day of Preparation of the Passover; it was about the sixth hour. (John 19:13–14)

---

had the trust and confidence of the king were given authority by him. The Romans adopted this Greek concept and terminology. But the term could also refer simply to the official representative of the emperor. Brown, *Gospel of John*, 2:879.

4   *Annals* 6.8. Sejanus was an equestrian by birth and had risen to become quite influential and head of the praetorian guard in Rome. But when Tiberius suspected him of disloyalty, Sejanus was executed, on October 18, AD 31. Sejanus is also known historically as a rabid anti-Semite who engaged in repressive measures against Jews in Alexandria (Philo, *Delegation to Gaius*, in *Works*, 159–61).

The location identified as The Pavement, or Gabbatha, has never been conclusively established.[5] The chief priests must have smiled with smug satisfaction when they saw Pilate ascend to the judgment seat.[6] They knew they had won at last. They knew Pilate had taken the judgment seat because he was about to sentence Jesus to death.

The irony is extraordinary: the Creator and King of all, he who will judge the living and the dead, has been rejected, judged, and condemned by his own creatures.

The Jewish Leaders and Crowd Blaspheme God

JESUS WAS STILL STANDING THERE in a pool of his own blood. The spiky crown of thorns embedded in his skull projected around his head like the glow of an imperial diadem. The blood-soaked burgundy robe stuck to his wounds. The entire sight was a macabre parody of kingly glory.

Pilate was seething with anger, furious with the Jewish leaders. He had suggested the prisoner release out of sensitivity to their situation, to avoid embarrassing them by releasing Jesus outright, but now the Sanhedrin had humiliated him. The chief priests were ungrateful. They had prevailed over Pilate, and everyone knew it. Pilate would comply with their extortion. He would do what they demanded. But he would make them pay for it. He would humiliate them as they had humiliated him. Now Pilate gestured toward Jesus, a gory

---

5   Two stone pavements have been unearthed at the Antonia Fortress in the course of archeological excavations, but the exact site of Gabbatha remains unknown. The word seems to have been a generic term that could apply to various types of stone pavements. Brown, *Gospel of John,* 2:881.

6   Some people have argued that the biblical text here is ambiguous. In Greek it literally reads, "Pilate hearing these words brought Jesus out and he sat down upon the judgment seat." Some commentators suggest that Pilate brought Jesus out and had *Jesus* sit on the judgment seat, because "he" could refer back to either Pilate or Jesus. It is a tantalizing image full of irony: Jesus with his crown and robe seated on the judgment seat as if on a throne, a fitting parody of kingship. But Jesus did not sit on Pilate's judgment seat. The verse was never understood that way by the early Church, and such an interpretation is not part of the patristic tradition. If John intended to suggest that or if that had actually happened, that detail would have come down to us through early Church tradition. Pilate had to pronounce judgment from the judgment seat, so he was the one who took the seat, not Jesus.

caricature of royalty, and mocked the Jewish establishment. "He said to the Jews, 'Behold your King!' They cried out, 'Away with him, away with him, crucify him!'"

Pilate's response was laden with sarcasm and contempt: "Shall I crucify your King?"

But the reply of the chief priests and their minions is shocking. Perhaps they were so determined to put Jesus to death that nothing else mattered at the moment. Their response was utter blasphemy and overflowed with hypocrisy: "The chief priests answered, 'We have no king but Caesar.'"

Once again, unexpectedly and unintentionally, the truth was spoken, but the implication of their words was shattering: they had rejected God. They had openly apostatized. To recognize anyone other than God as king, especially the Caesars, was blasphemy, not only because God alone can truly be king of Israel, but because Roman emperors were worshipped, and blasphemous titles of divinity were given to Caesars. But the assembled crowd not only publicly called Caesar king, but their only king: "We have no king but Caesar." Unwittingly, they had spoken the truth. Caesar was their king, since they had rejected the King of heaven, the Son whom the Father had sent. They had convicted Jesus on a charge of blasphemy, but they were the ones guilty of blasphemy now. They had broken the covenant and renounced their relationship to God as his chosen people. This was an especially poignant moment since the Feast of Passover recalled God's deliverance of his people and their unique and exclusive relationship.

The biblical prophecies, the responsibilities of the religious leaders, the messianic hopes of their people—all were ignored in order to ensure that Jesus was crucified. This was necessary that they might preserve their wealth, positions, and political power. A crowd was generated, instructed to call for Barabbas and to insist on Jesus' crucifixion. That this entire outcome was orchestrated by the religious authorities is confirmed by the extreme malice the crowd expressed: it demanded that Jesus be crucified. Many Jews had died under Roman occupation, and most Jews would have been quite disinclined to give the Romans yet another victim. Ordinary Jews had no malice toward Jesus, no motivation to demand his crucifixion.

The frenzied crowd was becoming uncontrollable. The sole purpose of the prisoner release was to dissipate tension and generate goodwill, to prevent a riot or rebellion. But a riot was about to occur if Pilate did not quickly succumb to the demand of the impassioned mob. He had done everything he could, but his foremost responsibility was to maintain order, and his foremost concern was to preserve his own life and position. It would be either Jesus or himself. He could only hope that Jesus was not a god in disguise.

The Blood Curse

PILATE LITERALLY WASHED HIS HANDS of the matter. Chrysostom observes that Pilate had consistently proclaimed Christ's innocence, and now he pronounced himself innocent. [7] "So when Pilate saw that he was gaining nothing, but rather that a riot was beginning, he took water and washed his hands before the crowd, saying, 'I am innocent of this man's blood; see to it yourselves'" (Matt. 27:24).

When Pilate said "See to it yourselves," he was not suggesting that the Jews themselves could physically crucify Jesus. He meant that although a contingent of Roman soldiers would carry out the execution on their behalf, he was not responsible. Pilate washed his hands to symbolically express that he did not agree with the death sentence. Both pagans and Jews were very concerned about being held responsible for shedding innocent blood and tried to distance themselves from it. [8]

But if Pilate did not want to take responsibility for the death of Jesus, the Jewish authorities gladly would. Roman law was irrelevant. Their law demanded that a false prophet or anyone who claimed to be the Son of God must be put to death. To emphasize their acceptance of responsibility, the

---

7   Chrysostom, Homily 84, *Homilies on the Gospel of John*, FOTC 41:419.
8   Deut. 21:6–9. Sophocles, *Ajax*, 774–54; Herodotus, *The Histories*, 1.35.1; Virgil, *Aeneid*, 2.717–18. When the Prophet Jeremiah was sentenced to death unjustly, he warned the people that by putting him to death, they would bring innocent blood upon themselves and their city (Jer. 26:15). They decided not to kill him because he had spoken to them in the name of the Lord. Jeremiah was sentenced to death for predicting the destruction of Solomon's Temple and was eventually killed by his fellow Jews in Egypt—stoned to death, according to Jewish tradition. *Jewish Encyclopedia*, s.v. "Jeremiah."

crowd called down a curse on themselves and their children. This has historically been called "the blood curse" or the "blood libel": "And all the people
answered, 'His blood be on us and on our children'" (Matt. 27:25).

Chrysostom was shocked by the statement but emphasized that God did
not accept the curse, either on their children or on themselves. Many Jews
came to faith in Christ after the crucifixion. "All the people answered" means
that those present spoke as a group, not that the entire Jewish race was cursed
by this statement, not even their children. God will judge each of us individually for whatever wrongs we commit, and children are not held responsible for
the sins of their parents. God would never allow that, because he loves humanity, and Christ came for the Jewish people first of all.[9]

The Lord forgave the disciples for abandoning him and Peter for denying him. No doubt he would have forgiven Judas too, if he had repented and
sought forgiveness, since there is nothing that God will not forgive. "His
blood be on us and on our children" should never be misunderstood as a curse
on all the Jewish people, either then or today. The Fathers of the Church did
not interpret it in that manner either.

> See here too their great madness . . . you curse yourselves; why do you draw
> down the curse upon your children also? Nevertheless, the Lover of Mankind,
> though they acted with so much madness, both against themselves and against
> their children, so far from confirming their sentence upon their children, did
> not even confirm it on them, but from the one and from the other received
> those that repented, and counts them worthy of good things beyond number.
> For indeed Paul was of them, and the thousands that believed in Jerusalem.[10]

But the statement, "His blood be on us and on our children," has an even
deeper, paradoxical significance. Forgiveness in Judaism occurred by shedding the blood of a sacrificial animal offered to God. By taking responsibility

---

9   "I have come for the lost sheep of the house of Israel" (Matt. 15:24). The same Gospel
     that reports this shocking statement, "His blood be on us and on our children," intro-
     duced the birth of Christ by explaining the meaning of his name, Jesus: "For he will save
     his people from their sins" (Matt. 1:21).
10   Chrysostom, Homily 86, *Homilies on Matthew*, NPNF-1, 10:494.

for the death of Christ, the crowd ironically speaks the truth without realizing it: his blood will be upon them, for it will be shed for the remission of their sins. The plan of God for salvation is at work, even though they appear to be rejecting it.

Chrysostom has no sympathy for Pilate, who had "surrendered himself over completely to the interests of this life." Pilate would not be heroic. He would not choose to do the right thing, even though his wife's dream concerned him, and even though Jesus' demeanor and statements had terrified him. "On the contrary, nothing influenced him for the better, nor was he moved at all by unworldly considerations, but handed Christ over to them."[11]

The Sixth Hour

PILATE ASCENDED THE JUDGMENT SEAT to condemn Jesus to death. The Evangelist John notes the precise moment the sentence was pronounced. The day and hour hold great significance for Jesus' purpose and sacrifice. "Now it was the day of Preparation of the Passover; it was about the sixth hour" (John 19:14).

John described Jesus as the "Lamb of God," but the profound meaning of that description only now becomes apparent. The "sixth hour" was twelve noon. On that day and at that hour, Jews began assembling at the Temple with their paschal lambs. The plan of salvation would soon culminate in the perfect sacrifice of the Lamb of God.

---

11   Chrysostom, Homily 85, *Homilies on the Gospel of John*, FOTC 41:428.

PART III

The Cross

CHAPTER 22

Crucifixion: Stigma and Spectacle

The History of Crucifixion

THE ROMAN ORATOR CICERO DESCRIBED crucifixion as "the cruel-
est and most disgusting penalty" and "the extreme and ultimate punishment of slaves."[1] Crucifixion means "fixed to a cross," from the Latin verb *cru-
ciare*, "to torture" or "to torment." Originally, people were literally affixed to
trees, which is one reason the cross is sometimes poetically referred to as "the
tree."[2] Later, actual crosses were constructed for executions. Crucifixion was
specifically designed to be painful, slow, and humiliating.

Crucifixion was not invented by the Romans. It reportedly originated in
Persia in the sixth century BC, but a wide variety of foreign nations that the
Romans considered barbarians used it: Indians, Assyrians, Scythians, Celts,
Germani, Brittani, Numidians, and especially the Carthaginians, from whom
the Romans likely learned it.

Although crucifixion was not a typical Greek penalty, the Greeks employed
it too.[3] Both Greek and Roman historians stressed that crucifixion came from
"barbarians." Associating it with foreigners implied that it was appropriate for
barbaric people, namely slaves and foreigners, which in many instances were

---

1   *Against Verres* 2.5.165 and 2.5.169 respectively. Gaius Verres, the Roman governor of
    Sicily, crucified a Roman citizen, an illegal and inappropriate act. This inspired Cicero's
    speech denouncing Verres.
2   The Greek word for "wood" and "tree" is the same: *xylon*.
3   Hengel, *Crucifixion*, 22–23.

one and the same, since slaves were acquired by conquering other nations. The Romans considered themselves models of nobility, distinction, and justice, but their self-image was incongruous with the violence and cruelty by which Rome retained power. They attempted to distance themselves from crucifixion by identifying it as barbaric, but the Romans perfected it, proliferated it, and made it infamous. Crucifixion became identified with ancient Rome more than with any other culture.

Crucifixion was so abominable that few literary descriptions of it exist.[4] We can gather some information about the Roman practice of crucifixion from references scattered throughout various genres of ancient writing. In spite of their brevity, the Gospels provide more details of the process than almost any other ancient source. Ancient authors came from the educated upper class and considered themselves too refined and cultured to describe crucifixion. It was gruesome, unbefitting an aristocratic author, and inappropriate for polite society and sophisticated circles, where lofty topics of conversation were preferred. Furthermore, virtually everyone had witnessed crucifixions; therefore, no description was necessary.

Crucifixion took a variety of forms. One could be nailed or tied to a tree, to a wooden cross, or even to a simple upright stake.[5] Regardless of the instrument, the purpose was always to subject the individual to the greatest possible degree of pain and humiliation. Crucifixion was reserved for the lowest offenders of society, those who did not deserve to die with even a shred of dignity.

Roman legal digests and ancient authors who discuss criminal penalties always listed crucifixion first as the supreme punishment, the *summa supplicia*.[6] Often the specific word "crucifixion" is not used, but it is implied and recognized as the worst punishment.[7] Greek sources also sometimes

---

4   Hengel, *Crucifixion*, 38.

5   Hengel, *Crucifixion*, 24. In addition to the word "cross" (*stauros*), other terms are used to refer to the implement of crucifixion, including *skolpos* ("stake") and *xylon* ("tree"). Brown, *Death of the Messiah*, 2:945n23.

6   For example, Paulus, *Sententiae*, 5.17.2; Minucius Felix, *Octavius*, 9.4; Lucan, *De Bello Civili*, 10.365. See Hengel, *Crucifixion*, 33–34.

7   The Roman jurist Ulpianus comments on punishment for those who falsify gold coins: "Persons who, on the one hand, shave down gold coins or on the other hand wash [with

describe crucifixion as *anōtato timōria* or *kolasis* ("highest punishment"). The second worst punishment in the Roman Empire was *crematio* (burning alive). The aggravated death penalty ranked third worst varies between *decollatio* (beheading) or *damnatio ad bestias* (being given over to beasts). In the latter case, the victim was tied to a post, and hungry wild animals were let loose upon him to eat him alive.[8]

The philosopher Seneca expressed the common Roman opinion that no punishment surpassed crucifixion:

> Can anyone be found who would prefer wasting away in pain dying limb by limb, or letting out his life drop by drop, rather than expiring once for all? Can any man be found willing to be fastened to an accursed tree, long sickly, already deformed, swelling with ugly weals on the shoulders and chest, and drawing the breath of life amid long, drawn out agony?[9]

Initially crucifixion was exclusively a punishment for slaves and for soldiers guilty of desertion or insubordination. The large slave population and the necessity to maintain discipline among soldiers required a punishment sufficiently horrific as to inspire absolute obedience and discourage any thought of revolt, desertion, or insubordination. Crucifixion never lost its association as a slave punishment (*servile supplicium*). Since slaves were frequently charged with theft or rebellion, eventually that penalty expanded to include robbers, traitors, rebels, the poor, and anyone of low social status—*humiliores*—especially foreigners, the peregrini. Crucifixion was rarely applied to the upper

---

gilt] or cast [other coins], if they are freemen should be thrown to the beasts, if slaves, sentenced to the extreme penalty." Ulpianus, *Digest of Justinian*, 48.10.8, 4:339.

8   Hengel, *Crucifixion*, 33–34. Christian martyrs suffered all these punishments. Throwing someone to the beasts was usually reserved for the entertainment of the masses and was carried out only when festivities were already planned or underway and wild beasts were available. Hengel, 35. When Polycarp, Bishop of Smyrna, was arrested, the crowd in the arena called for his execution by wild beasts, but none were available. Therefore, the crowd demanded his execution by being burned alive. *Martyrdom of Polycarp*, 12. Crucifixion was worse, but it was slow and held no crowd appeal unless wild animals were available to tear the crucified man to pieces while the spectators watched.

9   Seneca, *Epistle* 101 to Lucilius; Hengel, *Crucifixion*, 30–31.

class, the *honestiores*.[10] It was finally ended by Constantine the Great, who regarded hanging as more humane because it caused death almost instantly.[11]

Social Status and Crucifixion

CRUCIFIXION WAS CONSIDERED SO DEGRADING that to crucify a Roman citizen was to disgrace the Roman Empire itself.[12] By the first century, crucifixion had become the standard form of execution for anyone who was not a Roman citizen. Since citizenship was rare, almost everyone feared this punishment.[13]

The cross was the classic, prototypical slave punishment because slaves would always be regarded as *hostes*, enemies, since they were acquired through war and came from the vanquished population.[14] The slave population was quite sizable, and fear of a slave rebellion or the murder of a master by his slave was considerable. Crucifixion ranked as the most effective deterrent against slave revolt.[15] The master of the house had absolute power over his slaves, including the right to scourge them to death or to crucify them without any restrictions or involvement by civil authorities.[16] A cruel master might even crucify a slave on a whim,[17] and slaves often pessimistically resigned themselves to this grim fate.

---

10   J. Collins, "Exegetical Notes," 155; Hengel, *Crucifixion*, 51.
11   Hengel, *Crucifixion*, 29.
12   Sometimes even Roman citizens were crucified, although any official who ordered this could be subject to serious criminal prosecution himself.
13   Toward the end of the pagan Roman Empire, the situation deteriorated to the extent that citizens often faced crucifixion when previously that would have been unthinkable. J. Collins, "Exegetical Notes," 156. But even after all inhabitants of the empire were granted citizenship in AD 212, punishments were still aggravated or diminished on the basis of social class. Carucci, "The Spectacle of Justice in the Roman Empire," 222.
14   Aubert, "Double Standard," 129.
15   If a master was murdered, all the slaves of the household were crucified. Hengel, *Crucifixion*, 59. Romans lived in such fear of their slaves that if a slave consulted an astrologer about his master's future, the sentence of crucifixion was to be imposed. Paulus, *Sententiae* 5.21.3ff. Hengel, *Crucifixion*, 59.
16   J. Collins, "Exegetical Notes," 156.
17   Hengel, *Crucifixion*, 60.

In one Latin play, a slave threatened with crucifixion is told, "I think that in that self-same position you will have to die outside the gates, when, with hands outstretched, you will be carrying your cross." The slave's sober response is matter-of-fact: "I know that the cross will prove my tomb; there are laid my forefathers, my father, grandfather, great-grandfather, great-great-grandfather."[18]

The city of Rome had a specific location for the punishment of slaves, the Campus Esquilinus.[19] Horace referred to the vulture as "the Esquiline bird" because everyone had seen vultures and other animals consuming the rotting corpses of crucified victims there.[20] Without a doubt, for every city in the Roman Empire a similar location existed, where the decaying remains of the crucified were displayed on the highways leading into the city.[21]

Crucifixion was employed to discourage or quell rebellion in the provinces,[22] and common thieves, pirates, highway robbers, and rebels typically suffered this punishment. Since criminals were often runaway slaves, the punishment was considered especially appropriate. The general populace was not sympathetic toward the condemned. Provincial inhabitants were grateful when the seas, roads, and towns were liberated from the danger posed by robbers, especially those who attacked travelers. Their crucifixions provided some satisfaction to crime victims and also served to deter others.[23] For this

---

18 *Miles Gloriosus* (The Braggart Captain), in *The Comedies of Titus Maccius Plautus*, 2 vols., Henry Thomas Riley, trans. (London: G. Bell and Sons, 1912), 1:88. See also Hengel, *Crucifixion*, 52.

19 Tacitus, *Annals*, 15.60.1, and *Annals*, 2.32.2. The Esquiline Hill later became a high-class neighborhood, but during the first century BC, the plain surrounding the hill lay outside the city and served as a cemetery and also a place of execution.

20 Juvenal wrote, "The vulture hurries from dead cattle and dogs and crosses to bring some of the carrion to her offspring." *Satires*, 14.77.

21 Except among Jews, since leaving a body unburied was not permitted by Jewish law.

22 When Herod the Great died (4 BC), some Jews saw an opportunity for freedom, and a revolt broke out. It was suppressed by the Roman legate Quintilius Varus, who crucified 2,000 people. When the Jews rebelled against the Romans during the Jewish War (AD 66–73), the Roman army surrounded the city of Jerusalem and put it under siege for three years. After Titus, the general in charge, conquered the city, thousands of Jews were crucified, "their number so great that there was not enough room for the crosses and not enough crosses for the bodies." Josephus, *JW* 5.449–51. See also Hengel, *Crucifixion*, 26; J. Collins, "Exegetical Notes," 155.

23 Hengel, *Crucifixion*, 47.

reason, the crucified were displayed prominently in a public location outside the city.[24] "Whenever we crucify the guilty, the most crowded roads are chosen, where the most people can see and be moved by this fear. For penalties relate not so much to the retribution as to their exemplary effect."[25]

Roman society emphasized distinctions between social classes, and great importance was placed on personal glory, respect, and receiving public honors. Punishment according to social status was not only widely accepted but defended as rational and appropriate. Inequality under Roman law was guaranteed. Pliny the Younger praised his friend Calestius Tiro, a provincial governor, for preserving distinctions in class and social status while administering justice in his province:

> I cannot restrain myself from sounding as if I were proffering advice when I mean to praise you for the way you preserve the distinction of class and rank; if they are thrown in confusion and disorder and mixed up, nothing is more unequal than the same equality.[26]

Even after all inhabitants of the empire were given citizenship, distinctions in punishment between high-class and low-class citizens remained. A wealthy woman condemned for attempted murder was exiled, but her slave was crucified. "Riches buy off judgment and the poor are condemned to the cross."[27] Slaves were always in the most precarious position, forced to navigate difficult and complex relationships with no legal protection whatsoever. They were expected to be loyal both to their masters and to the Roman state. A slave who

---

24   The most famous Roman slave rebellion, led by Spartacus (73–71 BC), was crushed by Pompey, who crucified 6,000 slaves and lined the Appian Way from Rome to Capua with their crosses. J. Collins, "Exegetical Notes," 156. This means that about twenty-five crucified slaves were displayed per mile, on both sides of the road, for the entire distance of 120 miles.

25   Quintilian, *Declamationes Quae Supersunt CXLV* 274, Constantin Ritter, ed. (Leipzig: B.G. Teubner, 1884), 124. Translation in Hengel, *Crucifixion*, 50n14.

26   Pliny the Younger, *Epistle*, 9.5.

27   *Anthologia Latina*, 794.35. Translation in Hengel, *Crucifixion*, 60n15.

reported his master for treason might be praised and rewarded for loyalty to the state and subsequently crucified for being an informant.[28]

The Social Stigma of the Cross

IN A SOCIETY THAT ESTEEMED glory, honor, and personal reputation above all, where slaves occupied the lowest rung of the social ladder, assigning a slave's punishment to someone who was not a slave was an intentional act of debasement. Crucifixion of free persons was "a conscious attempt to treat them as slaves and implied for the victim a total loss of legal status (*capitis deminutio maxima*)."[29] The condemned were crucified nude. In places such as Judea, where public nudity was forbidden under Jewish law, condemned criminals wore a loincloth. This was equivalent to being displayed and executed in one's underwear, a slight improvement over total nudity but nonetheless humiliating. The offender's nudity or near-nudity proclaimed his low status and added to his disgrace.

Clothing—its colors, style, fabric, and the stripes on a toga, including their number, color, and width—identified one's social class and status. Partial or complete public nudity visually presented the criminal as a barbarian, even if he was native born and not a slave. In other words, the condemned is represented as "other," a foreigner, one who does not belong, who does not conform to Roman values and society (or to Jewish values in the case of Jesus). He is isolated, displayed without the dignity of clothing, as one who has violated the law and is now literally exposed as a wrongdoer for all to see. Therefore, obviously (in the Jewish mind), all crucifixion victims were cursed by God himself.

Various additional elements added to the disgrace of public execution, effectively dehumanizing the condemned. When Tacitus described the first Roman persecution of Christians under Nero in the year 65, he specifically pointed to details that augmented the penalty:

28　Hengel, *Crucifixion*, 56–57.
29　Aubert, "Double Standard," 114.

And additional derision accompanied their end: they were covered with wild beasts' skins and torn to death by dogs; or they were fastened on crosses and, when daylight faded, were burned to serve as lamps by night.[30]

The "additional derision" (*addita ludibria*) was being torn to death by dogs in the arena, because the person was eaten by the animals and thus denied a burial. Romans considered remaining unburied—becoming food for dogs, birds of prey, and wild animals—to be the greatest degradation and ultimate humiliation. To be denied burial was among the most revolting and feared aspects of crucifixion, a prospect that filled the ancients with a horror modern people cannot fully appreciate. This feature of crucifixion served no purpose except deliberately to increase disgrace and dishonor. The Roman historian Livy described executions ordered by Pleminius during the Second Punic War, remarking that when the victims "had been mangled by every torment which a human body can endure, he put them to death and not satisfied with the penalty paid by the living, he cast them out unburied."[31]

Nothing was more shameful than the cross. Piso, the father-in-law of Julius Caesar, was serving as consul when he learned that Cicero, the famous states-man and orator, had been accused of violating the law. Because Piso refused to protect Cicero from the charges, he incurred the orator's hatred and invective. In one of his orations, Cicero fantasized about seeing Piso crucified, along with another notable Roman statesman, Gabinius: "If I were to see you and Gabinius fixed to a cross, would I feel a greater joy at the laceration of your bodies than I do at that of your reputations?"[32]

Cicero's comment reveals the Roman psyche, which was not content merely to execute by torture, but whose ultimate goal was the complete dis-grace and humiliation of the offender, even after death. That Cicero would derive as much pleasure from their loss of reputation as from their physical suffering illustrates the supreme importance of personal honor in Roman

---

30   Tacitus, *Annals*, 15.44.4. See Hengel, *Crucifixion*, 26.
31   Livy, *History of Rome from Its Foundation*, 29.9.10.
32   Cicero *in Pisonem*, 42. Translation in Hengel, *Crucifixion*, 31n23. While defeating a conspiracy against the Republic (the Catiline conspiracy), Cicero reportedly ordered the execution of some Roman citizens without a trial, a serious violation of law.

society and the threat crucifixion represented. Roman citizens might face exile and confiscation of all their property, but they found some consolation in not being subject to crucifixion. Wealthy Romans sentenced to death were often allowed to choose their manner of death, which was frequently suicide.[33]

In another speech, Cicero defended a Roman senator accused of treason against the unthinkable prospect of crucifixion, entreating that age and honor (citizenship) ought to "protect a man from flogging, from the executioner's hook and finally from the terrors of the cross." In fact, "the very word 'cross' should be far removed not only from the person of a Roman citizen but from his thoughts, his eyes and his ears . . . the expectation, indeed the very mention of them, that is unworthy of a Roman citizen and a free man."[34]

The extreme suffering, the loss of reputation, and the public debasement of crucifixion lent itself to a Roman curse that was discovered inscribed as graffiti on a wall in Pompeii: "Be crucified!"[35]

First-Century Jews and Crucifixion

CRUCIFIXION WAS NOT A JEWISH penalty, although it was occasionally employed by Jews.[36] The Mishnah lists four methods of execution: stoning,

---

33   Hengel, *Crucifixion*, 42. Even if a high-born Roman chose suicide (considered the dignified option and appropriate for his status), he might still face the shame of the cross. The last king of Rome (Tarquinius Superbus, d. c. 495 BC) crucified those who committed suicide. He "fastened the bodies of all who had died in this way to the cross to be seen by the citizens and to be torn by wild beasts and birds." Pliny the Elder, *Historia Naturalis*, 36.107. See Hengel, *Crucifixion*, 43. This shows that crucifixion was not merely a death penalty nor the worst punishment, but the definitive expression of loss of status, the ultimate humiliation.

34   Cicero, *Pro Rabirio*, 16. His client, Rabirio, was acquitted. Cicero appealed to the fears of the jury, who were likewise terrified at the prospect of crucifixion. Hengel, *Crucifixion*, 44.

35   *In cruce figarus!* This expressed a desire for the worst imaginable fate, equivalent to "Go to hell!" CIL. IV, 2082, Pompeii, strada di Olconio. Hengel, *Crucifixion*, 37. The cross was a "vulgar taunt among the lower classes" and "found on the lips of slaves and prostitutes." Hengel, 9. Another curse was *"in malam crucem!"* ("Go to the evil cross!")

36   The best-known example is Alexander Janneus, the Hasmonean king, who executed Jews by crucifixion. The Jewish historian Josephus gives several examples, referring to these "hangings" with the word *anastauroun* ("on the cross"). *Ant.* 13.14.2; *JW* 1.4.6. Fitzmyer, "Crucifixion," 505.

burning, slaying (by decapitation), and strangling.[37] Although it was rarely practiced by the Jews themselves, crucifixion carried the same, or even worse, stigma as other forms of capital punishment allowable under Jewish law. Furthermore, the Jewish definition of "hanging on a tree," which originally meant death by strangulation, during the Second Temple period came to include crucifixion. This is particularly relevant in the case of Jesus.[38]

> If a man has committed a crime punishable by death and he is put to death, and you hang him on a tree, his body shall not remain all night upon the tree, but you shall bury him the same day, for a hanged man is accursed by God; you shall not defile your land which the LORD your God gives you for an inheritance. (Deut. 21:22–23)

Long before any tensions developed between Jews and Christians that might prompt Jews to apply that passage to Jesus, first-century Jews regarded crucifixion as a hanging, which meant that Deuteronomy 21:22–23 applied.[39] The Sanhedrin was determined to have Jesus crucified because anyone who died by hanging was considered cursed by God. Numerous New Testament passages refer to Jesus hanging on the tree. One passage of the Mishnah surprisingly specifies that criminals who are stoned to death are to be hanged afterward, adding, "and sages say 'Only a blasphemer and one who worships an idol are hung.'"[40] Hanging a corpse may seem pointless to us, but to Jews

---

37 *Sanh.* 7.1. Punishment by "burning" was accomplished by forcing the mouth open and burning the person from the inside. Fitzmyer, "Crucifixion in Ancient Palestine," 505.

38 Fitzmyer, "Crucifixion," 505–7. The typical Aramaic word for "hanging" was used to refer to impalement, hanging with a rope, or crucifixion. Fitzmyer, "Crucifixion," 506. Comments found in the Dead Sea Scrolls also confirm that "hanging on a tree" meant crucifixion among first-century Jews. 4QpNah. See Fitzmyer, "Crucifixion," 512.

39 Fitzmyer, "Crucifixion," 509–10. That Jesus was put to death by "hanging on a tree" was routinely part of early Church preaching. See Acts 5:30; 10:39; 13:29; Gal. 3:13; 1 Pet. 2:24.

40 *Sanh.* 6.4. *Talmud of Babylonia,* 87. Since Jesus was convicted of blasphemy, the Jewish leaders regarded crucifixion as the appropriate sentence. Many offenses were punishable by stoning, but only the bodies of blasphemers and idolaters were hanged after they were stoned.

it reinforced the idea that God cursed and utterly rejected the wrongdoer.[41] Jesus suffered the extreme penalty not only under Roman law but in Jewish eyes as well, even if he was not stoned to death for blasphemy. Hanging was the Jewish *summa suplicia,* the ultimate penalty. Nothing surpassed crucifixion as a statement of culpability and rejection by God.

Divine Justice

IN ROMAN LITERATURE, THE DEATH of a villain was usually "particularly gruesome," and Romans expected this. The manner of death "summed up" the life of an evil person in an "appropriate way."[42] Romans found this satisfying, just as modern theater goers appreciate an evil character meeting his demise in a way that pleases our notions of poetic justice. This was especially true in ancient Rome when evil characters opposed or offended divine powers. Various offenses were expected to result in different kinds of death.[43] Roman audiences anticipated that wrongdoing would always result in Roman justice, imposed either by the gods or by civil authorities. Roman justice expressed the triumph of the state. The ideal outcome was "one where gods and men work together to deal with miscreants."[44]

Jewish notions of justice were no different, and the religious notion that divine retribution was at work prevailed with equal force in the Jewish mind and in the Roman. Wealth, high social status, long life, and children were blessings, considered proof of righteousness and God's approval. Conversely, illness, poverty, and other misfortunes confirmed that someone was cursed by God and was being punished. Furthermore, the gravity of the calamity was in direct proportion to the magnitude of the sin. Since no circumstance was worse than crucifixion, the Jewish leaders were determined that Jesus should meet with that particular death, since it alone provided irrefutable proof that he was a blasphemer, the worst of sinners, and utterly rejected by God.

---

41 Aubert, "Double Standard,"124.
42 Köster, "How to Kill a Roman Villain," 311.
43 Köster, 311n7.
44 Köster, 330.

Crucifixion as Public Spectacle and Public Repudiation

CRUCIFIXIONS WERE DESIGNED TO BE a public spectacle, amplifying the message that criminals were both punished and shamed.[45] Crucifixion was a slow process that did not involve a large amount of blood, unless the condemned were executed in arenas where wild beasts were unleashed against them.[46] With their hands stretched out or tied behind their backs, the victims were unable to defend themselves against the animals or even turn away. Roman mosaics depicted such brutal scenes, which are also described in Christian accounts of martyrdom. Even without beasts for added entertainment value, erecting crosses on major roads outside every city reinforced that the criminal had been physically removed from among his group and cast out. The public display visually expressed society's complete repudiation and rejection of the offender.[47]

Rather than evoking sympathy or pity for the crucified, making the execution public accentuated the social distance or religious gulf between the offender and the onlookers—between the righteous, who maintained the norms expected by society, and the lawbreakers, who deserved their fate.[48] The criminal was on display for all to see: his bloody and contorted body, his facial expressions, his extreme pain.

Spectators also played an important role in executions by being implicitly invested with a certain authority, confirming the verdict themselves, even if only "to impose their punitive and judgmental gaze upon the wrongdoers." But spectators in fact often actively participated with "vocal expressions and

---

45 Wrongdoers displayed in the amphitheater were called *noxii*, from the verb *nocere* ("to harm, injure"), used for those who have caused harm or injured others. Carucci, "Spectacle of Justice," 227.

46 Cook, "Crucifixion as Spectacle in Roman Campania," 80. Ordinarily, crucified persons died without significant bloodshed. The absence of large quantities of blood actually contributed in the Roman mind to the view of death by crucifixion as shameful, since it was unlike glorious or heroic deaths accomplished with bloodshed in battle. The crucified criminal was bloody from scourging, but the relatively small amount of blood produced by the act of crucifixion itself was regarded as unmanly, shameful, and dishonorable. Cook, 76.

47 Carucci, "Spectacle of Justice," 214.

48 Carucci, "Spectacle of Justice," 229, 232.

emotional reactions" affirming that the offender had violated the "established order."[49] In the case of Jesus, we see exactly this treatment. The Gospels describe hostile spectators at his crucifixion. His critics and adversaries mocked and heckled him while he was on the cross; even the thieves who were crucified with him reviled him. This was commonplace. In both the Roman and Jewish mind, crucifixions were a powerful visual affirmation of justice and the judgment of God.

---

49   Carucci, "Spectacle of Justice," 217.

CHAPTER 23

The Road to the Cross

The Titulus

THE *TITULUS*, A PLACARD ANNOUNCING the crime, was carried through the streets to the place of execution by a soldier at the head of the procession accompanying the condemned. The titulus was a wooden board covered in white gypsum on which the crime was written in black letters.[1] Sometimes the condemned wore the titulus hanging by a rope around his neck as he proceeded to the execution site. There it was attached to the top of the cross, giving public notice of the crime for which he had been convicted.

The titulus of Jesus was written in three languages: Hebrew, Greek, and Latin. Hebrew was the official language of the Jews. Latin was the official language of the empire, and the execution was an act of the Roman state. Greek was the international language, the common spoken language in the empire.

The Jewish leaders had blackmailed Pilate into condemning Jesus to the cross, and he was furious. Pilate had brought Jesus forward, bloody and battered, to stand before them. "Behold your king!" he proclaimed. Pilate was not mocking Jesus; he was mocking the Jewish authorities and their accusation of treason against Jesus, which Pilate knew to be untrue. The chief priests and elders insisted on crucifixion. They had played their hand well. They had won. They had manipulated, embarrassed, and humiliated Pilate. But now,

---

1   J. Collins, "Exegetical Notes," 156.

as he wrote the titulus, he retaliated through the sign itself, which ironically expressed the truth of Jesus' identity: "Jesus of Nazareth, King of the Jews."[2]

> Pilate also wrote a title and put it on the cross; it read, "Jesus of Nazareth, the king of the Jews." Many of the Jews read this title, for the place where Jesus was crucified was near the city; and it was written in Hebrew, in Latin, and in Greek. (John 19:19–20)

The chief priests were insulted. The shame of the cross would be shared by all of them if Jesus was proclaimed king of the Jews on the titulus. They protested to Pilate, "It should say that Jesus *claimed* to be king of the Jews, not that he *is* the king of the Jews!" (see John 19:21).

But Pilate was adamant and curtly rebuffed them. He refused to change the placard's inscription, saying, "What I have written I have written" (John 19:22).

Saint Augustine commented on the three languages of the titulus. They showed that Christ would reign not only over the Jews but over all the nations, and that "not even by killing Him could they manage not to have Him as their king."[3] Chrysostom also noted the irony of the titulus and the purposeful action of Pilate in writing the inscription as he did.

> [Pilate] silenced their tongues and the tongues of all who might wish to malign Him by pointing out that they had risen up against their own king. And so he set the inscription in place, as if it were to serve as a kind of trophy, giving voice to a splendid message, both proclaiming His victory and heralding His

---

2   The phrase "Jesus of Nazareth, the king of the Jews" is often abbreviated in Christian art and iconography as "INRI" or "INBI." Neither the Greek nor the Latin alphabet has the letter "J," so the name "Jesus" is written with an "I"—"Iesous" in Greek or "Iesus" in Latin. "I" would also be used for the word "Jews." In Greek, the titulus would read *Iesous o Nazoraios o Basileus ton Ioudaion* (INBI), and in Latin, *Iesus Nazorenus Rex Iudaeorum* (INRI). The difference between INRI and INBI is simply due to the fact that the Latin word for king is *rex*, but the Greek word for king is *basileus*.

3   Augustine, Sermon 218.5, W. Aug., *Sermons*, III.7.184.

sovereignty . . . not in one tongue only but in three languages . . . that no one would fail to be aware of Christ's vindication.[4]

The Walk to Golgotha

WE DO NOT KNOW EXACTLY what route Christ took to Golgotha,[5] but the condemned criminal was forced to carry his own crossbeam to the site of execution, as if to physically bear responsibility for his crime. A soldier holding the titulus on a pole marched in front of him, or Jesus may have worn the titulus on a rope around his neck. A team of four soldiers, a *quaternion,* or in Greek a *tetradion,* were assigned to this duty under the direction of a centurion, the *exactor mortis.*[6]

Contrary to most artistic depictions of Jesus carrying his cross, the entire cross could not be carried. Two wooden beams joined together as a cross would have been too heavy and awkward to carry, even for a man who had not been scourged. Only the crossbeam, the *patibulum,* was carried, and that alone weighed from 50 to 70 pounds (approximately 22–31 kg). The condemned man's arms were stretched out to his sides. The crossbeam was placed on his upper back across the shoulder blades and tied to his arms with rope, forcing him to bend forward under the weight.

Hunched over by the weight of the crossbeam, with the rough-hewn wood scraping against his lacerated back, Jesus was led from the praetorium through the streets of the city to the execution site outside the city walls. The distance would have been about one-third of a mile, not far for most people to walk but a considerable distance for a heavily scourged man carrying a large wooden beam. Jesus was already exhausted from severe mental and physical suffering; the scourging resulted in significant loss of blood and most likely also fractured many ribs. Fluid was accumulating in his chest cavity, and his breathing

---

4   Chrysostom, Homily 85, *Homilies on the Gospel of John,* FOTC 41:429–30.
5   Pilgrims to Jerusalem today who wish to follow the footsteps of Jesus on the way to his crucifixion follow a route popularly known as the Via Dolorosa (Way of Sorrows). In fact, that particular route was established by the Catholic Church during the Middle Ages and does not accurately replicate the actual route.
6   Brown, *Death of the Messiah,* 2:954–55.

was shallow and extremely painful due to bruised or broken ribs. The wounds on his head from the crown of thorns contributed additional agony, and severed nerves may have caused extreme pain in his scalp that radiated across his face and head with every tiny movement.

The Women of Jerusalem

IT WAS NEARLY MIDDAY AND people were out and about, finalizing their Passover preparations. Jesus struggled through the narrow cobbled streets of Jerusalem, bent over by the crossbeam weighing down his outstretched arms, his bloody tunic stuck to the wounds that covered his entire body. Only St. Luke recorded for us the shock and grief of the crowd now seeing him paraded through the streets, condemned and on his way to execution. The sight was particularly heart wrenching for the women, because they knew of Jesus' gentleness and special care for them.

Jesus welcomed women into his circle of disciples, something unheard of at the time. Rabbis did not speak to women in public, not even to their own wives, and they never allowed women to become disciples. Jesus spoke to women and treated them with a dignity and value equal to that of men. He even allowed them to follow him as he traveled from place to place. Women disciples were an integral part of his ministry and provided critical financial support (Luke 8:2–3). Jesus praised the choice of a woman to sit, listen, and learn as a disciple, and even said this was better than performing the traditional female duty of preparing and serving meals (Luke 10:41–42). Sometimes women approached him, even though they feared to do so because they were sinners (Luke 7:37–50), or Gentiles (Matt. 15:22–28), or ritually unclean (Mark 5:24–34). Yet Jesus always accepted and commended them for their faith and love. Now he was to be crucified, and suddenly seeing him like this—bloody, bruised, battered, and condemned to death—the women of Jerusalem were especially distraught, overcome with grief and disbelief.

And there followed him a great multitude of the people, and of women who bewailed and lamented him. But Jesus turning to them said, "Daughters of

Jerusalem, do not weep for me, but weep for yourselves and for your children."
(Luke 23:27–28)

Why does Jesus tell the women to weep for themselves and for their children? Because he had foretold the destruction of the Temple and the entire city of Jerusalem, which would come to pass during the Jewish War of 66–73.[7] Those who were trapped inside the city experienced some of the worst suffering that has ever been described at the hands of both Romans and their fellow Jews.[8]

Simon of Cyrene

THE GOSPELS DO NOT TELL us that Jesus ever fell down under the weight of the cross, but he must have had difficulty carrying it.[9] Condemned criminals were routinely scourged and then carried the crossbeam. As a healthy young man, Jesus should have been able to carry the crossbeam, but he was too weak, suggesting that the scourging he had received was more severe than the typical pre-crucifixion flogging. The sun was growing hotter, and he was struggling, thirsty, lightheaded, and in agonizing pain. He had lost a significant amount of blood. The centurion responsible for the execution must have been concerned that Jesus might die before he even arrived at Golgotha. Roman soldiers had the legal right to conscript labor, and now they forced a passerby, Simon of Cyrene, to carry the crossbeam for Jesus (Matt. 27:32).

---

7   Luke 23:29–31. These statements indicate that the situation for Jerusalem will become much worse. Elsewhere in Luke, Jesus makes specific prophecies about the destruction of Jerusalem (Luke 21:20–24).

8   The Romans surrounded the city for three years and tried to force the Jews to surrender by starving them. What took place inside the city during that period is horrific beyond description, and those who managed to survive the siege were crucified, enslaved, or condemned to the mines, which was considered a fate worse than death. The siege is described in detail by Josephus in *The Jewish War*.

9   The tradition that Jesus fell three times is a Catholic embellishment from the Middle Ages that was incorporated into their practice of the "Stations of the Cross," an act of Catholic piety during which Catholics symbolically follow and remember the events that happened to Jesus from his condemnation by Pilate through his burial.

Because Simon of Cyrene is mentioned by name, it is likely that he became a Christian later, and his children almost certainly became Christians. Saint Mark's Gospel describes him as "the father of Alexander and Rufus," a detail that suggests Alexander and Rufus were believers known to St. Mark's community (Mark 15:21). Cyrene was the capital of the Roman district of Cyrenaica, where the nation of Libya is located today. A large number of Jews had settled there about three hundred years before Christ, but many Cyrenian Jews lived in Jerusalem and had organized their own synagogue.[10]

Centuries later, gnostic heretics would claim that Jesus was never crucified, but rather Simon of Cyrene was crucified by mistake in his stead.[11] Gnostics denied the humanity of Christ, claiming his body was a mere illusion and his crucifixion never occurred. Later, the falsehood that Simon of Cyrene was crucified instead of Jesus was adopted by some Muslims, many of whom deny the reality of the crucifixion because they regard Jesus as a prophet and do not believe that God would allow his prophet to be crucified.[12] But the historical record that Jesus was crucified is solidly established, not only in the New Testament but among both Roman and Jewish sources. The soldiers knew who their prisoner was. Also, Simon had not been scourged, and he could never have been crucified by mistake.

Outside the City

THE PLACE OF EXECUTION WAS outside the city walls.[13] No doubt Jesus had seen many crucified victims as he entered the city of Jerusalem during his lifetime. He knew what terrible suffering awaited him. Saint John Chrysostom comments on the elevation of the cross, and the public nature of the execution.

---

10   For the Cyrenian synagogue in Jerusalem, see Acts 6:9. Cyrenian members of the early Church are mentioned in Acts 11:20 and 13:1.

11   Saint Irenaeus refers to this in *Against Heresies*, 1.24.4, ANF 1:349.

12   Mourad, "The Death of Jesus in Islam," 363–64.

13   The site of the crucifixion is now located inside the city walls, because after the time of Christ the city of Jerusalem was expanded to encompass more land. The place of Christ's crucifixion is within the huge Church of the Resurrection (also known as the Church of the Holy Sepulcher), which incorporates the places of both Christ's crucifixion and his resurrection.

Chrysostom interprets Jesus dying outside the city in the open air as pointing to the sanctification of the entire world and the fact that worship of the Lord would no longer be confined to one place. "For we are able in every place to lift holy hands, since the whole earth has become holy, holier than the holies inside."[14]

Golgotha

"AND THEY BROUGHT HIM TO the place called Golgotha (which means the place of a skull)" (Mark 15:22). Golgotha is never described by the Scriptures as a hill or a mountain, even though it is almost always artistically depicted that way. No one is even sure why it was called Golgotha, but its appearance provides a clue. Golgotha is a rocky knoll about fourteen feet high, and since its name is Hebrew for "the place of the skull," it was probably a rounded rock formation that protruded out of the ground and resembled the top of a skull.[15] Golgotha was rendered into Latin as *Calvaria*; hence the name Calvary is sometimes used in English.

Golgotha was also said to be the site where Adam had died and was buried. For this reason, some Orthodox icons of the crucifixion show a small skull beneath the base of the cross. Regardless of whether Adam was actually buried there, some Fathers of the Church mention this tradition because Christ's death on the cross conquered death. The icons express the deeper theological and spiritual meaning of Christ's accomplishment, reversing the curse of death that Adam had brought upon humankind. As Chrysostom explains:

> Some say that there Adam had died and lay buried, and that Jesus set up His trophy over death in the place where death had begun its rule. He went forth carrying his cross as a trophy in opposition to the tyranny of death, and, as it

---

14 Chrysostom, *Homily on the Cross and the Bandits*, 1.1. I am indebted to Mark Bilby for this and other translations quoted herein from Chrysostom's *Sermons on the Bandits* in Dr. Bilby's dissertation, "'As the Bandit I Will Confess You.' Luke 23:39–43 in Early Christian Interpretation."

15 Brown, *Death of the Messiah* 2:937.

is customary with conquerors, He also carried on His shoulders the symbol of His victory.[16]

Adam's sin brought death to humanity, estrangement from God, and the corruption of the created world. Now the Second Adam would ascend the cross, reversing the effects of Adam's fall, bringing life and sanctification not only to the human race but to all of creation. But to accomplish this great mystery, Jesus would endure an agonizing ordeal beyond our comprehension.

---

16 Chrysostom, Homily 85, *Homilies on the Gospel of John*, FOTC 41:428.

CHAPTER 24

Crucifixion:
The Procedure and Cause of Death

INITIALLY JESUS, AND THEN SIMON of Cyrene, carried the crossbeam to the execution site, but the upright beam of the cross would have been located at Golgotha as a permanent fixture. It is likely that multiple upright beams had been erected there, or possibly even scaffolding that could accommodate numerous crossbeams, since the Romans sometimes crucified several people simultaneously.

Crosses varied in shape, and even a simple upright stake could be used for an execution. Variations included the X-shaped cross, the type used for St. Andrew's martyrdom, now called St. Andrew's cross. Crosses that looked like a capital "T" are often termed a Tau cross. A cross with the upright beam extending above the crossbeam, forming the classic cross shape most familiar to us, is typically referred to as a Latin cross. It is likely that Jesus was crucified on that type of cross, since the Gospels refer to the titulus being placed above his head. Both Jewish and Roman authors mention different types of crosses. They also relate that Roman soldiers routinely amused themselves at crucifixions by nailing their victims in different positions, whether out of boredom or cruelty:

I see crosses there, not just one kind but made in many different ways; some have their victims with head down to the ground; some impale their private parts; others stretch out their arms on the gibbet.[1]

Occasionally, a wooden wedge was attached to the middle of the upright beam to support the weight of the crucified person somewhat by providing a little seat, called the *sedile*. Ancient writers sometimes refer to the crucified person being "seated" on the cross or "mounting" the cross.[2] The sedile might also be a wooden piece protruding from the upright beam like a horn, which the condemned man straddled between his legs.[3] If the purpose of the sedile was to prolong suffering by delaying death, it would have served that purpose. But Jewish victims of crucifixion were always removed from the cross before sunset. It is unlikely that Jesus' cross had a sedile, since delaying death was never an objective for executions in Jerusalem.

In addition to the shape of the cross, the height also varied. Some crosses were lower, with the victim's feet only about ten to eighteen inches off the ground; this was called a *crux humilis*. A higher cross, a *crux sublimis,* elevated the crucified person about three feet off the ground. The crucified were always elevated due to the public nature of the spectacle and to emphasize their shame. Jesus was likely on a high cross, since the sponge was placed on a reed so it could reach his mouth (Matt. 27:28; Mark 15:36; John 19:29).

Once at the site of execution, the criminal was stripped of his clothing to add to his dishonor; in Judea, however, as noted earlier, he was left with a loin-cloth. Blood from Jesus' innumerable wounds would have dried as he walked to Golgotha in the sun, and no doubt his clothes had stuck to his skin. Now the tunic was harshly yanked off him, dislodging scabs from the wounds and dispersing waves of pain throughout his body.

---

1   Seneca, *Dialogue* 6 (*De consolatione ad Marciam*), 20.3. Hengel, *Crucifixion,* 25.

2   Brown, *Death of the Messiah,* 2:952. For example, see Seneca, *Epistle* 101.12.

3   No footrest existed, in spite of artistic depictions that seem to show Jesus standing on the cross. No ancient literature mentions anything like a support for the feet. Part of the agony of the cross resulted from the severe muscular cramps and spasms caused by the lack of support for the body. A foot support would also contradict the concept of the crucifixion as a hanging.

The crucifixion itself was accomplished quickly, since the Romans were extremely adept at this form of execution. The crossbeam was taken from Simon of Cyrene and laid on the ground. Jesus was cast down to the ground on his severely lacerated back, and his arms were promptly stretched out along the length of the crossbeam. Two soldiers held down his arms and one restrained his legs while the fourth drove a nail into each hand and deep into the wood underneath, passing through the sensitive nerves in the wrists. Roman nails were rough and crude irons, several inches long and squarish in shape except for the pointed tip. Occasionally people might only be tied to the crossbeam, but the most common practice was to nail the criminal to the cross. This provided maximum psychological impact on the viewer and maximum pain for the condemned.

After the condemned had been affixed by nails to the crossbeam, called the *patibulum,* he was placed on the upright beam, known as the *stipes,* which was permanently located at the site of execution. The upright beams were much heavier and stronger in order to hold the weight of the crossbeam and the condemned man. For crucifixion on a crux humilis, four soldiers could easily lift the condemned man and drop the patibulum into a slot at the top of the upright beam. For a crux sublimis, ropes were attached to the crossbeam, and it was lifted with pulleys to the upright beam and dropped into place.[4]

At that point, the condemned was suspended in an upright position, arms nailed to the crossbeam and legs hanging freely for a short while until the feet were nailed. The legs were bent at the knees, the bottom of each foot was placed flat against the upright beam, and nails were driven through the arch at the top of the foot. Another technique was to spread the legs open so that the feet straddled the sides of the upright beam. Then each foot was nailed to the side of the upright beam through the tendon at the back of the ankle, just above the heel.[5] Spreading the legs apart and nailing the feet to the sides of

---

4   No literature describes the process of exactly how someone was lifted up onto the cross. Because of expressions like "ascending" the cross, some people suggest that perhaps a ladder or stepstool was placed against the upright beam and the crucified man was guided to climb backward up to a position where the crossbeam would have been dropped into a notch or slot in the upright. That process appears less likely because it would require the cooperation of the victim.

5   As common as crucifixion was in the Roman Empire, only one small piece of archeo-

the cross was a particularly humiliating position, especially in locales where offenders were crucified completely naked.

Piercing with Nails

THE PAIN CAUSED BY THE nails went far beyond the pain caused by puncturing of the skin and flesh itself. The iron nails damaged the nerves, rubbed and pressed against them continually, resulting in the kind of agony that has given rise to our English word for a pain beyond description: "excruciating," meaning literally "from the cross." The slightest movement or stimulus would cause "incessant, burning and searing pains."[6] In addition to the torment from nerve damage, terrible muscle cramps quickly developed in the legs from the sustained bent position. The chest and shoulders also began to feel tightness, and then severe spasms erupted from the fixed position of the chest and outstretched arms.

When nails pierced the Lord's hands and feet, he experienced one of the worst pains known in medical science, called *causalgia*,[7] injury to the median nerves of the hands and plantar nerves of the feet. The pain is reportedly so unbearable that victims can go into shock from the pain alone, which has been compared to lightning bolts traveling through the arms and legs. Doctors treating World War I veterans who suffered nerve injury from shrapnel

---

logical evidence for it exists. A tomb was discovered in Israel containing the bones of a crucified man. He was crucified with his feet nailed to the outside of the upright beam. One of his ankle bones still had the nail in it because the tip had bent and the nail could not be removed from the body. Amazingly, this discovery is the only archeological evidence for the Roman practice of crucifixion ever discovered. Nails were removed from the bodies and reused, or in some cases, people kept them as a kind of talisman. Shanks, "New Analysis of the Crucified Man," 109–13; Zias and Sekeles, "The Crucified Man from Giv'at ha-Mivtar."

6   Zugibe, *Crucifixion of Jesus*, 97.

7   *Causalgia* means "burn" (*causos*) and "pain" (*algos*). It is a descriptive term for the pain caused by nerve injury. As a chronic condition, it is called Complex Regional Pain Syndrome Type 2. Hassantash et al., "Causalgia." The authors note that "true major causalgia" should be distinguished "from other less well-defined post traumatic painful syndromes because it occurs from nerve injury caused when the body has been penetrated, something rarely seen except during wartime" (1226–27).

discovered that even morphine did not provide relief.[8] The slightest stimulus, even a breeze across the skin or ordinary sounds such as rustling paper, is unbearable in this condition. Victims of causalgia desperately attempt to remain absolutely still and avoid any movement at all since the slightest movement exacerbates their agony.[9] The condition also causes profuse sweating and absolute intolerance of direct sunlight.

Crucifixion Experiments

FREDERICK ZUGIBE, WHO SERVED AS the chief medical examiner of Rockland County, New York, from 1969 through 2002, conducted experiments to test theories about the cause of death by crucifixion. His experiments have called into question many key assumptions and conclusions accepted for decades and restated repeatedly without scientific confirmation.[10] Zugibe's considerable experience as a coroner who analyzed bodies from crime scenes and accident sites has informed his conclusions, in addition to actual experiments he performed with live human subjects.

Zugibe conducted experiments on healthy young men who volunteered to be attached to a special full-sized cross he had constructed. The men were not actually crucified but held in place with strong straps at the wrists and feet. Since they did not sustain any nerve damage, they experienced only the pain that developed from the fixed position on the cross, in the legs when

---

8 Zugibe, *Crucifixion of Jesus,* 63. Zugibe notes that many patients became addicted to opiates, committed suicide, or went into shock because of the pain alone. Zugibe, 92.

9 Hassantash, et al., 1230.

10 Zugibe documented his many experiments, precise calculations, methodology, and conclusions in a number of publications. His most comprehensive book, entitled *The Crucifixion of Jesus: A Forensic Inquiry,* is not for the squeamish, as it contains descriptions and photographs taken by Zugibe during the course of his career as a coroner. Zugibe's conclusions conflict with theories about the physical death of Christ that have been repeated for decades without actually being tested. These theories were popularized by Dr. Pierre Barbet in *A Doctor at Calvary.* Zugibe subjected Barbet's hypotheses to careful scientific experiments, which he documented. Zugibe, a strong believer in the authenticity of the Shroud of Turin (which contributes to some of his conclusions), has published many articles on the Shroud. However, his decades of experience as a medical examiner and the scientific experiments he conducted on crucifixion are unmatched and very valuable.

the soles of their feet were secured to the upright beam, and cramping in the chest, arms, and shoulders from the sustained outstretched position of the upper body. None of the men could endure the pain that resulted from the leg cramping alone for more than forty-five minutes. They all had to be taken down, some after only fifteen minutes.

The pain in the chest and shoulders was alleviated somewhat by the feet, which supported the body's weight; but the fixed, bent position of the legs resulted in other pains. "After a short period of time on the cross, the severe cramps, numbness and coldness in the calves and thighs, caused by the compression due to the bent knees, would force Jesus to arch his body in an attempt to straighten his legs."[11] But to relieve the extreme cramping in his legs by arching his back, a crucified man would be forced to put pressure on his feet, which had been pierced by the nails through the plantar nerve, resulting in additional excruciating pain. This would continue throughout the entire period the condemned remained on the cross.

Controversy over the Place of the Nails

IN ART AND MOVIES, CHRIST is generally depicted as nailed to the crossbeam through the palms of his hands. The Gospels simply say that after the Resurrection, Jesus showed the disciples the wounds in his *cheiras*, which is typically translated into English as "hands" (John 20:20; Luke 24:39). We picture Jesus as being nailed through his palms. But the Greek language has only one word for the entire appendage, *cheir*, which means both "hand" and "arm." Similarly, only one word, *pous*, was used in ancient Greek for both "foot" and "leg."

The idea that Jesus was nailed through the palms presents some issues. First, the small bones of the hand could not support the weight of the body. The nails would have torn through the hand. Dr. Pierre Barbet performed an experiment in 1937 in which he drove a nail through the middle of the palm of a freshly amputated arm and then suspended an 88-pound (40 kg) weight from the elbow to simulate the force that would be exerted on the arm if it

---

11   Zugibe, *Crucifixion of Jesus*, 97.

were holding half the weight of an average man hanging from it. Within ten minutes, the nail tore through the hand.[12] Barbet concluded that Jesus' arms must have been nailed through the wrist, partly based on this single question-able experiment with the amputated arm and partly because the Shroud of Turin shows a crucified man with a large amount of blood on his right *wrist*, not on the back of his hand.

But Barbet never actually measured the amount of force exerted by a man hanging from a cross, nor did he take into consideration the fact that a cruci-fied man was not simply hanging from two nails in his hands or wrists. The hands never supported the entire body weight. Rather, the body's weight would have been supported by the legs and feet, which were nailed to the upright beam. Nonetheless, on the basis of this one experiment and the Shroud image, Barbet concluded that Christ's arms were nailed through the wrists. Barbet is also the person primarily responsible for the theory that Jesus died of asphyxia (lack of oxygen) because the position of the body made res-piration difficult. Barbet's theories dominated the discussions about Christ's crucifixion during the twentieth century.

But when Zugibe investigated the murder of a young woman, he acci-dentally learned that victims of crucifixion could have been nailed through the palms if the nail was inserted in the region called the thenar eminence muscles—the bulky or fleshy portion at the base of the hand.[13] If you look at your palm, the center of the palm is the thinnest point on the hand. That is not where Romans would have driven the nail, since it is weak. But you will notice two plump areas that extend down from the base of the thumb (thenar eminence) and the base of the little finger. These muscles allow the thumb and little finger to flex or bend toward each other. If you touch your thumb to your little finger, a deep furrow is created. This is called the thenar furrow. If a nail

---

12 Dr. Barbet never followed standard scientific procedures nor tested his hypotheses by conducting true experiments. Serious flaws in his methodology have led scientists to question Barbet's conclusions regarding the placement of the nails and Christ's cause of death.

13 Zugibe, *Crucifixion of Jesus*, 77. The victim had been stabbed to death, and Zugibe docu-mented every puncture wound she received as she attempted to fend off her attacker. She was stabbed through the thenar furrow. The entrance wound was at the lower part of the palm, but the exit wound was at the wrist.

is angled toward the wrist and driven through the base of the thenar furrow close to the wrist, the nail will exit at the back of the wrist. This means that the crucified man would be affixed to the cross through the bones of the wrist, which would provide much more support than the center of the hand.

The nail was not driven through the inside of the wrist, as Barbet imagined, but through the lower portion of the palm, at the base of the thenar furrow, exiting through the back of the wrist and into the wood of the crossbeam. On the cross, the criminal's palms were facing outward. Jesus would have had puncture wounds on the insides of his hands, at the base of the palms, but the exit wounds would be located at the wrists.

Zugibe also gives a strong argument for Jesus' feet being nailed separately, not together as some suppose. It would have been more difficult to restrain a crucified victim and hold both of his feet down, one on top of the other, to pound in a single nail. Additionally, a single nail a few inches long would not have been sufficient to penetrate both feet; something akin to an iron spike would be required, which would damage the feet considerably.[14] Zugibe noted that artistic depictions showing both of Christ's feet affixed with a single nail did not become popular until the eleventh century. The Romans likely would have chosen the easier and more efficient method, securing the feet by driving a nail through each foot.

Cause of Death

THE SCIENTIFIC AND MEDICAL COMMUNITIES have discussed the physical cause of the death of Jesus especially since the beginning of the twentieth century. From a theological perspective, Jesus Christ as Son of God cannot have a cause of death because he died willingly. The death of Christ is voluntary not simply because he allowed himself to be arrested and crucified, with full knowledge of what was about to happen. It was voluntary primarily because he allowed himself to die, which is not natural to his divinity. It is also true, from a theological perspective, that death does not belong to our

---

14   Zugibe, *Crucifixion of Jesus,* 93–95. The Apostle John testified that none of the Lord's bones were broken (John 19:33, 36). This was a fulfillment of the prophecy in Ps. 34:20 (33:21 LXX), "Not a bone of him shall be broken."

human nature, because God created us, but he did not create death. We cannot avoid death, because death is the consequence of sin. But it is theologically correct to say that Christ, as the only sinless human being who ever lived, would not have been subject to death, even in his human nature, had he not chosen to die. He allowed himself to die in order to defeat death by rising from the dead.[15]

As the Lord said in the Gospel of John, "For this reason the Father loves me, because I lay down my life, that I may take it again. No one takes it from me, but I lay it down of my own accord. I have power to lay it down, and I have power to take it again" (John 10:17–18).

So while we may speak of the physical death of Christ from a medical perspective, we should remember that theologically speaking, nothing would have killed him. That is, nothing could have taken his life. He willingly condescended to die. With this correct theological understanding firmly in place, let us nonetheless discuss the physical death of Christ from a medical perspective.

Medicine can never create a crucifixion experiment that is painless, humane, and ethical; therefore, no one can conclusively prove the cause of death by crucifixion. However, many theories that seem plausible cannot be substantiated by the available evidence. The immediate cause of death may have varied depending on the health, age, and physical condition of each particular victim, not to mention other circumstances, such as the weather or the severity of the scourging.[16] At least ten different theories have been proposed regarding what caused the physical death of Christ or other victims of crucifixion, but three theories dominate the discussion.

---

15 We must be careful when using expressions that suggest necessity (such as Jesus "had to" die), because God is not subject to necessity. The cross was not necessary, required, or demanded by the Father nor by circumstances. Conceptualizing the crucifixion of Christ as a transaction or obligation demanded by justice is a product of medieval theology and derives from conceptualizing sin as a crime against God, who demands or requires punishment. The idea that someone had to die to pay the penalty for sin was foreign to the mind of the early Church and is foreign to Orthodox Christianity, which sees sin primarily as spiritual illness and a departure from God.

16 Maslen and Mitchell, "Medical Theories on the Cause of Death in Crucifixion," 187.

1. *Asphyxia* (lack of oxygen). This is the most widely promoted theory, popularized by Dr. Pierre Barbet in the mid-twentieth century.[17] Its proponents say that the victim's position on the cross made breathing difficult. The individual could inhale but not exhale sufficiently to expel all the carbon dioxide from his lungs.[18] When we inhale air, we take in oxygen and send it throughout the body via the bloodstream, and we expel carbon dioxide when we exhale. In order to exhale completely, Barbet believed that a crucifixion victim had to raise himself up from a sagging position on the cross by pushing on his feet and lifting himself up with his arms.[19] Eventually a crucified man became exhausted, and carbon dioxide accumulated in the lungs until he died from lack of oxygen. This theory was proposed partly because of known cases of torture in which people were hung by the arms with their hands above their heads. They had difficulty breathing and were forced to pull themselves up with their arms in order to fully exhale and inhale.[20] The weakness of this theory is that Jesus' hands were not positioned above his head, and his legs were not dangling beneath him. His weight was partly supported by his feet and legs because they were nailed to the upright beam.

---

17 It also seemed to be supported in a rather famous article in the *Journal of the American Medical Association* that discussed the physical death of Christ. But the authors did not conduct any of their own experiments or test any theories but relied on Barbet's book and other articles that preceded their review. Edwards et al., "On the Physical Death of Jesus Christ."

18 "The weight of the body, pulling down on the outstretched arms and shoulders, would tend to fix the intercostal muscles in an inhalation state and thereby hinder passive exhalation. Accordingly, exhalation was primarily diaphragmatic, and breathing was shallow. It is likely that this form of respiration would not suffice and that hypercarbia would soon result." Edwards et al., 1461. In other words, because of the weight of the body pulling down on the arms and shoulders, the muscles in between the ribs would not be able to move, so the ribcage would not be able to expand. Jesus would be able to breathe in, but he would have difficulty fully exhaling and expelling the carbon dioxide from his lungs. The carbon dioxide would build up in the bloodstream and make the blood acidic, harming the organs and tissues of the body.

19 "Adequate exhalation required lifting the body by pushing up on the feet and by flexing the elbows and adducting the shoulders. However, this maneuver would place the entire weight of the body on the tarsals and would produce searing pain. . . . As a result, each respiratory effort would become agonizing and tiring and lead eventually to asphyxia." Edwards et al., 1461.

20 Zugibe, *Crucifixion of Jesus*, 103.

The volunteers in the experiments conducted by Zugibe had no difficulty breathing at any stage during their suspension on the experimental cross he had constructed. Their oxygen levels were tested and averaged between ninety-seven and ninety-nine percent. Readings of other vital signs, such as respiratory quotient (the ratio between carbon dioxide and oxygen in the lungs), lactic acid content (high levels would indicate a lack of oxygen), and cardiac output (pulse rate, blood pressure, etc.) were at acceptable levels. The crucifixion volunteers understandably exhibited stress initially, but their medical results indicated no difficulty with respiration. When questioned, all the volunteers confirmed that they had no difficulty breathing.[21]

Barbet presumed that the crucified man would be in a sagging posture. Rather than having his arms extended out to the sides, the body position would appear more like a "Y" than a "T." Barbet theorized that the sagging position would require the crucified man to lift himself up with his arms to fully inhale and exhale. But would a crucified man be able to move his arms or feet at all? Zugibe experimented with the position on the cross and adjusted the arms of the volunteers to this "Y" angle. The volunteers were told to push against the foot restraints as hard as possible and to attempt to raise themselves with their arms "as if their lives depended upon it." None of the healthy young men were able to lift themselves or change their position on the cross to any extent whatsoever, regardless of how hard they tried. With both knees bent and feet and wrists firmly attached to the cross, they found it impossible to straighten themselves or lift themselves in any manner. [22]

Zugibe's experiments question the theory that crucified people died of asphyxia. It is unproven that hanging from the cross adversely affected breathing. If it did not, there would also be no reason for a crucified man to attempt to straighten himself, particularly if the damaged nerves of the feet and wrists

---

21   Zugibe, *Crucifixion of Jesus*, 108–16.

22   Zugibe was surprised when the experiment volunteers found the pain resulting from the fixed position of the arms and feet intolerable. The crucifixion position led to tremendous pain from cramping in the arms and shoulders due to the strain on the chest from the suspension, and in the legs from their immobilization in a bent position. The volunteers were unable to move their arms or wrists at all to lift themselves, but they could arch their backs away from the upright beam of the cross in an attempt to straighten their legs to alleviate the pain. Zugibe, *Crucifixion of Jesus*, 99, 112, 116.

immediately radiated intolerable pain.[23] Secondly, it seems unlikely that a crucified man would be able to lift himself to facilitate breathing since Zugibe's volunteers, who were affixed to a cross by the wrists and feet, were not able to move at all.

2. A heart attack or ruptured heart. Many clergy were attracted to this hypothesis because it suggested that Jesus literally died of a broken heart because of the sins of humanity. While a ruptured heart can result from a heart attack, heart attack itself is extremely rare in a young, healthy person. The intense scourging Jesus suffered would not have caused sufficient injury to the heart to result in a heart attack. Furthermore, a ruptured heart, a rare occurrence in itself, happens days after a heart attack, and Jesus was on the cross for only a few hours.[24] However, this theory cannot be dismissed completely because Takotsubo cardiomyopathy ("broken heart" syndrome) has been reported and documented even among younger people who have experienced extreme stress.[25]

3. Shock. There are different kinds of shock, but the two types that could be factors in the physical death of Christ would be traumatic shock and hypovolemic shock. Traumatic (injury-related) shock occurs when a person sustains serious injuries, causing low blood pressure and reduced blood flowing to the tissues of the body. Hypovolemic (low fluid volume) shock results from inadequate fluid level in the body due to blood lost through trauma and other factors, such as dehydration caused by low fluid intake and excessive sweating. Low blood volume creates inadequate oxygen in the organs and tissues of the body. Losing as little as twenty percent of one's blood can lead to hypovolemic shock. Shock results from a combination of many different factors. Jesus' heart was pumping hard, especially on the cross, because he was in an upright position.

---

23 Zugibe, *Crucifixion of Jesus,* 117–18. Zugibe's experiments, while useful, have "limited relevance" since his volunteer subjects had not been subjected to a scourging, had not carried a heavy crossbeam, were not dehydrated, and did not remain on the experimental cross for a very long time. Maslen and Mitchell, "Medical Theories on the Cause of Death in Crucifixion," 187.

24 Oliva et al., "Cardiac Rupture, a Clinically Predictable Complication of Acute Myocardial Infarction"; Zugibe, *Crucifixion of Jesus,* 125–26.

25 Al-Tkrit et al. "Left Ventricular Free Wall Rupture in Broken Heart Syndrome."

His knees were bent, and his blood volume was already low from the blood and fluid loss he had sustained during scourging and from dehydration, making the circulation needed to sustain his organs even more difficult.

It is impossible to state with certainty a single cause of death for Jesus, since many factors probably contributed to his physical state. Some articles by physicians have arrived at the same conclusion: insufficient evidence exists to prove conclusively exactly how people died from crucifixion. There may have been different actual causes of death depending on the victim, but dehydration and hypovolemic shock are high on the list.[26] Jesus had lost a significant amount of bodily fluid. He had not consumed any liquid since the Last Supper the night before. He began to lose fluid as he anticipated his arrest in the garden. His excessive sweating from the profound anxiety and extreme stress he experienced is corroborated by the sweat "like great drops of blood" (hematohidrosis) as he prayed while awaiting his arrest. He began receiving beatings in the middle of the night after his conviction at his Jewish trial. He was struck even prior to the Jewish trial by a guard who interpreted Jesus' reply to Annas as disrespectful: "Is that how you answer the high priest?" (John 18:22).

Luke also describes the physical abuse of Christ while he was in the custody of the Jewish religious officials: "Now the men who were holding Jesus mocked him and beat him; they also blindfolded him and asked him, 'Prophesy! Who was it that struck you?' And they spoke many other words against him, reviling him" (Luke 22:63–65).

He lost blood from the rips and gouges created on his back and legs and the trauma to his chest from the scourging, possibly leading to pleural effusion (fluid around the lungs), which would also contribute to shortness of breath and hypovolemia. The brutal beating to the chest wall during the scourging, not to mention other ancillary beatings Jesus had received, could have caused fluid to build up around the lungs. This fluid mixed with blood would have

---

26 "The actual cause of death by crucifixion was multifactorial and varied somewhat with each case but the two most prominent causes probably were hypovolemic shock and exhaustion asphyxia. Other possible contributing factors included dehydration, stress-induced arrhythmias, and congestive heart failure with rapid accumulation of pericardial and perhaps pleural effusions." Edwards et al., "On the Physical Death of Christ," 1461.

developed slowly over a few hours after sustaining injuries to the chest, contributing to fluid loss, difficulty in breathing, and severe pain. An accumulation of blood, fluid, and mucus from such injuries is called acute lung injury or acute respiratory distress syndrome (previously known as traumatic wet lung), which it is highly possible Jesus experienced. This would be sufficient to cause traumatic shock,[27] exacerbated by the injury to the nerves of the scalp from the crown of thorns. Puncture of nerves in his scalp sent surges of pain across his head and face, intensified by the slightest movement or stimulus.

By the time he had arrived at Golgotha, Jesus was badly dehydrated. His pulse was faint and his heart rate rapid. His breathing was rapid and shallow because of the bruised or broken ribs, which made every breath very painful.[28] Everything just described occurred before he was actually crucified. Then, from the cross, severe pain and difficulty breathing would have continued, caused by the fluid accumulating for several hours around his lungs. The square iron nails in his hands and feet rubbed against the nerves and induced causalgia, excruciating and horrific pain. In an effort to relieve the terrible cramping created by the fixed and bent position of the legs, he may have attempted to straighten them by pressing on his feet and arching his body, which reactivated the intense nerve pain.

And yet, in this extraordinarily painful and debilitated physical condition, Jesus not only spoke from the cross but was in complete control of everything that took place around him.

---

27   Zugibe, *Crucifixion of Jesus*, 132.
28   Broken or bruised ribs are agonizing, causing the sufferer to avoid any movement because of intense pain that results when the lungs are inflated. The stiffening of a body part to avoid pain caused by an injury to that part of the body is called splinting. The term for shallow breathing after trauma to the ribcage is respiratory splinting.

CHAPTER 25

Events on the Cross

Dividing the Garments

AFTER JESUS WAS NAILED AND raised on the upright beam, the titulus was attached to the top of the cross: "Jesus of Nazareth, King of the Jews." Now the execution detail could take a break and divvy up the condemned man's property. When someone was convicted of a crime, all his property was confiscated by the Roman state, not just his clothes. Our word "confiscate" comes from the Latin word *confiscare,* meaning "to consign" or "transfer" to the *fiscus.* The fiscus was the state treasury. Wealthy families were impoverished when a husband or father was convicted of a crime because his money, lands, and home were seized. The only property Jesus owned was his clothes. Dividing the clothes of a condemned man was routine and regarded as a minor benefit or job perk for the soldiers. Cloth production was a time-consuming, multistep process. No disposable paper products existed. Even small pieces of fabric had value and were useful for a wide variety of daily purposes.

> When the soldiers had crucified Jesus they took his garments and made four parts, one for each soldier; also his tunic. But the tunic was without seam, woven from top to bottom; so they said to one another, "Let us not tear it, but cast lots for it to see whose it shall be." This was to fulfill the scripture, "They parted my garments among them, and for my clothing they cast lots." (John 19:23–24)

Jesus' clothing would have consisted of his undergarment, which he was still wearing; his sandals; a head covering; a cloth belt or sash; his tunic, which was the primary piece of clothing; and his mantle.[1] The garments were evaluated and divided equally among members of the execution squad. The most valuable object most people owned was their mantle, also sometimes called a cloak—the outer garment worn draped over one shoulder and hung diagonally across the body. The mantle was a large, rectangular piece of woolen cloth which served as a coat during the day and as a blanket at night.[2] The Law of Moses required that a mantle have a tassel on each corner (a *tzitzit*), sometimes translated as "fringe."[3] Mark tells us that many people tried to touch Christ's cloak, even just his tassels, because simply touching the fringe healed them.[4] What a remarkable mantle it was that cloaked the human flesh of the eternal God! That awesome cloak, through which so many had been healed, was cut into four pieces as bonus compensation for a soldier's chore.

The Seamless Robe

ONE GARMENT RECEIVED SPECIAL ATTENTION. The soldiers "cast lots" for that particular piece of clothing: his tunic. Often translated as "robe," tunics were long-sleeved and covered the entire body from the neck down to the ankles. This was the basic garment worn by both men and women. Other than the mantle, it was the only substantial piece of clothing. All the Gospels mention that the soldiers divided his clothing and cast lots for his robe. But only John tells us why they gambled for his clothes and precisely which garment was the prize for which they gambled: the blood-soaked tunic. Christ's

---

1   Brown, *Death of the Messiah* 2:955n45.
2   A mantle was often given as collateral for a loan since it was the only object of value most people owned. But it was so critical for comfort and survival that Jewish law required that anyone holding someone's mantle as collateral must return it to him or her every night before the sun went down (Ex. 22:26).
3   The many threads that create the tassels were intended to remind the Israelites of the requirements of the Law (Num. 15:38–39).
4   Mark 6:56. This is what the woman with the hemorrhage was trying to touch when she came up behind Jesus in the crowd. She said, "If I can only touch the fringe of his garment I shall be healed" (Luke 8:44; Matt. 9:20).

robe was unusual because it was seamless, making it valuable to the soldiers and highly significant to the Church.

A seamless garment was rare and required expert weaving skills.[5] The soldiers preferred not to tear it into parts, so they gambled for it as a prize. Matthew, Mark, and Luke use the term *ballein klēron*: the soldiers "cast lots," a common practice similar to throwing dice. It is unlikely that they had actual dice or lots; therefore, this was simply an expression to indicate that they gambled for the robe. John's Gospel uses the word *lagchanein*, "to obtain by chance" or simply "to gamble."[6] The soldiers may have played a simple game of chance similar to rock-paper-scissors, using hand signs or the number of fingers to determine the winner.

Jesus watched from the cross as the soldiers fulfilled the prophecy: "They divide my garments among them, and for my raiment they cast lots" (Ps. 22:18/21:19 LXX).

The prophecy was fulfilled because the soldiers wanted to win something valuable. But the Evangelist John was not trying to impress us with the fact that Jesus owned something rare or expensive. The detail that the tunic was seamless held great meaning: the Jewish high priest wore a seamless robe.[7] Christ was not a priest in his earthly ministry, but he is the Great High Priest of heaven, who sanctifies and blesses us.[8] The evening before his crucifixion, when he prayed to the Father, he consecrated himself for his sacrifice (John 17:19). As the heavenly High Priest, he was literally both the Priest performing the sacrifice and the sacrificial Victim, "both the Offeror and the Offered,"[9] offering himself "for the life of the world" (John 6:51).

---

5   To weave a single, seamless garment from top to bottom, including sleeves, was extremely difficult and required use of a complex technique called "tubular weaving." Anthropologist H. Ling Roth investigated ancient weaving techniques used by various cultures around the world and explained tubular weaving in the last of three articles on the subject of primitive weaving techniques. Roth, "Studies in Primitive Looms," esp. 118–20.

6   Brown, *Death of the Messiah*, 2:955.

7   Josephus, *Ant.* 3.7.4.

8   This is why in Orthodox iconography the fingers of Jesus' right hand form the priestly blessing. Jesus described himself as the one "whom the Father consecrated and sent into the world" (John 10:36).

9   The words of the priest as he prays silently during the Cherubic Hymn of the Divine

Christ's role as heavenly High Priest is beautifully developed in the Book of Hebrews, which tells us how Christ is different from all the Jewish high priests. They offered sacrifices for the people and for themselves, since they too had sin (Heb. 5:1–3). But Christ, the only sinless One, offered himself for the sin of the world—not for his own sin, since he had none. Through his blood he secured "an eternal redemption," and through his body we are sanctified (Heb. 9:12; 10:10). The tunic bore silent witness to the heavenly, mystical high priesthood of the Lord, who in that very moment was offering himself as the perfect Passover Lamb. Meanwhile, unaware of its true significance, the soldiers gambled for his seamless robe.

The Two Robbers

"THERE THEY CRUCIFIED HIM, AND with him two others, one on either side, and Jesus between them" (John 19:18).

Chrysostom notes that the prophecies proving that Jesus was the Christ were unwittingly fulfilled time and again by both Jews and Romans. The prophecies were not fulfilled by anything that was done to the thieves, only by what was done to Christ. Later, the extraordinary events that took place while he hung on the cross were also attributed to Christ alone, not to the thieves, even though the religious authorities wished to associate Jesus with thieves to destroy his reputation.[10] Rather than disproving that Jesus was the Messiah by crucifying him, the Jewish authorities unintentionally helped to fulfill the prophecy that he "was numbered with the transgressors" (Is. 53:12).

> Unwittingly they fulfilled the prophecy in this detail, also. Indeed, the very things which they did to revile Him were the ones that contributed to reveal the truth, in order that you might learn its power. I say this for the prophet had foretold this circumstance, also, from ancient times in the words "He was reputed with the wicked" (Is. 53:12).[11]

Liturgy of St. John Chrysostom.

10 Chrysostom, Homily 87, *Homilies on Matthew*, NPNF-1, 10:497.

11 Chrysostom, Homily 85, *Homilies on the Gospel of John*, FOTC 41:428–29.

Two were crucified with him, called "others" by John and "criminals" by Luke. They are described by Matthew and Mark as *lēstai* (plural of *lēstēs*), the word for a highway robber or revolutionary, like Barabbas. Placing Jesus between two *lēstai* was an attempt to associate him with violent political insurrectionists, whose ideas and philosophy were the opposite of what Jesus taught and the way he lived. That was no accident. Even if the other two were ordinary thieves, Jesus was crucified with criminals to portray him as a law-breaker. This was part of the shame of the cross and the reason Jewish leaders wanted Jesus to die by crucifixion.

The chief priests were infuriated by the Lord's cleansing of the Temple, when he insulted them and denounced their corrupt leadership of the Temple, the source of their power and wealth. This was the primary impetus and motivation for his crucifixion. "'My house shall be a house of prayer' but you have made it a den of robbers"(Luke 19:46), he said, using the same word used to describe the thieves now flanking Jesus on either side. He had described the chief priests as robbers (*lēstai*), but they made certain that Jesus would suffer the penalty of robbers, wear that label himself, and die with thieves, sharing their fate and considered guilty by association.

Being crucified as a criminal was considered proof that Jesus was a sinner, an evildoer, rejected by God. This too was prophetic fulfillment, as St. Augustine noted, citing the prophecy of Isaiah:

> Three men were crucified in the same place, the Lord in the middle because "he was reckoned among the wicked" (Is. 53:21). They placed the two robbers on either side, but they did not have a similar cause. They were flanking Christ as He hung there, but they were far removed from Him in reality. They were crucified by their crimes, but He by ours.[12]

The Mocking

AS CRIMINALS HUNG ON THE cross, they were defenseless against animals and human beings. The crucifixion of an enemy would certainly offer an

---

12   Augustine, Sermon 285:2, W. Aug. *Sermons* III.8:95.

opportunity to add extra insult, pain, and humiliation, not to mention gloat-ing. Spectators derided and cursed crucified criminals, spat on them, threw rocks at them, beat them, and even urinated on them. This was intentionally permitted to contribute to the shame and disgrace of this form of death. We know that Christ was mocked on the cross, but the Gospels do not indicate that anything else was done to him other than verbal taunting and insults. "And those who passed by derided him, wagging their heads" (Matt. 27:39; Mark 15:29).

The religious leaders had achieved their purpose; their plan had arrived at its culmination. They had schemed and plotted against Jesus for months, pres-suring Pilate to condemn him to the cross to demonstrate unequivocally that he was rejected by God. He was a false prophet, not the Messiah, and certainly not the Son of God. Although it was the day before Passover and important duties awaited them in the Temple, they made time to come to Golgotha to witness their triumph and enjoy their moment of satisfaction. They could not resist this opportunity to gloat and laugh at him, and they reveled in their vic-tory. "This insignificant preacher, Jesus of Nazareth, dared to challenge us? He got what he deserved!" Of that they were quite certain. The venom in their hearts came spewing forth in these taunts. The statements with which Christ was jeered, mocked, and insulted were tremendously ironic and theologically meaningful.

"You who would destroy the temple and build it in three days, save your-self!" (Matt. 27:39–40). The first taunt was the false charge brought against him at the Jewish trial: that Jesus said he would destroy the Temple and rebuild it, something he never said. Jesus had made a prophecy, not a threat, that the Jewish leaders would destroy "this Temple" (his body), and he would rebuild it (resurrect it) in three days. Once again, although unknowingly, the revilers were fulfilling his prophecy, destroying his Temple at that moment.

The taunting continued: "If you are the Son of God, come down from the cross!" (Matt. 27:40). The second taunt reflects the crime for which Jesus was convicted by the religious establishment: claiming to be the Son of God. This provocation has a rather sinister undertone since this exact phrase ("If you are the Son of God") was used by the devil to challenge Jesus when he was being tempted in the wilderness (Matt. 4:3, 6; Luke 4:3, 9). The evil one goaded

Jesus and challenged him to prove himself. But neither then nor now would Jesus act against the plan of the Father, follow his own desires, seek his own physical comfort or the self-satisfaction of proving his identity.

Members of the Sanhedrin who had convicted him joined in ridicule: "So also the chief priests, with the scribes and elders, mocked him, saying, 'He saved others; he cannot save himself'" (Matt. 27:41–42a). This third insult is also deeply ironic and quite personal on many levels. First, the word *sōzō* means both "save" and "heal." This double meaning expresses what Christ accomplished on the cross: salvation by the healing of humanity. The cross saves us not because it is payment for our sins but because through it we are healed of our spiritual illness and restored to wholeness and a relationship with God.

The statement by the chief priests "He saved others" was sarcastic, not an acknowledgment by them that Jesus had actually healed anyone, let alone saved them in any manner. Through this statement they were still attempting to discredit Jesus before the crowd for a very important reason: they wished to imply that Jesus never performed any miracles at all. If he could raise people from the dead, he should certainly be able to come down from the cross! They had accused him of using sorcery, tricks, or the power of Satan to perform miracles.[13] By saying "he cannot save himself" they implied that Jesus was now being exposed as a fraud.

"He saved others; he cannot save himself" is also deeply ironic and personal because salvation is embedded in his very name: Jesus (Yeshua), which means "God saves." His name embodies his identity and his purpose. Before he was born, both Mary and Joseph were told to name him Jesus, "for he will save his people from their sins" (Luke 1:31; Matt. 1:21). But from the cross he chose not to save himself, and by that choice he saved others and literally fulfilled his name and his purpose: "God saves."

"He is the King of Israel; let him come down now from the cross, and we will believe in him. He trusts in God; let God deliver him now, if he desires him; for he said, 'I am the Son of God'" (Matt. 27:42b–43). As the mocking continued, this third taunt was directed against Christ's kingship and

---

13 For example, Mark 3:22 and John 8:48. These slanders against Christ have been enshrined in the Talmud. Because they are found in the Talmud they continue to be read and believed by many Jews.

divinity, challenging Jesus to prove himself by coming down from the cross—
to prove that his miracles were genuine, that he is the King of Israel and the
Son of God.[14] God would not "deliver him," but not for the reason the Sanhedrin imagined. God would not deliver him because Christ's very purpose was
to deliver us from the slavery of sin and death. Their words drip with biting
sarcasm and fantastic irony, for in their minds his crucifixion is absolute proof
that God has categorically rejected Jesus. But sufferings and hardships do not
prove that one is unacceptable to God, even though this was the common
view among Jews at the time and remains so today.

This is the basis for the taunt "Let the Lord deliver him if he delights in
him." Once again, the religious authorities were responsible for fulfilling a
messianic prophecy: the mocking. "All who see me mock at me, they make
mouths at me, they wag their heads; 'He committed his cause to the LORD;
let him deliver him, let him rescue him, for he delights in him!'" (Ps. 22:7–
8/21:8–9 LXX).

In fact, the Father *did* delight in him: he delighted in the obedience of his
Son, who had fulfilled the plan of salvation. Suffering is not a sign that God
has abandoned us; the suffering of Christ clearly demonstrates that. Countless men and women have suffered injustice precisely because they were the
holy ones of God. Chrysostom condemns the taunts and reminds us of the
prophets who lived before Christ, who were also sent by God but abused, mistreated, and killed by their own people. Commenting on this particular taunt,
Chrysostom responds, "Deplorable, most deplorable! Were the prophets not
prophets nor the righteous not righteous because God did not rescue them
out of their dangers? They surely were, despite suffering these things!"[15]

The Darkness

"THERE WAS DARKNESS OVER THE whole earth." One of the most extraordinary details of the day Christ died was the strange darkness that covered

---

14   Saint Augustine remarked that in spite of the mocking, in fact "he did more than their
     mockery required of Him. There is, after all, more to rising from a tomb than to coming
     down from a tree." Augustine, Sermon 263:2, W. Aug. *Sermons* III.7:220.
15   Chrysostom, Homily 87, *Homilies on Matthew*, NPNF-1, 10:498.

the earth. We are not certain exactly what time Christ was crucified, although usually we say about noon.[16] Jews marked the time of day beginning with sunrise, which they referred to as the "first hour," about six AM. All evangelists agree that the Lord died at the ninth hour, or three PM, after a prolonged period of inexplicable darkness that began at noon, the sixth hour, when the sun would have been at its highest point. "It was now about the sixth hour, and there was darkness over the whole land until the ninth hour" (Luke 23:44; Matt. 27:45; Mark 15:33).

A popular explanation for the darkness is that it was a solar eclipse, but that is a demonstrable mistake, for a number of reasons. An eclipse is a natural occurrence, but this was an unnatural darkness. An eclipse does not last for three hours as this darkness did. According to scientists, the longest total solar eclipse was about twelve and a half minutes.[17] Also, no springtime solar eclipse visible in the Middle East occurred around the years when Christ was crucified.[18] An eclipse is predictable since it depends on the alignment of the sun, moon, and earth. By consulting astronomical charts and making calculations, scientists both in antiquity and today know precisely when an eclipse will occur in the future, as well as when and where eclipses have occurred in the past.

It can be said with absolute certainty that the darkness was not the result of an eclipse because Christ was crucified at Passover, which is always celebrated during a full moon. A full moon is large and luminous because the moon is behind the earth but is illumined by the sun. A solar eclipse occurs when the moon comes between the sun and the earth, blocking the rays of the sun.[19] Therefore, the darkness could not have been the result of an eclipse.

---

16 Only Mark states that he was crucified at the "third hour" (Mark 15:25), about nine AM. No one has ever arrived at a truly satisfactory explanation for why Mark differs in this detail, although many have tried.

17 According to NASA, this took place on December 7 in AD 150 and lasted twelve minutes and twenty-three seconds. https://eclipse.gsfc.nasa.gov/SEcat5/SEcatalog.html.

18 In the years AD 25–35 only two total solar eclipses occurred in the spring, and those both took place in the southern hemisphere and would not have been visible in Jerusalem. One took place in March of 33 southeast of Africa and the other in March of 34, just north of Australia. The NASA website has a solar eclipse search engine. Go to https://eclipse.gsfc.nasa.gov/SEsearch/SEsearch.php.

19 A new moon is positioned between the sun and the earth. This is what makes an eclipse

Some people deny that the darkness happened. They attribute it to legend or myth, or dismiss it as a dramatic embellishment by the evangelists, perhaps a symbol of spiritual darkness, an image of divine judgment inspired by Old Testament concepts (Amos 8:9; Joel 2:10; Jer. 15:9). The evangelists knew the word "eclipse," and if one had actually occurred at this time, they would have used that word and attributed it to the divine plan. But they did not call it an eclipse because no solar eclipse occurred, let alone a total solar eclipse, which is even rarer.

Nonetheless, an unnatural darkness enveloped the earth while Christ was on the cross. Evidence that an inexplicable darkness occurred was preserved in the earliest known historical reference to Christ outside the New Testament. About twenty years after the crucifixion, a pagan Greek historian named Thallos wrote a history of the eastern Mediterranean from the fall of Troy to his present day, around the year 55. Like most ancient literary works, Thallos's chronicle has not survived, but his assessment of the darkness that occurred when Christ died was preserved by an early Church Father, Julius Africanus (c. 160–240). Julius composed his own *History of the World* around the year 220, and he relied on and referred to Thallos's work and other ancient sources. Thallos, an eyewitness, wrote about the darkness, and Julius preserved his comments. Thallos chronicled and commented on the darkness because it was both a significant and an unusual historical event that had occurred rather recently, within Thallos's own lifetime and that of his readers.

Extremely noteworthy is that Thallos attempted to explain away the darkness in order to refute Christian claims that the darkness while Christ was on the cross was evidence of his divinity. Thallos disagreed with Christian claims and wrote that it was merely a natural occurrence, an eclipse, which is why Julius Africanus responded and proved that the darkness was not an eclipse.[20]

---

possible because the moon blocks the sun's rays: sun → moon → earth. But Passover always takes place during a full moon, which is the opposite phase, when the moon is on the other side of the earth: sun → earth → moon. Therefore, a solar eclipse would be impossible during the phase of a full moon, therefore impossible during the season of Passover.

20 Africanus wrote, "Thallos calls this darkness an eclipse of the sun, which seems to me to be wrong." Africanus also employed his knowledge of science to explain why a solar eclipse could not have occurred when Christ was crucified, because Passover is always

Julius Africanus refuted Thallos by checking the astrological records and determining that no eclipse happened that year.

Thallos unintentionally provided historical eyewitness proof of an extended period of darkness on the day Christ was crucified. This detail is particularly significant because Thallos wrote only about twenty years after Christ's crucifixion, the darkness was a recent historical event remembered by many, and Thallos was a pagan attempting to dispute Christian claims. He did not dispute that the darkness occurred, since so many had experienced it. He only disputed the cause, which Christians said was the crucifixion of the Lord.

Thallos was not the only pagan historian to confirm the unusual darkness that occurred the day Christ died. Although not personally an eyewitness to the darkness, Phlegon, another pagan Greek historian who wrote during the reign of Emperor Hadrian (AD 117–135), chronicled both the darkness (which he called an eclipse) and the earthquake that occurred when Christ died. Phlegon wrote:

> In the fourth year, however, of Olympiad 202,[21] an eclipse of the sun happened, greater and more excellent than any that had happened before it; at the sixth hour, day turned into dark night, so that the stars were seen in the sky, and an earthquake in Bithynia toppled many buildings of the city of Nicaea.[22]

---

celebrated during a full moon. Africanus's *History* was also lost, but his discussion of the event and his refutation of Thallos was copied by a Byzantine historian, George Syncellos, around the year 800 in his work *Chronicle*.

21 The Greeks marked their years by the Olympiads, which took place every four years. The fourth year of the 202nd Olympiad would have been between our dates AD July 32 and June 33. January was not the first month of the year for the ancients; therefore, their years do not precisely correspond to our dates.

22 Like the history written by Thallos, Phlegon's original composition has not survived, but he was quoted by several other ancient writers who preserved these comments for us, including Origen (*Contra Celsum*, 2.33), Julius Africanus (*Chronography*, 18.1), St. Jerome (quoting Eusebius of Caesarea's *Chronicle* for the eighteenth through nineteenth year of Tiberius), and John Philoponus (a sixth-century Greek Christian philosopher and scientist in *On the Creation of the World*, 2.21.2). See Brown, *Death of the Messiah*, 2:1042.

Both Thallos and later Phlegon attributed the darkness to an eclipse, but Julius Africanus proved that the darkness that occurred could only have been supernatural—the work of God, not of nature. The sun inexplicably grew dark, and it was very dark for a very long time on the day of Christ's death, supporting this detail of the Gospel narrative.[23]

> When they had ceased mocking, when they were satiated with their jeerings, and had spoken all that they were minded, then He shows the darkness, in order that at least so (having vented their anger) they may profit by the miracle. For this was more marvelous than coming down from the cross, that being on the cross He should work these things.[24]

The darkness expressed the reality of who Christ is: eternal God. But the humiliating events, the taunts, the mockery, the association with criminals, the horrific suffering, and the dreadful crucifixion itself were all in fulfillment of prophecy. The Sanhedrin should have remembered that the prophets foretold not only a glorious, triumphant Messiah, Son of David, but a different kind of messiah, one who would suffer: the Messiah, Son of Joseph.

---

23   For more details on the discussion concerning Thallos and his comments, see Van Voorst and Evans, *Jesus Outside the New Testament*, 20; Harris, "References to Jesus in Classical Authors," 323–24; and Prigent, "Thallos, Phelgum et le Testimonium Flavianum: Temoins de Jesus?" 329–34.

24   Chrysostom, Homily 88, *Homilies on Matthew*, NPNF-1, 10:501.

CHAPTER 26

The Messiah Son of Joseph

B IBLICAL PROPHECIES ABOUT THE MESSIAH engender debate among the Jews then and now. What will the Messiah be like, and when will he come? The reason for the confusion is that prophecies about the Messiah in the Bible seem contradictory. Some prophecies foretell a kingly warrior Messiah who will vanquish his enemies, while other prophecies predict that the Messiah will be rejected, suffer, and die. Some prophecies predict a glorious figure who will come on the clouds of heaven, while others speak of a humble Messiah who will ride on a donkey. The Messiah will have the Spirit of the Lord, will be a healer and the righteous Servant of the Lord, and will judge with true judgment.

The disagreements reflected in the Talmud, which was written after the time of Christ, are ongoing in Judaism today. The wide variety of prophecies resulted in many discussions and different ideas about the Messiah. How could all these different qualities be embodied in one person? Disagreements over the interpretation of these prophecies existed during the first century also. Some scholars say that the Jews anticipated a wide variety of Messiahs, and they point to figures such as Elijah, Melchizedek, and even Abraham as messianic.[1] But these were associated with apocalyptic expectations, specu-

---

1 The Qumran community (the Jewish religious community that created the Dead Sea Scrolls) expected two messiahs, the "Messiahs of Aaron and Israel" (Manual of Discipline 9.11).

lations about the end times that involved the possible appearance of various Jewish personalities from long ago. Those figures are not actually messianic.

While it is true that no single idea about the Messiah was universally accepted among all first-century Jews, there is no question that the Davidic Messiah predominated. Because prophecies about the role, actions, and person of the Messiah seem contradictory, a notion existed even before the time of Christ that there would be two Messiahs: the victorious warrior king, Son of David, and a suffering Messiah who would die, called the Messiah Son of Joseph. Recent scholarship has confirmed that this idea existed in Judaism even before the first century, but it developed further and was especially embraced after the failure of the last Jewish revolt, the Bar Kochba Revolt (AD 132–136).[2]

The Suffering Messiah: Isaiah 53

THE IDEA OF A SUFFERING Messiah, known as the Messiah Ben Joseph (Messiah, Son of Joseph), is very alive in Judaism today. The expectation of two Messiahs "holds an important place in Jewish theology . . . a standard article of faith, early and firmly established and universally accepted."[3] The idea of two

---

2   About one hundred years after the time of Christ, Simon bar Kosiba claimed to be the Messiah and organized a short-lived, unsuccessful military revolt in Judea against the Roman Empire. He changed his name from bar Kosiba to bar Kochba, which means "son of the star," because of a messianic prophecy: "A star shall come forth out of Jacob, and a scepter shall rise out of Israel" (Num. 24:17). One of the most famous Jews of the day, Rabbi Akiva, who is still a revered authority in Judaism, believed that Simon Bar Kosiba was the Messiah, and Akiva supported the war against Rome. Both were killed by the Romans, along with many other Jews. The Bar Kochba Revolt was the last time the Jews rebelled against Rome.

3   He is also sometimes referred to as the Messiah Son of Ephraim. Torrey, "The Messiah Son of Ephraim," 253. Torrey discusses the various messiahs and the possible reasons for their development from a Jewish perspective. Ideas about the Messiah Son of Joseph grew and developed considerably after the Bar Kochba Revolt, especially the idea that this Messiah would die in battle. Joseph Heinemann asserted that the Messiah Ben Joseph idea developed to explain the famous Rabbi Akiva's mistaken belief that Simon Bar Kosiba was the Messiah and to protect Rabbi Akiva's reputation. Heinemann, "The Messiah of Ephraim and the Premature Exodus of the Tribe of Ephraim." But examination of Jewish writings prior to the Christian era has conclusively established that a suffering Messiah expectation already existed before the time of Christ. Torrey notes

messiahs with very different destinies developed because the rabbis and Jewish sages were not able to reconcile the apparent contradictions in the biblical prophecies about the Messiah, especially because these incongruities perfectly fit Christian claims about Jesus. Even more surprising is recent recognition among Jewish scholars of pre-Christian statements in Jewish writings that identify the Messiah Son of Joseph as the Son of God who dies for his people.[4]

Isaiah 53, typically referred to as the Suffering Servant passage, is perhaps the most extraordinary biblical prophecy fulfilled by Christ.

Who had believed what we have heard?
  And to whom has the arm of the LORD been revealed?
For he grew up before him like a young plant,
    and like a root out of dry ground;
He had no form or comeliness that we should look at him,
    and no beauty that we should desire him.
He was despised and rejected by men;
    a man of sorrows, and acquainted with grief;
and as one from whom men hide their faces
    he was despised, and we esteemed him not.
Surely he has borne our griefs
    and carried our sorrows;
yet we esteemed him stricken,
    smitten by God, and afflicted.
But he was wounded for our transgressions,
    he was bruised for our iniquities;

---

that after the devastations caused by the Jewish revolts, rabbis downplayed messianic expectations (Torrey, 256).

4 Knohl, "The Messiah Son of Joseph." Knohl believes that the Messiah Son of Joseph who was killed goes back to the first century BC or early first century AD and even that his death would be for others. Knohl cites a number of statements in Jewish pseudepigrapha. For example, in *The Testaments of the Twelve Patriarchs*, Jacob tells Joseph that the "sinless one would die for the sake of impious men." Kee, "Testaments of the Twelve Patriarchs," 826. See also Second Esdras (4 Ezra) 7:28–31 and similar ideas in the Apocalypse of Baruch. The pseudepigrapha are not Jewish Scriptures, but they are useful to scholars because they express Jewish thoughts, beliefs, and expectations around the time of Christ.

upon him was the chastisement that made us whole,
   and with his stripes we are healed.
All we like sheep have gone astray;
   we have turned everyone to his own way;
and the LORD has laid on him
   the iniquity of us all.
He was oppressed, and he was afflicted,
   yet he opened not his mouth;
like a lamb that is led to the slaughter,
   and like a sheep before its shearers is dumb,
   so he opened not his mouth.
By oppression and judgment he was taken away;
   and as for his generation, who considered
that he was cut off out of the land of the living,
   stricken for the transgression of my people?
And they made his grave with the wicked
   and with a rich man in his death,
although he had done no violence,
   and there was no deceit in his mouth.
Yet it was the will of the LORD to bruise him;
   he has put him to grief;
when he makes himself an offering for sin,
   he shall see his offspring, he shall prolong his days;
the will of the LORD shall prosper in his hand;
   he shall see the fruit of the travail of his soul and be satisfied;
by his knowledge shall the righteous one, my servant,
   make many to be accounted righteous;
   and he shall bear their iniquities.
Therefore I will divide him a portion with the great,
   and he shall divide the spoil with the strong;
because he poured out his soul to death,
   and was numbered with the transgressors;
yet he bore the sin of many,
   and made intercession for the transgressors. (Isaiah 53)

Isaiah foretold that the Messiah would be ordinary in appearance. To the world it would seem that he was cursed by God, but his sufferings were on the people's behalf, and they were healed through his wounds. He was condemned as a lawbreaker and as a false prophet. He was crucified between two thieves even though he was without sin. He suffered silently even though he had harmed no one and was completely truthful.

The Suffering Servant would be humiliated but would also be vindicated by God because he was willing to die. His suffering would bear much fruit. Others would become righteous because of his actions.

This remarkable prophecy about the person and mission of the Messiah profoundly and accurately describes what happened to Jesus Christ and strongly supports Christian claims. But Isaiah 53 has led to deep conflicts among rabbis and Jewish scholars about its interpretation. They can never accept that the passage refers to Jesus, but they cannot arrive at a consensus as to its meaning. It became such an uncomfortable issue that the entire chapter of Isaiah 53 has been removed from the Jewish lectionary. Even devout Jews who attend the synagogue consistently throughout the year will never hear this prophecy.[5] To refute Christian claims that Jesus fulfilled Isaiah 53, many Jewish interpreters resort to weak and novel interpretations. During the Middle Ages, Jewish interpreters began to explain the Suffering Servant as referring to the Jewish people, who have suffered wrongly.[6] They support this interpretation by pointing to some Old Testament passages that refer to all the people of Israel collectively in the singular as "Israel, my servant."

But Israel as the servant of the Lord does not always refer to the nation collectively in the Scriptures. The "servant of the Lord" can also refer to a single individual. This is especially true and obvious in the section of Isaiah, called the Servant Songs, that describes the Messiah (Is. 42:1–4; 49:1–6; 50:4–9; 52:13—53:12). The Servant of the Lord cannot be the people of Israel because

---

5   The passage has not been removed from their Scriptures, but Jews are not likely to come across it in their Bibles, because Jews typically do not study the Bible. They study the Talmud, the collection of rabbinic interpretations of the Law of Moses.

6   This is probably the most common Jewish explanation today. See Rembaum, "The Development of a Jewish Exegetical Tradition Regarding Isaiah 53."

it describes a single innocent man who suffers for the people of Israel, and by his sufferings they are healed. The Jews have suffered unfairly many times in history, yet they are not sinless, as the Suffering Servant is described to be. They have not suffered on behalf of others, and their sufferings did not save others. The nation of Israel cannot simultaneously be both the innocent Suffering Servant who is saving others and the people who are being saved. Jewish people cannot be their own messiah; otherwise they would be suffering for their own sins and then healed by their own suffering. The prophecy is clear: a single, innocent individual will suffer and die for the nation, and because of his suffering others will be healed.[7]

The Church's understanding of Isaiah 53 as messianic prophecy did not originate with the Church, nor was that interpretation developed after the time of Christ. Jewish interpreters, rabbis, and commentators regarded Isaiah 53 as messianic prophecy before the time of Christ.[8] But today, because of its uncanny similarity to what happened to Jesus, Jews rejected it as a messianic prophecy. The fact that the chapter has been excluded from the Jewish lectionary is strong evidence of its application to Jesus and proof of the weakness of the Jewish interpretation that denies it is a messianic prophecy fulfilled by him.

The Dead Messiah: Zechariah 12

NOT ONLY ISAIAH, BUT OTHER prophets also described a suffering Messiah. The Book of Zechariah especially contains many prophecies fulfilled by Christ (see Zech. 9—13). He described a shepherd who cared for the flock, in contrast to the Jewish leaders, who exploited their people and did not care about them. This shepherd was to be God's ruler over his people, but he would be rejected by them, pierced and smitten, and mourned like a firstborn son

---

7   For an easily accessible discussion, see Efraim Goldstein's article "Who's the Subject of Isaiah 53? You Decide!" at https://jewsforjesus.org/publications/issues/issues-v13-n06/whos-the-subject-of-isaiah-53-you-decide/. Although Goldstein presents Christian beliefs, he marshals a number of pre-Christian rabbinic traditions to support the view that many during the era of Second Temple Judaism believed that the Messiah would suffer.

8   See Janowski and Stuhlmacher, *Suffering Servant*.

and only child: "When they look on him whom they have pierced, they shall mourn him, as one mourns for an only child, and weep bitterly over him, as one weeps over a first-born" (Zech. 12:10b).

This prophecy of the piercing is specific and important. It was also recognized as messianic before the time of Christ and is still interpreted that way by Jews. This prophecy generates discussion among Jews about the meaning and interpretation of what seem to be conflicting passages. One Jewish scholar remarkably admitted that he cannot explain these prophecies and concluded that they are eschatological, not to be fulfilled by any historical person. Interestingly, this scholar wrote of the future Messiah Son of Joseph "that he died for his people through no fault of his, but because they failed him, is clearly indicated in the present passage [Zech.12:9–12] as the [Jewish] commentators agree—though they vainly suppose the martyr to be a historical personage."[9] According to the Babylonian Talmud, the Messiah Ben Joseph would be pierced, killed, and mourned like an only child and firstborn son.[10] The idea of a suffering messiah is undeniable in Judaism. Because the Messiah Ben Joseph suffers and dies, many Jews have concluded that he must be a different person from the Davidic Messiah, who will appear at some later date after the death of the Messiah Son of Joseph.[11]

---

9   Torrey, "Messiah Son of Ephraim," 273.

10   *Sukk.* 5. Rabbis of later periods also came to this conclusion; see, for example, Rashi's commentary on Tractate Sukkah 52:71. Rashi, whose full name is Rabbi Shlomo Yitzchaki (1040–1105), wrote commentaries on the Bible and on the Talmud. He is one of the most influential interpreters of Jewish tradition, and his commentaries are still widely read. Rabbi Moshe Alshich (1508–1593) also wrote that the Messiah will willingly suffer for the sins of Israel and that he will die by piercing. This is also expressed in the *Yalkut Shimoni* of the Talmud, a famous work by Simeon, a medieval Jewish scholar in Germany, who created a compilation of Jewish interpretations called "the Yalkut," which means "anthology."

11   As time progressed, additional expectations were added to the Messiah Son of Joseph figure, including the idea that he would die in battle, but this was definitely not part of the early Jewish interpretation. This elaboration was created after the time of Christ. Today, among Jews who still believe that the Messiah will be an actual person, both messianic figures are typically connected to eschatological Jewish expectations.

Why "Son of Joseph"?

BUT WHY JOSEPH, AND WHICH Joseph? Messiah Ben Joseph does not refer to Joseph, the stepfather of Jesus, nor to Joseph of Arimathea, but to the Joseph whom the Orthodox Church refers to as Joseph the Comely (Handsome), who lived nearly four thousand years ago and whose story is told in the Book of Genesis (chs. 37; 39–50). This Joseph, the son of Jacob and the great-grandson of Abraham, is the model for the suffering and dying Messiah because of his life of righteous suffering and his remarkable character.

Jacob had twelve sons, each of whom later became the head of a family group, a tribe, which took the name of that son.[12] Joseph was the favorite son of Jacob and the first son of Rachel, Jacob's beloved second wife. Even at a young age, Joseph possessed many virtues. He also had prophetic dreams and the ability to interpret dreams. Jacob showed his love for Joseph by giving him an expensive cloak, traditionally described as a "coat of many colors" (Gen. 37:3). His older brothers were jealous of him, and when they were far from home tending the flocks, they impulsively sold Joseph as a slave to a passing caravan on its way to Egypt. They told their father Jacob that Joseph had been killed by wild animals, and Jacob mourned Joseph deeply for years. But Joseph was alive and living as a slave in Egypt.

Joseph did not change his character after becoming a slave but was hard working, honest, capable, and trustworthy. Soon his master gave him responsibility over the entire household. Joseph was a handsome young man, and his master's wife attempted to seduce him; but Joseph fled from sin, spurning her advances. She falsely accused him of attempted rape, and Joseph was put into prison. There he correctly interpreted the dreams of his cellmates. Eventually he came to Pharaoh's attention when Pharaoh had a dream he did not understand. Joseph explained that a period of plentiful harvest would be followed by a great famine.

The Pharaoh was so impressed by Joseph that he put Joseph in charge of preparing for the famine and managing the grain. Joseph became the right

---

12 The Twelve Tribes of Israel are named for the sons of Jacob, except for Joseph, who does not have a tribe named after him. Instead, Joseph's two sons have tribes named for them, Ephraim and Manasseh.

hand of Pharaoh and the second most powerful man in all Egypt. He was loved and highly respected by the Egyptian people, who owed him their lives. When his brothers came to Egypt to buy grain during the famine, Joseph recognized them and eventually revealed his true identity to them. He brought the entire family to Egypt because the famine was to continue for several years. Joseph forgave his brothers for selling him as a slave, telling them, "You meant evil against me; but God meant it for good" (Gen. 50:20).

Joseph as a Type of Christ

JOSEPH IS A UNIQUE AND important figure in the Jewish Scriptures. Although he was consistently godly and virtuous, he nonetheless suffered wrongly at the hands of others more than once, precisely because of his virtue. He is a figure of salvation because he saved the nation of Egypt from death by starvation through his interpretation of Pharaoh's dream and his wise management of the grain Pharaoh entrusted to him. Joseph saved his own entire family from starvation as well. Since Jacob and his twelve sons are the ancestors of all the tribes of Israel, the Jewish people exist today because of Joseph.

The idea of a salvific figure who was despised and misunderstood, and who suffered even though he was virtuous and innocent of any wrongdoing, led the Jews to entitle the righteous savior Messiah who suffers undeservedly as the Messiah Ben Joseph. The early Church also recognized the similarities between Joseph and Jesus. Joseph is a type or foreshadowing of Christ. It is not by accident that the Orthodox Church highlights this typology in the services of Holy Week. Both Jesus and Joseph were virtuous but were rejected by their own people. They were believed to be dead and were mourned, although Jesus was actually killed and Joseph was not. Both were wrongly and falsely accused, and both suffered, although blameless. Both resisted temptation and maintained their virtue. Both were despised and became servants, even though they were not in fact slaves. Both were sold for silver coins, both were about thirty years old at the important transition point of their lives, and both were accepted and became great among Gentiles while remaining unrecognized for who they truly were among their own people. What was done to both Jesus and Joseph was evil, but God used that evil for good.

The Jews had difficulty reconciling the different messianic prophecies and consider them incompatible. This is why many Jews, both then and now, have believed there would be two messiahs, one who suffered and one who would be a triumphant king. But human beings are incapable of understanding the wisdom and ways of God. The apparent contradictions about the identity, role, and destiny of the Messiah are combined and perfectly fulfilled in the one person of Jesus Christ, who both suffered unjustly and was victorious. He is both Messiah Son of Joseph and Messiah Son of David. The Isaiah 53 prophecy and other prophecies foretold that the Servant of the Lord would suffer and die, but he would also prevail. Christians recognize that both messianic expectations were profoundly and mysteriously fulfilled in the one person of Jesus Christ.

CHAPTER 27

The Last Words

E ACH EVANGELIST TOLD THE STORY of Christ in his own manner, emphasizing what he believed to be most important about Jesus. This does not mean that the evangelists were careless or dishonest. Each simply chose certain stories and details to include in his Gospel and consequently excluded other details. They did not attempt to tell us every detail of Christ's life, death, or ministry, but only what they considered most noteworthy and important.

The Lord made seven statements from the cross. None of the Gospels contains all of them. Each evangelist chose to include the statement(s) he believed to be most important for conveying his particular message about Christ.

> And about the ninth hour Jesus cried with a loud voice, "Eli, Eli, lama sabach-thani?" that is, "My God, my God, why hast thou forsaken me?" And some of the bystanders hearing it said, "This man is calling Elijah." And one of them at once ran and took a sponge, filled it with vinegar, and put it on a reed, and gave it to him to drink. But the others said, "Wait, let us see whether Elijah will come to save him." And Jesus cried again with a loud voice and yielded up his spirit. (Matt. 27:46–50)

Elijah

THE GREAT OLD TESTAMENT PROPHET Elijah, an important figure in the Jewish imagination, is associated with the end times because of the prophecy in Malachi that Elijah would return before the "Day of the Lord" to prepare the way (4:5–6). Elijah was also considered a precursor of the Messiah. This is why John the Forerunner was identified with Elijah, because Jesus was both the Messiah and the Lord. By the first century, a Jewish tradition had also developed that a righteous person could call on Elijah for help in times of distress.

The bystanders at Christ's crucifixion believed Jesus was calling on Elijah. This suggests that Jesus' contemporaries considered his preaching of the Kingdom of God to be a proclamation of the nearness of the end. For this reason, other bystanders stopped the man who attempted to offer Jesus some of the vinegar, saying, "Wait; let's see whether Elijah will come and save him." This is consistent with Jewish expectations at that time.[1]

"Why Have You Forsaken Me?"

MARK'S GOSPEL, WRITTEN FOR A Gentile audience, emphasized Jesus as the powerful Son of God. He also emphasized the mysterious nature of Christ's saving ministry, a feature commonly referred to as the "messianic secret." Among all the Lord's last words on the cross, "My God, my God, why hast thou forsaken me?" (Ps. 22/21:1; Mark 15:34; Matt. 27:46) is by far the most misunderstood. It is not a cry of despair or abandonment, as we will see below.

Among the evangelists, St. Mark most vividly highlights Christ as the suffering Messiah. The Passion narrative dominates his Gospel, and in his presentation of the crucifixion scene, Mark reports only one statement of Jesus from the cross: "My God, my God, why hast thou forsaken me?" This final statement of Christ fits with Mark's purpose and theme. It is the first line of Psalm 22, another messianic prophecy that dramatically captures the agony of the Suffering Servant of God foretold in Isaiah 53.

---

1   Kittel and Bromiley, *Theological Dictionary of the New Testament*, 2:931–34.

"My God, my God . . ." is also the only statement Matthew's Gospel records Christ making from the cross. Saint Matthew addressed his Gospel to an entirely different audience from Mark's. Matthew's community consisted of Jewish Christians—Jews who believed that Jesus was the Christ, the Messiah. Matthew focused on what was most important to his original readers: proving that Jesus fulfilled the messianic prophecies. For that reason, Matthew quoted from numerous Old Testament prophecies, far more than any other evangelist. "My God, my God . . ." draws our attention to Jesus' fulfillment of these.

When he said, "My God, my God, why hast thou forsaken me?" Jesus was not expressing a feeling that God had abandoned or forsaken him. He was not expressing fear or doubt, nor was he responding to that moment of crisis out of his human nature, as an ordinary person might do. "My God, my God, why have you forsaken me?" is the first line of the psalm we know as Psalm 22.[2] Everyone knew this hymn from the synagogue services. Jesus was quoting this particular psalm as prophecy, perhaps even praying it, and calling on those around him to recall it as well.

Psalm 22 describes the crucifixion scene and its aftermath in many striking ways. Let us look at a few of its verses.

[1] My God, my God, why hast thou forsaken me?
[4] In thee our fathers trusted;
     they trusted, and thou didst deliver them.
[6] But I am a worm, and no man;
     scorned by men, and despised by the people.
[7] All who see me mock at me,
     they make mouths at me, they wag their heads,
[8] "He committed his cause to the Lord; let him deliver him,
     let him rescue him, for he delights in him!"
[14] I am poured out like water,
     and all my bones are out of joint;
my heart is like wax,

---

2   Or Psalm 21 in the Septuagint (LXX) numbering. The Scriptures originally had no chapter or verse numbers, so the psalms were not numbered. The psalms were sung as the hymns of the Jews. The title of a hymn was always the first line of the psalm.

> it is melted within my breast;
> ¹⁵ my strength is dried up like a potsherd,
>> and my tongue cleaves to my jaws;
>> thou dost lay me in the dust of death.
> ¹⁶ Yea, dogs are round about me;
>> a company of evildoers encircle me;
>> they have pierced my hands and feet—
> ¹⁷ I can count all my bones—
>> they stare and gloat over me;
> ¹⁸ they divide my garments among them;
>> and for my raiment they cast lots. (Ps. 21/22)

Many details describe the crucifixion scene, in particular the speaker's physical distress, the piercing of his hands and feet,[3] the dividing of his garments and casting of lots for his clothes, the gloating and mocking by the spectators, and even their statements.

Perhaps most surprising is not only the fulfillment of the prophecy during the crucifixion itself, but that it foretells the unexpected reversal of this terrible situation. The first two-thirds of the psalm express the extreme distress of the suffering person. His situation is so grim that survival appears impossible, but the psalm abruptly changes in verse 22 to become a psalm of praise, glorification, and vindication. The last third of the psalm foretells his triumph and that "the nations" (the Gentiles) will come to the LORD because of his suffering. They will remember what took place.

> ^{22/23} I will tell of thy name to my brethren;
>> in the midst of the congregation I will praise thee:
> ^{23/24} You who fear the LORD, praise him!

---

3   In the Masoretic text (c. AD 1000), the current Hebrew Bible used by Jews, this verse was changed to read "like a lion they are at my hands and my feet" rather than "they have pierced" (literally "dug"). This occurred intentionally, when a tiny change was made to medieval Hebrew manuscripts by changing one letter, a *vav* ו to a *yod* י. If "like a lion" was the original wording, the prophecy would not apply to Jesus. However, first-century Hebrew manuscripts, the Dead Sea Scrolls, and the Septuagint (c. 250 BC) all read "they have pierced."

all you sons of Jacob, glorify him,

and stand in awe of him, all you sons of Israel!

24/25 For he has not despised or abhorred

the affliction of the afflicted;

and has not hid his face from him,

but has heard, when he cried to him.

27/28 All the ends of the earth shall remember

and turn to the LORD;

and all the families of the nations

shall worship before him.

30/31 Posterity shall serve him;

men shall tell of the LORD to the coming generation,

31/32 and proclaim his deliverance to a people yet unborn,

that he has wrought it. (Ps. 21/22)

When Jesus called out "My God, my God, why hast thou forsaken me?" he was not expressing a belief or sense that God had abandoned him. He was expressing the opposite. He was praying the psalm, and by calling out the first line perhaps he was also prompting others to recall it. By bringing this psalm to their minds, he was sending a message to those looking on—both those who loved him, gathered at the foot of the cross, and those who were jeering at him from afar. It was as though he was saying, "It may look bad for me now, but I will rise again. I will once again speak of God to my brethren and praise him in the congregation."[4] Jesus was saying that his Father had not abandoned him but had heard him and approved of him, and that he would rise again.

The psalm foretells an amazing mystery: through the cross, a horrific instrument of torture, the entire earth will worship the Lord. Future generations will be taught that the Lord has brought deliverance and salvation through this moment. The concluding message of the psalm is triumphant: deliverance and salvation will come to the nations (the Gentiles) and even to

---

4   In the LXX the word translated as "congregation" is *ecclesia*, the Greek word for church. This appropriately expresses the ultimate victory of Christ and the cross and its proclamation in the Church.

those yet unborn. Far from being a statement of despair, Jesus was expressing confidence in his ultimate victory over sin and death—assurance that through the cross, salvation will be accomplished and the Lord will draw all the nations of the world to himself. This was always the purpose of the cross and had been foretold by the Lord during his ministry: "And I, when I am lifted up [meaning crucified] from the earth, will draw all men to myself" (John 12:32).

The words "My God, my God, why have you forsaken me?" were spoken so that we might recall and reflect on the entire psalm. For Mark, whose Gospel emphasized the hidden, mysterious, and paradoxical nature of Christ's mission, this statement expressed that Jesus was truly the prophesied but unrecognized Messiah, the Suffering Servant of Isaiah 53. For Matthew, whose Gospel emphasized Jesus' fulfillment of prophecy, this psalm confirms not only that the crucifixion fulfills prophecy, but also the victory of Christ through the Resurrection, as well as the acceptance and worship of the Lord by the Gentiles and their salvation. Matthew's Gospel ends with the Great Commission, when the Lord sent the disciples out to "make disciples of all nations" (Matt. 28:19).

"Father, Forgive Them"

"FATHER, FORGIVE THEM, FOR THEY know not what they do" (Luke 23:34). This extraordinary statement by Christ on the cross was preserved for us only by St. Luke, whose Gospel strongly emphasizes the theme of forgiveness. After they had unjustly sentenced him to death, scourged him, mocked him, beat him, spat on him, and finally crucified him, our Lord Jesus gave us the greatest possible example of humility, longsuffering, and forgiveness. His behavior was emulated by the Protomartyr St. Stephen, who also forgave those who killed him (Acts 7:60), as well as by thousands of later martyrs who would take up their crosses and follow Christ. Countless accounts of martyrdom relate how Christian martyrs forgave their persecutors in imitation of their Lord. What sublime doctrine! It is indeed beyond amazement and comprehension that the Lord of all creation should accept this treatment from the hands of his creatures. Rather than responding with threats of divine retribution, he spoke only loving, gentle words of forgiveness and care.

Saint John Chrysostom remarks that by the words "Father, forgive them," he showed they could be forgiven even for this unspeakable act, just as St. Paul was forgiven even though he had persecuted the Church. The Lord prayed to the Father that they might be forgiven, for they did not know what they were doing. Chrysostom asks exactly what was it that they did not know? They were not only ignorant about who he was but also about the mystery of salvation that was being accomplished through this event. "For Christ did not say 'for they do not know *me*,' but 'for they do not know what they *do*,'" Chrysostom remarked.[5] The purpose of the cross was the salvation of the world. Therefore, even though Christ was treated with extreme cruelty, to his very last breath he did everything for the salvation of all, praying for their forgiveness and salvation.

Chrysostom used the verse to instruct his congregation: "This is how we ought to love our enemies, thus to imitate Christ. . . . This is to love God. Who has ordered it. Who has given it as His Law. To imitate him is to love our enemy."[6] Saint Augustine also spoke of the healing Christ brought us through the cross:

> Even while He was being killed, the Doctor was curing the sick with His blood. He said, you see, "Father forgive them, for they do not know what they are doing." Nor were these words futile or without effect. And of those people, thousands later on believed in the One they had slain, so that they learned how to suffer for Him who had suffered both for them and at their hands.[7]

"Today You Will Be with Me"

"TODAY YOU WILL BE WITH me in Paradise" (Luke 23:43). The Gospel of St. Luke offers many profound lessons, but it is here, in the example of Christ on the cross, that Luke's themes of repentance, humility, and forgiveness reach the summit of perfection. It is Luke alone who tells us that Jesus not

---

5   Chrysostom, Homily 7, *Homilies on 1 Corinthians*, NPNF-1, 12:36.
6   Chrysostom, Homily 7, *Homilies on Ephesians*, NPNF-1, 13:84.
7   Augustine, Sermon 302:3, W. Aug. *Sermons* III.8:302.

only forgave those responsible for his horrific death but also opened the doors of Paradise to the repentant thief while on the cross.

In the minds of the Jewish leaders, Jesus was cursed by God. As far as they were concerned, this was an incontrovertible fact, because Jesus was put to death as a common criminal along with other criminals. But something extraordinary would happen from the cross, exemplifying the saving purpose of the cross and serving as an important lesson for us.

Initially both thieves reviled Jesus, an extraordinary circumstance in itself. Matthew and Mark attest to this. But at some point, one of them apparently had an epiphany. Chrysostom explains that when the thief on the right observed the extraordinary signs that were taking place, he changed inwardly and recognized Christ. According to Chrysostom, Matthew and Mark show the repentant thief "while he is still retaining his former wickedness in order that you may perceive that his conversion was effected from within and out of his own heart assisted by the grace of God and so he became a better man."[8]

> One of the criminals who were hanged railed at him, saying, "Are you not the Christ? Save yourself and us!" But the other rebuked him, saying, "Do you not fear God, since you are under the same sentence of condemnation? And we indeed justly; for we are receiving the due reward of our deeds; but this man has done nothing wrong." And he said, "Jesus, remember me when you come into your kingdom." (Luke 23:39)

The first thief, on Jesus' left side, also recognized that Jesus was the Christ: "Are you not the Christ? Save yourself and us!" He acknowledged that Jesus had the power to save himself and them! Yet in spite of this knowledge, he did not gain Paradise because he did not acknowledge his own sin. He lacked repentance and humility.

On the other hand, the thief on the right confessed his sin and defended Jesus as innocent of any wrongdoing. Chrysostom describes the repentant thief as a teacher who rebukes and corrects the first thief, in spite of the fact

---

8   Chrysostom, *Homily on the Paralytic Let Down through the Roof* 3, NPNF-1, 9:214.

that both were suffering extraordinary pain and feeling the nails in their flesh. "Do you see his insight and teaching? Quickly from a cross he leapt up into heaven. Then, from his wealth of insight, he silences him, 'Are you still not afraid,' he said, 'since we are in the same judgment?'"[9]

The quick action on the part of Christ to accept the repentance and confession of the thief and to reward him with Paradise is a lesson for us all, St. Augustine noted. Even while hanging on the cross, the Lord was teaching both the robber and us. "The cross was a classroom. That's where the Master taught the robber. The tree He was hanging on became the chair He was teaching from."[10] Chrysostom observes that the thief on Christ's right side confessed his sin by acknowledging his crime, and only after his confession did he ask the Lord to remember him.

> For, lest you think because of the fellowship of punishment that he made him a companion of sin, he brings forward a correction, saying: "And we rightly; for we have suffered what is worthy of what we have done." Do you see a conclusive confession? Do you see how he stripped his transgressions at the cross? For, he says, "You first must tell your sins, that you may be justified." No one compelled him. No one constrained him. . . . And after these things he says: "Remember me, Lord, in your kingdom." He did not dare first to say, "Remember me in your kingdom," until after, through his confession, he had laid aside the burden of sins. Do you see how great the confession is? He confessed, and he opened paradise. He confessed, and he received such confidence as to ask a kingdom after robbery.[11]

Both thieves were hanging on a cross, but only the repentant thief recognized Jesus as the Lord. The faith he expressed is extraordinary. Chrysostom marvels that the thief should possess such insight in spite of the fact that he had not witnessed any of the miracles that Jesus performed during his ministry, nor did he receive promises such as those Christ had made to his disciples.[12]

---

9 Chrysostom, Homily 1.3, *Homilies on the Cross and the Bandits.*
10 Augustine, Sermon 234:2, W. Aug. *Sermons* III.7.37.
11 Chrysostom, Homily 1.3, *Homilies on the Cross and the Bandits.*
12 Chrysostom, Homily 1.2, *Homilies on the Cross and the Bandits.*

Chrysostom contrasts the direct experience of Christ the Jewish authorities possessed, having witnessed his teaching and his many miracles, with the knowledge and disposition of this simple thief. He recognized the divinity of Christ when the learned, educated religious leaders of Israel did not.

> But the bandit did not hear the prophets or see wonders. Only seeing Him nailed upon the cross, he did not focus on dishonor or see disgrace. Instead, he saw divinity itself within. "Remember me," he says, "in your kingdom." This is novel and paradoxical. You see a cross, and you remember a kingdom? What did you see worthy of a kingdom? A crucified man, beaten, mocked, accused, spat upon, flogged. So, tell me, are these worthy of a kingdom? Do you see that he saw with the eyes of faith, and was not scrutinizing visible things? For this reason God was not scrutinizing his bare words. But just as he saw divinity within, thus God saw the bandit's heart within and says, "Today you will be with me in paradise."[13]

Chrysostom contrasts the sin of Adam and its consequence with the sins of the thief and his reward. Adam lost Paradise because of one misdeed, and yet Christ brought this thief, who was guilty of countless sins, into Paradise. Even more extraordinary was that he entered Paradise before anyone else in the world, including the apostles, only because of the extraordinary love of Christ for humanity. The thief simply said, "Remember me in your kingdom." Even then, it was not his words that mattered but his heart, which God alone sees. Chrysostom points to this scene as a powerful reminder that we should never lose hope of our salvation.[14]

"Woman, Behold Your Son"

TO BE ALONE AND ELDERLY with no children and no income, unable to care for oneself, was a terrible predicament to face in the first century. No social services, pensions, senior housing, or nursing care facilities existed.

---

13 Chrysostom, Homily 7, *Homilies on Genesis,* Bilby trans.
14 Chrysostom, Homily 7, *Homilies on Genesis,* Bilby trans.

Elderly parents were cared for by their children, and as he was dying, Jesus was concerned for his mother.

> When Jesus saw his mother, and the disciple whom he loved standing near, he said to his mother, "Woman, behold, your son!" Then he said to the disciple, "Behold, your mother!" And from that hour the disciple took her to his own home. (John 19:26–27)

This touching and beautiful moment is preserved for us only by the Evangelist John, the beloved disciple to whom Jesus entrusted the care of his own mother. Jesus was the only child of Mary, and here he shows his love, concern, and respect for his mother. If he had not been her only child, he would have had no need to ask the beloved disciple to care for his mother.[15]

The first appearance of Mary in the Gospel of John is at the wedding at Cana, when she informs Jesus that the host has run out of wine. Jesus responds by saying, "O woman, what have you to do with me?" (2:3–4). Basically, he is saying that the situation is not their business. He adds, "My hour has not yet come," referring to the hour when his public ministry will begin. The fact that Jesus addresses his mother as "woman" has been cited by some as proof that Mary was simply an ordinary woman and that he had no particular respect for her. Others say that she had overstepped her bounds, or even that he was rebuking his mother and speaking to her harshly. But Jesus frequently addressed women as "woman." Not only was this customary for him, but it was even a term of gentleness and affection (John 4:21; 20:15).

The idea that Jesus disregarded his mother or did not respect her is entirely disproven here, as we see him express his concern for her from the cross. Although experiencing tremendous pain and facing death, he expressed love and concern for his mother, certainly not rebuking her. Saint Augustine commented on the moment:

---

15   The statement by the Lord, "Woman, behold your son," is also is the strongest evidence that the "brothers" of Jesus mentioned in the Gospels (Mark 3:31) were not children of Mary but children of Joseph by a prior marriage—Mary's stepchildren.

That on the cross He acknowledged His mother and entrusted her to the beloved disciple aptly indicated His human affection at the time when He was dying as a man. . . . You see, He had not received from Mary the power He had in His divinity, but He had received from Mary what was hanging on the cross.[16]

Saint John Chrysostom also spoke about the importance of caring for our parents:

While crucified He gave His mother to his disciple's keeping, to instruct us to take every care of our parents, even to our last breath. Why was it that He made no mention of any other woman, though others also were standing there? To teach us to give more to our mothers than to any others. For just as we must not even recognize parents who act as an obstacle to us in spiritual affairs, so also when they do not hinder us in any way, we must give them everything that is their due and place them ahead of all others, in return for their bringing us into existence, in return for their care of us, in return for the numberless ways in which they have helped us.[17]

"I Thirst"

WATER IS AN IMPORTANT SYMBOL in practically every religious tradition because of its association with life. Jesus had once stood in the Temple and proclaimed, "If any one thirst, let him come to me and drink" (John 7:37). On another occasion, after requesting water from a Samaritan woman at a well, he offered to give her "living water," water so satisfying that she would never thirst again (John 4:10). Of course, he was referring to the Holy Spirit and the water of eternal life, which he would provide.

In his humanity, Jesus needed physical water as much as anyone else. On the cross, he was suffering from hypovolemic shock—low bodily fluids—and by now his thirst was beyond description. He was not simply thirsty in the

---

16   Augustine, Sermon 218:10, W. Aug. *Sermons* III.6:185.
17   Chrysostom, Homily 85, *Homilies on the Gospel of John*, FOTC 41:433.

same manner we have all experienced. His thirst was critical and life threatening. Since the Last Supper the evening before, he had received no fluids at
all. He had been sweating profusely from the extreme stress in Gethsemane
as he anticipated his arrest and crucifixion. His apprehension was so extreme
that his capillaries burst and he apparently sweat blood. He was beaten, both
by the Jewish authorities that night and by the Romans in the morning. These
beatings may well have broken his ribs and led to a gradual accumulation of
fluid in his chest. The Romans also administered the most severe chastisement
at their disposal, a scourging, resulting in tremendous blood loss. Sweating
and bleeding, Jesus struggled in the sun attempting to carry the crossbeam to
the execution site, and now his blood pressure was dangerously low. His heart
labored to pump blood and bring oxygen to the vital organs. The posture of
Christ on the cross also contributed to hypotension (abnormally low blood
pressure) because blood would pool in the lower part of the body, adding to
the difficulty of the heart in circulating blood.

Water is so basic to survival that severely dehydrated people become desperate, delirious, obsessed with water, and even violent. We have all experienced craving for water, a dryness of the mouth and throat. This ordinary
thirst is easily ameliorated by consuming liquids or by the body secreting
more saliva. But when no liquid is received, after this initial stage of thirst the
mucus and saliva in the nose and throat become dry and sticky. Every lungful
of air feels hot, and the tongue sticks to the teeth and the roof of the mouth.
The sensation of a lump in the throat begins to arise, and even repeated swallowing cannot alleviate it. As dehydration progresses, the tip of the tongue
becomes hard and heavy, and the eyelids become stiff and immobile.[18] Such
was the thirst of the Lord.

"They offered him wine to drink, mixed with gall; but when he tasted it, he
would not drink it" (Matt. 27:34; Mark 15:23). It was customary for Jewish
women to offer wine to condemned criminals as an act of mercy.[19] The wine

---

18 Zugibe, *Crucifixion of Jesus*, 131.
19 The Talmud also mentions the Jewish tradition of giving wine with incense (*lebona*) to
    condemned criminals. Rabbinic writings suggest that groups of Jewish women would
    attend executions to give some comfort to the criminal, including offering wine mixed
    with certain substances. Berkowitz, *Execution and Invention*, 119 (see chapter 4, "Per-

was mixed with another substance, described either as "wine mixed with gall," in Matthew, or "wine mixed with myrrh," according to Mark. This was fulfillment of prophecy: "They gave me poison for food, and for my thirst they gave me vinegar to drink" (Ps. 69:21/68:22 LXX).

The Hebrew word for "gall" is *rosh:* "they gave me *rosh* for food." The word *rosh* literally means "head" but is often translated as "poison" because *rosh* was an abbreviation for *rosh hobel*, the head of the poppy plant. Eventually *rosh* became a general term in Hebrew for various bitter or poisonous substances, including myrrh, wormwood, and even hemlock. Although these substances were known to be poisonous in large quantities, they were used medicinally in small doses. In the Septuagint translation of the psalm, *rosh* is rendered in Greek as "gall" (*cholē*), which is the word Matthew uses. "Gall" simply indicates a bitter taste; the bitterness could come from any number of substances. It is described as "myrrh" in Mark's Gospel. Myrrh or incense comes from tree resin. The terms "myrrh," "incense," and "gall" were used interchangeably, since all those words referred in general to any bitter aromatic substance that might be mixed into wine for medicinal purposes. Opium poppies were known and cultivated and were used medicinally for pain relief. Poppy extract was also employed as a sedative by the ancient Greeks and Romans.[20]

At a crucifixion, any of these bitter substances—myrrh, poppy seeds, or possibly another plant, such as the mandrake—might be prepared, then mixed into wine and offered as an anesthetic to condemned criminals to alleviate some of the suffering of crucifixion. Sponges soaked in mandrake-laden wine were routinely used at crucifixions. This concoction, called *morion*, was

forming Execution 1" notes 106–9.) Raymond Brown noted that perfumed wine was prized in antiquity and cites Pliny that "the finest wine was spiced with myrrh" (Pliny, *Natural History*, 14.15). But Brown believed that the comfort offered to the condemned may not have been primarily from any narcotic effect but in the alcohol itself (Brown, *Death of the Messiah*, 2:941). Wine in antiquity was stronger with a higher alcoholic content than wine today. Some ancient wines were more like brandy and were even flammable. Haupt, "Alcohol in the Bible," 77.

20 Significant archeological and literary evidence exists for the use of the opium poppy in ancient Greece and Rome. Merlin, "Archeological Evidence for the Tradition of Psychoactive Plant Use in the Old World," 303.

a sedative often referred to as "death wine," since people who received it could appear dead.[21]

"After this Jesus, knowing that all was now finished, said (to fulfil the scripture), 'I thirst.' A bowl of vinegar stood there; so they put a sponge full of the vinegar on hyssop and held it to his mouth" (John 19:28–29). The Gospels mention both the bitter wine and the vinegar. These served different purposes and were offered at different times during the crucifixion process. The wine mixed with a bitter narcotic substance was offered to him immediately when he arrived at Golgotha, prior to the actual crucifixion. The vinegar was for thirst and did not contain any foreign substance. This was offered at the end of the process just before his death.

While it seems odd that a "bowl of vinegar" (John 19:29) was present at the site of the crucifixion, in fact that was rather common. The wine of common Roman soldiers and ordinary laborers was a sour, vinegary wine (*posca*), designed to quench thirst. The Greek word for this drink is *oxos*. John writes that Jesus "received" the vinegar. But the Gospels all agree that Jesus refused to drink the wine mixed with bitter gall, knowing that it contained narcotics intended to dull the pain.[22] Having accepted the cup of suffering, the Lord refused even the slightest diminishment of pain or loss of consciousness while on the cross.

When John wrote that Jesus said "I thirst" "to fulfil the scripture," he was not saying that Jesus deliberately spoke these words in order to fulfill the prophecy, but rather that what took place in fact fulfilled a prophecy made hundreds of years before the time of Christ: a sponge was filled with the vinegary wine, put on a reed, and offered to him (John 19:29).

---

21   Carter, "Narcosis and Nightshade," 1631. Romans routinely used sponges soaked in ether or chloroform and held under a person's nose for inhalation as a form of anesthesia for medical procedures. It was known as *spongia somnifera*. Mandrake extract was especially effective when blended with extracts from the opium poppy. The sponge and the Roman lance or spear are associated with each other because these narcotics could be so effective as to make someone appear dead. Because of this, crucifixion victims were sometimes lanced, which will be discussed below.

22   Matthew and Mark both distinguish between the wine (*oinos*), which Jesus refused (Matt. 27:34; Mark 15:23), and the vinegar (*oxos*, Matt. 27:48; Mark 15:36) that was put on the reed. Luke mentions that soldiers offered Jesus *oxos*, but that it was offered as part of their mocking and taunting (Luke 23:36), not as a gesture of compassion.

John alone mentions that the sponge was put on a stalk of hyssop, leading to much discussion and debate, because a stalk of hyssop is slender and supple, unable to support a liquid-soaked sponge. Because of this and because of similarity between two Greek words, some speculate that the word "hyssop" (*hyssopos*) was a manuscript error and the word should be *hyssōs*, the Greek word for "round," referring to a soldier's lance. They claim that the sponge was put on the end of a Roman soldier's lance and held up to Jesus' mouth. But that is not correct. The word "hyssop" was not an error by John or any manuscript copyist.[23] John knew its significance, which is why he specifically identified the kind of reed.

Hyssop was associated with Passover and with sacrifice. During the Exodus, the Hebrews used hyssop to sprinkle the blood of a lamb on their doorposts to protect them from the angel of death (Ex.12:22). Hyssop was used in many temple ceremonies and was identified with forgiveness—for example, "Purge me with hyssop, and I shall be clean" (Ps. 50/51:7). Because of its association with Passover and temple rituals that removed impurity and imparted forgiveness of sin, John specifically noted the use of hyssop here.[24]

"It Is Finished"

"WHEN JESUS HAD RECEIVED THE vinegar, he said, 'It is finished'; and he bowed his head and gave up his spirit" (John 19:30). By "it is finished" Jesus was not saying that his suffering was over. Rather, this statement means that he had completed the plan of salvation and that all had been accomplished according to the will of the Father. The Greek verb used here is *tetelestai*, from

---

23 Nonetheless, that mistaken idea has even been incorporated recently in some Bible translations. The J. B. Philips translation, *The New Testament in Modern English* (1972), has "spear," and *The Message*, by Eugene Peterson (1993), translates it as "javelin." One translation tried to combine the two and rendered it as "hyssop round" (Darby), while many added "stick," "stalk," or "branch," perhaps to compensate for the flimsiness of the hyssop. But this is not well supported because the word "spear" is not found in any of the early manuscripts. It appears in only two manuscripts dating only as far back as the Middle Ages.

24 Because a hyssop stalk was often weak, it was strengthened by combining it with a reed. The hyssop was used, not the reed alone, because hyssop was used for ritual cleansing or avoiding ritual defilement. See Beetham and Beetham, "A Note on John 19:29."

the noun *telos*, which means "end" or "goal." This one-word sentence can also be translated as "it is accomplished" or "it is completed." The goal had been reached. The plan had arrived at its appointed end.

During his earthly ministry, Christ had said, "My food is to do the will of him who sent me, and to accomplish [*teleioso*] his work" (John 4:34). Jesus repeatedly stated that he had come to earth to do the will of the Father (John 5:30; 6:38–39). The *oikonomia*, the plan of salvation, was put into place before the creation of the world by the Holy Trinity. The Father sent the Son into the world, and the Spirit supported the Son in his work. With one word, Jesus expressed that his work for the salvation of humankind had been completed. With his death, all that was involved in his earthly ministry was complete: becoming incarnate, growing from infancy to adulthood, the calling of disciples, the constant teaching, preaching, and healing of thousands, his instruction to the Twelve, patiently enduring the debates, arguments, opposition, and accusations of the religious authorities, his institution of the Eucharist, the betrayal, the arrest, the trials, the beatings, the scourging, the mockings, the humiliation, and lastly the excruciating pain of the crucifixion itself. It was over. It was accomplished. His work was done, completed to perfection, exactly according to plan. He had achieved his goal. Tetelestai.

John the Evangelist writes that Jesus bowed his head and "handed over his spirit" (translated as "he gave up his spirit"), which means his breath or his life, since *pneuma* ("spirit") is also the Greek word for breath. Ordinarily a person dies and then his head falls forward. But Christ, knowing that he had completed everything necessary for our salvation, lowered his head and then allowed himself to die. This means that Christ was in complete control of his life because, as God, he is the source of life. Chrysostom wrote:

> It is not *after* bowing one's head that one expires ordinarily. Here, however, it was just the opposite. For it was not when he expired that he bowed his head, as is the case with us, but, after he bowed His head *then* he expired. By all these details the Evangelist made it clear that Christ Himself is Lord of all.[25]

---

25   Chrysostom, Homily 85, *Homilies on the Gospel of John*, FOTC 41:434.

Chrysostom observed that everything Christ did showed that he was in complete control of events. He was calm, orchestrating everything from the cross.

The Evangelist endeavored in every way to show that this death was something new; in fact, every detail was controlled by the One who was dying, and that death did not enter His body until He Himself willed it, and He willed it only after all had been fulfilled. That is why he had said: "I have the power to lay down my life and I have power to take it up again" (John 10:18). Therefore, knowing that all things were now accomplished, He said, "I thirst," in this once again fulfilling a prophecy. . . . Offering him a sponge soaked in wine they gave Him a drink in the way in which they offered it to condemned criminals . . . therefore when He had taken it He said, "It is accomplished." Do you see that all things were done calmly and authoritatively?[26]

The critical detail is that the life of Jesus did not ebb away slowly. Rather, his death was accompanied by many amazing signs. He died with power and in complete control of when and how he would die. No one took his life. He gave it up.

There were indeed three crucified but Jesus alone was glorified, that you might learn that it was His power that was in control of everything. Even though it was when the three were fastened to the cross that miracles took place, no one attributed anything of what took place to any one of the others, but to Jesus only. . . . Not only then did He not diminish His glory by the crucifixion, but He even augmented it not a little.[27]

"Into Your Hands I Commit My Spirit"

"Then Jesus, crying with a loud voice, said, 'Father, into thy hands I commit my spirit!' And having said this he breathed his last" (Luke 23:46).

---

26 Chrysostom, Homily 85, *Homilies on the Gospel of John*, FOTC 41:434.
27 Chrysostom, Homily 85, *Homilies on the Gospel of John*, FOTC 41:429.

All the evangelists note that Christ said something just before he died. Mark writes that "Jesus uttered a loud cry and breathed his last" (Mark 15:37), and Matthew states that he "cried again with a loud voice and yielded up his spirit" (Matt. 27:50). Neither Matthew nor Mark wrote down exactly what Jesus said when he gave up his spirit. That detail was provided by St. Luke's Gospel.

The evangelists did not feel compelled to record everything Jesus said and did, either during his ministry or from the cross. The different accounts complement each other; they are consistent and in full agreement regarding the important theological message: Christ was in complete control of his life and death. In every instance, the words of Christ from the cross demonstrate this, including "Into your hands I commit my spirit" and "It is finished." Jesus "cried out with a loud voice" to show that he died "with power," Chrysostom writes. "The centurion for this cause most of all believed, because He died with power. This cry rent the veil, and opened the tombs and made the house desolate."[28]

Jesus "expired" or "gave up his breath." The link between breath, spirit, and life is clear in Hebrew, Greek, and Latin. The English word for breathing, "respiration," also reflects the idea that to breathe is to receive life or spirit (not the Holy Spirit). Similarly, to "expire" means to let your breath/life out—in other words, to die. Two Gospels say that Jesus "let out the spirit/breath" (*exepneusen*), translated as "he breathed his last" (Luke 23:46; Mark 15:37). Matthew writes similarly, "he gave up the spirit" (*afēken pneuma*, Matt. 27:50), and John has "he handed over the spirit" (*paredōken to pneuma*, John 19:30). In all cases, the idea remains the same: Jesus controlled his death.

Jesus was not a victim of circumstances beyond his control. He decided whether he would be arrested, where he would be arrested, and when it would take place. He allowed himself to be crucified, and he decided when he would die. Cyril of Jerusalem is in full agreement with the other Fathers of the Church that this statement, in which he gave his spirit to the Father, shows that Christ was in control because he himself is eternal God.

---

28   Chrysostom, Homily 88, *Homilies on Matthew*, NPNF-1, 10:502.

Of no small account was He who died for us; He was not a literal sheep; He was not a mere man; He was more than an Angel; He was God made man. . . . And do you wish to know how it was that He laid down His life not by violence, nor yielded up the spirit against His will? He cried to the Father, saying, *Father, into Thy hands I commend My spirit*; I commend it, that I may take it again. And having said these things, *He gave up the spirit*; but not for any long time, for He quickly rose again from the dead.[29]

The Lord's body hung on the cross, the Lamb of God, liberating humanity from the slavery of sin and death, just as the blood of the lamb had saved the Hebrews from death and liberated them from slavery in Egypt. Now the True Ram of God is revealed, perfecting what had been seen before only in shadow, the ram caught in the thicket by its horns and offered by Father Abraham as a sacrifice (Gen. 22:13). He was foreshadowed by Isaac also, the only begotten and beloved son of his father, willing to die as a sacrifice of love and obedience. The Suffering Servant was despised, rejected, stricken, pierced, and mourned, yet in him the prophecies of Isaiah, Zechariah, and other prophets were not only fulfilled but perfected. He hung on the cross as Messiah Son of Joseph, the righteous, innocent servant, against whom unjust and evil actions were committed, but God used those evil actions for good. Flayed and slain, bloody and battered, the immaculate body of the Lord hung on the cross as the perfect sacrifice, the slaughtered Passover Lamb.

---

29 Cyril of Jerusalem, Lecture 13.33, FOTC 64:27.

CHAPTER 28

Christ, the Slaughtered Passover Lamb

Prefiguring the Crucifixion: The Connection to Passover

WHILE THE SECOND TEMPLE STOOD, certain customs connected to Passover presented an interesting, even eerie, foreshadowing of the crucifixion of the Savior. Today Jews no longer eat lambs at Passover, but while the Temple stood and lambs were sacrificed, certain procedures were obligatory. Among other requirements, the lamb must be roasted, not over an open fire lengthwise, but in an oven created especially for Passover and used only once. These new, unfired clay ovens were prepared annually specifically for the roasting of Passover lambs.[1]

Passover ovens were dome shaped, tall but not wide, since the procedure required that the lamb be roasted upright in the oven. A wooden skewer was inserted from the bottom of the lamb up to the head. Another wooden skewer was inserted across its back with its forelegs spread out and tied to the skewer along its back. The lamb looked as though it had been crucified, and, adding to the analogy, it was impaled on wood since metal skewers or spits were prohibited.[2] Justin the Martyr and Philosopher, one of the earliest Fathers of the Church, actually witnessed this practice and described it:

---

1   Tabory, "Crucifixion," 402.
2   A metal spit was prohibited because any meat that touched a metal skewer would be cooked from the inside by contact with the hot metal in addition to being roasted from the outside. The lamb also could not touch the sides of the oven, since in that instance the meat would be considered grilled rather than roasted.

For the lamb, which is roasted, is roasted and dressed up in the form of a cross. For one spit is transfixed right through, from the lower part up to the head, and one across the back, to which are attached the legs of the lamb.[3]

Soon after the destruction of the Temple, rabbis forbade eating lamb at Passover in recognition that the Temple, where the Passover lambs were sacrificed, no longer existed. But evidence suggests that for a long time after the destruction of the Temple, many Jews continued to observe the custom of roasting a lamb at Passover in spite of rabbinic objections.[4]

While it seems odd that a lamb would be roasted in an upright position, this may reflect another strong Jewish tradition that links the near-sacrifice of Isaac by his father Abraham with the Passover and even with the Passover lamb.[5] As we have already seen, the Akedah (the "Binding" of Isaac) is strongly associated with Passover because, according to Jewish tradition, Isaac was bound for sacrifice on 14 Nisan, just before the start of Passover.[6] Furthermore, the Akedah was considered to have something akin to a salvific effect on the descendants of Isaac, or at least to have brought them divine favor that manifested itself at the Exodus event.

Some scholars have argued that the connection between the Akedah and the Passover was created by Jews in response to Christian claims about the sacrifice of Jesus. Jews believed that the sacrifice of Isaac (c. 1800 BC) prefigured the Passover sacrifice of lambs that would occur hundreds of years later with Moses and the Exodus (c. 1250 BC). This conviction existed before the first century.[7] The rabbis expressed an even more striking connection between

---

3   Justin Martyr, *Dialogue with Trypho* 40, ANF 1:215. This is one of the earliest Christian documents. It relates a discussion between Justin and Trypho, a Jew. It preserves the beliefs and debates common among Jews and Christians at that time.

4   Tabory, "Crucifixion," 396.

5   This tradition goes back to Gen. 22:13. After Abraham was told not to sacrifice Isaac, he saw a ram trapped in a thicket and caught by its horns. The implication was that it was standing upright with only its back legs touching the ground. Tabory, "Crucifixion," 404.

6   Leviticus 23:5 requires that Passover is to be celebrated on the evening of the fourteenth day of the first month of the year, which is the month of Nisan. Jesus was crucified on that exact date, 14 Nisan.

7   Tabory, "Crucifixion," 405.

the Passover, Isaac, and crucifixion when discussing the binding of Isaac. Genesis states that Isaac carried the wood for the sacrificial fire as he walked with Abraham toward Mt. Moriah, and rabbis describe Isaac as carrying the wood for his own sacrifice just as "one who carries his cross on his back."[8]

Saint Paul remarked, "Christ, our paschal lamb, has been sacrificed" (1 Cor. 5:7). The impaling of the Passover lamb on two crossed wooden spits would prompt anyone to think of the cross. The followers of Jesus easily identified him as the Passover Lamb, the perfect sacrifice, the Only and Beloved Son offered by his Father, in completion and fulfillment of what had merely been hinted at by Abraham's binding of his beloved and only begotten son, Isaac, who also willingly consented.

A New Covenant

THE JEWS CELEBRATE PASSOVER BECAUSE God commanded that they remember their deliverance from slavery in Egypt (Ex. 12:1–28; Num. 9:1–14). When Moses led the people of Israel to freedom, they immediately went to Mt. Sinai, where they received the Law and entered into the covenant that was to guide the Jewish people until the coming of the Messiah. Moses brought freedom from slavery and led the Hebrews to the promised land of Canaan. Jesus brought freedom from sin and death and leads us to the Kingdom of heaven. The first Exodus and Passover were only a type, a bare sketch of salvation, a hint of what was to come. The Christian Passover is the glorious, colorful, complete fulfillment of the Jewish Passover.

As St. John wrote in his Gospel, "The law was given through Moses; grace and truth came through Jesus Christ" (John 1:17). Hundreds of years before the coming of Christ, the prophet Jeremiah foretold there would be a New Covenant, a spiritual one, to replace the Law of Moses:

> "I shall make a new covenant with the house of Israel and the house of Judah,
> not according to the covenant I made with their fathers in the day that I took
> hold of their hand to bring them out of the land of Egypt; for they did not abide

---

8   Tabory 405, citing *Genesis Rabbah* 56.3.

in My covenant, and I disregarded them," says the Lord. "For this is the covenant I will make with the house of Israel after those days," says the Lord. "I will surely put my laws into their mind and write them on their hearts." (Jer. 31:31–33/38:31–33 LXX)

Christ, as the New Moses, fulfilled the Law and inaugurated the New Covenant, one unlike the covenant created on Mt. Sinai, which was based on the blood of irrational animals. Christ the sinless Son of God himself would be sacrificed, a perfect lamb without blemish, a sacrifice to end all sacrifices. His followers would worship God "in spirit and truth" (John 4:23). The New Covenant would be "rational," "spiritual" worship (Rom. 12:1) in which the faithful would offer their voices, their uplifted arms, their souls, their very selves in worship, rather than the blood of irrational animals.

Jesus inaugurated the New Passover and this New Covenant on the evening before his crucifixion, when he gave his disciples his own precious Body, which would soon be broken, and his own immaculate Blood, which he would soon pour out for the forgiveness of sins. "Do this," he said, "in remembrance of me" (Luke 22:19). This ritual was not to be a merely memorial meal. He did not say "Do this in *remembrance* of me," but "Do this in remembrance of *me*." From then on, at Passover, the disciples would no longer remember Moses and the Exodus but Jesus, his sacrifice on the cross, and his Resurrection. Every time they observed the sacred rite instituted that night, they would mystically participate in the liberation from sin and death accomplished through the cross.[9]

The Hebrews were forbidden to consume blood, according to the Law of Moses, for "the life is in the blood" (Lev. 17:11). This is one of the strictest Old Testament prohibitions and is repeated several times. The depth of this truth was revealed when the Lord inaugurated the Mystery of Holy Communion. Indeed, "the life is in the blood," for eternal life is found through partaking of his Body and Blood.

---

9   For this reason, it is wrong and inappropriate for Christians to revert to celebrating the Jewish Passover, somehow thinking that they are imitating the early Church. To adopt Jewish practices is forbidden by the Church canons because it amounts to a denial of Christ and the salvation he brought at Passover.

Jesus was crucified on 14 Nisan, the Day of Preparation, which would have begun at sunset the evening before (what we would call Thursday night) and continued until sunset on Friday.[10] Passover itself would begin on Friday at sunset. When Jesus held his Last Supper with the Twelve the evening before his crucifixion, he knew he would not be alive to share the Passover with them. Even though he sent two disciples to prepare the Passover meal, the Last Supper was not actually a Passover meal. No lamb meat was roasted and consumed at the Last Supper, since the lambs would not be sacrificed until the following day. But the True and Spotless Lamb, "who takes away the sin of the world" (John 1:29), presided over that supper and gave himself to his disciples at that first Holy Communion.

The Day of Preparation

THE EXQUISITE TIMING OF THE suffering and death of Christ at Passover, the deep and profound meaning it holds, and its many connections to the traditions, spirituality, history, and worship of Israel are utterly amazing and reveal to us how God's remarkable plan of salvation was brought to perfect completion. Jesus died at the moment lambs began to be slaughtered in the Temple. The Evangelist John notes simply that when Jesus was condemned to the cross by Pilate, it was the Day of Preparation, about noon (19:14). Matthew, Mark, and Luke tell us that he died at the ninth hour, or three PM.

The significance of those details required no explanation for the first Christians. As Christ hung on the cross on the Day of Preparation, huge crowds were filing into the Temple courtyard, carrying the lambs they would offer as their Passover sacrifice. The ritual began at noon, when the crowd assembled in three groups, since the courtyard could not accommodate the huge numbers of worshippers all at once. When Pilate ascended the judgment seat and sentenced Jesus to death at noon, the sixth hour, the first group was gathering. Thousands of priests were on duty to receive the lambs to be sacrificed. With

---

10 Because no Jewish Temple exists today, and therefore no lambs are sacrificed, Passover begins for the Jews on 15 Nisan. 14 Nisan is still recognized as a Day of Preparation, during which Jews remove all yeast and other leaven from their homes.

the blast of a shofar, the sacrifice began.[11] At three PM the blood of the first lamb was shed, followed by thousands and thousands more. After sacrifices for the first group were completed, the entire courtyard was washed down, the gates were opened again to admit the second group, and after them, the third group in its turn. People returned home with their sacrificed lambs to roast them that evening.

Thousands of lambs were being offered within a short period of time. The Court of Israel was unable to accommodate the huge crowd, so the lambs were sacrificed in the outer courts. Dozens of priests formed a long line stretching all the way from the courtyard to the Temple altar. As one priest sacrificed the lamb, another priest collected the blood into a gold bowl and passed it to a priest next to him, continuing down the line until the priest at the end of the line nearest the altar flung the blood on the altar. The empty gold vessels were quickly returned to the priests sacrificing lambs at the head of the line to receive more blood from more lambs. As bowl after bowl of lamb's blood was thrown at the base of the altar, the area was quickly flooded with blood, covering the once-pristine Temple floor, streaming into gutters that overflowed.

While the sacrifice was being offered, the Levites chanted the Hallel, Psalms 113—118 (112—117 LXX), which included many memorable and highly significant verses, such as:

> I will lift up the cup of salvation
> > and call on the name of the LORD,
> I will pay my vows to the LORD
> > in the presence of all his people.
> Precious in the sight of the LORD
> > is the death of his saints.
> O LORD, I am thy servant;
> > I am thy servant, the son of thy handmaid.
> (Ps. 116:13–15/115:4–6 LXX)

---

11   The procedure described is found in the Mishna, *Pesachim* 5. The shofar is the traditional trumpet made from a ram's horn used on Jewish holidays.

I shall not die, but I shall live,
    and recount the deeds of the LORD.
The LORD has chastened me sorely,
    but he has not given me over to death.
Open to me the gates of righteousness,
    that I may enter through them
    and give thanks to the LORD.
This is the gate of the LORD;
    the righteous shall enter through it.
I thank thee that thou hast answered me
    and hast become my salvation.
The stone which the builders rejected
    has become the head of the corner.
This is the LORD's doing;
    it is marvelous in our eyes.
(Ps. 118:17–23/117:17–23 LXX)

After each lamb was slain and its blood collected, the priests prepared the lamb to be roasted later. They skinned each lamb by hanging it on a hook with its forelegs outstretched, much like the pure and spotless Lamb, who at that moment was hanging with his arms outstretched outside the city walls. At the very moment the priests shed the blood of the first lamb in the Temple, at three PM, the sacrifice of the Perfect Lamb of God was accomplished, and he committed his spirit to the Father.

CHAPTER 29

The Death of Jesus:
The Veil, the Earthquake, and the Piercing

The Veil of the Temple

"A ND BEHOLD, THE CURTAIN OF the temple was torn in two, from top to bottom" (Matt. 27:51).

One of the most enigmatic events associated with the death of Christ is the tearing of the Temple curtain, or veil. The uncertainty of its meaning has perplexed Christians since the earliest centuries. This veil was nothing like an ordinary curtain or drapery that we might see in a home, church, or theater, but rather a massive blue-and-purple curtain, as thick as a hand width, expertly woven and elaborately embellished with embroidery.[1] To remove and wash this curtain required three hundred priests.[2] A curtain of this size, weight, and thickness could have been torn from top to bottom only as an act of God.

The tearing may be associated with the earthquake at the time of Christ's death. Saint Jerome and other ancient historical sources remark that a massive stone lintel in the Temple broke in two. Jerome connects the lintel breaking to

---

1   It was about 80 feet high and presented an image of the entire universe, Josephus remarked. It may have been decorated with stars in the form of constellations. *JW* 5.212–14.

2   *Shek.* 8.5; Jeremias, *Jerusalem in the Time of Jesus*, 203.

the tearing of the curtain and points to an ancient gospel written in Hebrew as his source of information:

> The curtain of the Temple was torn, and all the mysteries of the Law that were previously woven together were made known and passed to the Gentile people. In the gospel we have frequently mentioned, we read that the upper lintel of the Temple, which was of immense size, was broken and split in two.[3]

The veil of the Temple separated God from humanity. Not only physical but even visible access to God was restricted, because God is holy. Reverence for God was expressed by recognizing the sanctity of the Holy Place, into which few people could venture. The tearing of the temple veil has been endlessly discussed, and its meaning cannot be conclusively resolved because key questions remain unanswered. First, was there one veil or two? Secondly, if there were two, which of the two was torn?

Moses was instructed to hang two veils. According to Exodus, an outer curtain was to separate the Holy Place from the rest of the Tabernacle, and a second inner curtain would separate the Holy Place from the Holy of Holies, the most sacred space into which only the high priest ventured once a year (Ex. 26:33–37). Unfortunately, we cannot rely on Exodus for information, since by the first century many of the original significant requirements were no longer observed in Judaism and the Temple. Even the Mishnah's description of the Temple curtain(s) does not match the biblical requirements.[4] The most reliable witness is probably Josephus, who was a priest himself and had served in the Second Temple on countless occasions. Josephus mentions only one temple curtain.

---

3   Jerome, *Homilies on Matthew, Commentary on Matthew* 27:51, FOTC 117:320. Saint Jerome, who knew Hebrew, occasionally referred to a gospel written in Hebrew that was still in use by Jewish Christians, whom he calls "Nazarenes," noting that some people believed this was the original gospel of Matthew (141). It is widely attested in antiquity that Matthew wrote the first gospel in the Hebrew language, but no gospel written in Hebrew survives today.

4   Written c. AD 200, the Mishnah describes features of the Second Temple before its destruction in AD 70, but we cannot be certain about its accuracy.

The meaning of this dramatic sign is inextricably connected to the number of curtains, and if there were two, knowing which veil was torn would be key to understanding. Some scholars believe there was only one veil, since Josephus attests to only one, and he is the only person who gives us an eyewitness, firsthand description of the Temple during the first century. Others say there were two curtains, because the Bible states there must be two. If there were two curtains, some insist that the inner veil must have torn because of its greater significance as a barrier between God and humanity, which was eliminated on the death of Christ. Others agree it was the inner curtain, because the Greek word here is *katapetasma,* ordinarily used by the Septuagint for the inner curtain, whereas *kalymma* was typically used for the outer curtain. But *katapetasma* could have been used even if only one curtain existed.

Other scholars conclude that it must have been the outer curtain that tore because the centurion witnessed the tearing, something I dispute and discuss below. They also assume that if the inner curtain was torn, that would not have become known, since it would not have been visible to most people, and the tearing might even have been so shocking it was kept secret. But the torn curtain would have to be replaced, and three hundred priests were needed to remove it. It could hardly remain a secret! The tearing of the veil would have been so unprecedented that it would have been discussed and become known to all priests.[5] In short, scholarly opinion is divided regarding the number and location of the curtain(s); and yet the ultimate meaning of the sign is dependent on these uncertain details.

Unfortunately, the evangelists do not explain the meaning of the torn veil. Perhaps they assumed the first Christians knew the number of veils, which one tore, and what it meant. Quite often, the meaning of a biblical saying or event has been passed down through early church tradition. The Fathers of the Church are fairly consistent in their interpretations, but even in antiquity, multiple explanations of the torn veil existed. Ephrem the Syrian, in his

---

5   We know that Jewish priests were among the members of the early Church, and whether it was the inner curtain, the outer curtain, or a single curtain, the apostles most likely would have learned of the tearing of the curtain after the event. "And the word of God increased; and the number of the disciples multiplied greatly in Jerusalem, and a great many of the priests were obedient to the faith" (Acts 6:7).

commentary on the *Diatessaron,* mentioned several interpretations without choosing any one of them.[6] The torn veil remains a mystery, or it may have more than one interpretation. The following have been proposed:[7]

1. The tearing of the veil marked the end of Jesus' earthly ministry, which began with his baptism. At that moment, St. Mark wrote the heavens were "torn" open (1:10), the Spirit appeared as a dove, and the Father's voice proclaimed that Jesus is the Son of God. Describing the heavens as "torn" is rather strange, but he used that same word to describe the tearing of the veil of the Temple on the death of Christ, followed by the centurion's words, "Truly this man was the Son of God!" (Mark 15:39). The temple veil was a beautiful blue-purple color, decorated with stars and symbols that represented the heavens. Both the precise beginning and the precise ending of Christ's earthly work are marked by the revelation that Jesus is the Son of God through the "tearing" of the heavens.[8]

2. The tearing was a sign of divine displeasure. It was customary to tear one's clothing as an expression of grief. The curtain(s) were like a garment for God, and the tearing might be a symbol of God's anger or grief, according to some interpreters.

3. The tearing was a sign of divine power. When Jesus died, Mark literally writes, "He breathed out" (*exepneusen*) (15:37). The Greek word for "spirit" (*pneuma*) is also the word for "breath." When Jesus exhaled his final breath/ let out his spirit, it was so powerful as to tear the temple curtain. The torn veil is proof of Christ's divine power, the beginning of his Resurrection, and a transition into a new phase of salvation history.

4. The Temple was no longer sacred nor the dwelling place of God. All ancient people, both Jews and pagans, recognized temples as sacred spaces, places where God (or the gods) dwelt. A destroyed temple signified that the god(s) had departed. The veil separated the holy from the profane, and tearing it open meant "destroying the special character or holiness that made the

---

6   Ephrem the Syrian, Commentary 21:4, *Saint Ephrem's Commentary on Tatian's Diatessaron.*

7   See Gurtner, *The Torn Veil.* Gurtner gives a comprehensive overview of the various scholarly and early Church opinions in his introductory chapter.

8   Ulansey, "The Heavenly Veil Torn," 123–25.

place a sanctuary."[9] The torn veil indicated that God had departed and gone to the Gentiles, or God departed because the sacrifice of animals was no longer needed since Christ had offered the perfect sacrifice.

5. That which was previously hidden from the Gentiles has been made manifest. Origen mentions this interpretation. Saint Jerome gives this explanation as well, that "the mysteries of the Law ... were made known and passed to the Gentile people."[10] The veil enclosed the most sacred space, where the LORD had made his dwelling. He was accessible to the Jews alone, through the sacrificial system of the Temple. Through animal sacrifice, sin was removed and the relationship between Israel and God was maintained. Gentiles were strictly forbidden from approaching the sacred space of the Temple, but now what had been hidden and restricted to the Jews is open to all. But this interpretation is insufficient since it was not the soreg (the low wall beyond which Gentiles could not pass) that was torn when Christ died. The veil was torn; therefore, the significance must be much greater than simply opening the mysteries to the Gentiles, because the tearing opened the Holy of Holies to everyone. The most sacred space, access to which was previously restricted to the high priest once a year, is now accessible to all humankind. This brings us to the last two interpretations, which are the most compelling.

6. Jesus' death has removed the barrier between God and humankind, which the veil represents. Sin separated or alienated humanity from God. The Jewish high priest mediated between the people of Israel and God. The Jews had no direct access to nor direct experience of God. Temple priesthood and rituals emphasized the holiness and inaccessibility of God through ritual purity and progressively restricted spaces. God remained distant from all that was not sacred. But Christ eliminated all barriers and the restrictions of ritual purity, and gave everyone access to God. We commune and communicate with God without mediation, receiving God directly through the sacred Body and Blood of Christ, for "there is one mediator" (1 Tim. 2:5).[11]

---

9   Brown, *Death of the Messiah,* 2:1101.

10 Jerome, *Homilies on Matthew* 27.51, FOTC 117:320. Origen also mentions the idea that the tearing was an expression of mourning. Origen, *Fragments on Matthew* no. 560.

11 That verse is sometimes cited as a justification for rejecting Christian priesthood, ritual, liturgy, and sacraments. But its point is that the Jewish Temple, priests, and rituals no

The Book of Hebrews reflects this interpretation and uses the Septuagint word for the inner curtain, *katapetasma*. During Great Lent, most of the Sunday epistle readings in the Orthodox Church come from the Book of Hebrews. We hear the readings describe Jesus going inside the Holy of Holies, behind the curtain (*katapetasma*), as a forerunner on our behalf, having become a high priest after the order of Melchizedek (Heb. 6:19–20). Hebrews 9 explains that the holiest objects for the Jews, such as the ark of the covenant and the mercy seat, were located behind the *katapetasma*. This was the most sacred area into which only the high priest ventured once a year, bringing the blood of an animal for his sins and for those of the people. But when Christ appeared, he entered into the Holy Place—not the one made with hands (the earthly Temple) but the true sanctuary in heaven. He brought not the blood of animals but his own blood, erasing our sin by sacrificing himself.

Hebrews 10 explains that since Christ has offered himself as a sacrifice, we now have confidence to enter the sanctuary, "by the new and living way which he opened for us through the curtain (*katapetasma*), that is, through his flesh" (Heb. 10:20). In that verse, Hebrews is telling us that the curtain is the flesh of Christ, through which we enter the sanctuary—the place of intimate encounter with God. It is this flesh, which he assumed as God for our salvation, that was torn and hanging on the cross. Through the breaking of the body of Christ, the tearing of the veil of his flesh, the sacred, the divine, is opened to us. This happened not because someone had to pay for sin but because God loved the world and chose the cross to graphically demonstrate that his love is without limits. We directly participate in the life of God, because Christ was incarnate, and through the sacrament of Holy Communion we physically commune and dwell with him and he in us. The depth of meaning is profound and inexpressible.

7. The tearing of the veil was a sign of the coming destruction of the Temple. This is also a widely accepted explanation, and many early Christian interpreters believed that the tearing of the curtain confirmed that the Temple would be destroyed. Christ predicted the destruction of the Temple and said that in the future God would be worshipped spiritually (John 4:23–24). The

---

longer forgave sins because Christ had accomplished that.

crucifixion of the Son of God fulfilled and perfected the Law, putting an end to animal sacrifice. The destruction of the Temple was also seen as a judgment upon Israel. After the long list of woes Jesus pronounced on the Pharisees, he lamented over Jerusalem: "Behold, your house is forsaken and desolate" (Matt. 23:38; also Luke 13:35). Rending the veil foreshadows the destruction of the Holy Place or symbolizes its impending ruin.

Early Jewish writings preserve reports of strange events that occurred forty years prior to the destruction of the Temple in AD 70, portending its demise. Of course, they reject the idea that these events and the destruction of the Temple were in any manner connected to the death of Jesus. But from a Christian perspective, it is impossible to ignore the timing of these fascinating and bizarre incidents, especially since they are preserved in Jewish historical and religious sources, such as Josephus and the Talmud, and by early Christian writers as well.[12] The Talmud was compiled after the time of Christ, but it preserves first-century Jewish traditions about these events that coincided with the time of Christ's ministry and death.[13] Multiple Jewish sources confirm that at least four strange phenomena occurred forty years before the unimaginable catastrophe of the Temple's destruction.

According to Josephus, certain odd occurrences in the Temple were recognized as omens of its future destruction. Among other things, many priests serving in the inner courts of the Temple heard mysterious voices saying "Let us depart from here." Also, the huge brass gate of the inner courtyard (probably the Nicanor Gate) opened by itself in the middle of the night. This door was so massive that it ordinarily required twenty men to open and close it. When it opened of its own accord, it was only closed again with great difficulty. This was interpreted to mean that the security of the Temple was ending.[14]

---

12 To this day, Jews do not agree as to the reason God allowed the Temple to be destroyed. However, they agree that something changed in Judaism afterward, and God seems more distant.

13 The number forty in the Bible is usually understood to be an approximation, not an exact number. But whether these events occurred exactly forty years before, at the beginning of Christ's ministry (around the year 30), or about forty years before, which still coincides with the death of Jesus (around the year 33), the precise dating for these signs is not essential to link them to the ministry, death, and Resurrection of Christ.

14 Josephus, *JW* 6.290–300. The presence of strange signs that hinted at the coming

Both the Palestinian Talmud and the Babylonian Talmud record the following signs forty years before the event, signifying the future destruction of the Temple:

a. The heavy gates of the Temple would open by themselves at night.

b. The "western light" would burn out for no apparent reason. What Jews called the "western" light is actually what we would consider the center light of the seven-branched menorah. Typically, that central light would remain lit much longer than the lights on the other branches. It was considered a sign of God's presence and blessing. But forty years before the destruction of the Temple, that particular light began to extinguish itself for no apparent reason. This was understood as a bad omen: God had departed, or his blessing had been withdrawn.

c. Yom Kippur, the Day of Atonement, the most sacred day of the Jewish year, was the day when the high priest entered the Holy of Holies to sprinkle blood for the sins of the people of Israel and ask God to forgive their sins. On that day, a special thread would always miraculously change from red to white, an important sign that indicated forgiveness.[15] Forty years before the Temple was destroyed, the thread stopped changing from red to white, suggesting that the rituals and sacrifices of the Day of Atonement no longer operated to forgive people's sins.

d. Also on the Day of Atonement, lots were cast to determine which of two goats would be sacrificed. One goat was sacrificed to the Lord, and the other became the scapegoat.[16] The goat to be sacrificed was offered to the Lord for the sins of the people, but which goat it would be was decided by lot. Previously, "the lot for the LORD" had always come up in the high priest's right hand. This was considered auspicious, a good sign. The statistically impossible consistency of this outcome was miraculous and was interpreted as a sign of God's favor. But forty years before the destruction of the Temple, "the lot for

---

destruction of the Temple about forty years before the event, during the time of Christ, was noted by rabbis in the Mishnah, *y. Yoma* 6,43c and *b. Yoma* 39b in the Jerusalem and Babylonian Talmuds.

15   "Though your sins are like scarlet, they shall be as white as snow" (Is. 1:18).

16   Leviticus 16:8. The first goat was sacrificed, but the high priest placed his hands on the head of the scapegoat, ritually transferring the sins of the people to the scapegoat, which was then led out of the city.

the LORD" began always to come up in the high priest's left hand, which was considered a bad omen.[17]

Chrysostom believed the tearing of the veil had many meanings, including being a sign of the future destruction and end of Temple worship and sacrifice and of God's abandonment.

> The cry rent the veil, and opened the tombs and made the house desolate. And he did this not as offering insult to the Temple (for how should he who said, "Do not make my Father's house a house of merchandise") but declaring them to be unworthy even of his abiding there, like as also when he delivered it over to the Babylonians. But not for this only were these things done but what took place was a prophecy of the coming desolation and of the change into the greater and higher state, and as a sign of His might.[18]

Christians do not consume animals whose blood is offered for our forgiveness through the agency of the Israelite priesthood. Through the sacrifice of Christ, we approach and receive God directly for our sanctification. We consume the Holy One himself, the perfect Lamb, holy without blemish. By the crucifixion and Resurrection of Christ, the veil was rent, showing that heaven and God himself are accessible to us.

---

17 The process is described in *b. Yoma* 4.1. Two lots made of gold, one inscribed "To the Lord" and the other "Azazel" (meaning "Scapegoat"), were placed into a special urn. Without seeing them, the high priest removed one lot with his right hand and one with his left to determine which of the two goats would be sacrificed to the Lord and which would be taken out into the wilderness. The lot that represented something good, a positive outcome, was always pulled out by the high priest in his right hand. But forty years before the Temple was destroyed, year after year the "lot for the Lord" was removed by the high priest in his left hand, a bad sign. *Jewish Encyclopedia*, s.v. *"Lots."* About these signs, the Babylonian Talmud reads, "Our rabbis have taught on Tannaite authority: forty years before the destruction of the sanctuary the lot did not come up in the right hand, and the thread of crimson never turned white, and the westernmost light never shone, and the doors of the courtyard would open by themselves." *The Talmud of Babylonia: An American Translation. Yoma, Chapters Three through Five*, 49–50.

18 Chrysostom, Homily 88, *Homilies on Matthew*, NPNF-1, 10:502.

The Earthquake and the Dead That Were Raised

> And the earth shook, and the rocks were split; the tombs also were opened, and
> many bodies of the saints who had fallen asleep were raised, and coming out of
> the tombs after his resurrection they went into the holy city and appeared to
> many. (Matt. 27:51–53)

THE EARTHQUAKE IS ALSO A matter of much debate, just as mysterious but
not quite as complicated. Matthew is the only evangelist to record the earthquake. For this reason, its historical veracity is doubted by most interpreters,
who consider it poetic embellishment inspired by Old Testament apocalyptic symbols.[19] The Jewish saints whose tombs were opened by the earthquake
appeared after the Lord's Resurrection on Sunday, not at the moment of crucifixion.[20] The Fathers understood the appearance of the dead after the Resurrection of the Lord as foreshadowing the general resurrection. "They appeared
to many," St. Jerome noted, but not to all, since only some people were worthy
to see these saints.[21]

The earthquake might provide some explanation of how the Temple curtain was torn, particularly if the lintel that broke, mentioned by Jerome, had
provided support for the veil. As discussed in chapter 25, a Greek pagan historian, Phlegon, linked the earthquake to the darkening of the sun as happening
on the same day, providing historical support for Matthew's account.

> In the fourth year, however, of Olympiad 202, an eclipse of the sun happened,
> greater and more excellent than any that had happened before it; at the sixth

---

19 A sign of divine power (as in Joel 3:16), divine displeasure, or judgment (as in Nah. 1:5).

20 Resurrection of the dead was a common feature of Jewish end-times expectations.
Matthew does not explain the reason for delay, nor any other details, but it is generally
understood that these saints could not rise from the dead before the Lord himself rose.
Matthew would not have considered the timing nor an explanation to be important,
only the meaning and message of the event.

21 Jerome, *Homilies on Matthew, Commentary on Matthew* 27:52–53, FOTC 117:321. He
allows for the possibility that the "holy city" could mean either the earthly Jerusalem or
the heavenly Jerusalem.

hour, day turned into dark night, so that the stars were seen in the sky, and an earthquake in Bithynia toppled many buildings of the city of Nicaea.[22]

Many scholars entirely dismiss as unhistorical any extraordinary events described by the Gospels on the day Christ died—the darkness, the tearing of the veil, the earthquake—because ancient stories often included strange phenomena when a heroic figure died. The difference in the case of Christ's death, however, is significant. First, Christ was a real historical person, not a myth; and secondly, a variety of other ancient sources—Greek, Roman, Jewish, and Christian—independently confirm that amazing events or signs occurred during that period, even on the exact date of Christ's death. This corroboration, which is routinely ignored, should be taken into consideration as historical evidence that substantiates the historicity of the Gospels.

The Centurion

THE DEATH OF JESUS WAS a relief to the Jewish leaders, but it prompted fear, awe, and regret among many bystanders. The crowd reacted with deep remorse, beating their breasts in a classic gesture. "And all the multitudes who assembled to see the sight, when they saw what had taken place, returned home beating their breasts" (Luke 23:48).

Jesus had been taunted and challenged to prove he was the Messiah and the Son of God. But while he was on the cross, the sun had gone dark, and his death was followed by an earthquake and the tearing of the Temple veil. These impressive signs prompted the centurion to recognize the innocence, righteousness, and divinity of Christ. "When the centurion and those who were with him, keeping watch over Jesus, saw the earthquake and what took place, they were filled with awe, and said, 'Truly this was the Son of God!'" (Matt. 27:54).

The centurion represents and foreshadows the many Gentiles who would come to believe in Christ. Some Bible scholars believe that his statement "Truly this was the Son of God!" was sarcastic because Jesus had died as a

---

22   See Brown, *Death of the Messiah* 2:1042.

criminal. But the centurion had undoubtedly witnessed the crucifixion of countless men. If Jesus had simply died in the same manner, then perhaps his statement might be interpreted as sarcastic. But this death was unlike anything the centurion had ever experienced. Crucifixion was intended for humiliation. But rather than being diminished by the cross, the Lord was glorified, because from the cross itself he exhibited his power. The centurion witnessed "what took place," and this is why he made the statement. The Scriptures do not specify exactly what he saw, but the darkness, the earthquake, and even Christ dying with power would have been more than sufficient signs to prompt the centurion's exclamation.

Many interpreters assume that "what took place" included the tearing of the curtain. They use the centurion's statement to prove that the Temple had only one curtain or that the outer curtain must have torn, since the inner curtain behind it would not have been visible. If someone was standing in the Court of the Women, looking through the Nicanor Gate into the Court of the Priests, a curtain might be seen from that vantage point. But the centurion did not see and could not have seen the veil in spite of its immense size, for a number of reasons.

Golgotha was at a much lower elevation and outside the city walls, which were very high. The sacred spaces for which the curtain served as a barrier could not have been seen from Golgotha, not only because of the sight lines or the distance from Golgotha to the Temple, but because the back wall of the Holy of Holies faced Golgotha, not the front façade of the Holy Place, beyond which the curtain hung. The front of the Temple faced the opposite direction from Golgotha.

The centurion is noteworthy not as a witness to the events that took place but because of his remarkable statement that Jesus is truly the Son of God. Saint Jerome attributes his recognition of the divinity of Christ to the fact that Jesus "dismissed the spirit," meaning that he controlled his death.[23] The centurion's insight nearly rivals that of the repentant thief. With their physical eyes, both the thief and the centurion beheld a bloody and battered man

---

23   Jerome, *Homilies on Matthew, Commentary on Matthew* 27:54, FOTC 117:322.

dying as a condemned criminal. But with the eyes of faith, they recognized his divinity.

Jesus was very different from what he outwardly appeared to be. This contrast between the appearance and the reality mirrors the paradox of the cross itself. According to ancient church tradition, this centurion was named Longinos, and he eventually became a believer.[24] He was also among those soldiers assigned to guard the tomb of Christ and became a witness of the Resurrection. When the guards reported to the Jewish leaders what had taken place, Longinos refused to accept a bribe and falsely state that the disciples stole the body of Jesus while the soldiers were sleeping (Matt. 28:11–15).[25]

Breaking the Legs of the Thieves

Since it was the day of Preparation, in order to prevent the bodies from remaining on the cross on the sabbath (for that sabbath was a high day), the Jews asked Pilate that their legs might be broken, and that they might be taken away. So the soldiers came and broke the legs of the first, and of the other who had been crucified with him. (John 19:31–32)

A COMMON PRACTICE AMONG THE Romans if they wished to hasten death was to break the legs of those crucified. Crucifixion was intended to be a prolonged agony that could last for days, and ordinarily soldiers had no motive to hasten death. However, Jewish law required that anyone who had been hanged on a tree was to be buried before sunset, and this rule was strictly observed. As we have seen, crucifixion was considered a form of hanging. Josephus confirms the importance Jews placed on burying crucifixion victims.[26]

---

24 Longinos means "spear" or "lance," and for that reason some said it was he who pierced the Lord's side with the spear. However, according to the Great Synaxaristes, this is not correct.

25 Eventually Longinos was beheaded, becoming a martyr for Christ because he refused to deny the Resurrection and the extraordinary events he witnessed while Christ was on the cross. His feast day is October 16.

26 Josephus, *JW* 4.317.

This sunset was not only the end of the day and the beginning of the Sabbath, but this was an especially holy Sabbath, since Passover would begin at sunset. Jews were exceptionally concerned about maintaining ritual purity on important feasts, but in this case the purity of the land of Israel was at stake. Some pundits attempt to deny the Resurrection of Jesus by asserting that he was never buried but left to rot on the cross, since that was the typical Roman practice. But the historical sources are clear: burying a body—criminal or not—was always important to the Jews, especially in this type of circumstance. The legs of the thieves were broken for the express purpose of hastening their death so they could be buried before sunset.

Crurifragium was the brutal procedure of smashing the legs with a large iron mallet. No one is absolutely certain how this accelerated the onset of death, since the cause of death by crucifixion has not been conclusively determined. If the cause of death was asphyxia because breathing was difficult while hanging on the cross and the criminal had to raise himself by pushing with his legs, then crurifragium would hasten death by making it impossible to inhale enough oxygen and exhale sufficient carbon dioxide from the lungs. (As discussed above, this may have been a less likely scenario; see chapter 24.) But if crucifixion victims had no difficulty breathing and the cause of death was hypovolemic shock, then crurifragium would still result in death by accelerating the loss of blood. Smashing both femurs (the large bone of the thigh) would result in traumatic hemorrhagic shock, not to mention hypovolemic shock. Significant internal bleeding would result, up to four liters of blood from smashing only the two femurs, not to mention the bones in the lower part of the leg. The adult human body has about five liters of blood. The crucified would already have lost blood from the scourging. Significant internal bleeding from the crurifragium would result in a rapid demise, since not enough oxygen-carrying blood would circulate through the body to keep the criminal alive.

The Piercing of Christ

But when they came to Jesus and saw that he was already dead, they did not break his legs. But one of the soldiers pierced his side with a spear, and at once there came out blood and water. He who saw it has borne witness—his testimony is true, and he knows that he tells the truth—that you also may believe. For these things took place that the scripture might be fulfilled, "Not a bone of him shall be broken." And again another scripture says, "They shall look on him whom they have pierced." (John 19:33–37)

THE PIERCING OF CHRIST'S SIDE with a spear is related to us only by John, the fourth evangelist. Why did the soldier pierce him? Sometimes this action is interpreted as an unnecessary insult to the body. But actually, as discussed earlier, lancing a crucifixion victim was rather common because of the narcotic effects of some concoctions given to crucified criminals. Since a crucified person who appeared dead might be merely anesthetized, Roman soldiers were trained to check and ensure that the person had died. A spear thrust would accomplish that, or kill him if he had not already expired.

Jesus was already dead. His suffering on the cross was over, and perhaps that is why most Christians give little consideration to the piercing, except to think this was a gratuitous assault on the body. However, this detail was important to the Evangelist John, who adamantly emphasizes that he himself witnessed the piercing. "He who saw it has borne witness—his testimony is true, and he knows that he tells the truth—that you also may believe."

To what exactly is John bearing witness? He writes that he witnessed "these things," presumably the piercing, that Jesus' bones were not broken, and that blood and water came from his side. Why are these details so important that three times he emphasized that he was an eyewitness to them? (1) "He who saw it has borne witness"; (2) "his testimony is true"; and (3) "he knows that he tells the truth."

The piercing fulfilled important prophecy. Some say John was emphasizing his status as an eyewitness because he believed that the blood and water flowing out of Christ's side represented a miracle. Even if he considered it miraculous, John did not stress it for that reason or simply because a prophecy was fulfilled, thus adding weight to the accumulated collection of fulfilled prophecies and bolstering evidence that Jesus is the Messiah. Rather, these prophecies have specific importance and significance.

"Not a Bone of Him Will Be Broken"

JOHN QUOTES TWO PROPHECIES HERE. The first is the prophecy that none of Jesus' bones would be broken, taken from a verse of Psalm 34: "Not one of them is broken" (v. 20). It is useful for modern readers to remember that when a biblical author cited a verse, he intended to call to our attention the entire passage, not simply the single verse that was quoted. The first verse was important, but not in isolation. What is the thrust of the entire passage? This verse is a line from a beautiful psalm that begins, "I will bless the LORD at all times; his praise shall continually be in my mouth." The psalm affirms God's protection for the righteous person, and John certainly considered the psalm prophetic. "Many are the afflictions of the righteous; but the LORD delivers him out of them all. He keeps all his bones; not one of them is broken" (Ps. 34:19–20/33:20–21 LXX).

The proper celebration of Passover required the observance of a number of rules concerning the lamb, such as how it was to be roasted, that it must be shared and entirely consumed by morning, and that the Jews were forbidden to break the bones of the lamb in the process of eating it (Num. 9:12). John here affirms that none of Jesus' bones were broken, not only fulfilling the prophecy about the righteous man in the psalm but showing that Christ's death was consistent with his role as the Passover Lamb.

But "not one of them is broken" from Psalm 34/33 also has a eucharistic significance. This psalm is often sung by chanters and choirs during Holy Communion, including the verse, "Taste and see that the LORD is good" (34:8/33:9). It is sung at the conclusion of the Presanctified Divine Liturgy, and many of its verses are used during the Presanctified Liturgy and other services of the Church. The prophecy that no bones would be broken becomes eucharistically connected to the second prophecy, "They shall look upon him whom they have pierced," because blood flowed from the Lord's side, and now the faithful are invited to "taste and see that the LORD is good."

"They Will Look upon Me, upon Him Whom They Have Pierced"

THE SECOND HISTORICAL FACT TO which John bears witness, the piercing, has two extremely important implications. First, it is a fulfillment of one of the most important messianic prophecies. Jesus already fulfilled the prophecy in Psalm 22/21, "they have pierced my hands and my feet" (v. 16).

The second and far more amazing aspect of the prophecy, which we see in a verse from Zechariah, is that *God* is the One who is pierced. This supports Christian claims that the prophets also foretold that the Messiah would be the Son of God.

> I will pour out on the house of David and the inhabitants of Jerusalem a spirit of grace and mercy, so that when they look on me, on him whom they have pierced, they shall mourn for him, as one mourns for an only child, and weep bitterly over him, as one weeps over a firstborn. (Zech. 12:10, author's translation)

God is the speaker in this passage. He is the one who will pour out his spirit of grace and mercy, and he is the one being pierced. This is why the passage is so important, significant, and astonishing in its impact and meaning for John. The Messiah will be God himself—not the Father, but the Son of God, who is also God. This is so unexpected that the words "on me" ("they will look upon me") are ignored by many biblical interpreters, but "they will look upon me" is in the original Hebrew version of this passage and also in the Septuagint version (*kai epiblepsontai pros me*).

Blood and Water

JOHN ALSO BORE WITNESS TO the blood and water that flowed out of Christ's side. The pathophysiology of this occurrence has been widely discussed among physicians, because no consensus exists regarding how this took place. Physicians are perplexed because John mentions that blood came out of Christ's side, then water. Some biblical commentators have entirely dismissed it as a purely theological elaboration, because Jesus was already dead.[27] But three times John emphasized that he was an eyewitness, and that this is exactly what he saw.

At least eleven different explanations have been proposed by physicians and others. Some doctors opine that the lance might have pierced Jesus' heart. Other experts assert that blood would not have emerged from Jesus' body because blood begins to coagulate immediately upon death. However, certain factors, including asphyxia, can cause blood to resist clotting or to dissolve clots (fibrinolysis) and remain liquid or reliquify (rehemolyze). Furthermore, complete clotting of the blood does not occur instantly but over a period of about thirty to sixty minutes. Jesus had not been dead for long prior to being pierced with the lance.

Considering what we have established concerning the injuries Jesus suffered, it is possible that the clear fluid that emerged from his side was the result of a pleural effusion, that is, an accumulation of fluid around the lungs. The lungs are encased in two fibrous protective sacs called the *pleura*. A small amount of clear fluid normally lubricates the membrane. However, excess fluid can accumulate in the pleura for many reasons, including heart failure. In this case, the heart is unable to receive the pulmonary (lung) circulation, which increases the pressure in the tiny blood vessels (capillaries) inside the lungs, pushing the fluid from within the vessels to the tissues of the lungs (alveoli) responsible for the exchange of air. This causes difficulty in breathing as well as leaking of some of that fluid into the pleural space, which in turn results in more pressure around the lungs and further difficulty in breathing.

However, fluid can also accumulate in the sacs surrounding the lungs when a person experiences trauma to the chest. In that case, the pleural effusion would consist of blood that had entered the pleural sac from the injuries sustained. Broken ribs from the beatings and scourging Jesus endured could have

---

27 The argument is that no blood would have come out of the body because "circulation of the blood had ceased in someone who was already dead"; therefore, "the event is conceivable only as a miracle." Not every crucifixion victim was pierced, and some scholars dismiss this account as "a product of a young Christian scribalism." Haenchen, *Commentary on the Gospel of John*, 2:195. However, in certain types of traumatic deaths, such as by asphyxiation, blood rehemolyzes quickly and has even been observed in a liquid state at autopsies.

caused blood to collect slowly within these sacs. Upon death, blood stops circulating and begins to coagulate. In Jesus' case, a pool of blood and possibly other fluid, as described in the previous paragraph, had most likely already formed in the pleural sac because of his injuries. After blood has pooled somewhere in the body, because it has stopped circulating it begins to separate, with the heavier red blood cells settling to the bottom of the pool and lighter fluids, such as plasma and perhaps any other lighter liquid, forming a layer above it.

Jesus was in an elevated position on the cross. If the Roman soldier thrust his lance through Jesus' ribcage upward into the bottom of one of the sacs around his lungs, it would have pierced the bottom of the lung. Therefore the blood solids, being heavier, would have emerged first, followed by the lighter liquid, either plasma or ordinary pleural fluid that had accumulated in the pleural sac.

The Theological Significance of Blood and Water

VARIOUS FACTORS MIGHT PROVIDE A medical or scientific explanation for the appearance of "blood and water" when the side of the Lord was pierced. John emphasizes his eyewitness testimony to the blood and water because of the theological meaning of the event. The piercing was not a scribal embellishment. It really happened, as John testified. Whether or not it has a physiological explanation, that does not negate its theological meaning, which neither science nor medicine can address.

The first theological truth it points to is the sinlessness of the Lord. Because he was sinless, his body did not suffer corruption. That means it did not decay. Blood coagulating after death could be seen as an early manifestation of decay. Orthodox hymns of Great Friday mention this fact, and this was the teaching of the early Church from the beginning. When the tomb of Lazarus was opened, there was a stench because he had begun to decay. But this was not the case for the Lord, and that too was fulfillment of prophecy. As St. Peter preached to the people in Jerusalem on the Day of Pentecost, he pointed to the tomb of David, located not far from the Upper Room where the Church had received the outpouring of the Holy Spirit. He noted that David had died and was still buried in the tomb. But David had prophesied that his descendant, the Messiah, "was not abandoned to Hades, nor did his flesh see corruption" (Acts 2:29–32, quoting Ps. 16:10/15:10 LXX).

Secondly, the Church immediately associated the blood and water with the two most important Holy Mysteries: Holy Communion and Baptism. Water is usually associated with the Holy Spirit and with baptism; therefore, "the Church was created from both of these" elements, Chrysostom said. "Those in the Church know this—they are regenerated by water and fed by flesh and blood. Here those mysteries take their beginning so that when you approach the awe-inspiring cup, you may approach as if you are drinking from his very side."[28] Cyril of Alexandria also considered the blood and water an important sign: it was "God's way of giving us a kind of image and first fruits of the mystery of the Eucharist and holy baptism. Holy baptism comes from Christ and the power of the mystery of the Eucharist sprang forth to us from his holy flesh."[29] The fact that the Lord was pierced in his side also reminded the Fathers of the Church of the creation of Eve from the side of the sleeping Adam. Augustine wrote that while Christ, as the Second Adam, was asleep on the cross, his Bride, the Church, was formed from his side.[30]

The blood and water that emerged from the Lord's side confirm that Jesus truly died, a very important fact for two reasons: First, his death disproves the argument raised by some that Jesus never rose from the dead because he never actually died. Second, the blood and water bore witness to the humanity of Christ, something the early Church fought to affirm. Two serious early heresies, Docetism and gnosticism, denied the reality of Christ's physical body. These heresies insisted that Jesus only seemed to have a body but never truly became human.

The complete humanity of Christ is just as important as his complete divinity. If Jesus was not fully human, there was no Incarnation and no union of the humanity and divinity in the person of Christ. Without that, the deification of our human nature is not possible, nor is our sanctification. If Jesus was not human, there is no bodily resurrection, no salvation, no eternal life.

---

28   Chrysostom, Homily 85, *Homilies on the Gospel of John*, FOTC 41:435.
29   Cyril of Alexandria, *Commentary on John*, 12.104, ACT 2:354.
30   Augustine, *Tractates on the Gospel of John*, Tractate 120.2, FOTC 92:50.

The presence of blood and water testifies to the true humanity of Christ. He died in reality, not merely in appearance.

The Lord truly had a real human body that would need to be buried quickly. The sun was rapidly sinking. Passover was about to begin, and Joseph of Arimathea was already before Pilate asking for the body of Jesus.

CHAPTER 30

The Burial

Was Jesus Buried?

A COMMON ATTEMPT TO REFUTE the Resurrection of Christ is the claim that he was never buried, since the Romans did not bury crucified criminals. However, we know from many historical sources that Jews were always buried.[1] Romans altered their usual crucifixion procedures to comply with Jewish law in three ways: criminals were not crucified naked, they were never left on the cross after sundown, and they were always buried. These modifications were observed elsewhere in the empire also. Both Philo and Josephus confirm that crucified Jews were routinely removed from their

---

1   Even when non-Jews were crucified, Roman governors and other authorities frequently permitted families to bury their loved ones, unless the crime was treason or revolt. People crucified during a war would remain unburied, including Jews. But otherwise, the Roman jurist Ulpianus seems to suggest that releasing a body to the family was not uncommon and should not ordinarily be denied. "The bodies of those condemned to death should not be refused their relatives. . . . At present, the bodies of those who are punished are only buried when this has been requested and permission granted; and sometimes it is not permitted, especially when persons have been convicted of high treason." Ulpianus, *Digest*, 48.24.1. But Pilate did not consider Jesus guilty of treason, so refusing burial would have been inappropriate and even "morally reprehensible." Keener, *The Gospel of John*, 2:1160.

crosses and buried before sunset.[2] Jews considered burial a sacred duty that took precedence over even the circumcision of one's own son.[3]

Other skeptics claim that Christ would not have been buried as the Gospels describe because criminals were not buried in a family tomb, since they had been cursed by God and the presence of the body would defile the tomb. But this is a weak argument because Jesus was not regarded as a criminal by his followers. Anyone unjustly executed would not have been considered a criminal by his family or friends. Furthermore, no one could prevent the burial of a loved one in a family tomb. In fact, the only archeological evidence of crucifixion is a bone with a Roman nail embedded in it found in an ossuary within a family tomb.[4] Lastly, even if Jesus might technically have been considered a criminal or defiled because of his manner of death, this was irrelevant since the tomb is described by the evangelists as "new," a tomb "where no one yet had ever been laid" (Luke 23:53). Jesus did not share his tomb with anyone, so the presence of his body could not have defiled any other remains.

The Women Disciples

There were also many women there, looking on from afar, who had followed Jesus from Galilee, ministering to him; among whom were Mary Magdalene, and Mary the mother of James and Joseph, and the mother of the sons of Zebedee. (Matt. 27:55–56)

MATTHEW, MARK, AND LUKE MENTION that the women who had accompanied Jesus from Galilee to Jerusalem were present at his burial and noted the location of the tomb. This is important to the story because they would return to the tomb on Sunday morning only to find it empty. Luke also

---

2   Philo of Alexandria complained bitterly when the prefect of Egypt Flaccus refused to allow bodies of crucified Jews to be taken down from the crosses in AD 38. *Against Flaccus*, in *Works*, 9.61–72. This was considered outrageous and an egregious violation of Jewish rights in the empire. J. Collins, "Exegetical Notes," 157.

3   *Meg.* 3b. Even enemies were to be buried, since an unburied corpse defiled the land. Josephus, *Against Apion*, 2.211.

4   Zias and Sekeles, "Crucified Man."

tells us specifically that they "saw the tomb, and how his body was laid" and went home to prepare "spices and ointments" (Luke 23:55–56). Preparation of spices and even washing a body before burial were allowed on the Sabbath.[5] The women disciples served as witnesses to his death and burial, and later to his Resurrection. But Joseph of Arimathea is the person consistently identified in all four Gospels with the actual burial of Christ.

Joseph of Arimathea

And when evening had come, since it was the day of Preparation, that is, the day before the sabbath, Joseph of Arimathea, a respected member of the council, who was also himself looking for the kingdom of God, took courage and went to Pilate, and asked for the body of Jesus. And Pilate wondered if he were already dead; and summoning the centurion, he asked him whether he was already dead. And when he learned from the centurion that he was dead, he granted the body to Joseph. And he bought a linen shroud, and taking him down, wrapped him in the linen shroud, and laid him in a tomb which had been hewn out of the rock; and he rolled a stone against the door of the tomb. (Mark 15:42–46)

MATTHEW DESCRIBES JOSEPH AS A "rich man" who "was also a disciple of Jesus" (Matt. 27:57). He was a respected member of the council, but it was the Sanhedrin that had sentenced Jesus to death. Luke explains, however, that Joseph was "a good and righteous man, who had not consented to their purpose and deed, and he was looking for the kingdom of God" (Luke 23:50–51). John adds that Joseph "was a disciple of Jesus, but secretly, for fear of the Jews" (John 19:38).

Joseph of Arimathea is remembered by the Church and honored as *euschēmon*, a word from the Gospel of Mark often translated into English as "respected" or "noble." Hence, Orthodox hymns and prayers routinely refer to him as "the noble Joseph." The Gospels provide only a few facts about Joseph.

---

5   The Mishnah permits everything necessary for a burial to be done on the Sabbath (*Shab.* 23.5), including washing and anointing a body.

He was good, righteous, noble, respected, and wealthy. He must have had an excellent reputation and high social status since he was a member of the Sanhedrin. He must have lived in Jerusalem, because the tomb he commissioned was just outside the city walls, but he had come from Arimathea, a site we cannot identify with complete certainty.[6]

Some scholars claim, with no evidence, that Joseph was not a follower of Jesus but was acting for the Sanhedrin to ensure the burial and prevent the land's defilement. But this is not supported by the facts and cannot be correct. First, Joseph asked Pilate only for the body of Jesus, not for those of the thieves. If the Sanhedrin had assigned this task to Joseph to protect the land from defilement, he would have removed and buried all three men, not just Jesus. Second, he personally supervised taking Jesus down from the cross. Third, he did not bury Jesus in a mass grave or in just any tomb. He buried him with honor, carefully wrapping the body and placing it in his *own* tomb, presumably commissioned for himself and his family. Last, Joseph obviously could not have acted on behalf of the Sanhedrin, since they would not have wanted Jesus buried with any honors or special treatment. Joseph's actions are not those of a detached, disinterested, possibly even hostile person who was motivated by Jewish legal obligation or who had been assigned a task. Instead, the Gospels describe someone acting out of love, respect, and devotion. In fact, Joseph placed himself in opposition to the Sanhedrin and showed himself to be a disciple of Jesus.

Some speculate that, being wealthy, Joseph must have been well connected and may even have known Pilate. But the Gospels mention that Joseph "took courage" and approached Pilate to ask for the body, which does not suggest a prior acquaintanceship.[7] Joseph needed to take courage because his actions were risky and he had much to lose. By openly associating himself with Jesus, who had just been condemned for treason, Joseph made himself vulnerable to suspicion that he too might be disloyal to Rome.

---

6   This is because the Gospels were written in Greek, but most place names were Hebrew. Some people identify it as Ramathaim or Rathamin, and others have suggested Ramah or Ramallah.

7   Mark 15:43. Matthew and Luke write that Joseph "begged for the body of Jesus" (Matt. 27:58; Luke 23:52). The word is stronger than simply "to ask."

But the more significant negative consequences he risked would have come from his fellow members of the Sanhedrin. For a law-observant and righteous Jew to claim and bury a body, an obligation under Jewish law, ordinarily would carry no repercussions. But Joseph claimed and buried the body of Jesus, whom the Sanhedrin had condemned only the night before as a blasphemer. No doubt the words of Jesus still rang in their ears: "You will see the Son of man seated at the right hand of the Power, and coming on the clouds of heaven" (Matt. 26:34; Mark 14:62; Luke 22:69). Joseph buried Jesus, a blasphemer, and not in a mass grave simply to fulfill the Law, but with honor. He washed and wrapped the body in a brand-new linen shroud and laid it in his own expensive, rock-cut tomb.

Consider Joseph's actions, which were not clandestine. His behavior—the manner in which he cared for the body of Jesus—was a statement, public recognition of his high esteem for Jesus, regardless of the decision of the Sanhedrin. Jesus was dead, and Joseph could easily have decided not to become involved. The stakes were high, and he had much to lose, and yet he came forward, and with love and devotion he cared for the body of Jesus. He expected no appreciation or reward, only retribution, which is why he is such an admirable figure.

Joseph was a member of the council that made decisions for virtually all Jews worldwide. He was one among a small group of elders, the most wealthy, eminent, influential, and highly respected men in Jerusalem. He operated and participated within the inner circle of Jerusalem society, religious and political. He must have suffered a significant degree of social ostracism and the loss of many personal and business relationships because of his actions. But he is remembered to this day as the noble Joseph because he demonstrated his love and devotion to Christ regardless of any personal cost or negative consequences.

The Tomb

FAMILIES WITH MONEY AND STATUS had large tombs outside the city that were dug out of the limestone hills around Jerusalem.[8] Limestone is a soft rock that allowed caves to be cut into it. Jesus' tomb had been commissioned by Joseph for himself and his family but had not yet been used. Wealthy people had family tombs with elaborately decorated façades and even courtyards outside the entrance. Often benches were placed there for people to sit outside. Matthew mentions female disciples sitting outside the tomb: "Mary Magdalene and the other Mary were there, sitting opposite the sepulchre" (Matt 27:61).

The entrance to such tombs was low, requiring a person to bend over to enter. Once inside the main chamber of the tomb, the floor was sunken so people could stand upright. Cave tombs were large enough to hold more than one body, and families reused them over generations. These tombs had long niches, shelf-like recesses cut out from the rock, on which the body was initially laid. Once the body had decomposed, about a year after death, the family gathered and placed the bones of their loved one in an ossuary, a stone box. The ossuary was inscribed with the name of the person whose bones it contained, and often with other details such as their age or profession. The tomb contained smaller niches that had been carved out of the rock, and the ossuary was placed on one of the niches.

These cave-like tombs were protected from wild animals and thieves by a large stone placed in front of the entrance. The stone could be square and tumbled into place, but usually it was round, like an enormous coin, flat on two sides and sitting on its edge. This must have been the case with Joseph's tomb, since the Gospels refer to "rolling" the stone in front of the tomb. A long channel or groove that had been dug into the ground along the front of the tomb allowed the stone to be rolled back and forth across the entrance. However, the stone was extremely heavy and required more than one man to move it. It could not be moved from the inside at all.

---

8   Ordinary burials were done in the ground. Only the well-off could afford a family tomb. About eight hundred such rock-cut tombs carved out of the hillsides have been discovered in the vicinity of Jerusalem. Berlin, "Jewish Life before the Revolt," 454.

Nicodemus

After this Joseph of Arimathea, who was a disciple of Jesus, but secretly, for fear of the Jews, asked Pilate that he might take away the body of Jesus, and Pilate gave him leave. So he came and took away his body. Nicodemus also, who had at first come to him by night, came bringing a mixture of myrrh and aloes, about a hundred pounds' weight. They took the body of Jesus, and bound it in linen cloths with the spices, as is the burial custom of the Jews. Now in the place where he was crucified there was a garden, and in the garden a new tomb where no one had ever been laid. So because of the Jewish day of Preparation, as the tomb was close at hand, they laid Jesus there. (John 19:38–42)

UNLIKE JOSEPH OF ARIMATHEA, WHO is mentioned in all four Gospels but appears only at the very end to bury Jesus, Nicodemus is mentioned only by John but appears in his Gospel three times. We meet Nicodemus initially in John 3, when he comes to Jesus secretly "by night." Jesus tells him that he must be "born anew" or "born from above" to enter the Kingdom of heaven (John 3:3). Nicodemus does not understand this but clearly remains sympathetic to Jesus. Later in the Gospel, when attempts are made to arrest Jesus, Nicodemus calls upon the Jewish authorities to halt their rush to judgment and not to condemn him without even holding a hearing (John 7:51).

Nicodemus brought 100 pounds (approximately 45 kg) of myrrh and aloes for the burial of Jesus. The myrrh and aloes would have been in the form of a dry powder, not perfumed oil. Myrrh is a gum resin that is secreted from trees and becomes dry when its natural oils evaporate. Aloes were leaves of aloe plants that were dried and crushed into a powder.[9] The spices the women would prepare were mixed with oil and applied to the body; these are different from the dry ingredients Nicodemus brought.

---

9   Many plants and their medicinal uses were described by Dioscorides, a first-century physician and early pharmacologist who wrote a five-volume work in Greek, *Peri Hylēs Iatrikēs* (in Latin known as *De Materia Medica*). He discusses the ancient method for preparing dry myrrh in chapter 67 of volume 1. The entire first volume is devoted to an explanation of various aromatic substances.

The Grave Cloths and the Spices

THE BODY OF JESUS WOULD have been washed prior to being buried because this was part of the burial process. A body was anointed only after it was washed. Some academics maintain that he would not have been washed, since the Sabbath was rapidly approaching and there was no time. However, a body could be washed quickly and efficiently.[10] Jesus was covered in dirt, blood, and sweat. He would not have been buried without his body having first been washed.

The body was then perfumed with spices, according to the Jewish custom. Anointing or the application of spices had nothing to do with embalming or mummification. This was not an attempt to preserve the body. Spices were used primarily to minimize or mask the stench of decay. People visited the tomb, especially during the first few days after a death, even going inside the tomb to pray. Archeologists have found many perfume containers inside tombs excavated in Palestine/Israel. The anointing was done with oils, but Jesus was not anointed after death. The women disciples had gone home to prepare the perfumed oils and planned to return to the tomb on Sunday morning. The spices Nicodemus brought were dry powders of myrrh and aloes that were applied to the body. The body was then wrapped with cloth.

A significant debate exists among scholars as to exactly how Jesus' body was wrapped. The Scriptures refer to three different cloths connected with the burial of Jesus: a linen shroud (*sindon*), strips of cloth similar to bandages (*othonia*), and a cloth covering for the face or head (*soudarion*). Matthew, Mark, and Luke refer to Joseph of Arimathea wrapping the body of Jesus in a linen shroud, but John's Gospel describes Jesus being bound with strips of cloth, *othonia*.[11]

---

10   Frederick Zugibe, the chief medical examiner in Rockland County, New York, for decades, noted that on many occasions when time was of the essence because it was late on Friday afternoon, he witnessed ultra-orthodox rabbis wash the body of an Orthodox Jewish trauma victim in just a few minutes. *Crucifixion of Jesus*, 225–26.

11   *Sindon* (shroud) in Matt. 27:59; Mark 15:46; Luke 23:53 but *othonia* (cloths) in John 19:40. The cloth covering the face of Jesus, the *soudarion*, is not mentioned until after the Resurrection, in John 20:7.

John is very precise and knew Jewish burial customs well. He specifically states that the body of Jesus "was bound in linen cloths (othonia) with the spices that Nicodemus had brought, as is the burial custom of the Jews."[12] Although the process was undoubtedly hurried, John's point is that Jesus received a proper Jewish burial. The synoptic Gospels refer to Joseph of Arimathea wrapping the body in a linen shroud, something that John does not mention but which was an important aspect of an honorable Jewish burial. Some people believe that the terms for "shroud" and "cloths" were used almost interchangeably, both terms simply referring to burial cloths. Others say that only a shroud was used to wrap the body of Jesus, as strips of cloth required too much time.

No definitive answer is possible, but must it be one or the other? We need not choose between the evangelists nor harmonize the accounts. The use of the term *othonia* might simply suggest that more than one piece of cloth was needed to wrap the body, not necessarily dozens of tiny strips.[13] It is not impossible that Jesus could have been wrapped with strips.

The Gospels are brief and omit many details, such as the presence of helpers. But Nicodemus and Joseph certainly did not arrive at Golgotha alone. Nicodemus brought one hundred pounds of spices. Both he and Joseph of Arimathea would have been accompanied by several servants to assist with the process. Jesus may have been washed, wrapped with strips of cloth, and then enveloped in a shroud.[14] If several people were preparing the body simultaneously, there is no reason why the process could not have been completed quickly and efficiently, within minutes.

Another detail that provokes discussion is the quantity of spices brought by Nicodemus: one hundred pounds. A Roman pound equals twelve ounces, so this would amount to seventy-five pounds in modern usage. Some scholars say the quantity is so excessive that the number must be symbolic, ahistorical,

---

12   Interestingly, the Orthodox icon of the Resurrection in which the angel is sitting by the tomb showing the women the grave depicts the cloths as othonia, not a shroud.

13   Keener, *Gospel of John*, 2:1162–63. Supporting or denying the authenticity of the Shroud of Turin is irrelevant, since the reliability or historicity of the Gospels does not depend on establishing the authenticity of the Shroud.

14   Shamir, "Textiles from the 1st century CE in Jerusalem," 79.

or simply intended to indicate a large amount; it should not be regarded as an accurate number. Others have said that perhaps this amount is the result of a manuscript copyist's error. However, spending lavishly on burial spices for the funeral of someone important or one whom mourners wished to honor was quite common among first-century Jews.

Jesus was extraordinary in all that he said and did, even if his true divinity was not widely realized. In the disciples' minds, this was not the burial of an ordinary person. Nicodemus was a wealthy man who could afford the expenditure. The large quantity of spices highlights the importance of Jesus, suggests his true kingship, and testifies to the extremely high regard Nicodemus had for him. Jesus received a similar treatment during his lifetime with the lavish expression of love by Mary, the sister of Lazarus, when she spent a huge sum of money to anoint his feet (John 12:5). Furthermore, not all the dry spice was applied to the body. Some of it was scattered on the floor of the tomb, some was placed on the stone ledge where the body would be set, and some was burned as incense. Considering these factors, there is no reason to doubt the historical accuracy of what John reported as an eyewitness regarding the quantity of spices Nicodemus brought for Jesus' burial.

Passover, AD 33

AFTER CAREFULLY GIVING JESUS A proper and honorable burial, Joseph of Arimathea, Nicodemus, their entourage, and the women disciples went to their homes for the Passover. Could they have participated in the Passover, considering that they had been defiled by contact with a body and a tomb? It is possible that servants took care of the body while Joseph and Nicodemus supervised. But even if they had personally washed, applied the dry aromatics, and wrapped the body of Jesus, this would not disqualify them from participating in Passover. The Book of Numbers, which also contains the requirements for consuming the Passover lamb, states, "If any man of you or of your descendants is unclean through touching a dead body, or is afar off on a journey, he shall still keep the passover to the LORD" (Num. 9:10). They did participate in Passover, but it held no joy for the disciples of Jesus.

It was Friday night, April 3 of the year AD 33.[15] Pilate and his troops looked down from the Antonia Fortress on the Court of the Gentiles. All was now quiet. People had gone home with their sacrificed lambs. The sun had set. Sabbath and Passover had begun. Smoke rose from hundreds of homes as people roasted their lambs, drinking wine and no doubt discussing the surprising events of the day. Caiaphas and his family had concluded their Temple duties and were enjoying Passover festivities, confident that they had avoided disaster by removing the threat Jesus posed. Herod Antipas and his retinue were enjoying a delicious meal in his sumptuous palace. The crucifixion of Jesus had been nothing more than a brief, amusing distraction in an otherwise typical day.

But for the followers of Jesus, this Passover was one they could never have imagined and one they would never forget. Their hopes were dashed, their dreams shattered. Judas, one of their own, one of the Twelve, had betrayed him. Peter the Rock had denied him. They all felt vulnerable without Jesus' protection, his strength, wisdom, and calm, reassuring presence. They were unsure of what to do or where to go, frightened that they might meet the same horrible fate. The Feast of Passover celebrated the deliverance of the Hebrew people from slavery. The disciples had been convinced that Jesus would soon deliver Israel from the Romans, but instead he had been delivered—to the cross! How could everything have changed so quickly?

The situation would change again, just as suddenly, and the world itself would soon change forever with the Resurrection. But for now, the disciples were inconsolable in their grief. They had forgotten his words, spoken less than twenty-four hours before, by which he had tried to prepare them and reassure them:

---

15 Pinpointing a precise date for the crucifixion has its challenges, but this is the most likely date. During Pilate's tenure, Passover could have fallen on a Saturday in only four possible years: 27, 30, 33, and 34. The years 30 and 33 are the most likely. We know that John the Forerunner began his ministry during "the fifteenth year of Tiberius" (Luke 3:1), which would have been between August 19, 28, and August 18, 29. Thus John's ministry likely took place during the years 28–30. We know that Jesus' ministry lasted about three years, bringing us to the year 33.

"You will weep and lament, but the world will rejoice; you will be sorrowful, but your sorrow will turn into joy. . . . In the world you have tribulation; but be of good cheer, I have overcome the world." (John 16:20, 33)

CONCLUSION

King of Glory

THE CHRISTIAN FAITH STANDS IN stark contrast to all other value systems or philosophies, whether secular or religious, because of the cross. Only Christians affirm that God loved the world and humanity to the extent that he came into the world, became one of us, and lived among us. He came to share our life and to teach us by his own example who God is and what it is to be truly human. Only Christians believe that God himself died for us in the most shameful, brutal, and painful manner ever devised.

The cross is the heart of the gospel message. Its sheer irrationality defies logic, common sense, and credibility. The apostles faced this reality time and again as they evangelized the world. They were ridiculed, mocked, scorned, considered insane, and rejected as purveyors of a dangerous superstition. By preaching the gospel, the apostles became a "spectacle to the world," "fools for Christ's sake." Society treated the apostles like garbage, St. Paul commented, as "the refuse of the world, the offscouring of all things" (1 Cor. 4:9, 10, 13).

The very idea of a God who loves us and who was willingly crucified for us was preposterous to the world. In the Greco-Roman worldview, the gods did not create the world, they did not love humanity, and they certainly would never sacrifice themselves. In that culture, the Incarnation itself was impossible to accept, let alone the cross. This is hardly surprising, considering the behavior and character of the gods most people of the time worshipped. Why would a god become a human being and subject himself to all the difficulties and challenges of our existence? Such a notion was inconceivable, even among the Jews. Furthermore, most people reasoned that if a god were indeed to become a human being, he would be born a king and live in luxury. He certainly would not become incarnate as a poor Jewish rabbi to die on a cross! Neither Jews nor pagans ever ceased pointing to the disgraceful manner of Jesus' death, a slave's death no less, as absolutely repudiating any claim of his divinity.

Even the apostles initially struggled with both the Incarnation and the crucifixion. The prophet Isaiah had expressed the incredibility of it all: "Who has believed our report?" (53:1 NKJV). All that had taken place among the apostles, the events they personally had witnessed, were almost impossible to believe; and most astonishing of all was the voluntary crucifixion of Christ. They knew exactly who he was; they had experienced his grace and power. They also knew exactly what the cross meant culturally and what it involved physically. For Jesus to be willingly crucified defied not only all human reasoning but human imagination as well. In a culture built on the pursuit of honor, glory, power, wealth, and military strength, the idea that God would reveal his strength through weakness and shame was utterly incomprehensible. Indeed, the power and meaning of the cross can be accepted and appreciated only through the eyes of faith.

The horror of crucifixion, so removed from our life experience, was quite familiar to those first Christians. The shame of the cross was always a challenge and an obstacle to the gospel message. Saint Paul was forced to correct the attitude of early Christians at Corinth who boasted about their superior human wisdom. Paul recognized the divine wisdom of the cross as contrary to human wisdom, and he reproached the Corinthians with brutal candor: "but we preach Christ crucified, a stumbling block to Jews and folly to Gentiles" (1 Cor. 1:23). Saint Paul always advanced the cross and did not shrink from it. When the Galatians accepted the gospel, the cross was the stark message Paul presented to them, "before whose eyes Jesus Christ was publicly portrayed as crucified" (Gal. 3:1). Paul presented the image of the cross as if forcing his readers to confront the repulsive reality: *this* is our God.

Why did Paul continually challenge the Galatians and Corinthians with the cross? The cross was a shocking scandal. Jesus died in the most shameful manner possible. Saint Paul would not allow these early Christians to debate human wisdom or simply focus on the lovely teachings and miracles of Christ. He wrote that he was called "to preach the gospel, and not with eloquent wisdom, lest the cross of Christ be emptied of its power" (1 Cor. 1:17). The power of the cross lies in its very incongruity, in the unexpected, the unanticipated, the paradox and absurdity. It defies human logic and contradicts human expectations. The cross is the power and wisdom of God, greater than anything any human could imagine or accomplish: eternal life, power, and glory emerging from the most shameful, most painful death imaginable. "The foolishness of God is wiser than men, and the weakness of God is stronger than men" (1 Cor. 1:25). Paul challenged intellectuals to explain this conundrum with their limited and fallible human reasoning: "Where is the wise man? Where is the scribe? Where is the debater of this age?" God "made foolish the wisdom of the world" (1 Cor. 1:20) by saving us through the cross. For this reason, no human being can boast. Salvation through the cross lies so far beyond human comprehension and capability that the accomplishment belongs to God alone.

The Christian Faith was never an easy sell. We should not imagine that the gospel message was readily accepted because first-century people were ignorant or gullible. The cross was repulsive, and anyone who worshipped a crucified god was considered by society to be mentally disturbed. Saint Justin explained to the Roman emperor that Christian worship of Jesus Christ is considered "madness" by others because "they do not discern the mystery."[1] No human words of wisdom or eloquence could sugarcoat the brutal reality of the crucifixion.

The Mystery of the Cross

THERE IS NO CIRCUMVENTING THE conundrum of the cross. No rational explanation exists for why Christ died on the cross. One attempt at explanation favored by many Christians today—that the crucifixion of the Lord was necessary because Jesus had to die to pay the price for our sins or needed to appease the wrath of God—is, to Orthodox Christians, heretical. This idea

---

1   Justin Martyr, *First Apology*, 13, ANF 1:167.

(known as substitutionary atonement) suggests that God is the source of the problem between God and humanity, not us. But in truth, God neither needs nor demands anything from us. It was not he whose attitude required alteration. Rather it is *we* who need to change.

The bloody, painful death of the Son of God was not required for any reason. The death of Christ was a voluntary sacrifice made out of pure love, the ultimate example of humility. To regard the crucifixion as an element in a transaction robs the cross of its power. The crucifixion is an example to be imitated, not a payment of a debt. It is the paradigm par excellence of profound humility and unspeakable love, such as the world had never before experienced and could never imagine. The paradigm is so powerful that it compels us to examine our own lives and behavior, as St. John Chrysostom wrote:

> And you, O man, on hearing these things and seeing your Lord driven in fetters from place to place, have no esteem for the present life. Is it not a strange thing, indeed, if Christ has undergone such great sufferings for your sake, whereas you frequently cannot even bear up under harsh words? But He on the one hand was spat upon, whereas you adorn yourself with fine apparel and rings, and, if you do not meet with words of approval from all people, you consider life not worth living. Yes, He was insulted, endured jibes and mocking blows against His face, while you wish to receive honor at all times and cannot bear the dishonor received by Christ. Do you not hear Paul saying: "Be imitators of me as I am of Christ?" When someone ridicules you, then remember your Lord, that they bowed the knee to Him in mockery, dishonored Him both in word and deed and showed great hypocrisy toward Him. However, He not only did not reciprocate, but even gave back the opposite, namely, gentleness and kindness.[2]

The cross perfectly, profoundly, and wordlessly communicates the limitless, irrational, undeserved, and inexplicable love of God.

The Christian faith is not a religion. It has no merely human founder and does not concoct concepts to correspond with human reasoning. Christ did

---

2   Chrysostom, Homily 83, *Commentary on the Gospel of John*, FOTC 41:413–14.

not establish a religion but a Church that offers actual participation in the Divine, a deep personal relationship with Christ that can never be adequately articulated or understood. Like love, it can only be experienced.

> The Lord of earth and heaven, the creator and artificer of all, the King of kings and Lord of lords, He who is of such surpassing greatness in glory and majesty, the foundation of everything, and that in which all things exist and abide—for all thing exist in him (Col. 1:17)—he who is the breath of all the holy spirits in heaven, is scorned like one of us, and patiently endures buffetings, and submits to the ridicule of the wicked, offering himself to us as a perfect pattern of longsuffering, or rather manifesting his incomparable greatness of his godlike gentleness. Or perhaps even he thus endures to rebuke the infirmity of our minds, and show that the things of men fall far below the divine excellencies as our nature is inferior to his. For we who are of earth, mere corruption and ashes, attack at once those who would molest us, having a heart full of fierceness like savage beasts. But he, who in nature and glory transcends the limits of our understanding and our powers of speech, patiently endured those officers when they not merely mocked but smote him. . . . They ridicule, as if he were some ignorant person, him who is the giver of all knowledge and even sees what is hidden in us.[3]

"God Will Provide the Lamb"

"GOD WILL PROVIDE THE LAMB," Abraham told his son Isaac as he carried the wood for the sacrifice (Gen. 22:8). The binding of Isaac occurred on the very date on which Christ would later carry the wood of the cross and become the Lamb. At the very moment the Passover lambs were being slaughtered in the Temple, the Perfect Lamb of God offered himself for the salvation of the world.

Abraham was willing to sacrifice his only-begotten and beloved son to God, but ultimately both Abraham and Isaac were spared from undergoing such a horrific experience. Abraham was willing to sacrifice his son out of love

---

3   Cyril of Alexandria, Homily 150, *Commentary on Luke*, 594–95.

and obedience. The Father "did not spare his own Son" (Rom. 8:32) but willingly gave him, not out of obedience as Abraham had done, nor out of necessity because sin required it, but out of love—a love so completely selfless it can only be divine. God the Father had nothing to gain by giving us his Son. Neither did Jesus have anything to gain by voluntarily accepting the cross. But God the Father so loved the world that he gave us his Only-Begotten and Beloved Son (John 3:16).

Many concepts that seemed strange, mysterious, or contradictory in the Jewish Scriptures and in first-century Judaism converged and were fulfilled in the person of Jesus Christ. Judaism anticipated and hinted at what the Church fulfilled and made manifest: the willingness of Abraham to offer his beloved and only begotten son, Isaac's willingness to be sacrificed, the sacrifice of the Passover lambs offered on the same date as the binding of Isaac, the blood of the Passover lambs saving the Hebrews from death, and the simple readiness of Isaac to be sacrificed seen as an atonement or at least an eternal blessing for the people of God. In Christ, seemingly contradictory prophecies are united, fulfilled, and perfected: the Suffering Servant Messiah, son of Joseph, is also the victorious Messiah, son of David, but in a manner beyond human comprehension, defying human expectations. But Christ did not merely unite opposites; he transformed everything as he fulfilled the Law and the Prophets.

The apostles were shaken and distraught over the crucifixion of the Master on that Passover night. Perhaps they gazed on the Passover lamb that had been slaughtered earlier in the Temple. Now it was being roasted, held upright, forelegs outstretched, attached to wooden rods. The resemblance to the body of a crucified man was unmistakable, and perhaps they began to perceive the mystery.

Peter had tried to dissuade Jesus from going to Jerusalem (Matt. 16:22). James and John had sought to be at his right and left hand in his Kingdom, oblivious to what he meant by the cup he must drink (Mark 10:37–39). They anticipated a worldly kingdom established by Jesus, the glorious, victorious Messiah, Son of David. But what they witnessed was the suffering, pierced, dead Messiah, Son of Joseph. The apparent contradiction would be resolved only by the Resurrection.

Judaism maintained many strict taboos: against consuming blood, against direct contact with the sacred, against any possibility of communion with God or intimate knowledge of God. These religious boundaries were nullified by the cross. Christians see God, consume God, know God, experience God directly and without fear because "the Word became flesh," and that flesh died on the cross and rose from the dead. Because he became flesh and allowed his body to be broken, we receive and consume that very flesh, participating directly in his life and in the life to come.

"Isaac anticipates redemption but cannot achieve it."[4] Judaism anticipated redemption, but the Church received it. Judaism prepared the world for what the Church embraced. "Christianity brings to manifest expression much that remains latent in Judaism."[5] What is *latent* in Judaism is *patent*, or manifest, in Christianity.

The Jews could approach God only through mediators: only the priests could offer animal sacrifices. Furthermore, sacrifices could be offered only in the one Temple at Jerusalem. But the living Temple himself was crucified. God is no longer mediated or distant, because through and in Christ we commune directly with the living God. While the Temple stood, God remained hidden behind a thick curtain, the veil of the Temple, which shielded people from his awesome presence. Only the high priest could enter the Holy of Holies once a year. But when the perfect sacrifice occurred, of the perfect, spotless Lamb of God, the veil of the Temple was torn open. The Holy of Holies was exposed. God was open and available to all without the mediation of the Jewish priesthood or the offering of the blood of an irrational animal. Now sin would be forgiven anywhere and everywhere, for all time and for all people.

While the Lord walked the earth, his human body served as the veil of that amazing Divine Temple. The veil of his flesh was torn that we might participate in his life by partaking of that flesh. "We have confidence to enter the sanctuary by the blood of Jesus, by the new and living way which he opened for us through the curtain, that is, through his flesh" (Heb. 10:19–20). The flesh of Christ became the medicine of immortality, the means by which we

---

4   Rubenstein, "What Was at Stake," 101.
5   Rubenstein, "What Was at Stake," 101.

participate in eternal life. In Judaism, animals were sacrificed to God, the flesh was consumed, and the sacrifice had to be repeated. But the eternal sacrifice offered for us, Christ the Lamb of God, is consumed but is still alive. The "slain Lamb" is standing (Rev. 5:6). He conquered death by death, and because he lives, we too shall live.

The Curse

CHRIST DIED TO CONQUER DEATH. He "became a curse" to undo the curse (Gal. 3:13). The Scriptures declared that anyone hung upon a tree was accursed (Deut. 21:22–23), but Jesus voluntarily accepted the pain and humiliation of the cross to free us from the first curse, the primordial curse that had deprived our first parents of Paradise. The consequence of the ancestral sin affected all humanity. Adam and Eve were "indifferent" to God, Chrysostom observes, and lost Paradise because they followed their self-will.[6] Indifferent to the will of God, they chose the fruit of the Tree of the Knowledge of Good and Evil.

But Christ chose the tree of the cross in perfect obedience to the Father's will. If we follow his example, with the assistance of divine grace, we too can experience victory over sin and death. Christ invites us to participate in his victory: "If any man would come after me, let him deny himself and take up his cross and follow me" (Matt. 16:24). Our Lord never asks anything of us that he did not do himself. He demonstrated the way to salvation by his every word and action, and above all by the cross. He does not command us but invites us to follow his example, if we wish to be his disciples.

Without love and humility, we cannot be saved. The cross is the ultimate example of these virtues. To pick up our cross is not simply to accept the challenges and difficulties life has dealt us, but to make a free choice to go beyond what is necessary—just as Christ was not obligated to pick up his cross because circumstances demanded it. Likewise, we must actively choose to follow him, to willingly pick up our cross and follow his example of love and humility.

---

6   Chrysostom, Homilies 16 and 17, *Homilies on Genesis*, FOTC 74:215, 221, 242, 244.

Let us not then everywhere seek victory, nor everywhere shun defeat. There is an occasion when victory brings hurt, but defeat profit . . . for instance as in the case of those who are angry. He that has been very outrageous seems to have prevailed . . . but he that endured nobly, this man has got the better and conquered. . . . He who is wronged, and seems to have been conquered, if he has borne it with self-command, this above all is the one that has the crown. For never do we overcome by doing wrongfully, but always by suffering wrongfully. Thus also the victory becomes more glorious when the sufferer gets the better of the doer, because thereby it is shown that the victory is of God. . . . God has given you the might to conquer not by might but by endurance alone.[7]

The Lesson of the Cross for the Modern World

THE MYSTERY OF THE CROSS remains misunderstood and rejected by the world even today for one reason: it does not conform to human mentality or values. The cross is the wisdom of God; it defies, overturns, and confounds human judgment and expectations. The cross requires us to submit, to renounce our impoverished human logic, because it is in this that we are tempted to place our trust and hope. The cross invites us to surrender to something that confounds us: true glory and eternal life through self-sacrifice, love, and humility. The cross forces us to concede that to seek recognition or to promote ourselves through our human power, personality, achievement, or intellect is ultimately a futile effort that will pass away like dust.

Salvation through the cross is unacceptable to the human mind, "folly to those who are perishing." But "to us who are being saved it is the power of God" (1 Cor. 1:18). God chose the cross as the instrument of our salvation precisely for this reason. He chose something low, humiliating, and despised to save us so that none might glory or boast, that we would recognize that our salvation is the work of God alone. Salvation came to humanity in a manner contrary to any human expectation and in defiance of all human logic. Because of this it can be appropriated only by faith, not by logic or by historical or scientific proof.

---

7   Chrysostom, Homily 84, *Homilies on Matthew*, NPNF-1, 10:485–86.

From the beginning, Christians believed in spite of the cross, not because of it. The absurdity of the cross in its original cultural setting should remind us that our world continues to regard it as absurd. The cross is a call for faith (belief) and for faithfulness (unwavering adherence) in spite of what the rest of the world thinks. In our era, when people obsess over what others think of them—even others whom they know only through social media—this is a powerful mandate. It is a lesson and reminder lest we shy away from uncomfortable Christian truths that are contrary to what our society deems acceptable. Other religions reject the cross as an intolerable humiliation of God, but Christians revel in it as our hope, our pride, our boast, our comfort, our inspiration.

Every time we make the sign of the cross, we should remember the lessons Christ taught us through it.

> Why do you sign yourself with the cross? If you don't *act* the cross, you don't in fact sign yourself with it. Recognize Christ crucified, recognize His suffering, recognize Him praying for His enemies, recognize Him loving those at whose hands He endured such things and longed to cure them. If you do not recognize Him, repent.[8]

The pagan Roman world esteemed personal glory and honor above all else. Crucifixion was feared not only because of the intense pain it entailed but because of the shame and dishonor it conveyed. Christ himself spoke of being lifted up, an ironic double entendre that pointed to both exaltation (glorification) and crucifixion (being literally lifted up off the ground). The horror of crucifixion became the glory of God. Such a paradoxical opposition could be achieved only in the person of Jesus Christ, "for whom and by whom all things exist" (Heb. 2:10). The defeat was transformed into victory. The shame became glory, and the weakness revealed absolute power.

> Let us not be ashamed to confess the Crucified. Let the Cross, as our seal, be boldly made with our fingers upon our brow, and on all occasions, over the bread

---

8   Augustine, Sermon 110A:4, W. Aug. *Sermons* III.11.97.

we eat, over the cups we drink, in our comings and in our goings; before sleep, on lying down and rising up; when we are on the way and when we are still. It is a powerful safeguard; it is without price, for the sake of the poor; it is without toil, because of the sick; for it is a grace from God, a badge of the faithful and a terror to devils . . . for when they see the cross they are reminded of the Crucified.[9]

King of Glory

FAR FROM BEING A CURSE, the cross is the glory of Christ and of the Church. The Orthodox icon of the crucifixion is different from traditional Western religious depictions, which tend to emphasize the agony of Christ. Orthodox icons focus on the victory Christ achieved on the cross rather than on his suffering. This is not because Orthodoxy does not realize or appreciate what the Lord endured; rather, it is because iconography's purpose is to convey theological truths rather than to elicit an emotional response or depict historical events in a realistic fashion.

Orthodox iconography, prayer, and hymnology repeatedly emphasize the voluntary nature of Christ's crucifixion. Icons of the crucifixion do not depict Christ in agony because he willingly accepted the cross. He is portrayed with a relaxed posture, his eyes closed, as if resting on the cross. Small amounts of blood are shown emitting from his hands, feet, and side to indicate that he had a real human body and truly suffered as any human would. His hands are not clenched but open, and the backs of his hands are stretched out flat against the wood of the crossbeam, to emphasize that he went to the cross willingly for our sake. His face is serene and peaceful. His hair and body are perfect, clean, and neat. These details present the Church's theological lessons of the cross. For that reason, in most Orthodox icons we do not see INRI or INBI ("Jesus of Nazareth, King of the Jews") on the placard over his head; instead, the titulus reads "King of Glory." The eternal God, the King of Glory, was crucified, and he was glorified by the cross. This theological message is more profound and significant than any historically accurate portrayal or graphic depiction designed to elicit feelings of guilt or remorse within the viewer.

---

9   Cyril of Jerusalem, Lecture 13.36, *Catechetical Lectures*, FOTC 64:28.

Our Victory through the Cross

THE CROSS PRESENTS THE OPPOSITE of the world's values and turns our human concepts upside down.

> Christ was crucified in order to rule. He conquered the world, not in pride but in humility. He destroyed the devil, not by laughing but by weeping. He did not scourge, but was scourged. He received a blow, but did not give blows. Let us therefore imitate our Lord.[10]

Christ redeemed us from sin and death, rescuing us from the devil, blotting out our sins, and opening up Paradise, because he loves us. "God so loved the world that he gave his only Son," John wrote (John 3:16). Paul, possibly alluding to the offering of Isaac, wrote that God the Father "did not spare his own Son but gave him up for us all" (Rom. 8:32). This unspeakable mystery can be understood and accepted only through the lens of faith. Because of the cross, we recognize the vanity of this world and the futility of human thoughts and plans.

Only in the light of Christ do we see the plan of God, and only through the cross do we begin to realize the incomprehensible and limitless extent of God's love for humanity. Without faith, the story of Jesus Christ is the story of just another victim of Roman occupation. However, with faith, all the discordant and obscure elements of the Old Testament are transformed into a magnificent masterpiece of indescribable beauty, revealing the Holy Wisdom of God beyond human comprehension.

GLORY TO THY FORBEARANCE, O LORD, GLORY TO THEE!

---

10   Jerome, Homily 83, *Homilies of St. Jerome*, FOTC 57:184.

Bibliography

Primary Sources

Ambrose of Milan. *Exposition on the Holy Gospel According to St. Luke.* Translated by Theodosia Tomkinson. Etna, CA: Center for Traditionalist Orthodox Studies, 1998.

Assumption of Moses. The Assumption of Moses. Translated by R. H. Charles. London: A&C Black, 1897.

Augustine of Hippo. *Sermons.* 11 vols. Translated by Edmund Hill. The Works of Augustine. Edited by John E. Rotelle. Vols. 6, 7, and 16. New Rochelle, NY: New City Press, 1993, 1994, 1997.

———. *St. Augustine: Tractates on the Gospel of John.* Translated by John W. Rettig. 54 vols. The Fathers of the Church 78, 79, 88, 90, and 92. Washington, DC: Catholic University of America Press, 1988–95.

Cyril of Alexandria. *Commentary on John.* Translated by David R. Maxwell. 2 vols. Ancient Christian Texts, edited by Joel C. Elowsky. Downers Grove, IL: InterVarsity, 2015.

———. *Commentary on Luke. Cyril of Alexandria: Commentary on the Gospel of Luke.* Translated by R. Payne Smith. Studion, 1983.

Cyril of Jerusalem. *Catechetical Lectures.* In *The Works of St. Cyril of Jerusalem.* 2 vols. Vol. 2. Translated by Leo P. McCauley and Anthony A. Stephenson. Fathers of the Church 64. Edited by Roy Deferrari. Washington, DC: Catholic University of America Press, 1968, 1970.

Egeria. *Diary of a Pilgrimage.* Translated and annotated by George Gingras. Ancient Christian Writers 38. New York: Newman, 1970.

Ephrem the Syrian. *Saint Ephrem's Commentary on Tatian's Diatessaron.* Translated by Carmel McCarthy. *Journal of Semitic Studies,* supplement 2. Oxford: Oxford University Press, 1993.

Eusebius of Caesarea. *History of the Church.* In *Eusebius Pamphilus: Church History, Life of Constantine, Oration in Praise of Constantine.* Translated by Arthur Cushman McGiffert. Nicene and Post Nicene Fathers of the Church, 2nd ser., 1, edited by Philip Schaff and Henry Wace. Peabody, MA: Hendrickson, 1995.

The Great Synaxaristes of the Orthodox Church. Translated from the Greek. 14 vols. Buena Vista, CO: Holy Apostles Convent, 2002.

Irenaeus. *Against Heresies.* In *The Apostolic Fathers with Justin Martyr and Irenaeus.* The Ante-Nicene Fathers 1, edited by Alexander Roberts and James Donaldson. Grand Rapids, MI: Wm. B. Eerdmans, 1989.

Jerome. *Homilies. Homilies of St. Jerome.* Translated by Marie Liguori Ewald. Fathers of the Church 48 and 57. Edited by Roy Deferrari. 2 vols. Washington, DC: Catholic University of America Press, 1964, 1965.

———. *Homilies on Matthew. St. Jerome: Commentary on Matthew.* Translated by Thomas P. Scheck. Fathers of the Church 117. Washington, DC: Catholic University of America Press, 2008.

John Chrysostom. *Homilies on 1 Corinthians. St. Chrysostom: Homilies on the Epistles of Paul to the Corinthians.* Translated by Talbot W. Chambers. Nicene and Post Nicene Fathers of the Church 1st ser., 12, edited by Philip Schaff. Grand Rapids, MI: Wm. B. Eerdmans, 1979.

———. *Homilies on Ephesians.* In *St. Chrysostom: Homilies on the Epistles of Paul to the Galatians, Ephesians, Philippians, Colossians, Thessalonians, Timothy, Titus and Philemon.* Translated by Gross Alexander, John Broadus, and Philip Schaff. Nicene and Post Nicene Fathers of the Church, 1st ser., 13, edited by Philip Schaff. Grand Rapids, MI: Wm. B. Eerdmans, 1979.

———. *Homilies on Genesis.* Translated by Mark Bilby. "'As the Bandit I Will Confess You': Luke 23:39–43 in Early Christian Interpretation." Ph.D. diss., University of Virginia, 2012.

———. *Homilies on Matthew. St. Chrysostom Homilies on the Gospel of Matthew.* Translated by George Prevost. Nicene and Post-Nicene Fathers of the Christian Church, 1st ser., 10, edited by Philip Schaff. Grand Rapids, MI: Wm. B. Eerdmans, 1975.

———. *Homilies on Romans.* In *St. Chrysostom: Homilies on Acts of the Apostles and the Epistle to the Romans.* Translated by J. B. Morris and W. H. Simcox. Nicene and Post-Nicene Fathers of the Christian Church, 1st ser., 11, edited by Philip Schaff. Grand Rapids, MI: Wm. B. Eerdmans, 1975.

———. *Homilies on the Cross and the Bandits.* Translated by Mark Bilby. "'As the Bandit I Will Confess You': Luke 23:39–43 in Early Christian Interpretation." Ph.D. diss., University of Virginia, 2012.

———. *Homilies on the Gospel of John. St. John Chrysostom: Commentary on St. John the Apostle and Evangelist.* Translated by Sr. Thomas Aquinas Goggin. 2 vols. The Fathers of the Church 33 and 41. Washington, DC: Catholic University of America Press, 1957 and 1959.

———. *Homily against the Marcionists and Manicheans.* Translated by W. R. W. Stephens. In *St. Chrysostom: On the Priesthood; Ascetic Treatises, Select Homilies and Letters, Homilies on the Statues.* Nicene and Post-Nicene Fathers of the Christian Church, 1st ser., 9, edited by Philip Schaff. Grand Rapids, MI: Wm. B. Eerdmans, 1986.

John of Damascus. *An Exact Exposition of the Orthodox Faith.* Translated by Frederick H. Chase. Fathers of the Church 37. New York: Fathers of the Church, 1958.

Josephus, Flavius. *Against Apion.* Translated by William Whiston. In *The Works of Josephus.* Peabody, MA: Hendrickson, 1987.

———. *Antiquities of the Jews (Ant.).* Translated by William Whiston. In *The Works of Josephus.* Peabody, MA: Hendrickson, 1987.

———. *The Jewish War (JW).* Translated by William Whiston. In *The Works of Josephus.* Peabody, MA: Hendrickson, 1987.

Julius Paulus Prudentissimus. *Pauli Sententiarum Ad Filium Liber Primus.* Edited with comments by Ernst Levy. Ithaca, NY: Cornell University Press, 1945.

Justin Martyr. *Dialogue with Trypho.* In *The Apostolic Fathers with Justin Martyr and Irenaeus.* The Ante-Nicene Fathers 1, edited by Alexander Roberts and James Donaldson. Grand Rapids, MI: Wm. B. Eerdmans, 1989.

———. *First Apology to the Emperor.* In *The Apostolic Fathers with Justin Martyr and Irenaeus.* The Ante-Nicene Fathers 1, edited by Alexander Roberts and James Donaldson. Grand Rapids, MI: Wm. B. Eerdmans, 1989.

The Mishnah. Translated and edited by Herbert Danby. Oxford: Oxford University Press, 1933.

Origen. *Contra Celsum.* Translated by Frederick Crombie. In *Fathers of the Third Century.* Ante-Nicene Fathers 4, edited by Alexander Roberts and James Donaldson. Grand Rapids, MI: Wm. B. Eerdmans, 1989.

Philo of Alexandria. *The Works of Philo.* Translated by C. D. Yonge. Peabody, MA: Hendrickson, 1993.

The Talmud of Babylonia: An American Translation. Translated by Jacob Neusner. Brown Judaic Studies volume 295. Atlanta: Scholars, 1994.

Testaments of the Twelve Patriarchs. Edited by James H. Charlesworth. In *The Old Testament Pseudepigrapha.* New York: Doubleday, 1983.

Ulpianus. *Digest of Justinian.* Edited by Theodor Mommsen with Paul Krueger. Translated by Alan Watson. 4 vols. 1985. Revised English translation by Alan Watson. Philadelphia: University of Pennsylvania Press, 1998.

Secondary Sources

Abbot, Frank Frost, and Allan Chester Johnson. *Municipal Administration in the Roman Empire.* Princeton, NJ: Princeton University Press, 1926.

Al-Tkrit, Amna, Andrew Mekaiel, Mohammed Aneeb, et al. "Left Ventricular Free Wall Rupture in Broken Heart Syndrome: A Fatal Complication. *Cureus* 12, no. 11 (November 2020): e11316 DOI 10.7759/cureus.11316.

Andreopoulos, Andreas. *Gazing on God: Trinity, Church and Salvation in Orthodox Thought and Iconography.* Cambridge: James T. Clarke, 2013.

Applebaum, Shimon. *Judea in Hellenistic and Roman Times.* Studies in Judaism in Late Antiquity 40. New York: E. J. Brill, 1989.

Aubert, Jean-Jacques. "A Double Standard in Roman Criminal Law? The Death Penalty and Social Structure in Late Republican and Early Imperial Rome." In *Speculum Iuris: Roman Law as a Reflection of Social and Economic Life in Antiquity,* edited by Jean-Jacques Aubert and Boudewijn Sirks. Ann Arbor: University of Michigan Press, 2002.

Bahat, Dan. "The Second Temple in Jerusalem." In *Jesus and Temple: Textual and Archeological Explorations,* edited by James H. Charlesworth. Minneapolis: Fortress, 2014.

Bar, Eitan. *Refuting Rabbinic Objections to Christianity and Messianic Prophecies.* One for Israel, 2019.

Barbet, Pierre. *A Doctor at Calvary.* New York: Image Books, 1963.

Beetham, F. G., and P. A. Beetham. "A Note on John 19:29." *Journal of Theological Studies,* n.s., 44 (1993): 163–69.

Berkowitz, Beth. *Execution and Invention: Death Penalty in Early Rabbinic and Christian Cultures.* Oxford: Oxford University Press, 2006.

Berlin, Andrea. "Jewish Life before the Revolt: The Archeological Evidence." *Journal for the Study of Judaism in the Persian, Hellenistic and Roman Period* 36, no. 4 (2005): 417–40.

Berger, David. *Cultures in Collision and Conversation: Essays on the Intellectual History of the Jews.* Brighton, MA: Academic Studies, 2011.

———. "Three Typological Themes in Early Jewish Messianism: Messiah Son of Joseph, Rabbinic Calculations and the Figure of Armilus." *Association for Jewish Studies Review* 10, no. 2 (Autumn 1985): 141–64.

Besi, E., and J. M. Zakrzewska. "Trigeminal Neuralgia and Its Variants: Management and Diagnosis." *Oral Surgery* 13 (2020): 404–14.

Bilalis, Yiorgos. *Lazarus, the Friend of Christ: St. Lazarus in Literature and Icons, Hymns and Folk Songs.* Athens: Melodiko Karavi, 2001.

Bovon, Francois. *Commentary on Luke.* 3 vols. Hermeneia, edited by Helmut Koester. Minneapolis: Fortress, 2012.

Bowsher, David. "Trigeminal Neuralgia: An Anatomically Oriented Review." *Clinical Anatomy* 10 (1997): 409–15.

Bromiley, Geoffrey, ed. *International Standard Bible Encyclopedia.* Rev. ed. Grand Rapids, MI: William B. Eerdmans, 1979.

Brown, Raymond. "The Burial of Jesus (Mark 15:42–47)." *Catholic Biblical Quarterly* 50 (1988): 233–45.

———. *The Death of the Messiah.* 2 vols. New York: Doubleday, 1994.

———. *The Gospel of John.* 2 vols. The Anchor Bible 29 and 29a, edited by William Foxwell Albright and David Noel Freedman. Garden City, NY: Doubleday, 1970.

Bruce, F. F. "Palestine, Administration of (Roman)." In *Anchor Bible Dictionary*, edited by David Noel Freedman, 6 vols. New York: Doubleday, 1992.

Burton, G. F. "Proconsuls, Assizes and the Administration of Justice under the Empire." *Journal of Roman Studies* 65 (1975): 92–106.

Carr, David. M. *Holy Resilience.* New Haven, CT: Yale University Press, 2014.

Carter, Anthony John. "Narcosis and Nightshade." *British Medical Journal* 313, no. 7072 (1996): 1630–32.

Carucci, Margherita. "The Spectacle of Justice in the Roman Empire." In *Impact of Justice on the Roman Empire*, edited by Olivier Hekster and Koenraad Verboven. Leiden: Brill, 2019.

Cazares, Shelley M., et al. "Significance of Rib Fractures Potentially Caused by Blunt-Impact Non-lethal Weapons." In *Injuries and Complications of Blunt-Impact Non-lethal Weapons.*" Institute for Defense Analysis, 2017.

Chance, J. Bradley. "The Cursing of the Temple and the Tearing of the Veil in the Gospel of Mark." *Biblical Interpretation* 15 (2007): 268–91.

Chancey, Mark Allen, and Adam Lowry Porter. "The Archeology of Roman Palestine." *Near Eastern Archeology* 64, no. 4 (December 2001): 164–203.

Chapman, David W., and Eckhard J. Schnabel. *The Trial and Crucifixion of Jesus: Text and Commentary.* Peabody, MA: Hendrickson, 2019.

Charlesworth, James H. *Jesus and the Temple: Textual and Archeological Explorations.* Minneapolis: Fortress, 2014.

Chavel, C. B. "The Releasing of a Prisoner on the Eve of Passover." *Journal of Biblical Literature* 60 (1941): 273–78.

Clermont-Ganneau, Charles. "Une stèle du Temple du Jerusalem." *Revue Archéologique*, n.s., 23 (1872).

Cohen, Jeremy. "On Pesach and Pascha: Jews, Christians and the Passion." In *Engaging the Passion: Perspectives on the Death of Jesus*, edited by Oliver Larry Yarbrough. Minneapolis: Fortress, 2015.

Cohen, Shaye J. D. "The Destruction: From Scripture to Midrash." In "Catastrophe in Jewish Literature," special issue of *Prooftexts* 2, no. 1 (January 1982): 18–39.

Collins, Adele Yarbro. *Mark: A Commentary.* Edited by Harold W. Attridge. Minneapolis: Fortress, 2007.

Collins, John J. "Exegetical Notes: The Archeology of the Crucifixion." *Catholic Biblical Quarterly* 1 (1939): 154–59.

Constantinou, Eugenia Scarvelis. "Roman Criminal Procedure in the Provinces during the First Century of the Roman Empire." Master of theology diss., Harvard Divinity School, 1998.

———. *Thinking Orthodox: Understanding and Acquiring the Orthodox Christian Mind.* Chesterton, IN: Ancient Faith, 2020.

Cook, Christopher, Helen Tarbet, and David Ball. "Classically Intoxicated." *British Medical Journal* 335 (2007): 1302–4.

Cook, John Granger. "Crucifixion as Spectacle in Roman Campania." *Novum Testamentum* 541 (2012): 68–100.

Croke, Brian. "The Originality of Eusebius' Chronicle." *American Journal of Philology* 103, no. 2 (Summer 1982): 195–200.

Crook, J. A. *Legal Advocacy in the Roman World.* London: Gerald Duckworth, 1995.

Das, Andrew A. *Paul and the Stories of Israel.* Minneapolis: Fortress, 2016.

Davies, Philip, and Bruce Chilton. "The Aqedah: A Revised Tradition History." *Catholic Biblical Quarterly* 40 (1978): 514–46.

De Jonge, M. "Matthew 27:51 in Early Christian Exegesis." *Harvard Theological Review* 79, no. 1/3 (January–July 1986): 67–79.

Derwacter, Frederick M. "The Modern Translators and John 19,13: Is It 'Sat' or 'Seated'"? *Classical Journal* 40, no. 1 (October 1944): 24–28.

DeVries, LaMoine. *Cities of the Biblical World.* Peabody, MA: Hendrickson, 1997.

Dietler, Michael. "Alcohol: Anthropological/Archeological Perspectives." *Annual Review of Anthropology* 35 (2006): 229–49.

Dijkhuizen, Petra. "'Buried Shamefully': Historical Reconstruction of Jesus' Burial and Tomb." *Neotestamentica* 45 (2011): 115–29.

Edwards, William D., Wesley Gabel, and Floyd Hosmer. "On the Physical Death of Jesus Christ." *Journal of the American Medical Association* 255 (1986): 1455–63.

Ellershaw, John E., Jane M. Suttcliffe, and Cicely M. Saunders. "Dehydration and the Dying Patient." *Journal of Pain and Symptom Management* 10 (April 1995): 192–97.

Eppstein, Victor. "The Historicity of the Cleansing of the Temple." *Zeitschrift für die Neutestamentliche Wissenschaft* 55 (1964): 42–58.

Evans, Craig A. "Jesus' Action in the Temple: Cleansing or Portent of Destruction?" *Catholic Biblical Quarterly* 51, no. 2 (April 1989): 237–70.

———. *Jesus and His Contemporaries.* Leiden: Brill, 2001.

———. *Jesus and His World: The Archeological Evidence.* Louisville, KY: John Knox, 2012.

———. *Mark.* 2 vols. Word Biblical Commentary 34a and 34b, edited by Bruce Metzger. Nashville, TN: Thomas Nelson, 2000.

Ferda, Tucker S. "Matthew's Titulus and Psalm 2's King on Mount Zion." *Journal of Biblical Literature* 33 (2014): 561–81.

———. "Naming the Messiah: A Contribution to the 4Q246 'Son of God' Debate." *Dead Sea Discoveries* 21, no. 2 (2014): 150–75.

———. "The Soldier's Inscription and the Angel's Word: The Significance of 'Jesus' in Matthew's 'Titulus.'" *Novum Testamentum* 55 (2013): 221–31.

Fiensy, David A. *Christian Origins and the Ancient Economy.* London: James Clarke, 2014.

Finegan, Jack. *The Archeology of the New Testament: The Life of Jesus and the Beginning of the Early Church.* Princeton, NJ: Princeton University Press, 1992.

Fischer, Zoltan. "Sacrificing Isaac: A New Interpretation." *Jewish Bible Quarterly* 35, no. 3 (2007): 173–78.

Fitzmyer, Joseph A. "Crucifixion in Ancient Palestine." *Catholic Biblical Quarterly* 40 (1978): 493–513.

———. "4Q246: The 'Son of God' Document from Qumran." *Biblica* 74, no. 2 (1993): 153–74.

———. "The Sacrifice of Isaac in Qumran Literature." *Biblica* 83, no. 2 (2002): 211–29.

Flowers, Michael. "The Bystanders at the Cross and Their Expectations about Elijah." *Catholic Biblical Quarterly* 80, no. 3 (July 2018): 448–69.

France, R. T. *Matthew.* Grand Rapids, MI: William B. Eerdmans, 1985.

Freedman, David Noel, ed. *Anchor Bible Dictionary.* 6 vols. New York: Doubleday, 1992.

Friedberg, Arthur. *Coins of the Bible.* Atlanta: Whitman, 2004.

Friedländer, Ludwig. *Roman Life and Manners under the Early Empire.* 4 vols. Originally published as *Sittengeschichte Roms.* Translated by Leonard A. Magnus. New York: Barnes and Noble, 1968.

Gafni, Isaiah. "The Historical Background." In *Jewish Writings of the Second Temple Period,* edited by Michael E. Stone. Philadelphia: Fortress, 1984.

Gambeta, Eder, Juliana G. Chichorro, and Gerald W. Zamponi. "Trigeminal Neuralgia: An Overview from Pathophysiology to Pharmacological Treatments." *Molecular Pain* 16 (January 2020): 1–18.

Garnsey, Peter. "The Criminal Jurisdiction of Governors." *Journal of Roman Studies* 58 (1968): 51–59.

———. "The *Lex Iulia* and Appeal under the Empire." *Journal of Roman Studies* 56 (1966): 167–89.

———. *Social Status and Privilege in the Roman Empire.* Oxford: Clarendon, 1970.

Goodman, Mark. "Trajan and the Origins of Roman Hostility to the Jews." *Past and Present,* no. 182 (February 2004): 3–29.

Goodman, Martin. *The Ruling Class of Judea.* Cambridge: Cambridge University Press, 1987.

Gordon, A. E. "Seven Latin Inscriptions in Rome." *Greece and Rome* 20, no. 59 (June 1951): 75–92.

Grabbe, Lester L. *Judaism from Cyrus to Hadrian.* 2 vols. Minneapolis: Fortress, 1992.

Gurtner, Daniel M. *The Torn Veil: Matthew's Exposition of the Death of Jesus.* Cambridge: Cambridge University Press, 2007.

———. "The Veil of the Temple in History and Legend." *Journal of the Evangelical Theological Society* 49 (2006): 97–114.

Haenchen, Ernst. *A Commentary on the Gospel of John.* 2 vols. Hermeneia. Minneapolis: Fortress, 1988.

Hagner, Donald. *Matthew.* 2 vols. Word Biblical Commentary 33a and 33b, edited by Bruce Metzger. Nashville, TN: Thomas Nelson, 1995.

Hammer, Reuven. *Akiva: Life, Legend, Legacy.* Philadelphia: Jewish Publication Society, 2015.

Harper, George McLean. "Village Administration in the Roman Province of Syria." Ph.D. diss., Princeton University, 1924. Reprinted from Yale Classical Studies 1, Yale University Press, 1928.

Harrington, Daniel J. *The Gospel of Matthew*. Sacra Pagina 1, edited by Daniel J. Herrington. Collegeville, MN: Liturgical, 1991.

Harris, Murray. "References to Jesus in Classical Authors." In *Jesus Traditions outside the Gospels*, edited by David Wenham. Sheffield, UK: Sheffield University Press, 1982.

Hart, H. St. J. "The Crown of Thorns in John 19:2–25." *Journal of Theological Studies*, n.s., 3, no. 1 (April 1952): 66–75.

Hassantash, S. Ahmad, Maryam Afrakhteh, and Ronald Maier. "Causalgia. A Meta-analysis of the Literature." *Archives of Surgery* 138 (November 2003): 1226–31.

Haupt, Paul. "Alcohol in the Bible." *Journal of Biblical Literature* 36 (1917): 75–83.

Hayward, C. T. R. "The Sacrifice of Isaac and Jewish Polemic against Christianity." *Catholic Biblical Quarterly* 52, no. 2 (April 1990): 292–306.

Hegg, Tim. "Separating the Holy from the Most Holy": The 'Veil' in the Tabernacle and First and Second Temples." Paper presented at the Northwest Regional Conference of the Evangelical Theological Society, Portland, OR, 2000.

Heinemann, Joseph. "The Messiah of Ephraim and the Premature Exodus of the Tribe of Ephraim." *Harvard Theological Review* 6, no. 1 (January 1975): 1–15.

Hengel, Martin. *Crucifixion*. Philadelphia: Fortress, 1977.

Hobson, Deborah L. "The Impact of Law on Village Life in Roman Egypt." In *Law, Politics and Society in the Ancient Mediterranean World*, edited by Baruch Halpern and Deborah W. Hobson. Sheffield, UK: Sheffield Academic, 1993.

Honoré, Tony. *Emperors and Lawyers*. London: Gerald Duckworth, 1981.

Horsley, Richard A. *Bandits, Prophets and Messiahs: Popular Movements at the Time of Jesus*. San Francisco: Harper and Row, 1985.

———. "High Priests and the Politics of Roman Palestine: A Contextual Analysis of the Evidence in Josephus." *Journal for the Study of Judaism in the Persian, Hellenistic and Roman Period* 17, no. 1 (June 1986): 23–55.

———. "Popular Messianic Movements around the Time of Jesus." *Catholic Biblical Quarterly* 46 (1984): 471–95.

Huizenga, Leroy Andrew. "Obedience unto Death: The Matthean Gethsemane and Arrest Sequence and the Aqedah." *Catholic Biblical Quarterly* 71, no. 3 (July 2009): 507–26.

Hurtado, Larry. "The Staurogram: Earliest Depiction of the Crucifixion of Jesus." *Biblical Archeology Review* 39 (2013): 49–53.

Jackson, Kent. "Revolutionaries in the First Century." *Brigham Young University Studies* 36, no. 3 (1996–97): 129–40.

Janowski, Bernd, and Peter Stuhlmacher, eds. *The Suffering Servant: Isaiah 53 in Jewish and Christian Sources*. Translated by Daniel Bailey. Grand Rapids, MI: Wm. B. Eerdmans, 2004.

Jerajani, H. R., Bhagyashri Jaju, M. M. Phiske, and Nitin Lade. "Hematidrosis: A Rare Clinical Phenomenon." *Indian Journal of Dermatology* 54, no. 3 (July–September 2009): 290–92.

Jeremias, Joachim. *Jerusalem in the Time of Jesus*. Philadelphia: Fortress, 1969.

The Jewish Encyclopedia. 12 vols. Edited by Isidore Singer. New York: Funk and Wagnalls, 1901–09.

Jolowicz, H. F. *Historical Introduction to the Study of Roman Law*. Cambridge: Cambridge University Press, 1952.

Jones, A. H. M. *The Cities of the Eastern Roman Provinces*. Oxford: Clarendon, 1971.

———. *The Criminal Courts of the Roman Republic and Principate*. Oxford: Basil Blackwell, 1972.

———. *The Greek City*. Oxford: Clarendon, 1940.

———. *Studies in Roman Government and Law*. Oxford: Basil Blackwell, 1960.

Jouanna, Jacques. "Wine and Medicine in Ancient Greece." In *Greek Medicine from Hippocrates to Galen*, translated by Neil Allies, edited by Philip van der Eijk. Studies in Ancient Medicine 40. Boston: Brill, 2012.

Juster, Jean. *Les Droits Politiques des Juifs dans L'Empire Romain*. Paris: Librarie Paul Geuthner, 1912.

———. *Les Juifs dans L'Empire Romain*. 2 vols. Paris: Librairie Paul Geuthner, 1914.

Keener, Craig S. *The Gospel of John: A Commentary*. 2 vols. Peabody, MA: Hendrickson, 2003.

Kelly, J. M. *Roman Litigation*. Oxford: Clarendon, 1966.

Kennard, J. Spencer. "The Burial of Jesus." *Journal of Biblical Literature* 74, no. 4 (December 1955): 227–38.

Kittel, Gerhard, and Geoffrey W. Bromiley, eds. *The Theological Dictionary of the New Testament*. 10 vols. Grand Rapids, MI: William B. Eerdmans, 1964.

Kluger, Nicholas. "Hematidrosis (Bloody Sweat): A Review of the Recent Literature." *Acta Dermatovenerologica Alpina, Panonica et Adriatica* 27 (June 2018) 2:85–90.

Knohl, Israel. *The Messiah before Jesus: The Suffering Servant of the Dead Sea Scrolls*. Translated by David Maisel. Berkeley: University of California Press, 2000.

———. "The Messiah Son of Joseph." *Biblical Archeology Review* 34, no. 5 (September/October 2008): 58, 60–62.

Köster, Isabel. "How to Kill a Roman Villain." *Classical Journal* 109, no. 3 (February–March 2014): 309–32.

Krikorian, Abraham D. "Were the Opium Poppy and Opium Known in the Ancient Near East?" *Journal of the History of Biology* 8 (1975): 95–114.

Lapin, Hayim. *Early Rabbinic Civil Law*. Brown Judaic Studies 307. Atlanta: Scholars, 2020.

Lattey, Cuthbert. "The Praetorium of Pilate." *Journal of Theological Studies* 31, no. 122 (January 1930): 180–82.

Lavoie, Bonnie, Gilbert Lavoie, Daniel Klutstein, and John Regan. "In Accordance with Jewish Burial Custom, the Body of Jesus Was Not Washed." *Sindon*, no. 30 (December 1981): 1–10.

Lémnon, Jean-Pierre. *Pilate et le Gouvernement de la Judée*. Paris: Librarie Lecoffre, 1981.

Levenson, Jon. *The Death and Resurrection of the Beloved Son: The Transformation of Child Sacrifice in Judaism and Christianity*. New Haven, CT: Yale University Press, 1993.

Levine, Lee I. *Caesarea under Roman Rule*. Studies in Judaism in Late Antiquity 7, edited by Jacob Neusner. Leiden: E. J. Brill, 1975.

Lewis, Karoline. *John*. Minneapolis: Fortress, 2014.

Lintott, Andrew. *Imperium Romanum: Politics and Administration*. New York: Routledge, 1993.

Longenecker, Bruce W. *The Cross before Constantine: The Early Life of a Christian Symbol*. Minneapolis: Fortress, 2015.

Luz, Ulrich. *Commentary on Matthew.* Translated by James E. Crouch. 3 vols. Hermeneia, edited by Helmut Koester. Minneapolis: Fortress, 2005.

MacMullen, Ramsay. *Roman Social Relations.* New Haven, CT: Yale University Press, 1974.

Magie, David. *Roman Rule in Asia Minor to the End of the Third Century after Christ.* 2 vols. Princeton, NJ: Princeton University Press, 1950.

Mahoney, Aidan. "A New Look at the 'Third Hour' of Mk 15:25." *Catholic Biblical Quarterly* 28 (1966): 292–99.

Maier, Paul L. "The Fate of Pontius Pilate." *Hermes* 99, no. 3 (1971): 362–71.

———. "Sejanus, Pilate and the Date of the Crucifixion." *Church History* 37 (1968): 3–13.

Marcus, Joel. "Crucifixion as Parodic Exaltation." *Journal of Biblical Literature* 125 (2006): 73–87.

———. "Mark 14:61: 'Are You the Messiah-Son-of-God?'" *Novum Testamentum* 31, fasc. 2 (April 1989): 125–41.

Marshall, J. Howard. "Church and Temple in the New Testament." *Tyndale Bulletin* 40 (1989): 203–22.

Maslen, Matthew, and Piers D. Mitchell. "Medical Theories on the Cause of Death in Crucifixion." *Journal of the Royal Society of Medicine* 99 (April 2006): 185–88.

McCane, Byron. *Roll Back the Stone: Death and Burial in the World of Jesus.* Harrisburg, PA: Trinity Press International, 2003.

McGing, Brian C. "Pontius Pilate and the Sources." *Catholic Biblical Quarterly* 53 (1991): 416–38.

Meinhardt, Molly Dewsnap, ed. *Jesus: The Last Day.* Washington, DC: Biblical Archeology Society, 2003.

Merlin, M. D. "Archeological Evidence for the Tradition of Psychoactive Plant Use in the Old World." *Economic Botany* 57 (2003): 295–323.

Mierow, Herbert Edward. "The Roman Provincial Governor as He Appears in the Digest and Code of Justinian." Ph.D. diss., Colorado Springs College, 1926.

Millar, Fergus. *The Emperor in the Roman World.* Ithaca, NY: Cornell University Press, 1984.

———. *The Roman Near East.* Cambridge, MA: Harvard University Press, 1993.

———. *Rome, the Greek World and the East.* 3 vols. Vol. 3, *The Greek World, the Jews and the East.* Edited by Hannah M. Cotton and Guy M. Rogers. Chapel Hill: University of North Carolina Press, 2006.

Møller-Christensen, Vilhelm. "Skeletal Remains from Giv'at ha-Mivtar." *Israel Exploration Journal* 26 (1975): 35–38.

Montanari, Massimo. *Medieval Tastes: Food, Cooking and the Table.* New York: Columbia University Press, 2012.

Montiglio, Silvia. "Wandering Philosophers in Classical Greece." *Journal of Hellenic Studies* 120 (2000): 86–105.

Moore, George Foot. "The Rise of Normative Judaism: To the Reorganization at Jamnia." *Harvard Theological Review* 7 (1924): 307–73.

Mourad, Suleiman. "The Death of Jesus in Islam: Reality, Assumptions and Implications." In *Engaging the Passion: Perspectives on the Death of Jesus,* edited by Oliver Larry Yarbrough. Minneapolis: Fortress, 2015.

Muirhead, James. *Historical Introduction to the Private Law of Rome.* 2nd ed., revised and edited by Henry Goudy. London: Adam and Charles Black, 1899.

———, trans. and ed. *The Institutes of Gaius and the Rules of Ulpian*. Edinburgh: T&T Clark, 1880.

Murphy-O'Connor, Jerome. "What Really Happened at Gethsemane?" In *Jesus: The Last Day*, edited by Molly Dewsnap Meinhardt. Washington, DC: Biblical Archeology Society, 2003.

———. "Where Was the Antonia Fortress?" *Revue Biblique* 111, no. 1 (January 2004): 78–89.

Nicholas, Barry. *An Introduction to Roman Law*. Oxford: Clarendon, 1962.

Nippel, Wilfried. *Public Order in Ancient Rome*. Cambridge: Cambridge University Press, 1995.

Nodet, Étienne. "On Jesus' Last Supper." *Biblica* 91, no. 3 (2010): 348–69.

O'Herlihy, Donal J. "The Year of the Crucifixion." *Catholic Biblical Quarterly* 8 (1946): 298–305.

Oliva, B., S. C. Hammill, and W. D. Edwards. "Cardiac Rupture, a Clinically Predictable Complication of Acute Myocardial Infarction: Report of 70 Cases with Clinicopathologic Correlations." *Journal of the American College of Cardiologists* 22, no. 3 (September 1993): 720–26.

Pate, J. W. "Chest Wall Injuries." *Surgical Clinics of North America* 69 (Feb. 1989) 1:59–70.

Patton, Callum. "Tomb of Jesus Christ, Dated for First Time, Revealing Ancient Crypt Built Far Earlier Than Experts Believed." *Newsweek*, November 28, 2017, https://www.newsweek.com/tomb-jesus-christ-dated-first-time-revealing-ancient-crypt-724507.

Plummer, Robert. "Something Awry in the Temple? The Rending of the Temple Veil and Early Jewish Sources That Report Unusual Phenomena in the Temple around AD 30." *Journal of the Evangelical Theological Society* 48 (2005): 301–16.

Pomeranz, Jonathan A. "Did the Babylonian Sages Regard the Ammei-ha'Aretz as Sub-human?" *Hebrew Union College Annual* 87 (2016): 115–43.

Pope, Michael. "The Downward Motion of Jesus' Sweat and the Authenticity of Luke 22:43–44." *Catholic Biblical Quarterly* 79, no. 2 (April 2017): 261–81.

Porcel, José M. "Pleural Effusions from Congestive Heart Failure." *Seminars in Respiratory Critical Care Medicine* 31 (2010) 6:689–97.

Prigent, Paul. "Thallos, Phelgum et le Testimonium Flavianum: Temoins de Jesus?" In *Paganism, Judaïsme et Christianisme*. Paris: Boccard, 1978.

Reeder, Rhonda J., and Diane M. Danis. "Penetrating Chest Trauma." *American Journal of Nursing* 101, no. 9 (September 2001): 15–18.

Reich, Ronny. "A Note on the Population Size of Jerusalem in the Second Temple Period." *Revue Biblique* 121, no. 2 (April 2014): 298–305.

Rejali, Darius. "Why Social Scientists Should Care How Jesus Died." In *Histories of Victimhood*, edited by Steffen Jensen and Henrik Ronsbo. Philadelphia: University of Pennsylvania Press, 2014.

Rembaum, Joel E. "The Development of a Jewish Exegetical Tradition Regarding Isaiah 53." *Harvard Theological Review* 75 (1982): 289–311.

Richardson, J. S. "The Purpose of the Lex Calpurnia de Repetundis." *Journal of Roman Studies* 77 (1987): 1–12.

Ritmeyer, Leen. "Imagining the Temple Known to Jesus and to Early Jews." In *Jesus and Temple: Textual and Archeological Explorations*, edited by James H. Charlesworth. Minneapolis: Fortress, 2014.

Ritmeyer, Leen, and Kathleen Ritmeyer. *Jerusalem: The Temple Mount.* Jerusalem: Carta, 2015.

Robinson, O. F. *The Criminal Law of Ancient Rome.* Baltimore: Johns Hopkins University Press, 1995.

Rogers, Robert Samuel. *Criminal Trials and Criminal Legislation under Tiberius.* Philological Monographs, edited by Joseph William Hewitt. Middletown, CT: American Philological Association, 1935.

Rosenberg, Roy. "Jesus, Isaac and the 'Suffering Servant.'" *Journal of Biblical Literature* 84, no. 4 (December 1965): 381–88.

Rosenblatt, Samuel. "The Crucifixion of Jesus from the Standpoint of Pharisaic Law." *Journal of Biblical Literature* 75 (1956): 315–21.

Rostovtzeff, M. *The Social and Economic History of the Roman Empire.* 2nd ed. 2 vols. Oxford: Clarendon, 1957.

Roth, H. Ling. "Studies in Primitive Looms." *Journal of the Royal Anthropological Institute of Great Britain and Ireland* 48 (1918): 103–44.

Rousseau, John, and Rami Arav. *Jesus and His World: An Archeological and Cultural Dictionary.* Minneapolis: Fortress, 1995.

Rubenstein, Richard. "What Was at Stake in the Parting of the Ways between Judaism and Christianity?" In "Jesus in the Context of Judaism," special issue of *Shofar* 28, no. 3 (Spring 2010): 78–102.

Sanders, E. P. *Judaism: Practice and Belief, 63 BCE–66 CE.* Minneapolis: Fortress, 2016.

Sava, A. G. "The Wound in the Side of Christ." *Catholic Biblical Quarterly* 19, no. 3 (July 1957): 343–46.

Schäfer, Peter. *Jesus in the Talmud.* Princeton, NJ: Princeton University Press, 2007.

Schisas, Pandias M. *Offenses against the State in Roman Law and the Courts Which Were Competent to Take Cognisance of Them.* London: University of London Press, 1926.

Schmidt, Thomas. "Jesus' Triumphal March to the Crucifixion." In *Jesus: The Last Day*, edited by Molly Dewsnap Meinhardt. Washington, DC: Biblical Archeology Society, 2003.

Schoeps, Hans Joachim. "The Sacrifice of Isaac in Paul's Theology." *Journal of Biblical Literature* 65, no. 4 (December 1946): 385–92.

Schürer, Emil. *The History of the Jewish People in the Age of Jesus Christ.* 4 vols. Edinburgh: T&T Clark, 1986.

Schwartz, Joshua. "Lessons from Inter-communal Conflict during the Second Temple Period." *Jewish Political Studies Review* 12, no. 3/4 (2000): 39–52.

Segal, Alan. "'He Who Did Not Spare His Own Son . . .': Jesus, Paul and the Akeda." In *From Jesus to Paul*, edited by Paul Richardson and John C. Hurd. Waterloo, ON: Wilfrid Laurier University Press, 2006.

Seo, Pyung-Soo. *Luke's Jesus in the Roman Empire and the Emperor in the Gospel of Luke.* Eugene, OR: Pickwick, 2015.

Shamir, Orit. "Textiles from the First Century C.E. in Jerusalem." In *Ancient Textiles*, edited by Carol Gillis and Marie-Louise B. Nosch. Oxford: Oxbow Books, 2014.

Shanks, Hershel. "New Analysis of the Crucified Man." In *Jesus: The Last Day*, edited by Molly Dewsnap Meinhardt. 2nd ed. Washington, DC: Biblical Archeology Society, 2003.

Sherwin-White, A. N. *The Roman Citizenship.* Oxford: Clarendon, 1973.

———. *Roman Society and Roman Law in the New Testament.* Oxford: Clarendon, 1963.

Shisley, Steven. "The Cross in the Roman World." *Biblical Archeology.*

Smith, Mark. D. *The Final Days of Jesus.* Cambridge: Lutterworth, 2018.

Spiegal, Shalom. *The Last Trial.* Translated by J. Goldin. New York: Random House, 1967.

Stevenson, G. H. *Roman Provincial Administration.* Oxford: Basil Blackwell, 1939.

Strachan-Davidson, James Leigh. *Problems of the Roman Criminal Law.* 2 vols. Oxford: Clarendon, 1912. Reprint, Littleton, CO: Fred B. Rothman, 1991.

Swarney, Paul R. "Social Status and Social Behavior as Criteria in Judicial Proceedings in the Late Republic." In *Law, Politics and Society in the Ancient Mediterranean World,* edited by Baruch Halpern and Deborah W. Hobson. Sheffield, UK: Sheffield Academic, 1993.

Sylva, Dennis D. "The Temple Curtain and Jesus' Death in the Gospel of Luke." *Journal of Biblical Literature* 105, no. 2 (June 1986): 239–50.

Tabory, Joseph. "The Crucifixion of the Paschal Lamb." *Jewish Quarterly Review* 86 (1996): 395–406.

Tallmadge, G. Kasten. "Anesthetics of Antiquity." *Journal of the History of Medicine and Allied Sciences* 1 (1946): 515–20.

Taylor, Joan. "Where Was Gethsemane?" In *Jesus: The Last Day,* edited by Molly Dewsnap Meinhardt. Washington, DC: Biblical Archeology Society, 2003.

Torrey, Charles. "The Messiah Son of Ephraim." *Journal of Biblical Literature* 66, no. 3 (September 1947): 253–77.

Turner, David. *Israel's Last Prophet: Jesus and the Jewish Leaders in Matthew 23.* Minneapolis: Fortress, 2015.

Tzaferis, Vassilios. "The Archeological Evidence for Crucifixion." In *Jesus: The Last Day,* edited by Molly Dewsnap Meinhardt. Washington, DC: Biblical Archeology Society, 2003.

Ulansey, David. "The Heavenly Veil Torn: Mark's Cosmic Inclusio." *Journal of Biblical Literature* 110, no. 1 (Spring 1991): 123–25.

Ulmer, Rivka. "The Contours of the Messiah in 'Pesiqta Rabbati.'" *Harvard Theological Review* 106, no. 2 (April 2013): 115–44.

Urch, E. J. "Procedure in the Courts of the Roman Provincial Governors." *Classical Journal* 25, no. 2 (November 1929): 93.

Van Voorst, Robert. *Jesus outside the New Testament.* Grand Rapids, MI: Wm. B. Eerdmans, 2000.

Walsh, Carey. "Christianity: Traditional Christian Interpretation of Genesis 22." In *Interpreting Abraham: Journeys to Moriah.* Minneapolis: Fortress, 2014.

Walther, James A. "The Chronology of Passion Week." *Journal of Biblical Literature* 77 (1958): 116–22.

Wuenschel, Edward A. "The Shroud of Turin and the Burial of Christ II—John's Account of the Burial." *Catholic Biblical Quarterly* 8, no. 2 (April 1946): 135–78.

Zeitlin, Solomon. "The Crucifixion of Jesus Re-examined." *Jewish Quarterly Review* 31 (1941): 327–69.

Zias, Joseph, and Eliezer Sekeles. "The Crucified Man from Giv'at ha-Mivtar: A Reappraisal." *Biblical Archeologist* 48 (1985): 190–91.

Zugibe, Frederick. *The Crucifixion of Jesus: A Forensic Inquiry.* Lanham, MD: M. Evans, 2005.

———. "Experimental Studies in Crucifixion." In *The Shroud of Turin: Unraveling the Mystery,* edited by A. Adler, D. I. Piczek, and M. Minor. Proceedings of the 1998 Dallas Symposium on the Shroud of Turin. North Carolina: Alexander Books, 2001.

————. "Forensic and Clinical Knowledge of the Practice of Crucifixion: A Forensic Way of the Cross." In *The Turin Shroud: Past, Present and Future*, edited by S. Scannerini and P. Savarino. Torino, Italy: Effata Editrice, 2000.

————. "The Man of the Shroud Was Washed." *Sindon*, n.s., 1 (June 1989): 1–8.

————. "Pierre Barbet Revisited." *Sindon*, n.s., 8 (December 1995): 109–21.

Index

kingship, 173; on Jesus' last words, 273,
274–75, 286; on Joseph of Arimathea, 318; on
Judas' betrayal, 122; reliability of, 8; on scourging, 183; on seamless robe, 248; on time of
Christ's death, 292; on vinegar, 282n22; on
walk to Golgatha, 227; on women disciples at
Christ's burial, 317–18

M
Maccabees, 22–23. *See also* Hasmonean Kingdom
mandrake, 282, 282n21
mantles, 89, 89n10, 247, 247nn2–4
Marcion, 15
Mark (evangelist): on Barabbas, 195; on grave
clothes, 323–24; on Jesus' agony in the
garden, 109, 109n7; on Jesus as suffering
Messiah, 269–70, 273; on Jesus' clothes, 247,
248; on Jesus' kingship, 173; on Jesus' last
words, 286; on time of Christ's death, 254n16,
292; on two robbers, 250; on veil's tearing,
298; on wine and vinegar, 282n22; on women
disciples at Christ's burial, 317
marriage, levirate, 85–86, 85n7
Mary (Theotokos), 47n12, 278–79
Mary and Martha, 32, 34, 35–36, 98, 325
Matthew (evangelist): on Barabbas, 195; gospel
written by, 296n3; on grave clothes, 323–24;
on Jesus' agony in the garden, 109; on Jesus'
kingship, 173; on Jesus' last words, 270,
286; on Joseph of Arimathea, 318; on Judas'
kiss, 122; on seamless robe, 248; on time of
Christ's death, 292; on two robbers, 250;
on wine and vinegar, 282n22; on witnesses
against Christ, 145; on women disciples at
Christ's burial, 317
McGing, Brian, 166n20
Messiah: divinity and, 151–52, 151n13, 152n14;
Jesus as, 39–40, 150–51, 267; Jewish expectations, 22, 23–24; prophecies and disagreements about, 258–59, 258n1; as son of David,
90–92; suffering Messiah (Messiah Son
of Joseph), 259–63, 259n3, 260n4, 262n6,
263n7, 264–65, 264n10, 265n11, 266–67,
269–70; Temple and messianic expectations,
148–49
mikveh, 48, 48n13, 52
Mishnah: introduction, 26n1; on burial, 318n5;
on execution, 219–20; on Jewish criminal
courts, 143; on pilgrim festivals, 45n5;
reliability for Temple descriptions, 55n33,
296n4; on "second tithe," 46n10; on Temple
veil, 55, 296
mocking, 186–87, 187–88, 189, 251–54, 253n14.
See also humiliation
Moses, 55, 290, 296
Mount of Olives, 105. *See also* Gethsemane

mourning rituals, 33, 33n2
myrrh, 281–82, 322

N
nails: pain from, 235–36; placement of, 237–39
names: numerical equivalent of, 98n3; sacred
name of God, 134n4
New Covenant, 290–91
Nicene Creed, 14
Nicodemus, 322–23, 324, 325

O
Origen, 175, 177, 257n22, 299
Orthodox Christianity, 9, 15

P
Palm Sunday, 39–40
parables: Two Sons, 76–77; Wicked Tenants,
77–78
paradise, opening the doors of, 274–77
parents, caring for, 279
Passion. *See* Jesus Christ
The Passion of the Christ (Gibson film), 11–12
Passover: about, 45n6; *Akedah* (Binding of Isaac)
and, 113, 113n4, 289–90, 289n5; burial of
Christ and, 325–26; custom to release a
prisoner during, 193, 194; Day of Preparation,
196, 292–94, 292n10; Holy Communion
and, 291–92; Jesus' arrest and, 105–6; New
Covenant and, 290–91; ordinary priests and,
60; parallels to crucifixion, 288–90, 289n6,
310, 332, 333; Pilate and, 158, 182; pilgrimage
requirement, 45; Roman concerns, 161–62,
193–94
patristics. *See* Church Fathers
Paul (apostle): administration of Jewish law and,
169, 169n24, 186n9; on apostles, 328; appeal
to Caesar, 172n29; beaten with rods, 188n12;
on Christ as paschal lamb, 290; on Christ's
voluntary and sacrificial death, 118, 119; *coercitio* and, 184n1; on foolishness and mystery
of the cross, 329–30, 339; forgiveness of, 274;
on Jews, 15–16; on scripture, 18; zealotry of,
97n2
Pentecost (*Shavuot*), 32, 45, 45n6
Peter (apostle), 67n6, 103, 124–25, 129–32,
131n8, 150, 313–14
Pharisees, 26–28, 27n2, 28n3, 29–30, 90. *See also*
Jewish leaders
Philo of Alexandria, 46n10, 116, 316–17, 317n2
Phlegon, 256–57, 257n22, 304–5
piercing, of Christ, 308–11, 313
pilgrim festivals, 45, 45n5
Pliny the Elder, 281n19
Pliny the Younger, 216
Polycarp, Bishop of Smyrna, 171n26, 213n8